BELFAST: APPROACH TO CRISIS

Also by Ian Budge

Scottish Political Behaviour (with D. W. Urwin)
Agreement and the Stability of Democracy
Political Stratification and Democracy (with
J. A. Brand, Michael Margolis and
A. L. M. Smith)

Also by Cornelius O'Leary

The Irish Republic and its Experiment with
Proportional Representation
The Elimination of Corrupt Practices in British
Elections 1868–1911

Belfast:
Approach to Crisis

A STUDY OF BELFAST POLITICS
1613–1970

IAN BUDGE
Reader, Department of Government
University of Essex

CORNELIUS O'LEARY
Reader, Department of Political Science
The Queen's University of Belfast

MACMILLAN
ST. MARTIN'S PRESS

First published 1973 by
THE MACMILLAN PRESS LTD
London and Basingstoke
Associated companies in New York Toronto
Dublin Melbourne Johannesburg and Madras

SBN 333 01708 0

Library of Congress catalog card no. 72–85194

Printed in Great Britain by
R & R CLARK LTD
Edinburgh

Contents

List of Tables

Introduction

Belfast now dominates the headlines. The Northern Ireland crisis, spawned in Londonderry, is at the time of writing being fought on the streets of Belfast: not the first time that the fate of the Province has been settled in its capital. The onrush of events has conflated immediate problems with political scientists' traditional concern for political stability, that is to say the continued functioning of basic institutions and procedures without serious disruption. Our attempts to isolate influences producing tension and unrest in Belfast thus have a practical as well as a theoretical interest: they help us to understand the preconditions of crisis better, and in so doing we may be better prepared for future crises, not only in Belfast but in polities where similar circumstances prevail.

When we began our investigation in 1966 we could not anticipate the violent turn which would be taken by events three years later. In 1966 the most likely projection was the success of the attempt by the Northern Ireland Prime Minister, Captain Terence (now Lord) O'Neill, to achieve a reconciliation with the Catholics. But recent history was enough to mark Belfast as a city in which basic antagonisms divided one set of citizens from another, where political compromises were as a result difficult to obtain and established institutions perpetually under threat. In all these respects it contrasted with cities of the British mainland, such as Glasgow, where similar investigations offered a basis for comparison. We discuss the Belfast–Glasgow comparison in more detail below.

Tensions were such even in 1966 that it was generally thought impossible to mount a political survey in Belfast. Our own research, initiated in the early summer of 1966, included the first political survey ever to be undertaken in Northern Ireland. Its success, especially during a riot and just after a political murder, encouraged several public opinion polls and a further academic survey, all of which cast further light on Northern

Irish politics. Because of our concern with political tensions in Belfast, the information we collected – both survey and historical – is capable of answering many of the questions which subsequent developments prompted us to put to it. We could, for example, see how far the present riots resemble those of the past. We could ask whether a majority of Unionists, activists as well as followers, supported Captain O'Neill's initiatives in 1966. We could discover whether there was more basic hostility between Catholics and Protestants in Belfast than in other parts of Britain. We could enquire whether the Unionist leaders' reforming policies ever carried much conviction at the popular level. These and similar questions answered in the following chapters all obviously relate to the origins of the present crisis.

Nevertheless, there are limitations on answers from particular sets of respondents, located in one city at a specific time – even when these are supplemented by fairly extensive historical investigation. For full understanding of such constraints we need first to describe the exact shape taken by our investigation. Then we must consider the restrictions imposed by our focus on Belfast, rather than on the Province as a whole, and by the staging of the survey in 1966 rather than later. The uses of the Belfast–Glasgow comparison in isolating factors associated on the one hand with political compromise and on the other with intransigence and disorder can also usefully be considered. Following these specific points we can assess the general advantages and disadvantages of our data in understanding the present crisis and enumerate the various stages of our discussion.

During the winter of 1965–6 three surveys were carried out in Glasgow:[1] interviewees consisted of a systematic probability sample of Glasgow residents, all Glasgow councillors willing to answer questions, and a group of party workers. Starting in June 1966, two surveys were carried out in Belfast using questionnaires as similar to those used in Glasgow as different local conditions would permit: interviewees consisted of a systematic probability sample of Belfast residents, and all Belfast councillors willing to answer questions. These surveys are described in detail in the Appendix. In addition to residents and councillors we interviewed the correspondents who supplied local papers and local television with political news from Belfast. We were also favoured by interviews with a number of senior officials of Belfast Corporation who wish to remain anonymous.

Obviously the attitudes and perceptions elicited by our surveys were formed not in isolation but as reactions to preceding events. Particularly in Ireland, where the past often carries more emotive force than the present, we could not fully understand the survey responses without putting them into their historical context. The functioning of institutions, too, often depends greatly on their historical evolution and origins. For these reasons we made a study of the political history of Belfast, the most intensive to date. In the historical analysis we paid particular attention to questions of contemporary relevance, such as the conditions contributing to Unionist hegemony in the city and the link between economic conditions and religious rioting.

Our reason for extending the original surveys from Glasgow to Belfast lay in the unique combination – as between the two cities – of basic institutional and social similarities with strong political divergences. The natural procedure through which to discover factors associated with instability is by comparisons between a stable and an unstable city: characteristics found in the latter and not in the former can be taken to have some connection with instability. The trouble is that there can be so many. Where the cities resemble each other on basic social characteristics, as Glasgow and Belfast do, fewer differences will appear but these are more likely to be strongly associated with instability.

It is general knowledge that Glasgow, in contrast to Belfast, shares general British tendencies to political compromise. Scottish nationalist activities in Glasgow have taken the form of peaceful pressure-group and electoral activities, and these have also characterised Socialist and Labour movements. An orderly transfer of power from the Labour Party to the opposition Progressives took place in 1968. These behavioural dissimilarities occur within an institutional framework common to British cities, where the Council, whose members are elected from wards for a three-year term, combines local legislative and executive functions, both of which are exercised through a complex committee structure. The institutional differences between Glasgow and Belfast are two. First there are different methods of selecting the Council – through an annual election of a third of the councillors in Glasgow, and three-yearly 'general elections' in Belfast of all councillors and one half of the aldermen. Second, the local franchise was more restricted in Belfast, where property qualifications contrasted with universal adult suffrage in Glasgow. Nevertheless, as a result of regular elections and consequent party competition, both cities can be regarded as democracies.[2]

Reinforcing the broad institutional resemblances between Glasgow and Belfast are the social similarities. Belfast has, of course, less than half the population of Glasgow, but since Northern Ireland has less than half the population of Scotland, it is equally dominant within its region. Both Glasgow and Belfast are nineteenth-century industrial cities which rose on the basis of textiles and heavy engineering and now face similar problems of a declining industrial base, considerable unemployment and the need to diversify. Hard data also underline the cities' close socio-economic similarities. There is an almost exact correspondence between the proportions of the work force at various levels of socio-economic status, apart from the higher ratio of skilled to unskilled manual workers in Glasgow.[3] The ratio of Catholics to non-Catholics in both cities is one to three and in both Presbyterianism is a leading Protestant denomination.[4] Social tension between Catholics and Protestants is high in both cases, and affrays between the sects are common – centring in Belfast on political and social questions and in Glasgow on football. Catholics in both Glasgow and Belfast tend to have Southern Irish connections, while Protestants tend to be of Northern Irish, Scottish or English extraction. As a result of heavy Irish immigration in the nineteenth century Glasgow politics have experienced the impact of historical Irish divisions, although obviously not to the same extent as Belfast. Their main continuing influence lies in the solid voting support given by Catholics to the Labour Party in Glasgow. Generally, however, Glasgow politics have centred round the opposition of class interests familiar in most British cities and seemingly no more bitter or divisive than elsewhere.[5] This is in strong contrast to sectarian suspicions and political rivalry in Belfast. Socio-economic similarities thus made possible a reasonably controlled investigation of conditions associated with compromise in Glasgow and overt violence in Belfast. We will emphasise below the importance of having in the Glasgow situation a norm by which to evaluate politically significant differences in Belfast.

Belfast is not an exact microcosm of Northern Ireland, even though it contains a quarter of the Northern Irish population. There is some question of how far any investigation centred on the city can produce information relevant to the problems of the whole Province. Even if our interest were solely in the politics of Belfast there is the further problem of how far tension and violence can be attributed to causes operating purely within the city, and not to causes operative within the Province as a whole.

Taking the last question first, it is true that to consider any polity in isolation is to some extent to segregate it artificially from influences in the wider environment. This is as true of Northern Ireland as of Belfast. It can be argued that the Provincial crisis will not be fully understood until it is placed in the wider Irish or even British context. But whatever the antecedent causes or wider influences, they cannot operate directly to produce tension or violence: they can only produce such effects through intervening attitudes and behaviour present in the locality. And the investigation of local attitudes and behaviour takes us quite far back in the explanation of local tensions and violence.

Moreover, Belfast Corporation is an autonomous body which in its present form long antedates the Stormont Parliament.[6] Local problems in Belfast generate issues, most of which are within the jurisdiction of the Corporation rather than of the Stormont Parliament. (For example, of the five local issues current in Belfast in 1966 which we investigated in detail, only one directly involved Stormont.) It was in fact the very freedom of local governments in Northern Ireland to regulate such matters as housing and employment that touched off the initial stages of the present crisis.[7]

This effect of local government operations underlines the usefulness of studying them as autonomous units, as we shall study Belfast in this book. Simultaneously, however, the effect points to the way in which the politics of local government in some respects reflect the politics of the whole Province. The division between Catholics and Protestants is repeated at local level, and the distaste of Catholics for the Protestant-dominated government at Stormont was extended to the Protestant-dominated local authorities. While issues differ, divisions and behaviour in the localities may reveal a great deal about what goes on at the provincial level. Quite apart from Belfast's numerical weight in the province we thus feel able at many points to extrapolate from relationships among residents and activists in Belfast in 1966 to such relationships in the Province as a whole; and from these to suggest an interpretation for the immediate development of the crisis.

Quite apart from the ability to generalise, an investigation into Belfast politics has its own justification at this point in time. For the Corporation itself has fallen victim to civil disorders in the city streets. As part of reforms designed to placate Catholic opinion, the Unionist Government at Stormont in a series of policy statements from October to December 1970 clarified its intention of accepting the Macrory Report, which recommends the transfer of all significant local powers to the central Government and the reduction of all local authorities (Belfast among them) to district councils. In practical terms, therefore, our historical study is coterminous with the whole of the Corporation's existence as an effective decision-making body and the detailed statistical analysis covers the whole modern period during which the city was governed within the framework of the Act of 1896. Our gratification at the definitiveness thereby given to our study is tempered by regret for the passing of an institution of venerable, though not always respectable, antecedents.

If our information is limited spatially to Belfast the detailed survey answers are limited temporally to 1966, two years before the first open signs of crisis in Northern Ireland. The survey findings are of course supplemented by our historical analysis and, interpreted in the light of the historical evidence and our later experience of 1969 and 1970, can be brought to bear quite directly upon later events. In 1966 the moderate Unionist attempt to win over Catholics was at its height. This attempted rapprochement heightened Catholic aspirations while splitting the Unionist party internally and failing to produce any recognisable improvement in Catholic well-being. Disillusion with the moderate Unionists is usually thought to have spread in 1968, because that was when the first overt protests were staged. Our evidence indicates a credibility gap between moderate Unionists and population which existed from the very start of O'Neill's opening to the Catholics (Chapters 11 and 12). Difficulties in communication rather than an absence of majority support for reform seem to have been at the heart of the crisis. The fact that this discovery was made for 1966, when Right-wing Unionist and Left-wing Catholic opposition was muted, supports an interpretation in communication terms more strongly than if the finding was made for later years when political waters had already been muddied. In some respects, therefore, it is an advantage to have detailed information from an earlier year, since the factors isolated can be clearly seen to be preconditions of crisis rather than results of the initial protest.

Very often the kind of explanation evolved depends on the type and extent of the information used. Thus, if the investigation starts by focusing upon a single factor as the explanation for Irish ills, the materials collected on that premise will be likely to support the explanation. For example, a major influence upon present discontents is the feeling on the part of a third of the Northern Irish population that the Unionist Government has no claim on their obedience or loyalty. However, as an interpretation of the present crisis an explanation in terms of Catholic alienation alone would be inadequate, since the Unionist Government has been rejected by the same section since its inception, yet it was shaken by crisis only in 1968 after functioning efficiently for almost fifty years.

Our own strategy has therefore been to take as many factors as possible into account in explaining the tensions which led to crisis. Thus our historical analysis devotes attention to industrial development in Belfast and the effects this had on the composition of the population, as well as to overtly political events. Our survey material permits the investigation of voting behaviour, recruitment to political office, political representation and communication, as well as the direct support given to established political institutions. A particular feature of discussion is the way in which residents and activists behaved in relation to five issues current in 1966, four of which were directly related to O'Neill's policy of conciliation.

Besides examining popular attitudes, we focus as much or more on those of political activists. It is by now a platitude that the shape taken by popular feeling is always moderated or sharpened by élite reactions. Any explanation of the origins of crisis which ignored the latter is bound to be incomplete. Our concurrent interviews with councillors, correspondents and residents on a set of related topics also permit an examination of interrelationships between them, so that we have some idea of how activist initiatives affected the populace, and how far activists responded to popular feeling.

In keeping with the general strategy of explanation just outlined we review a variety of attitudes and behaviour before narrowing discussion to those which seem to have a real effect on political instability. In winnowing out the directly relevant factors we do not need to rely only on our unaided judgement supplemented by findings from Belfast: only where specific attitudes or behaviour do not appear in Glasgow and do appear in Belfast must we credit their influence on political instability.

Our discussion begins with analyses of the main areas of political activity in Belfast, as these have evolved over time and as they manifested themselves in 1966. The first five chapters trace the economic, social and political development of Belfast from its origins to the crisis of 1968–9. (Although we may refer to specific events later, we do not generally carry our discussion beyond the beginning of 1970.) In Chapter 1 we sketch the development of the town from the grant of a charter by James I in 1613 to the passing of the Great Reform Act, which gave Belfast two members elected by the £10 householders. Chapter 2 describes the beginnings of party organisations and their development up to 1855. Chapters 3 and 4 carry the story further to the mature development of the politico-religious antagonisms characteristic of the city. In Chapter 4, to prevent tedious repetition, the strict chronological pattern is abandoned when discussing economic and social factors and in these cases the story is carried up to the present day. Otherwise, developments after the setting up of Northern Ireland in 1920 are confined to Chapter 5.

Linking the more general historical discussion with the detailed review of survey data is our analysis of the institutional context of Unionist hegemony in the city, using ward election returns from 1897 to 1967 (Chapter 6). Chapter 7 carries on the discussion of party competition by examining popular reactions to the parties in 1966 and the social factors correlated with residents' choice of party. The next two chapters deal with questions arising from the voting analysis. Since class and religion affect voting most powerfully of all social factors it is of interest to study their correlates and consequences (Chapter 8). In Chapter 9 we see how far party, class and religious divisions affect popular perceptions and political preferences.

Turning from population to activists, we examine first the basic question of how councillors were recruited for the office they hold – this analysis also bears on the problem of how far Belfast activists are socially representative of the population, compared with those in Glasgow (Chapter 10). In Chapter 11 we go to the related question of how far their issue-preferences reflect those of population and constituents and how far councillors even have accurate knowledge of what population groups are thinking. This leads naturally into an examination of communication (Chapter 12).

The issues of daily politics are debated within the context of procedures and institutions which sometimes determine their outcome. Chapter 13 examines the degree of support for established institutions which existed in Belfast compared with Glasgow in 1966. Lack of support for basic procedures might be one explanation for instability: other explanations based on the particular shape taken by distributions of political preferences and of social characteristics in Belfast are also confronted with our data. Our Conclusions (Chapter 14) integrate the results of the various analyses into a coherent description and explanation of the current crisis, distinguishing as far as possible between basic conditions which always made a crisis possible and the short-term factors which actually triggered the crisis of late 1968. If these Conclusions aid understanding of the complex political problems of Northern Ireland, our investigation will have proved worthwhile. Our concurrent description of municipal affairs during the last days of the Corporation should at any rate commend the work to contemporary historians.

Our research would not have been possible without financial help from the Nuffield Foundation, the Social Science Research Council, the Universities of Essex and Strathclyde and the Queen's University, Belfast. To our universities, colleagues and students generally we are indebted for much help. We should especially mention Mrs S. E. Baker, Dr R. J. Baxter, Dr J. A. Brand, Dr S. Elliott, Mr M. Marsh, Mr N. May, Mr E. Roughley, Mr A. J. Skinner, Mr A. L. M. Smith and Mr M. J. Taylor, who helped us in various ways with research, computing, statistics and interviewing. To Michael Margolis particularly we owe a model for the conduct of our survey and for our discussion of representation and communication. To Professor J. C. Beckett and Professor E. R. R. Green, who read the manuscript in part and offered much useful advice, we are also grateful. To many municipal councillors, officials, journalists and other citizens of Belfast we owe interview material on which much of our discussion is based. In such a controversial area as the politics of Belfast, we should, however, make it very clear that we ourselves bear sole responsibility for the findings and judgements made in this book.

NOTES

1. These are described, and findings reported in Ian Budge, J. A. Brand, Michael Margolis and A. L. M. Smith, *Political Stratification and Democracy* (London, 1972) and *Class, Religion, Politics: Glasgow* (forthcoming).
2. See the discussion of this point at the end of Chapter 6.
3. See Table 8.1, below.
4. See the discussion of Table 8.10, below.
5. For comparisons of class feeling in Glasgow and other British cities see Chapter 8 of Ian Budge and D. W. Urwin, *Scottish Political Behaviour* (London, 1966).
6. The Northern Ireland Parliament and Government, which meet at Stormont, a suburb of Belfast, are popularly termed the Stormont Parliament and Stormont Government, in order to distinguish them from the corresponding British bodies meeting at Westminster. The Govern-

ment and Parliament of Northern Ireland were suspended in March 1972 and replaced by a Secretary of State and two junior Ministers.

7. A general argument for regarding all polities as located at some point on a continuum between complete autonomy and complete subordination in decision-making is made in the introduction to *Political Stratification*. Governments will not fall at either extreme point because none are completely free from external constraints and none are completely subordinated, whatever the formal relationship between national and local governments.

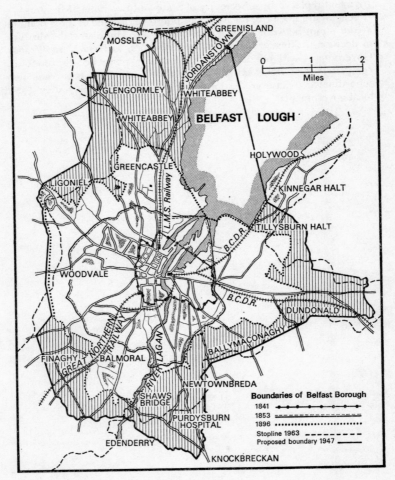

BELFAST

Map showing the Belfast municipal boundary as established in 1897, together with the new boundary proposed by the Corporation in 1947.

(Of the shaded area, the part lying south of the River Lagan is in County Down, the remainder in Antrim.

1 The Early Years:
1613–1832

BELFAST alone among the great towns of Ireland has been a political community almost from its beginning, which can be dated precisely to the first decade of the seventeenth century. Like all the other towns, with the exception of Kilkenny, it was built on tidal water at a ford across the river Lagan. Although some habitations existed since prehistoric times, they were insignificant until the conquest of Ulster under Elizabeth and James I. During the first five hundred years after the Norman invasion the ford of Belfast was the object of a long struggle between the Anglo-Normans and the Irish, and a twelfth-century castle was built there, not twenty miles from the first and greatest Norman castle of Carrickfergus. From the fourteenth to the sixteenth century Belfast was in the hands of native chiefs who dominated the whole of Ulster except Carrickfergus, and a small part of County Down. The next efforts to gain control of Belfast were almost contemporary with the coming of the Reformed religion to Ireland, and the reign of Elizabeth witnessed the subjugation of the Gaelic chiefs and the granting of the castle and harbour of Belfast to a succession of royal retainers, including Essex. The conquest was complete after the final desperate rebellion of the remaining Ulster chiefs, the Earls of Tyrone and Tyrconnell in the last years of Elizabeth's reign, their submission and eventual flight to the continent in 1607.

The castle and land of Belfast were granted in 1603 to Sir Arthur Chichester, the military genius who as Lord Deputy (1605–15) consolidated the conquest of Ulster and in the years after the 'flight of the Earls' planted the territories formerly ruled by the O'Neills and the O'Donnells (comprising the present counties Armagh, Londonderry, Fermanagh, Tyrone, Cavan and Donegal)[1] with English and Scottish settlers, lured

by the promise of generous helpings of the confiscated lands.
The main purpose of the plantations enthusiastically promoted
by Chichester was to strengthen the tiny Protestant interest in
Ireland, since both the native Irish and the Old English (i.e.
descendants of pre-Reformation settlers) remained Catholic,
and were persistently, though unjustly, suspected by the Dublin
Government of potential disloyalty and sympathy with King
James's foreign enemies – the first time in Irish history that the
profession of religion was equated with disloyalty. With English
settlers came English law and English political forms. Even
before the plantation Ulster had been divided into nine counties
and sub-divided into baronies. Assizes were held, commissions
of the peace established and, most important of all, between
1610 and 1613 forty towns were given charters entitling them
to return two members to the Irish Parliament in Dublin, and
endowing them with the other attributes of a parliamentary
borough.

The creation of these new boroughs was explicitly designed to
counter the Roman Catholic majority in the county seats and
to enable the parliament of 1613 – the first in nearly thirty
years – to proceed with legislation against recusancy.

The charters for the forty boroughs[2] established between 1610
and 1613 were in strange contrast with those created in previous
reigns. Although a freeman element was allowed with a very
limited share in the municipal government, the right to send
two members to parliament was exclusively vested in approximately a dozen 'free burgesses', members of a self-perpetuating
Protestant Corporation. From the start, therefore, Belfast,
Enniskillen and Coleraine were close boroughs by contrast with
Dublin, Cork or even Carrickfergus, where the freemen were
the most numerous element in the constituency, and the Irish
corporation boroughs loomed far larger in the Irish political
scene than their counterparts in Britain.

The narrowness of the franchise made the Irish boroughs
created by James I particularly liable to fall into the clutches of
a patron, especially in the next century when parliaments sat
regularly and seats in the House of Commons came to be
prized. Moreover, some of the borough charters gave certain
named aristocrats or gentry exclusive rights in municipal government and none more so than Belfast, the Lord Deputy's own

borough. By the charter the Lord of the Castle, Sir Arthur Chichester (later Baron Chichester of Belfast),[3] and the constable appointed by him were to be members of the Corporation *ex officio*; the Sovereign, or head of the Corporation, was to be selected annually by the free burgesses from a list of three furnished by the Lord of the Castle – whose approval was also required for the municipal bye-laws. The charter included a popular element in the constitution – freemen 'without limit',[4] who were not endowed with any elective function but might act with the Sovereign and free burgesses to make bye-laws and assessments on the rest of the inhabitants – the normal functions of a Corporation grand jury in Ireland.

During the first century of its corporate existence Belfast as a trading port enjoyed steady development, interrupted only by occasional wars, e.g. the Dutch wars of the 1660s and 1670s. In the beginning there were the Castle, a few houses, a market and little more.[5] But soon it became a natural growth point for the settlers coming from Scotland and England to Antrim and Down – the two counties not included in the original plantation but lying closest to the 'mainland'. The early records of the Corporation show the names of families from the north of England and south of Scotland who flourished in trade during these years – Vesey (the first Sovereign), Le Squire (Chichester's agents), Leathes (shippers), Waring (tanners), and most prominent of all, Macartney (millers and sugar refiners).[6] These were mainly engaged in the export trade – and before long they were even building their own ships.

By the 1690s Belfast's sea-going trade was six or seven times that of Carrickfergus (previously the largest port in the North) and its merchants were dealing with most of Europe and the American colonies. Its population was at least 1,000 in the 1660s – 2,000 at the accession of James II in 1685. The Irish wars of religion did not affect Belfast greatly. The first in 1641 was caused by an unexpected rising of the dispossessed Irish of the North, who hoped to make common cause with the Catholic gentry of the South and exact from the much-troubled King a measure of religious freedom – with the possibility of some restoration of the forfeited estates. That rising, though instigated in Ulster, spread to three provinces and eventually to the three kingdoms; but the outcome was the decisive defeat of the Catholics, Irish and Old English, and the consolidation of the new order.

The town of Belfast was protected from the depredations of the native Irish by a Scottish army, which in its six years' stay in the city established the Presbyterian religion (shared by most of the Scots settlers) on a firm foundation. During these years, too, Belfast was the centre of the Government of East Ulster (the Commissioners of the Belfast Precinct). The Restoration of 1660 involved the re-establishment of Protestant episcopacy in Ireland, Presbyterian clergy were deprived of the livings they had acquired during the Commonwealth by declaration of the Dublin Parliament, and all persons were obliged to conform to the Established Church. In spite of these grievances the Presbyterian community in Belfast, as elsewhere in Ulster, continued to grow. By the end of the century – although proof is difficult, since the records are meagre – Presbyterians appear to have outnumbered the Church of Ireland community.[7]

Although they were free to practise their religion and their profession or trade – rights which were afterwards denied to their Catholic fellow-countrymen – Presbyterians in Belfast, as elsewhere in Ulster, do not seem to have played a part in municipal affairs. All free burgesses of Belfast until 1690 were members of the Established Church. From its inception the Corporation was manned by friends and retainers of the Patron. The Sovereign was re-elected for years until Lord Donegall decided on a replacement.[8] (The same was true of the two members of parliament.) But from the start the Corporation was hampered by the lack of a regular income. The sources prescribed in the Charter, custom and tolls, from the market,[9] fees for admission to the freedom and fines imposed by the Borough Court of Record were inadequate. When extra money was needed for any purpose it had to be met either from voluntary subscription (as the provision of a water supply) or by subvention from the Patron (as the building and endowment of a town school), or by assessment on the inhabitants (as the building of the Town Hall in 1664). In the last case the Corporation grand jury – the freemen – joined with the burgesses and expected in return to be associated in the making of by-laws. (There are a number of entries in the Corporation records between 1662 and 1694 which show that these privileges were reciprocal.)[10]

But even this small share by the inhabitants in the town government was grudged by the Corporation. The right of inhabitants to the freedom was gradually eroded and in 1671 when the Corporation (vainly) petitioned the Lord Lieutenant and Council in Dublin for a modification of the Charter to provide for a mayor, aldermen and common council, and for fresh revenue – through imposing wharfage, quayage and cranage on all foreign ships using the port of Belfast – they pointedly excluded the freemen from any share in the making of by-laws.[11] The confines imposed on the municipal government by the Charter of 1613 were already being narrowed and the power of the Patron maximised.

The events of the unhappy reign of James II must be dealt with briefly. At his accession the all-Protestant Corporation and 126 inhabitants[12] sent an effusive address of welcome to the King, one of the earliest to be received. Nor did it offer any more than the most formal resistance to the King's demand in 1687 for a surrender of the Charter.[13] This demand was simultaneously made to all Irish Corporations at the time in order to hasten the entry of Catholics to the corporate posts from which they had been excluded. The new Charter,[14] granted on 16 October 1688 (4 James 11), just a month before the arrival of William of Orange at Torbay, did not prove of much advantage to the Belfast Catholics (of whom there were then very few), but broke the oligarchy of the Lord of the Castle[15] and the Established Church. The number of free burgesses was increased from 12 to 35, and they, with the Sovereign and other officers, were made removable by the Crown. One interesting consequence of the revocation of the old Charter was that the new Corporation (all of whom were nominated by the Crown) was divided almost equally between Presbyterians – who included the Sovereign, Thomas Pottinger, a well-known merchant and shipper – and Catholics.

Belfast was occupied by King James's forces during the revolution, after which there was a large exodus of Protestants – including the second Earl of Donegall and his family – to Scotland. However, the Sovereign kept at his post and secured from James protection for those who remained, and leave to

return for those who fled (June 1689). When Marshal Schomberg (August 1689) invested the city with 10,000 Williamite
troops, Pottinger dutifully paid the expenses of quartering and
servicing them, for which he was afterwards reimbursed by
William and Mary.[16]

William himself, who spent four days in Belfast,[17] confirmed
the restoration by Schomberg of the old Corporation. Although
there was no formal change in the Charter, Presbyterians were
nominated as free burgesses and dominated the Corporation
between 1691 and 1704.

The Great Revolution ensured the predominance of the
Protestant religion in the public life of Ireland. The Catholics,
beaten for the second time in fifty years, were cowed into
submission and fresh privations were in store for them. The
laws for the suppression of popery, passed by the Irish Parliament from 1703, excluded Catholics from Parliament itself,[18]
from corporate offices, and finally (1727), deprived Catholics
and freeholders of the parliamentary franchise. But the
restrictions aimed primarily at the Catholics also affected the
Dissenters. The Act which imposed a sacramental test for
holders of public office also hit the Presbyterians. Six members
of Belfast Corporation, including the Sovereign, David Butle,
and one of Belfast's two parliamentary representatives[19] had to
resign (1704), and this disability in the Irish Parliament was
not entirely counterbalanced by the extension of the *Regium
Donum*,[20] the annual grant for the upkeep of the Presbyterian
Church introduced by Charles II in 1672. For the rest of the
century Ulster Presbyterians could engage to their hearts'
content in commerce or agriculture, but public office and entry
to the only University, Trinity College, Dublin, was denied
them.[21]

The effect of the Popery Laws, as far as Belfast was concerned,
was to eliminate the right of the majority of the inhabitants to a
share in the government of the town.

From the time when Butle and his fellow-Presbyterians were
replaced by six Episcopalians the Corporation slowly but
irreversibly deteriorated into a complete, though ineffectual,
oligarchy. The right of freedom through inhabitancy fell into
abeyance; the Corporation grand jury was discontinued; the
Corporation itself merely elected the Sovereign and the M.P.s

at the behest of the Patron; the Borough Court of Record and Manor Court[22] declined. Abuses also crept into the administration of the town. Money voted for specific purposes was not used and the unexpended balances accumulated. The Sovereign (by the Charter) was entitled to the income from the markets. This by the end of the eighteenth century was £500 a year, but the town received no corresponding benefits – since the Sovereigns would not even perform magisterial duties. Late in the eighteenth century the Irish House of Commons heard a petition claiming that the Earl of Belfast (who was both a peer and a minor) had voted as a member of the Corporation.[23] Nor did any significant change occur when the old Irish Parliament was abolished by the Act of Union and Belfast survived with one member at Westminster. By the end of the eighteenth century the divorce between Corporation and people was complete[25] – even the Catholic Relief Act of 1793 failed to produce (as in Londonderry) any Catholic freemen – and the grave judgment of *Rep. Comm. Mun. Corp.* in 1835 sums up the last century of the unreformed Corporation's history:

> The Corporation, as now conducted, embraces no principle of representation and confers on the inhabitants no benefit. No power of control or check is preserved; the proceedings are carried on without publicity and the consequences have been that great neglect and abuse of trusts reposed in the body have occurred, and have remained so long concealed, that the utmost difficulties now lie in the way of any attempt to correct them.[26]

Apart from calling a few town meetings – to consider the riot of 1813 and to protest against Catholic Emancipation[27] – the old Corporation scarcely impinged on the consciousness of the citizens during the first three decades of the nineteenth century. In politics throughout they merely reflected the aspirations and prejudices of the Donegall family, who were in no way distinguished from the general run of Irish peers, unimaginative 'Church and King' Tories.

One of the consequences of the disabilities imposed on the Presbyterians was a brain drain to Scotland, at whose tolerant universities many of the best-known citizens secured the higher education denied to them at home and where some of the most illustrious remained to teach – Joseph Black, Professor of Chemistry at Edinburgh, being the outstanding example. The Scottish universities indeed were a source of the radical ideas that percolated back to Belfast at the end of the century. Meanwhile the city for the first half of the century as before was a thriving port, and with a population of 8,000 in 1757 started to develop an industrial base.[28] The cotton industry was established on a factory basis in the 1780s[29] but it was 'an exotic growth developed from a combination of existing textile production and easy access to the new technology in Great Britain, but restricted to the narrow base of a domestic market'.[30]

But while the much older linen industry remained on a cottage basis the cotton boom provided the impetus for Belfast's population expansion – from 8,000 in 1757 to 13,000 in 1782 and 20,000 in 1800.[31] Inevitably such a population increase created a demand for more houses and more urban amenities. But the supine Corporation did little and the Patron seemed content with his reputation as the peer with the largest rent roll and with trying to acquire the status symbol of the Irish grandees – a parliamentary following. In spite of efforts to influence the elections in the neighbouring counties of Antrim and Down, Lord Donegall[32] by the time of the Union did not control more than three members – the two from Belfast and one for Carrickfergus. The prosperous merchants took the initiative and, by founding independently a number of civic bodies, made good the deficiency left by Patron and Corporation – a Chamber of Commerce (1783); a Ballast Board founded in 1784 to develop the port (by 1800 a graving dock was built); a Charitable Society (1752) to provide material relief and hospitalisation for the destitute;[33] a poorhouse built in 1768. The centre of the town was laid out tastefully by a number of enterprising merchants having purchased the sites from Donegall.[34] It was not surprising, therefore, that the composition of the Police Board set up in 1800 should have excluded the Patron and Corporation.

Up to this point the development of Belfast has resembled that of the other boroughs in the planted province – such as Lisburn, Londonderry and Coleraine: aristocratic patrons, typical products of the Anglo-Irish Protestant (i.e. Episcopalian)

Ascendancy monopolising civic power, and the Presbyterian merchant and working classes assiduously pursuing their avocations. But now we come to an extraordinary interlude of sixteen years when Belfast becomes for the first and last time the centre of Irish radical thought while other Ulster boroughs remain largely unaffected. These are the years between the founding of the Volunteer movement in 1782 and the rebellion of 1798.

The story has often been told before and therefore may be recounted here briefly.[35] From 1778, when France and Spain seemed about to intervene in the American war, Ireland was largely denuded of troops. To make good this deficiency Protestants all over Ireland formed companies of volunteers armed and equipped at their own expense. By 1782 over 100,000 were enrolled. By this time the danger of foreign invasion had passed but the Volunteers soon realised their potential as a pressure group and had exacted from a frightened Dublin Government the repeal of all the legislative disabilities gradually imposed on the Irish Parliament by the British, and a Renunciation Act which declared that the exclusive right of the Irish Parliament to legislate for Ireland was to be forever unquestionable.[36]

Although the Protestant landlord class from which the Irish Parliament was almost exclusively drawn believed that the newly acquired autonomy would benefit themselves alone, the middle-class Protestants who formed the rank-and-file of the Volunteers and the unenfranchised mass of Roman Catholics[39] hoped for the abolition of close boroughs and extension of the franchise. On this issue, brought into the open almost immediately after the settlement of the constitutional dispute with England, three main attitudes developed over the next decade. First, there were those who firmly opposed any extension of the franchise to the Catholics on the ground that it would inevitably lead to the subversion of Protestant ascendancy. These included the government party in the House of Commons, most Irish peers, prelates of the Established Church, and some dissenters. Secondly, there were those who wished a gradual enfranchisement of the Catholics – £50 householders, £20 householders, even £10 householders. These included most of the Patriot Party (who had supported legislative independence) some established clergy, a considerable number of Presbyterian clergy, and, incidentally, some Catholic landed gentry. Lastly, there were those who desired the total abolition of political discrimination between the religions – the bulk of the Catholics and the United Irishmen (to be discussed below).

The Volunteers were split by the controversy[38] and several conventions meeting to discuss parliamentary reform presented resolutions without mentioning the Catholics. But Ulster seemed to lead the liberals. By allowing Catholics formally to join their ranks the Ulster Volunteers gave (in 1784) a lead to the rest of the country.[39] (They were later dissuaded by their timorous general, Charlemont, from pressing for full enfranchisement of the Catholics.) The Synod of Ulster, the governing body of the Presbyterian Church in Ulster,[40] passed a declaration in favour of complete abolition of discrimination; the Belfast companies of Volunteers paraded at the opening of the first Catholic Church, St Mary's, in 1784, and were thanked by the parishioners in an address in which gratitude struggled with surprise; a town meeting[41] was called in Belfast to discuss the resolutions passed by a similar meeting in Dublin. They approved the Dublin resolution with one emendation:[42] 'the *gradual* extension of suffrage to our too long oppressed brethren the Roman Catholics, preserving unimpaired the Protestant Government of this country', and sent a memorial to Pitt which the latter refused to forward to the King.

But by 1790 the more advanced reformers pessimistically believed that the dead weight of the landed interest was too strong to permit the Irish Parliament to reform itself. However, the success of the French Revolution gave a new boost to their sagging morale. In 1790 there was established in Belfast the Society of United Irishmen – 'To unite the whole people of Ireland, to abolish the memory of all past dissensions and to substitute the common name of Irishman in place of the denomination of Protestant, Catholic and Dissenter' – the most important radical group ever to emerge in Ireland, dedicated to the setting up of a republic in which all Irishmen, Catholic and Protestant, would share the same national commitment and in which privilege would be abolished. Apart from the leader, Theobald Wolfe Tone, a Dublin barrister of Protestant background but no religious affiliation, and Thomas

Russell, a devout Anglican from Cork, the rest of the executive committee were from Ulster. Of the leading Belfast United Irishmen, Dr William Drennan, McTier, Neilson, Henry Joy McCracken (grandson of the founder of the *Belfast News Letter*), and Rev. Steele Dickson (Moderator of the Synod of Ulster), were all from Belfast or its environs. Although at the outset the United Irishmen aimed merely at Catholic Emancipation and parliamentary reform, by 1794 they were committed to complete separation from England.

The United Irishmen spread rapidly. They had in Belfast a thriving newspaper, *The Northern Star.* Nor were they deflected from their aims by the Catholic Relief Act of 1793 which gave the vote to the Catholics on the same basis as the rest of the electorate (i.e. the 'wretched tribe' of forty shilling freeholders in the counties and the customary medley of borough franchises), but continued to exclude them from Parliament.[43] Unfortunately this measure of relief prevented their making much headway among the apathetic Catholic masses. When eventually the United Irish rebellion took place, in 1798, it was evident that outside Ulster only a few hundred belonged to the organisation.

The Irish Government, gravely worried by the development of a movement that they could not regard as other than subversive, encouraged county authorities to raise fresh companies of exclusively Protestant volunteers. And in Ulster the latent prejudice against Catholics was soon exploited, since the new companies in many areas sang anti-Catholic songs and provoked the emergence of rival groups. In County Armagh, in particular, open warfare developed between armed bands of Protestant and Catholic farmers which the magistrates and the Government were not particularly anxious to put down, since this dissension was the best antidote to the United Irish poison.

Out of a battle in Armagh in 1796 between the Peep of Day boys (Protestant), and the Defenders (Catholic), which the latter lost, emerged the Orange Order,[44] a militant and classless Protestant secret society which in its first public pronouncement included among its goals, in addition to the Constitution and the Protestant religion, the maintenance of the Established Church. To the hard-pressed Government, central and local, this appeared a godsend. Before long the Order found a considerable number of recruits not only in Ulster but also among

Protestants in Dublin and in the Midlands. The original bucolic leaders were supplanted by people of quality. The first Grand Master, Thomas Verner, was the son of Lord Donegall's brother-in-law, and the Grand Secretary was one of the ubiquitous Beresford family whose name recurs among lists of leading Government officials throughout the century. Several of the largest landowners joined the Order, though Charlemont held aloof and deplored the fickleness of the people who only ten years before had been ready to ruin 'themselves and their country by giving up all to the Papists'.[45]

With official encouragement several corps of Yeomanry, consisting largely of Orangemen, were set up, but it was noticed that wherever the United Irishmen were strong the Orangemen found difficulty in recruiting.[46] Belfast, in particular, was for them a stony ground.[47]

After two years of severe military repression in which the Orangemen joined with some British regiments, the United Irishmen in 1798 sprang a rebellion. It was confined to the two opposite ends of the east of Ireland – Wexford and Antrim. The Wexford revolt, which deteriorated into a *jacquerie* involving the massacre of some Protestants, did not help the cause in the North where memories were still fresh of the massacre of Protestants during the rebellion of 1641. The revolt was easily put down. Although the rebels fought bravely there were only two skirmishes – at Antrim and Ballynahinch. Most of the leaders were executed, including Henry Joy McCracken, William Orr and Rev. William Porter. All those executed and transported from Ulster were Presbyterians – it was estimated that out of 183 Presbyterian ministers in Ulster eighteen were known sympathisers with the rebellion,[48] and ten were imprisoned; two of them were executed. The Catholics of Ulster remained largely quiescent: at Ballynahinch some fought on the rebel side, but many more served with the militia.

During the rebellion Belfast was quiet, since it was heavily garrisoned, and a local corps of yeomanry was formed to supplement the militia. After 1798 most of the radical leaders were dead or exiled. Only Drennan, who had withdrawn from the United Irishmen in 1794, and the Simms brothers lived on quietly in Belfast. The brief episode in which 'Ulster joined Ireland' was over.

In the aftermath of the rebellion the Government introduced its scheme for a legislative union (with a half promise of satis-faction of the remaining Catholic claims). Again this was a cause of conflict between Patron and town.[49] Several groups of merchants and almost all the Orange lodges submitted petitions against the Union. The first Marquis of Donegall[50] was believed to be anti-Union, and his three members voted against the government in January 1799. But in the same month the Patron died and his son was bought over by permission to raise his own yeomanry corps. In 1800 the two anti-Unionist members[51] for Belfast were replaced by Edward May (father-in-law to the second Marquis), who voted for the Union, and a Belfast merchant who never took his seat. The Union passed into law on the same day as the Belfast Police Act.

We have dwelt so long upon the volunteer movement and its aftermath because of its unexpected character – a liberal episode in the history of a highly conservative city. Unexpected it certainly was, and to a large extent inexplicable, both as to its inception and decline. Several questions immediately arise. Was radicalism both in its political and religious forms an exotic growth soon to perish in the sharp Ulster climate, or did it take slow root, its development inevitably stunted by the repression of 1798 and the Union, to re-emerge forty years later? Was the enthusiasm for Catholic emancipation confined to a very small and enlightened element in the community, or not sincerely felt even by these? How could the mutually exclusive United Irishmen and Orangemen flourish in the same city within a short time of each other?

All historians of the period tackle these questions: none satisfactorily answers them. The answer given by Dr Rogers[52] appears to us the most plausible – that the early demands for reform, including admission of the Catholics to the franchise, were born of momentary enthusiasm, but that before long traditional counsels of prudence were bound to prevail in Ulster: 'The Irish Protestant still remained a firm believer in the necessity for an essentially Protestant State. Catholics might share the rights of citizenship, but only to a certain extent, to the extent which would make then contented and loyal subjects, but which would deprive them of political power, such as their numbers might demand.'

It is impossible to conjecture just how many Ulster Presbyterians were genuinely in favour of the Catholic claims. As Rogers hints, the enthusiasm may have been only skin deep.[53] The one significant group which was incontrovertibly tolerant and egalitarian was the United Irishmen and their main centre was Belfast,[54] the 'headquarters of disaffection in the north' as Castlereagh called it. But the United Irishmen were an elitist group, recruited from the professional classes. It is also clear that in the 1790s Belfast had fewer Catholics than any Ulster town; while in the rural areas, like Armagh (where it originated) the Orange Order greatly flourished. There Catholics and Protestants were almost equal in numbers and, in an era of rapid population growth, competing for the same land.

1800–1832

After 1800 Belfast receded into the background of Irish politics. The second Marquis of Donegall was weak-willed, if not weak-minded. Benn, the historian of Belfast, described him charitably as 'benevolent and always generous to the town (but) destitute of that firmness of character, and that commanding talent, necessary to deal with so great and rising a place as Belfast'.[55]

Although his rent-roll was the largest in Ireland, when he succeeded to the title Lord Donegall had already pawned the greater part of his inheritance in order to pay off gambling debts and throughout his life was constantly harassed by creditors. In the 1820s he disentailed his estates, selling off the properties to the various tenants, at considerable profit to them. Thus, by his death in 1844, the Donegall estates, though rapidly increasing in value, had passed almost entirely out of the hands of the family. Had the Marquis been more prudent the family might eventually have rivalled the Grosvenors in London or the Stanleys in Liverpool.

During this period, too, the old Corporation became even more alienated from the life of the city. The Patron to an even greater extent than his predecessors restricted his political patronage to his kinsmen: all the M.P.s representing Belfast at Westminster between the Union and the Reform Act were close relatives – father-in-law, cousins and son.[56] The Sovereigns of

Belfast were also for the most part close relatives and one of them was also appointed Vicar of Belfast. Meanwhile the Corporation at various times got into bad odour, through mismanagement of funds of the Charitable Society and through the exactions of a police magistrate who charged far more than the scale of fees allowed – it was argued that if the Sovereign did his duty and acted as a magistrate the police court would be unnecessary. The setting up of Police Boards[57] on which the Sovereign and burgesses sat, if resident (and sometimes as many as half were not), together with an equal number of other leading citizens, was interpreted as a slap in the face for the Corporation. Apart from the Sovereign's role in summoning town meetings, which could be requisitioned by the 'better class citizens' and in acting as honorary chairman of any voluntary civic body – like the soup kitchen committee set up in 1800 to alleviate the distress caused by an almost total crop failure, or the Dispensary and Fever Hospital (established in 1802) – the original civic authorities had ceased to be an object of interest to the inhabitants.[58]

As a result, Belfast Corporation was from the beginning of the nineteenth century increasingly superseded by police commissioners set up under the Belfast Police Act,[59] one of the last major pieces of legislation passed by the old Irish Parliament. (This new institution was not peculiar to Belfast – similar police boards were set up in Dublin.) A two-tier structure was established – twenty-one commissioners of police, the first listed *nominatim* in the Act with powers to fill casual vacancies, and another body of twenty-one, the Committee of Police, elected annually as an executive.[60]

To qualify for the Police Committee one had to be a householder, with a personal estate worth at least £1,000; to be a Police Commissioner one had to be an M.P., a peer, the heir apparent of a peer, or to possess a personal estate of £2,000 or an annual income of £100 from rent and profits of land. The electorate for the Police Committee was restricted to ratepayers of not less than twenty shillings per annum. The Police Commissioners were given responsibility for paving, lighting and cleaning the streets, and also for providing a fire service and a night watch, with powers to detain people arrested in breach of the peace, burglary or felony until they could appear before a

magistrate,[61] who held court twice weekly. Another Act in
1816 expanded the powers of the Commissioners. The basis of
the police tax was specified – a sliding scale ranging from sixpence for a house of £5 clear annual value to 1s. 6d. for a
house of £80 and upwards, and four qualified valuators were
to act as applotters. The Commissioners were also given power
to make more extensive by-laws. While the electorate for the
committee was narrowed to householders paying £2 a year in
rates (and for the Commissioners, £4), the qualification to
serve both as a Commissioner and committee member was
reduced to payment of rates to the amount of £4 and £2
respectively.

Using these powers the Police Boards proceeded to plan new
streets, to pave old ones, and to set up a night watch, a fire
brigade, and a magistrate's court.[62] But the Police Boards also
incurred censure. Under the second (private) Police Act the
valuation was applotted yearly by four professional 'valuators'
and there were many complaints that the valuation was too
high.[63] There was also the problem of overlapping jurisdictions:
in some functions the police committee was entirely independent of the Commissioners (appointing scavengers and night
watchmen), in others each had to consent to the others' acts
(borrowing), while in still others the two boards had to act
together (contracts for paving, lighting and cleansing).

Concurrently, Belfast experienced rapid population growth,
though not to the fantastic extent that the rest of the century
was to witness. It was far more extensive than any other
Irish city, and was equalled by only a few industrial cities in
England. (For a general discussion of the population explosion
see Appendix to this chapter.)

Meanwhile the economic character of the town was changing.
It was still a large market town with an export trade in agricultural produce and ancillary industries, such as brewing,
distilling and tanning. But it was also becoming an industrial
centre. Foundries, rope works, sugar refining, and vitriol
factories were all established by the 1790s. The main factor in
Belfast's conversion from a commercial to an industrial centre,
the foundation of her prosperity, was cotton. The cotton
industry had started in the 1780s (when the war of independ-

ence was impeding importation of cheap cotton goods from America). Its establishment in Belfast was due to an accident – the visit by Robert Joy, owner of a paper mill and son of the founder of the *Belfast News Letter*, [64] to Scotland where he became acquainted with the new cotton-spinning techniques of Hargreaves and Arkwright. Subsequently, he formed a partnership with another entrepreneur and, since risk capital and a supply of trained labour was lacking, persuaded the Belfast Charitable Society to allow the children in the Poorhouse to learn the trade of spinning. Subsequently Joy with his brother-in-law, John McCracken, founder of Belfast ropeworks (and father of Henry Joy McCracken) started a small spinning mill on the Falls Road. The first mill in Ireland had, however, been built at Whitehouse, on the Antrim side of Belfast Lough, by Nicholas Grimshaw, a Lancashire textile printer who had built and installed the machinery in the Belfast poorhouse. [65]

The cotton industry developed very rapidly, especially in Antrim and Down, where for a century the linen industry had already been established on a cottage basis. The fact that muslin weavers could earn three times as much as linen weavers (and also the fact that cotton is much easier to weave than linen) resulted in the almost complete extinction of linen weaving in Belfast. The spinning machinery was operated by water power more often than by steam (the first steam-powered mill was established in 1790), and the mills were not just concentrated in Belfast but were built within a ten-mile radius, close to streams and rivers. The supersession of linen by cotton in Belfast and its environs may be shown in the following table:

TABLE I.I

*Numbers of Linen and Cotton Looms in
Belfast 1760–1810*

	1760	1791	1806	1810
Linen looms	400	129	4	—
Cotton looms	—	522	629	860

While the total number employed in the cotton industry soared from 13,500 in 1800 to 33,000 in 1811, in Belfast alone in 1806 2,108 people were thus employed – that is, 10 per cent

of the entire population and about fifteen per cent of the
labour force.[66] Belfast was by 1811 importing over three
quarters of the total Irish imports of raw cotton. Cotton quickly
captured the Irish domestic market from linen (which in 1800
was three times as dear), but had little success in exporting to
England. (High protective duties were gradually scaled down
after the Union: in 1808 they reached 10 per cent, where they
remained until their total abolition in 1824, under Huskisson's
free trade policies.) It is worth noting that only the spinning side of the industry was mechanised: although power
looms were in use in Lancashire in the early years of the century this was not the case in Ulster, and by 1831, when the
industry was past its peak, weaving was still largely done by
hand.

The cotton boom, sustained by the buoyant wartime economy,
lasted until the end of protection in 1825, although through
overproduction every three years or so there were pockets of
acute unemployment, especially among the weavers.

Although it was generally admitted by those giving evidence
to House of Commons inquiries and Royal Commissions during
the 1820s and 1830s that cotton was the mainstay of the economy
during the first quarter of the century, it was clear that
prosperity was not evenly diffused throughout the industry.
Spinners, who constituted nearly two thirds of the labour force,
were paid fantastically high wages (15 to 30 shillings a week)
and weavers (particularly those of coarser cloths) considerably
less (12 to 16 shillings in good periods, 5 to 8 shillings a week in
1832). The latter were always affected by the occasional
depressions. At the end of the eighteenth century cotton weavers
appear to have been prosperous, but after 1815 they worked
not like the spinners, in mills, but in small stifling houses; their
food was very poor, their working hours from four in the
morning to midnight, their average wage in times of depression
4s 6d per week.[67]

During the periodic depressions between 1800 and 1820 the
weavers resisted efforts to lower their wages further: there was
a weavers' riot in 1815 and an attempt to form a weavers'
association in 1824; but as if by an inexorable law the standard
of living of the handloom weavers continued to deteriorate.

In the cotton industry wages were forced down by more than

a third after the post-1815 depression. In the next twenty years they fell another third and 'slumps, followed by mass unemployment, were common'.[68] In 1815 the muslin weavers marched to Belfast and left their unwoven webs with their employers. In 1816 two muslin weavers were convicted and hanged for setting fire to the home of a cotton manufacturer. In 1817 George Maxwell, the President of the Muslin Weavers' Society, was fatally wounded on a journey to Lisburn. He claimed while dying that John McCann, a muslin manufacturer, had shot him; but McCann was acquitted.

After the depression of 1825 the cotton industry declined. Wages in all levels of the industry fell by about a third. Worse still, the abolition of protection meant that the finer English muslins and cottons could outsell the coarser Irish fabrics. The weavers were at once threatened with starvation, and over the next five years public meetings were held to assist 'this most patient and peaceable class'[69] by a temporary measure (e.g. providing them with food at half-price) and ultimately to help them to emigrate. Many went to the United States on assisted passage but as late as 1838 there were still about 12,000 to 15,000 cotton weavers within ten miles of Belfast and few, if any, elsewhere.[70] By 1861 the families of the remaining weavers in Belfast were 'subsisting on a type of food that a careful farmer would not have given his stock'.[71] The cotton famine of 1862–3 finally wiped them out.

However, most of the cotton spinners were saved by a well-timed development in textile technology. During this period the production of fine linen by hand had continued, though at a much reduced rate. But the development of the wet-spinning process in England in 1825 meant that even the finest yarns could be mill-spun. This could have marked the end of the long-established linen trade in Ulster.

But at the crucial moment – in 1828 – a cotton manufacturer, Thomas Mulholland, when rebuilding his burnt-out mill, decided, on account of the keen competition from England and Scotland and since the linen trade was 'the natural business of Ireland',[72] to adapt it for flax-spinning instead of cotton-spinning. The experiment was very successful and within five years there were a dozen flax mills in Belfast. Farmers found it more profitable to grow flax than any other crop, and although the capacity of the industry soon outstripped the local supply of raw material, and raw flax had to be extensively imported, there was a ready supply of labour (including the ex-cotton spinners) available for training. The lack of power looms capable of weaving fine linen cloth, coupled with the cheapness of the cottage system, encouraged the manufacturers to rely on hand-loom weavers. Not until the early 1860s was steam power applied on any considerable scale to the weaving of linen. The flax-spinning mills brought the weaver no additional prosperity, as the cotton mills had done forty or fifty years before. His earnings remained static at about a shilling a day. Wages began to rise after the great decrease in population consequent on the famine, but the manufacturers counteracted this by the belated introduction of the power loom.

Unlike the cotton masters, the linen magnates relied on women and juveniles of both sexes for spinning – throughout the second half of the century the ratio of women to men remained constant at seven to three – and this, of course, meant that low levels of wages were established quite early in the history of the industry. Wage rates did not rise until the introduction of power looms, and the factory weavers were always paid better than the spinners, as well as having work that was much less arduous and unhealthy. Thus, as conditions in the linen industry developed, the status of the spinners relative to the weavers was the reverse of that which had prevailed in the cotton industry.

Spinners enjoyed continuous employment – except occasion-ally when there were not enough weavers to process the yarn – but little else. Linen masters showed a typically Victorian distaste for improving conditions of work or even installing adequate safety devices in their mills, although, when intro-duced, workers were also reluctant to use them. Most of the operatives, especially the hacklers, worked in an atmosphere permeated with flax dust. Some women became so debilitated that they had to rely on drink to get through the day's work, and the average life expectancy of hacklers was a mere forty-five years.[73]

The transformation of the Belfast textile industry during these years may be quickly summarised. In 1832 there were in the town 'and neighbourhood' nineteen cotton mills[74] and just one flax mill. Five years later there were fifteen flax mills and six cotton mills.[75] The number of flax mills in 1840 was eighteen; in 1852, twenty-four; in 1861, thirty-two, and in the last year there were just two cotton factories.[76] The labour force showed a corresponding increase: in 1836 there were 2,000[77] employees of the linen industry; in 1862, 15,000. By 1835 over half the total exports from Belfast were linen,[78] and at that time Belfast was the first port in Ireland in value of trade (though second to Dublin in tonnage) – £7,900,000 against Dublin's £6,900,000. Thirty years before the Belfast share of Ireland's total of exports (in terms of value) was one sixth.[79]

With the successive development of the cotton and linen industries the improvement of the port of Belfast became a necessary condition for further growth. Although it had existed since the seventeenth century and had been placed under the control of various short-lived public authorities,[80] the Belfast port at the beginning of the nineteenth century was little better than an anchorage. There were only two quays with three small docks, all built by private enterprise: the largest town dock was at the end of the main street (High Street), but on account of the shallow water only small sailing ships could anchor there. Large vessels had to anchor in the deep water of Garmoyle pool in Belfast Lough, some three miles away, and their cargoes had to be carried by lighter along the tortuous course of the Lagan through great bends before reaching the small and crowded town quays. The Ballast Board in the year of its foundation formed a scheme to cut a deep channel to link the quays with Garmoyle. But nothing came of it and in 1791 the Board was expressing its thanks to the first Marquis of Donegall for his promise (never carried out) to build dry and wet docks. Between 1785 and 1824 the only significant improvements were the deepening of the harbour by the ingenious method of using sand from the channel as ballast for outgoing vessels and the building of a graving dock in 1800 – by John Ritchie, the first Belfast shipbuilder. From 1820 on, the Board considered various schemes for enlarging the port, the most elaborate being submitted by the famous engineers, John Rennie and Thomas Telford, but the Board hesitated on account of the cost envisaged (ranging from £250,000 to £400,000), and angled for Government support. When it became clear

that no support would be forthcoming, the Board decided to
go ahead on their own and eventually accepted a less expensive
scheme proposed by another firm of engineers (Walker &
Burgess), involving two cuts across the bends of the river
Lagan eventually creating a single straight channel between the
town and Garmoyle, new quays in front of the small existing
ones, and a further deepening of the harbour. In 1831 a private
bill promoted by the Board (and resisted by some businessmen
on the ground of expense) authorised them to raise the tonnage
dues and purchase the private docks and quays.[81] But it was
another seven years before they were able to raise the £60,000
necessary to start the scheme and work on the first cut did not
begin until April 1839.

With the rapid development of the textile industry and steady
growth in the engineering industry, it is not surprising that
there followed a substantial increase in the numbers employed
in consumer industries. Between 1820 and 1836 there was a
tenfold increase in the number of shoemakers, stockingmakers,
dressmakers, and a slightly smaller increase in the numbers
involved in the provision trade.

Another important feature of this period was the development
of the Orange Order in the former headquarters of the United
Irishmen.

Since 1798 the Order had had its ups and downs. It so
dominated the yeomanry corps, established throughout Ulster
during the Napoleonic wars, that some regiments were able to
veto the admission of Catholics to their ranks. Like the masons,
it was professedly classless, but although its membership
embraced dukes and unemployed labourers, the higher
echelons of the Institution were dominated by the aristocracy
in Ireland, and to an even greater extent in England, where the
Dukes of Northumberland and Gordon held prominent office
even before the royal Dukes of York (1821) and Cumberland
(1828) were elevated to the grand mastership. As the century
wore on the clergy of the Established Church in both countries
joined in large numbers.[82]

The Grand Committee of the Order in Ireland in 1834
contained thirteen grand chaplains, all from the Church of
Ireland and including four archdeacons – one a future primate.

(In England the Bishop of Salisbury was grand chaplain.) In Dublin 'everyone' of the Anglican clergy was allegedly in the Institution. Dissenting clergy, however, were very few. Politically, the Order in both countries espoused High Tory causes – not only did it strenuously oppose Catholic Emancipation, but several English members were expelled for supporting the Reform Bills of 1830 to 1832.

In Ulster Orangemen resumed their practice of the 1790s, marching armed through hostile neighbourhoods 'for the purpose of provoking attack'.[83] When attacks came, as they frequently did, the Catholics generally came off worse; but the magistrates trying those involved in outrages generally turned a blind eye to the depredations of the Orangemen.[84] To the Orange psyche, crimes committed against Catholics were a continuation of an ancient feud, a form of warfare which no Protestant courts had the right to punish. Carrying arms was a privilege which had been exclusive to Protestants and should remain so.[85]

But before long the Orangemen attracted the unfavourable attention of the Commons. The first hostile motion, proposed in 1813, claimed that they were a cause of dissension in Ireland. Peel (then Chief Secretary), refused an inquiry on the soon-to-be-familiar ground that it would exacerbate the situation. But the Institution was put on the defensive and changed its rules several times in order to avoid censure. In the 1820s successive Tory Governments had to deal both with O'Connell's perfectly constitutional attempts to organise the six million Catholics into a disciplined pressure group and with the Orange protestations of loyalty and readiness to fight the former. In 1825 the Catholic Association was banned as subversive; but Brougham and the Whigs insisted that the Orange Order be also banned. Both managed to circumvent the prohibitions. The Catholic Association was reconstituted under a different name and the Grand Lodge of England (unaffected by the law) quietly issued warrants under which new lodges were set up in Ireland.[86] Former Orangemen were also enrolled in 'Brunswick Clubs'. In 1828 the Act lapsed and the Order was reconstituted in Ireland with the Duke of Cumberland as Grand Master in both countries. But the radicals were now on its track, and in spite of efforts in the next six years to avoid attention by issuing instructions (generally ignored) to Irish lodges to refrain from marching on 12 July, the Order was unable to escape a thorough investigation by a Select Committee, set up in 1835 (shortly after the Whigs returned to office) under the chairmanship of Joseph Hume, its most persistent enemy in the Commons. The evidence given to the Committee, which filled three blue books 'established beyond doubt what had been general knowledge in Ireland since 1795 – that is, that the Orangemen controlled the Irish yeomanry, had lodges in the Army, enjoyed a certain immunity from justice in Ulster, and were frequently engaged in civil disturbances'.[87] It was the infiltration of the Order into the army in both countries rather than the other findings which damned it in the eyes of the Commons and, following a broad hint (in reply to an address moved by Hume in February 1836) that legislation would be introduced against the Order, the Duke of Cumberland formally dissolved the Order in both countries.

The dissolution was much more effective in Great Britain than in Ireland. Just as the Irish lodges (during the six years since 1828) had persistently ignored the annual warnings from Cumberland against parading, so they now went underground, but only just.

In the report of the Select Committee,[88] the name of Belfast hardly occurs. The processions there were small and poorly attended, and the Belfast lodges generally joined those of Lisburn and several adjoining towns in a procession to Hillsborough (Co. Down). No figures[89] are available in the report for the number of Orangemen existing in Belfast in 1835, and still less for any previous year. But it is clear that some prominent Belfast citizens, including Thomas Verner, Sovereign, and a relative of the first Orange Grand Master, belonged to the Order in the early nineteenth century. In 1810 the general commanding the militia in Ulster complained of 'inveterate' animosity between Orange yeomen and the Catholics.[90] In 1813 Belfast experienced its first religious riot[91] which, though on a small scale, exhibited some of the features that were later to become all too familiar. A small Orange procession returning from Lisburn on the 'Twelfth' clashed with a crowd in a street mainly inhabited by Roman Catholics. The Orangemen retreated to a public house where they were quickly provided with arms, and then fired into the crowd, killing two (Protestants) and wounding four (Catholics). When the perpetrators came up for trial the judge directed the jury to consider the right to self-defence and verdicts of manslaughter, not murder, were returned. Some witnesses testified that Orange processions had previously passed off without incident, and a further indication that the incident was not less novel than deplorable is provided by the stern editorial comment of the *Belfast News Letter*:

> When the intelligence reaches London, how will the subject be taken up, and what severe animadversions will it give rise to against this town, which has so long been the theme of eulogism, alike distinguished by its internal peace, its opulence and its industry.[92]

In the same year (1813) occurred the first public meeting of Belfast Catholics to petition for further emancipation – as part of a general campaign throughout Ulster. It was attended by the leading Catholic merchants and also by Dr Drennan. One of the most significant speeches was given by a Protestant, who urged the Catholics to pursue their objectives in a strictly constitutional manner since their enemies were just waiting for them to resort to violence. The meeting also passed a vote of thanks to the Synod of Ulster for supporting their claims.[93]

The next eruption of violence occurred in 1825 when, thanks to the Act of that year, the Grand Lodge of Ireland was trying hard to prevent lodges from marching. The violently anti-Orange, *Northern Whig*, wrote that 'If the surviving dregs of the Orangemen should presume to celebrate their revolting orgies' the magistrates should prevent them.[94] One magistrate tried to do this, but was hooted for his pains by the lodges insisting on marching to Lisburn. A clash followed with Catholics, and a small number were injured.

In 1825, too, the House of Lords Select Committee on the State of Ireland heard a good deal of evidence about the Orange disturbances, but none in relation to Belfast. Two witnesses are worth quoting – the Rev. Dr Henry Cooke, Moderator of the Synod of Ulster and later Principal of the Presbyterian College, who gave his opinion that since the Orange bands, whom he then disliked, were merely continuing

an eighteenth-century tradition, they could not be regarded as
the *cause* of the current dissensions between Catholic and
Protestant. By contrast, Right Rev. Dr Crolly, Catholic
Bishop of Down and Connor and former parish priest of Belfast,
later to become Archbishop of Armagh, gave quite an optimistic
forecast. He believed that with increasing prosperity inter-
denominational relations were already improving and would
improve further.[95]

In the years before 1829 there were a number of petitions
from town meetings against the Catholic claims, but perhaps
the meeting that is most relevant to our study was one held to
petition for parliamentary reform, just before the fall of Well-
ington's Government. Among those attending was the nucleus
of Belfast's Liberal Party for the next quarter century, and the
Rev. Henry Montgomery, minister of the First Presbyterian
congregation in Rosemary Street,[96] who deplored the fact that
he was the only clergyman present and warned that the
Presbyterian body might soon be a prey to illiberal influences.
A few respectable Catholics also attended.

So far we have seen far-reaching changes in the social and
economic character of Belfast between 1800 and 1830: the
gradual change from a market town into an industrial centre,
accompanied by a waning of the radical tradition (Drennan, its
last exponent, died in 1820), and the first beginnings of religious
dissension.

The abrupt change in the social temper of Belfast in the half-
century between 1798 and 1857, the year of the first major riot,
has often been remarked upon by historians. The prevailing
verdict is that of David Owen, who asserted that Catholic-
Protestant relations began to deteriorate in the late 1820s when
O'Connell's campaign for emancipation was reaching its
height, and it was clear that the six million enfranchised
Catholics, able to return their own members, would speedily
swamp the Irish Protestant representatives in the House of
Commons. Beckett in his most recent work says that the
animosities really began to develop in the 1850s when the
Catholics constituted one third of the population and were in
competition with Protestants for jobs.[97] But these arguments
are open to objection. As is shown in the Appendix to this

chapter, the Catholic share of the population was very nearly at its peak in 1834 and scarcely altered during the succeeding years. There is no evidence of job competition in the 1820s (we will see later whether it was relevant in the 1850s): the Catholics came in at the lowest rung of the economic ladder – unskilled labouring. As to O'Connell's responsibility for provoking a hostile reaction in the city, the first religious disturbance occurred ten years before the founding of the Catholic Association, which may be regarded as a cause of continuing the religious antipathy, but scarcely as a primary cause.

All these writers[98] appear to have underestimated the divisive influence of the Orange Order, and the possibility that to its development rather than to any of the causes assigned above may be attributed the growth, if not the inception, of religious rivalry in Belfast. It was making headway there by the 1830s, though admittedly by no means as strong as in the neighbouring counties. It is, nevertheless, remarkable that the familiar pattern of sectarian rioting in Belfast should have been established as early as the first quarter of the nineteenth century.

APPENDIX

Note on Population Growth in Nineteenth-Century Belfast

The immediate corollary of industrial expansion in Belfast was population growth. Table 1.2 spotlights the dramatic upsurge of population associated with the initial textile boom, especially in the early nineteenth century. In the first third of that century Belfast borough alone doubled its population (within the same boundaries): suburbs growing up on what had previously been open country added even more to the partly qualitative change from large market town to manufacturing centre. The growth rate between 1821 and 1901 considerably exceeded that of any major British city.

As a manufacturing centre Belfast's sustained expansion throughout the nineteenth century continued to boost population. Both absolutely and in terms of percentage rate of increase, the middle decades of the nineteenth century surpassed the rapid growth of earlier years, and were in turn surpassed by the

TABLE I.2

Population of Belfast Borough 1801–1961

Year	Number	% Increase
1801	19,000*	—
1811	27,832*	46·47
1821	37,277*	33·93
1831	53,287*	42·95
1841	70,447	32·20
1851	87,062	23·58
1861	121,602	39·67
1871	174,412	43·43
1881	208,122	19·33
1891	255,950	22·98
1901	349,180	36·43
1911	386,947	10·82
1926	415,151	7·3
1937	438,086	5·5
1951	443,671	1·3
1961	416,094	−6·2

Sources: 1801 – estimated. 1811 – returns by Constables appointed under Belfast Police Act (*B.N.L.*, 20 August 1813). 1821–1911 – Census of Ireland. Thereafter Census of Northern Ireland.

* The figures given for 1801–1821 inclusive relate to the 'Town' of Belfast; those for 1831 to the Town and suburbs (a separate figure of 39,146 is given for the borough) and those for subsequent years to the area of the Borough or County Borough as constituted at the date of each Census.

1880s and 1890s, as shipbuilding and heavy engineering added their labour demands to those of the prosperous linen industry. Although these industries continued to prosper until the end of the First World War, their slower rate of expansion is reflected in a slackening of population growth. Nevertheless by the 1920s Belfast contained the roughly 400,000 inhabitants which it still counted in the mid-1960s. Static population is associated in part with the unchanged political boundaries of the borough in this period, but much more strongly with industrial stagnation, decline, and high unemployment, during these forty years. We shall discuss these, as background to political developments, in the following chapters.

Just as the twentieth-century equilibrium was associated with unchanging municipal boundaries, so nineteenth-century expansion followed in part from extensions to the boundaries

TABLE 1.3

Comparative Population Growth

(in thousands)

Decade	Birmingham	Belfast	Glasgow	Liverpool	Manchester	Newcastle-on-Tyne	Sheffield	Greater London
1801	71	19	77	82	75	33	46	1,117
1811	83	28	101	104	89	33	53	1,327
1821	102	37	147	138	126	42	65	1,600
1831	144	53	202	202	182	54	92	1,907
1841	183	70	275	286	235	70	111	2,239
1851	233	87	345	376	303	88	135	2,685
1861	296	122	420	444	339	109	185	3,227
1871	344	174	522	493	351	128	240	3,890
1881	401	208	587	553	(341) 462*	145	285	4,770
1891	478	256	658	630	505	186	324	5,638
1901	522	349	762	685	544	215	381	6,586
1951	1,113	444	1,090	789	703	292	513	8,348

* Area change.

which incorporated populous suburbs. The major areal expansions are displayed in Table 1.4.

TABLE 1.4

Area within Belfast Municipal Boundaries:
At Dates of Major Expansions 1613–1966

Date	Area in Acres
1613–1841	160 (approx.)
1841–1853	970
1853–1897	6,421
1897–1959*	16,504
1959–	18,052

*1959 extension due to reclamation in Belfast Lough

However, the very fact that the suburbs grew, and that areal extensions came to be perceived as politically necessary, can ultimately be traced to industrial expansion just as much as the growth of population within the old boundaries. Growth of this kind derived from two sources: a high birth rate, which, as local sanitary and health services improved, increasingly outpaced the high death rate; and immigration from outside the city. Immigration was undoubtedly the major factor in the earlier growth of population: as population increased, more growth was met by its natural increase, but immigration remained a major factor, Some idea of the extent to which growth resulted from immigration as compared to natural increase can be obtained from the census figures on birthplaces of the population.

TABLE 1.5

Birthplaces of Belfast Population 1841–1961

(Percentage)

	1841	1861	1881	1901	1911	1961
Antrim, Down or Belfast City	84·8	75·2	77·3	76·7	77·8	85·1
Rest of Ulster	10·5	15·8	13·8	12·6	10·9	5·8
Rest of Ireland	2·1	3·3	3·05	3·24	3·26	3·2
England, Wales and Scotland	2·36	5·14	5·17	6·64	7·21	4·6
Abroad	0·23	0·57	0·74	0·83	0·83	1·3

Unfortunately no distinction was drawn in these figures between persons born in Belfast itself and in the adjacent counties of Antrim and Down. Difficulties in social and economic adjustment would probably be less severe for inhabitants of these counties, and the figures do enable us to distinguish between immigration from the rest of Ulster (heavy), and from Britain, and from the provinces of Munster, Leinster and Connaught (negligible). Regional origins provide some indication of the probable social standing of immigrants: those from the South and West of Ulster were most probably Catholic peasants, while immigrants from East Ulster were more likely to be Protestants from industrial areas or at least areas of commercial farming, where social relationships resembled those of industrial society. It is noteworthy, therefore, that immigration from Ulster itself was always heaviest, while immigration from Great Britain usually equalled immigration from Southern Ireland: in fact, in the censuses from 1851 to 1871 the English- and Scottish-born were proportionately double the Southern-born, and at all periods those born in the city itself and the neighbouring counties constituted three quarters of the population. With the stabilisation of population in the twentieth century the native born constituted an overwhelming 85 per cent of the population.

Regional origins are, however, a relatively imperfect indicator of social status: for example, an immigrant from the Ulster counties of Tyrone or Fermanagh was more likely to be Catholic than Protestant (an immigrant from Donegal even more so), while many notable immigrants from further south were Protestant.

Table 1.6 accordingly presents direct estimates of Catholics in the population, which also have the advantage of covering a longer time-span than the figures on birthplace. The proportion of Catholics in the population had shrunk in the eighteenth century to a mere 6 to 8 per cent. The dramatic upsurge in their share of the population is probably attributable to the labour demand created by the cotton boom. This inference is supported by a contemporary account of 1811: 'The population in a random way may be estimated at thirty thousand of which four thousand are Catholics. These are almost entirely working people. A few years ago there was scarcely a Catholic in the place.' Twenty-five years later another writer commented: 'Within a few years some four or five thousand raw, uneducated Catholic labourers from the South and West had poured into the city', and were 'rapidly increasing in proportion to the rest'.[99]

TABLE I.6

Roman Catholics in the Belfast Population:
Various Dates 1659–1961

Date	Number of Roman Catholics	Percentage of Roman Catholics in population
1659	223	38
1757	556	6
1776	256 (families)	8
1784	1,092	8
1808	4,000	16
1834	19,712	32
1861	41,406	33·9
1871	55,575	31·9
1881	59,975	28·8
1891	67,378	26·3
1901	84,992	24·3
1911	93,243	24·1
1926	95,682	23·0
1937	104,372	23·8
1951	115,029	25·9
1961	114,529	25·5

Note: Sources: 1659 – W. Petty, *Census of Ireland* (the first), ed. S. Pender, 1939, p. 8. 1757 – the first local census in Belfast, cf. Benn, *A History of Belfast*, Vol. 1, p. 622. 1776 – from a Public Record office return for the Parish of Belfast cited by Rev. Dr Patrick Rogers in *The Belfast Volunteers and the Catholic Question* (1778– 1793), p. 5 (unpublished D.Litt. thesis for Queen's University, Belfast). (Here the percentage is adjusted to cover only the town.) 1784 – from work by Andrew Boyd (shortly to be published). The 1808 figure is from a return from the Belfast parish cited by Rev. Dr Rogers in *Essays . . . in honour of J. E. Todd* (London, 1949), p. 233. (Here the population figure is estimated.) The 1834 figure is the first to be fully authenticated – from the *Report of the Royal Commission on Public Institutions*, 1834, which gives the Church of Ireland population as 16,388 and the Presbyterians as 25,576. Figures from 1861 onwards are taken from the Census of Ireland or Census of Northern Ireland for the relevant dates. The Census of 1861 was the first to give religious statistics.

These statements imply that the Catholic immigration consisted largely of unskilled labourers. Although more marked than elsewhere, this was part of a general population shift throughout Ireland during these years. The legacy of the Penal

Laws meant that there were scarcely any Catholics in the professions or in manufacturing or the higher levels of commerce. With continued expansion in the textile industries, the proportion of Catholics continued to rise, until in 1834 they numbered about a third. As it happened, their share of the Belfast population remained constant thereafter, although the absolute numbers of Catholics increased in line with the expansion of the total population. (Professor Emrys Jones, observing that the 1841 census shows 15,334 Belfast residents to have been born in Ireland, though outside Belfast, concludes: 'although the majority came from Ulster where the proportion of the two religious sects was approximately 50/50, *very many* [our italics] came from the other three provinces, where the Catholic population accounted for about 9 in 10 of the total.'[100] This is an exaggeration. The census figures to which he alludes show that of these 15,334 only 1,565 came from Munster, Leinster or Connaught, as against 1,778 from Great Britain.) To some extent the stable proportion of Catholics in the later nineteenth century is explained by the counterbalancing immigration from Great Britain, discussed previously in relation to Table 1.4.

The rapid increase in relative numbers of Catholics in the first third of the nineteenth century probably helped to create a *laager* mentality among Protestants, which contributed to the growth of the militant Orange Order. No doubt the threat which Catholics were felt to pose was exacerbated by job competition with unskilled Protestant labourers, although generalising from the later experience of Glasgow[101] it is also possible that Catholic immigrants took the dirtiest, most menial jobs. Even so, occupational distinctions of this kind were well able to feed Protestant prejudices, already exacerbated by the alien peasant background and customs of the Catholic immigrants.

NOTES

1. Cavan and Donegal are in the Irish Republic; Antrim and Down were not included in the plantation; in them the native Irish were not so important.
2. E. Porritt, *The Unreformed House of Commons* (London, 1926), Vol. I.
3. In the years between the initial grant of the Castle and lands and the incorporation of the town, Chichester had to face a lawsuit concerning

his title. Cf. B. C. S. Wilson in J. C. Beckett and R. E. Glasscock, *Belfast. The Origin and Growth of an Industrial City* (London, 1967) (hereinafter referred to as *Belfast*), p. 23.

4. Admitted by the Sovereign on payment of a fee. It appears to have been intended by the charter that inhabitancy should confer freedom. *Rep. Comm. Mun. Corp. P.P. 1835*, XXVIII, 254 (P.P. is used throughout as the contraction for Parliamentary Papers).

5. *Belfast*, Chapter 3. For the Belfast industries of the seventeenth century cf. ibid., 29–35.

6. G. Benn, *A History of the Town of Belfast* (Belfast, 1877), Vol. I, pp. 236–269. Of these names only the last two are found in Belfast today.

7. Beckett and Glasscock, *Belfast*, pp. 37–8, 39; also Beckett, *The Making of Modern Ireland 1603–1923*, (London, 1966), pp. 123–6. Beckett points out that the disturbed state of Scotland following the Restoration attempt to restore episcopacy during these years may have influenced the Church of Ireland, equally conscious of its minority position, not to press too hard its advantages under the law.

8. Cf. *P.P. 1835*, XXVIII, 254–6.

9. These went mainly to maintaining the market.

10. Cf. *P.P. 1835*, XXVIII, 255–6.

11. Benn, op. cit., p. 150.

12. Ibid., pp. 153–4.

13. One of the first acts of King James was to dismiss James, Duke of Ormond, from the Lord-Lieutenancy, thereby ending a career of fifty years in the forefront of Irish political life, a record which has been equalled only by Mr de Valera.

14. The new Corporation lasted only from October 1688 to August 1689. A list of members is given in Benn, *A History of Belfast*, Vol. I, App. XI.

15. Colonel Arthur Chichester, a strong supporter of Charles I, was created first Earl of Donegall on 30 March 1647, at Ormond's instigation. He died in 1675.

16. Benn, op. cit., pp. 162–8. Robert Leathes, the pre-1687 Sovereign, was restored to office. Pottinger continued his lucrative business undisturbed and lived until 1715. (He was buried with great pomp.)

17. He landed at Carrickfergus (14 June), went directly to Belfast whence he issued his proclamation promising liberty and just government for all, went south to win the Battle of the Boyne, (12 July), and returned to England.

18. In practice, they had been excluded since the 1660s.

19. In Londonderry 10 out of 12 aldermen and 14 out of 24 burgesses were turned out of office. Porritt, op. cit., II, 343.

20. And defrayed originally out of the Customs of the Port of Belfast.

21. The test, however, was virtually suspended from 1719 and was repealed in 1780.

22. See *Rep. Comm. Mun. Corp. P.P. 1835*, XXVIII, 257–9. The Borough Court of Record had jurisdiction up to £20. By 1835 it was 'long since neglected'. The Manor Court, however, met once a year to appoint

constables, appraisers and applotters for the following year. It survived the municipal overhaul of 1840 and in 1847 Bernard Lennon (a Liberal solicitor) was brought before it for refusing to pay £5 to an agent who had thoughtfully paid rates to that amount for some Liberal electors to make them eligible to vote in the annual municipal elections. *Belfast News Letter*, 4 May 1847. (Henceforth cited as *B.N.L.*)

23. Porritt, op. cit., II 302, quoting *H. of C. Journals*, II, 746.

24. The two criteria applied by the Chief Secretary, Castlereagh, for borough representation after the Union were population and rate of contribution to hearth money and window tax. Under both of these criteria Belfast took third place. *Castlereagh Correspondence* III, 345, quoted by Porritt, II, 517.

25. In 1825 the Town Clerk, Stephen Daniel, was dismissed for misconduct.

26. *P.P. 1835*, XXVIII, 257.

27. and – with a bad grace, following a requisition – to present a petition for reform, cf. *Town Meeting for Reform*, 1830.

28. The earliest mills were in Smithfield.

29. Largely through Robert Joy's visit to Scotland to see Arkwright's cotton-spinning machinery. See below, p. 17.

30. E. R. R. Green in Beckett and Glasscock, *Belfast*, p. 84.

31. By 1805 cotton weavers were earning twelve to sixteen shillings per week (*Report on State of Poor, P.P. 1836*, XXX, 42), when the average labourer was earning seven shillings and sixpence. By 1806 there were two thousand weavers out of a total population of twenty-two thousand.

32. Arthur Chichester, fifth Earl of Donegall, born 1739, succeeded 1757, created a British peer in 1790, elevated to Marquis 1791, died January 1799. Although his rent roll was the largest of any Irish peer he was so anxious to augment his income that when tenants' leases fell in he levied fines as a condition of renewal. Some tenants in Antrim refused, but two Belfast merchants paid the fines, occupied the farms and raised the rent. The upshot was an agrarian secret society, the Hearts of Steel, and many outrages.

33. And the Charitable Society also enterprisingly took upon itself the task of supplying water to the town, the profits being devoted to the poorhouse. After 1800 it also had its own graveyard. This situation prevailed until 1840. See below, p. 112.

34. The most important late eighteenth-century buildings were the White Linen Hall (on the site of the present City Hall), built in 1784, the Exchange and Assembly Rooms (1769), St Anne's Church (1774). From this period date Donegall Street and Donegall Place, two of the finest streets in the city.

35. The literature on this subject is considerable. See especially P. Rogers, *The Volunteers and Catholic Emancipation* (London, 1934) and the bibliography in J. C. Beckett, *The Making of Modern Ireland*.

36. As Beckett writes, op. cit., p. 222, 'Far more truly than the parliament in College Green they represented the spirit of the protestant nation'.

37. Two million, compared with 600,000 Protestants.

38. While Lord Charlemont, the general of the Volunteers, opposed any

extension of the franchise to Catholics, the Earl-Bishop of Derry, Frederick Hervey, their second most prominent figure, favoured complete enfranchisement.

39. This occurred on 13 May 1784, just two months after the defeat of the Volunteer Reform Bill; cf. Rev. P. Rogers, *The Volunteers and Catholic Emancipation*, p. 147.

40. And in Ireland, too, until the General Assembly was instituted in 1840. Alone among the Irish Churches the Presbyterian Church has always had its headquarters in Belfast.

41. Town meetings or assemblies of the 'most respectable citizens' were not uncommon in eighteenth-century Ireland. Usually they were summoned by the civic head. The Dublin meeting referred to here was summoned by the High Sheriffs; the Belfast one by the Sovereign; cf. C. Dickson, *Revolt in the North: The '98 Rebellion in Antrim and Down* (Dublin, 1961).

42. This has been interpreted as due to the Belfast citizens having been more diffident about the Catholic claims than the Dubliners. However, it must be remembered that while Catholics were certainly present at the Dublin meeting, no evidence exists that any were present at the Belfast one.

43. In gratitude for the passing of the Act of 1793, the Catholic Committee in Dublin awarded Wolfe Tone £1,500 (he had served for a time as their secretary), William Todd Jones, M.P. for Lisburn and their leading supporter in the North, another £1,500, and £2,000 as a mark of their fealty to 'the best of Kings', George III, to erect a statue in his honour. (It was erected in front of Trinity College and blown up in 1920.)

44. The Orange Order was not a unique creation. Similar bodies commemorating the establishment of Protestant ascendancy in 1690, armed with rituals and songs, had existed mainly in Dublin at various times in the century. But the tradition was dying out until it received this unexpected and permanent accession of strength; cf. H. Senior, *Orangeism in Ireland and Britain, 1795–1836* (London, 1966).

45. *Charlemont Mss. H.M.C.*, II, p. 7, quoted by Rogers, p. 196.

46. It must be remembered that the Orange Order from its inception spread all over Ireland. Apart from Dublin, to which its headquarters were moved in 1798, the midlands (especially County Meath) were a stronghold of Orangeism and there were pockets of Orangeism even in County Cork.

47. Senior, op. cit., pp. 60–62.

48. G. C. Bolton, *The Passing of the Irish Act of Union* (Oxford, 1966), p. 135.

49. G. C. Bolton, op. cit., pp. 135–9, 175–6.

50. For an appreciation of the first Marquis, see C. E. B. Brett in Beckett and Glasscock, *Belfast*, pp. 69–70.

51. One of them, Alexander Hamilton, resigned his seat and also a lucrative sinecure, the cursitorship of the Exchequer, rather than support the Union. Benn, *A History of Belfast*, Vol. II, pp. 735–6.

52. P. Rogers, *The Irish Volunteers and Catholic Emancipation 1778–93*, p. 163. Dr Rogers is here referring to a specific incident – the success of Charle-

mont in getting the Volunteers to emasculate their original proposals for Catholic enfranchisement: it is equally appropriate as a judgement on the whole period.

53. The Rev. William Campbell, one of the few Presbyterian ministers to oppose openly any franchise concession to the Catholics, believed that the majority of northern Protestants were of his way of thinking – but he conceded that Belfast and Lisburn were exceptional. Rogers, op. cit., p. 165.

54. Another indication of the strength of radical feeling in Belfast was the drop in the sales of *B.N.L.* in 1796 when it began to take the 'Dublin Castle' line in 1797. Senior, *Orangeism in Ireland and Britain*, p. 62.
Even in 1793 there were four undisguised societies of United Irishmen in Belfast, and in the latter part of 1794 'several additional societies, of a similar political character'. J. A. Pilson, *History of . . . Belfast and the County of Antrim* (Belfast, 1846), pp. 21–2.

55. Benn, *A History of Belfast*, Vol. II, p. 13.

56. Sir Edward May (father-in-law), M.P., 1800–1818, his son, Sir Stephen May, 1814–18; Arthur Chichester (cousin), 1818–20, and the Earl of Belfast (son), 1820–1830. The Mays each served six years as Sovereign.

57. For the police boards see *P.P. 1835*, XXVIII, 261–7; *P.P. 1837*, XI, Pt 1, 18–37, 43–48.

58. In 1823 Stephen Daniel, Town Clerk since 1814, was accused of several acts of misconduct and although defended by Verner, the Sovereign, was dismissed in 1825.

59. *40 Geo. III. C. 37* (Irish).

60. But their decisions had to be ratified by the Commissioners. Much friction ensued.

61. Since neither the Sovereign nor J.P.s were willing to perform magisterial duties, a special police magistrate had to be appointed at a salary of £200. Two men (a father and son) had held this post up to 1835 and their decisions were openly distrusted on the ground of partiality, while they were also reputed to charge fees 'some of which were double or more than double the amounts authorised by statute and some of which were not authorised at all' (*P.P. 1835*, XXVIII, 261).

62. The Corporation Records for the last 92 years of the Corporation's history (1750–1842) cover a mere 362 pages. The Police Committee minutes (1800–1804) extended to 459 pages. Cf. J. J. Monaghan, 'A Social and Economic History of Belfast, 1801–25' (unpublished Ph.D. thesis, Queen's University, Belfast, 1940), p. 39.

63. It was claimed before the Select Committee on fictitious votes that the police valuators undervalued houses because they generally confined themselves to an external inspection of the house. Assistant barristers in the 1830s valued at £10 houses applotted at £8 or even £7 in the police books. *P.P. 1837*, XI, Pt 1, 19–35, 48–53.

64. The oldest newspaper in the British Isles, founded in 1737.

65. On the development of the cotton industry in Belfast, secondary works are few. G. O'Brien's *Economic History of Ireland* (London, 1921) is

generally useful, though somewhat out of date. See also J. J. Monaghan 'The rise and fall of the Belfast Cotton Industry', in *Irish Historical Studies*, III (March 1942), pp. 1–17; and 'The Cotton Handloom weavers in the North-East of Ireland', *U.J.A.*, Series, 3, VII, 31; also E. R. R. Green, *The Lagan Valley 1800–50*. Linen has a more extensive bibliography. Apart from O'Brien, see E. R. R. Green, *The Lagan Valley*, (London, 1949), especially Chapter 3; Conrad Gill, *The Rise of the Irish Linen Industry* (Oxford, 1925); also Hugh McCall, *Ireland and her Staple Manufactures* (Belfast, 1870) ('one of the best authorities for the Irish linen industry and almost the only one for the cotton industry': Green, op. cit., p. 167); William Charley, *Flax and its Products in Ireland* (Belfast, 1862). See also a very useful short article, D. L. Armstrong, 'Social and Economic Conditions in the Belfast Linen Industry 1850–1900', *Irish Historical Studies*, VII (September 1951), pp. 235–69. For a valuable, though brief, survey of the history of both textile industries up to 1840 cf. E. R. R. Green, 'Early Industrial Belfast' in Beckett and Glasscock, *Belfast*, pp. 78–87.

66. Cf. Monaghan, op. cit. It is extremely difficult to get statistics of employment in Belfast alone for this period. The first Irish census (of 1801) did not furnish them. Apart from the 1806 figure (which is based on a census of the city taken in that year by Arthur Thomson) the statistics refer to the area within ten miles of Belfast.

67. Linen also suffered from a considerable fall in prices (with consequential effects on wages) between 1816 and 1820. Green, *The Lagan Valley*, pp. 66–8; Gill, *The Rise of the Irish Linen Industry*, pp. 264–80.
    In the *Northern Whig*, 13 July 1826, there is a report of a memorial forwarded by the Belfast cotton weavers praying for aid to emigrate before the winter weather makes their state worse. They blame their distress on an overstocked market and on 'continual introduction of machinery'.
    For a description of working conditions of cotton weavers, see Monaghan, op. cit., pp. 1–17. See also *Northern Whig*, 19 January 1826, where factory spinners agitating against a cut in wages were reminded that they were already very well off. (This paper is henceforth cited as *N.W.*)

68. Green, *The Lagan Valley*, p. 107.

69. Monaghan, op. cit., p. 17.

70. Green, *The Lagan Valley*, p. 105.

71. Monaghan, op. cit., p. 17.

72. Cited in E. R. R. Green, in Beckett and Glasscock, *Belfast*, p. 85. Until 1850 linen continued to be woven by hand, and although the few existing handloom linen weavers had more than enough work to occupy them, the unfortunate cotton weavers could not all be absorbed into the new industry. A different loom was necessary and the poorest weavers were unable to raise the capital. In Belfast in 1852 there was only one power loom; in 1862, 6,000 (E. Jones, in Beckett and Glasscock, *Belfast*, p. 109). For the early development of machine-spinning in Ireland, see C. Gill, *The Rise of the Irish Linen Industry*, pp. 316–22.

73. D. L. Armstrong, op. cit., pp. 243–53, gives a graphic description of conditions in the early flax mills. See also C. D. Purdon, *Sanitary Conditions in the Linen Industry.* (Purdon was city medical officer in the 1850s: his son held the same post in the 1890s.)

74. *Belfast Chamber of Commerce Records, PRONI,* D. 1857/2, No. 1, p. 301. (The Public Record Office of Northern Ireland is hereinafter cited as PRONI.)

75. *Second Report of the Railway Commissioners,* 1837 (*P.P. 1837–8,* XXXV), p. 481.

76. *Report on the State of the Poor in Ireland, P.P. 1836,* XXX, 41 (which gives a breakdown of the numbers employed in each mill). *Report of the Belfast Chamber of Commerce, PRONI,* D. 1857/2, No. 3.

77. Armstrong, op. cit., p. 240, gives figures relating to the total employment in linen for the whole of Ireland (but mainly for Ulster): 1850, 21,000; 1862, 34,000.

78. E. R. R. Green in Beckett and Glasscock, *Belfast,* p. 86. *Second Report of Railway Commissioners, P.P. 1837–8,* XXXV, 7–15.

79. Benn, *History of Belfast,* Vol. II, pp. 119–22.

80. For the early history of the port see above, p. 8. In 1729 an Act for preserving ports of Cork, Galway, Sligo, Belfast and Drogheda established ballast offices under the direction of the town corporations, and laid down a scale of charges for home and foreign ships, but included no provision for building quays or docks. In 1785 an Act dealing with Belfast alone admitted that the 1729 Act had failed and repealed it completely: in its place was established the 'Corporation for preserving the Port and Harbour of Belfast' (popularly known as the Ballast Board), comprising the Earl of Donegall and fourteen nominated members including the Sovereign of the day. Unlike their predecessors the Ballast Board was authorised to use the surplus from ballast charges to improve the harbour by building dry and wet docks. Cf. D. J. Owen, *A Short History of the Port of Belfast* (Belfast, 1917), pp. 7–20.

81. It also altered the composition of the Board. Henceforth it contained *ex officio* the Lord of the Castle, the Sovereign, the members of parliament for Belfast, Carrickfergus, Downpatrick, and Counties Antrim and Down, and sixteen others: the first nominated, their successors elected by the Board and by others of 50 tons registered shipping, and having paid £4 per annum in police taxes, and not living more than seven miles from the town.
   The growth of the port between 1785 and 1830 may be illustrated thus:
   Customs revenue: 1784 – £101,900. 1813 – £393,000.
   Number of vessels using port: 1786 – 772; 1813 – 1,190; 1830 – 2,423
   Number of vessels belonging to port: 1785 – 55; 1830 – 251
   Revenue of port: 1786 – £1,558; 1813 – £4,848; 1830 – £7,094
   (Owen, *A Short History of the Port of Belfast,* p. 23.)

82. The only comprehensive lists of officers of the Irish and English grand lodges is provided in the appendices to the report of the Select Committee of 1835. *P.P. 1835,* XVI, 281–88.

83. Senior, *Orangeism in Ireland and Britain*, p. 147.

84. *P.P. 1835*, XVII, p. 381.

85. Senior, op. cit., p. 185. Senior argues that without the armed Orange yeomen the Ulster Catholics would have attacked their Protestant neighbours. No evidence is adduced in support of this assertion. The Catholic secret society, the Ribbonmen (who took a secret oath of loyalty to the King), arose as a direct response to the challenge of Orangeism.

86. *P.P. 1835*, XVII, p. vi. Senior does not mention this important fact.

87. Senior, op. cit., p. 268.

88. The Select Committee found that in 1835 there were 220,000 Orange-men in Ireland. This was stated in evidence by the deputy grand secretary. At the processions in 1835 a mere 3,000 paraded in Dublin and 5,000 at Bandon (the other centre in the south), while 30,000 paraded in Cavan (the southernmost county of Ulster), and 75,000, representing the lodges of Counties Antrim and Down, at Hillsborough. *P.P. 1835*, XVII, pp. xvi and xxvii.

89. The first authentic figure available is 1,335 (*Report, Grand Lodge of County Antrim 1851*) (Dublin, 1852), but several lodges had been established between 1835 and that year.

90. Senior, *Orangeism in Ireland and Britain*, pp. 183–4.

91. In 1759 a food riot had occurred, during a time of near-famine.

92. *B.N.L.*, 13 July 1813. (See also 11–12 August 1813.)

93. *B.N.L.*, 26 October 1813.

94. *N.W.*, 7 July 1825.

95. *P.P. 1825*, IX.

96. In 1840 Montgomery and his followers seceded from the Synod of Ulster and established the Non-Subscribing (Unitarian) Presbyterian Church. With their departure the Presbyterian Church in Ulster lost its most liberal minded element. See below, p. 42.

97. Beckett and Glasscock, *Belfast*, pp. 187–8.

98. D. J. Owen, *History of Belfast* (Belfast, 1921), pp. 198–208.

99. J. Gamble, *Sketches of Dublin and the North of Ireland* (Dublin, 1811), p. 34. J. Barrow, *A Tour around Ireland* (Dublin, 1835), p. 37.

100. E. Jones, 'The Distribution and Segregation of Roman Catholics in Belfast', *Sociological Review*, New Series, IV (1956), 169.

101. Ian Budge *et al.*, *The Political Development of Modern Glasgow* (unpublished MS.), Chapter 3.

2 The Age of John Bates:
1832–55

I

THE first election after the Reform Act (which doubled the Irish electorate) marked the emergence all over the country of political clubs and societies characterised by their devotion to political principles, but also by the more utilitarian purpose of managing the registration system at its first trial. Two main parties emerged generally, but not uniformly.[1] The Liberals, or Reformers, were prevalent throughout the three southern provinces and to a lesser extent in Ulster. They had been agitating for Catholic emancipation and parliamentary reform, and the agitation over the previous fifteen years for these objects had provided them with a rudimentary organisation. The conservatives relied on family influence and patronage. But it is incorrect to label all the non-Liberal borough proprietors as Conservatives or Tories. Some had pursued an eclectic course in the years before 1832 – Lord Donegall, for example, voted against Catholic emancipation but in favour of parliamentary reform, and it was not until the late 1830s that such great Ulster families as the Downshires and Ranfurlys were definitely aligned with the Tories. They wished to conserve their family influence but were otherwise independent.

It was to be expected that in Belfast, as elsewhere, rival political societies would emerge to manage the new registration system so hastily established by the Reform Act, and to compete for the two seats with which the borough was now endowed.[2] Nevertheless they were not formed immediately. The existence of the Reform Party can be traced back to a town meeting of 15 November 1830, attended by two thousand of the 'wealthy and influential' inhabitants, which passed resolutions for reform, attacked the all-pervading Donegall interest and rejoiced in the non-denominational character of its membership. Among those present were names which would recur in Belfast politics over the following decades – Dr Robert Tennent, Robert Grimshaw (linen merchant), Edmund Getty (banker), the Rev. Henry Montgomery (leader of the secessionist non-subscribing Presbyterians), James Simms (editor of the *Northern Whig*), and James Emerson, a young barrister, who on marrying into the Tennent family took the name of Emerson Tennent.[3]

The first candidate in the field was Lord Arthur Chichester (son of the second Marquis), whose campaign manifesto was couched in the most unexceptionable platitudes but whose real aim was to continue the Donegall interest. That the reformers would feel bound to oppose him was inevitable. But the method of candidate selection proved crucial. Emerson Tennent and his cousin, Robert James Tennent, both coveted the nomination and they apparently agreed to accept the party committee's decision. However, the committee decided to nominate R. J. Tennent, and a radical landowner, William Sharman Crawford of Crawfordsburn, County Down. On 6 September Emerson publicly spoke of the selection method as not having been 'in accordance with the constitutional principles which have always been a bond of our party'[4]. The Donegall faction then seized the opportunity and with the blessing of the *Belfast News Letter*, which to this date had simply supported Chichester, a requisition signed by five hundred 'merchants, gentry and respectable inhabitants' ('rabble', wailed the *Northern Whig*) urged Tennent to stand with Chichester. But two public meetings were required to persuade him to desert his old party and accept the draft (on 13 September).

The rest of the campaign was predictably acrimonious, Emerson and his erstwhile colleagues bombarding each other with open letters to the papers. In the welter of debate and recrimination the religious issue was the one most frequently obtruded. Grimshaw asked Emerson whether he still held the low opinion of the Established Church that he had expressed a few years before.[5] At the end of the campaign Tennent complained[6] that Orange voters were presumed to be hostile and not worth calling on. Ireland, he said, had been depressed for too long by respecting 'political religion'. (No formal organisation had yet entered the field on behalf of Chichester and Emerson, but a speech of Crawford in November admitted that they had the advantage over the Liberals in having barristers to watch the registry.)[7] At the end of November a Conservative organisation at last appeared – The Belfast Constitutional Club 'to unite men of moderate views but of sound constitutional principle', the founder of which was Jonathan Cordukes.[8] Its first secretary was one John Bates.

The poll was extremely rowdy. A large crowd of artisans, presumably Roman Catholic, shouted down Emerson and Chichester and would listen only to R. J. Tennent. On the second day two mobs stoned each other and had to be separated by the military. When the result[9] was announced on Christmas Eve many hours' consultation was held before it was decided to chair the victors through the town. All went well from the Court House (now Howard Street) through Donegall Place and High Street, but the procession led by an Orange band playing party tunes unwisely turned into Hercules Street – a narrow, ill-lit street full of butchers' shops and mainly Catholic: there they were attacked with hatchets and knives, as some witnesses averred. The victorious candidates escaped to friends' houses, the Sovereign who came to read the Riot Act was dragged to safety by police, and then police and military fired on the crowd, killing four people. The inquest proved inconclusive.[10]

In a post-mortem on the election the *Whig* claimed that Emerson had won under Orange patronage and denounced the survivors of 1798 who had 'disgraced their hoary heads' by failing to vote for Crawford and Tennent.[11] The *News Letter*[12] pooh-poohed the suggestion that Orange influence was dominant; admitted that during the final day large numbers had been parading the streets, with fifes, drums and flags; but rather unconvincingly claimed that they had nothing to do with Emerson. Unexpectedly, the *News Letter* agreed with the *Whig* that only two hundred Protestants had voted for the Liberals and that the remainder of their support came from Roman Catholics. This is borne out by a contemporary reprint of the poll-book, which indicates that almost all the Roman Catholics and some Presbyterians voted for the reformers, while Episcopalians and Methodists, plus the bulk of Presbyterians, supported Chichester and Emerson.[13]

It is worth treating the election of 1832 in such detail if only because it exhibits so many of the features that were to characterise Belfast elections later in the century – the inextricable

confusion between religious and political loyalties, the superior
organisation of the Tories, and the sensitivity of the politicians
to wider issues in Irish politics. The fact that Crawford favoured
a federal union between Britain and Ireland and not the larger
measure of autonomy demanded by O'Connell did not suffice
to protect him from allegations of being a crypto-repealer – or,
indeed, a charge that he refused to employ Catholic domes-
tics.[14]

Although his name was not mentioned in the contemporary
accounts it appears that the Conservative organisation was
managed mainly by one man, John Bates, then an apprentice
solicitor. From then until his death he acted as Conservative
agent at every election except the general election when his
principal was the agent to the Liberal candidates. As we shall
see, his position as chief Conservative agent was not deemed
to be incompatible with the post of Town Clerk to which he was
elected when the Corporation was reformed in 1842.

That Bates was endowed with all the qualities of a machine
politician is clear, not only from his subsequent career – dictator
of Belfast from 1842 until his downfall after the unfortunate
Chancery suit of 1854 – but from his insight into the intricacies
of registration, a system then completely new. Owing to the
careless haste with which the assistant barrister, John O'Dwyer,
had performed his duties, the register contained hundreds of
duplicate entries, and since the Irish Reform Act provided that
a name remain on the register for eight years there was in
consequence a fruitful field for personation or 'manipulation'.
Bates and the Constitutional Society attended with great
energy to the annual revision of the register and used the
complexities of the electoral law to benefit his own party and
disconcert his opponents. In 1835 he persuaded John O'Dwyer
(now assessor) to reject about eighty certificates of registration
granted by himself in 1832 on the ground that they stated 'house
and shop' instead of 'house, shop' as the qualification in question, and thereby ensured that the Liberals lost a by-election.
(For this the indignant Liberal Attorney-General sacked
O'Dwyer as Crown counsel for the Leinster circuit.) In 1837
O'Dwyer's successor, Philip Fogarty, was prepared to register
claimants with legal possession though not in residence; to this
Bates objected strenuously, though he was unable to sustain

his objection when questioned by O'Connell before the Select Committee on Fictitious Votes later that year.[15] A grudging tribute was paid to him by Durham Dunlop, otherwise a highly prejudiced witness: 'Ready in conception, unscrupulous in action – prompt, energetic and determined – capable of sustaining great bodily and mental fatigue, with a mind fitted to embrace all the ramifications of the machinery with which he had to work.'[16]

While Bates, under the approving eye of Emerson Tennent, was building up the party, attending to the registry and arranging entertainments for the 'Belfast Society', as the Belfast Constitutional Society was popularly known, the Liberals had their own municipal association with a number of distinguished names, but no formal agent and as yet inadequate appreciation of the importance of registration.

When the general election of 1835 came up Sharman Crawford transferred his attention to Dundalk where he secured election as an O'Connellite. The Belfast Liberals put forward a relative nonentity named John French (who secured three votes) and John McCance, a well-known linen merchant. Since Emerson Tennent's popularity stood high, the contest was really between McCance and Chichester, with the Donegall family straining every nerve for the return of Lord Arthur. Although extra police were drafted into the town by the Police Commissioners and public pleas were made that the chairing of the successful candidates be waived, the announcement of the result – McCance beating Chichester into third place – so provoked the Conservative partisans that they tried to force their way into the street where McCance had his tally rooms and had to be repulsed by a body of cavalry. Fourteen people were subsequently charged for rioting.[17]

The Liberals had wrested one of the borough's seats from the Tories;[18] but their triumph was short-lived. McCance died in August 1835. At the by-election in the same month R. J. Tennent was again put in nomination against a Tory – George Dunbar – Tennent making clear that he was opposed to repeal of the Union and to the Irish Church establishment, and did not wish to see a Catholic ascendancy 'any more than do the Catholics, themselves, of the town'.[19] His electoral fortunes were ruined, however, by Mr Fogarty's 'house and shop' decision, and the poll was prematurely closed with Dunbar securing 161 votes to Tennent's 84.[20]

The frustrated Liberals decided at the general election following the accession of Queen Victoria to nominate the strongest possible team. Robert Tennent withdrew disinterestedly and the candidates selected were James Gibson, a Presbyterian merchant – the first parliamentary candidate to come from Belfast's largest sect – and the Earl of Belfast[21] who had been member for Carrick from 1818 to 1820, for Belfast from 1820 to 1830, and since then for County Antrim. Although he had held a junior post in the administration of Lord Grey and his attitudes were mildly Liberal, the eldest son of Lord Donegall was not the most desirable candidate in the eyes of the *Whig*, who impressed on his lordship the necessity of 'turning over a new leaf'. When it appeared, Lord Belfast's[22] election address was devoid of policy content – merely stressing his desire to represent the wishes of Belfast.[23]

The campaign, while less disorderly than the previous three, was more redolent of theological disputation than normal electioneering. The Conservatives ignored Lord Belfast and concentrated their fire on Gibson. His orthodoxy was called in question – during the recent dispute in the Synod of Ulster he had opposed the 'great men' of the Synod (Cooke, Stewart and Reid) and every elector 'who wished to uphold Protestantism' was urged to vote for Tennent and Dunbar.[24] Cooke himself preached on the text: 'When the enemy shall come in like a flood, the spirit of the Lord shall lift up a standard against him.'[25] Mr Dunbar refused to think of extending to the Catholics any further privileges and his agent, in what may well be the most recondite of electioneering allusions, derided Gibson as 'an old light Presbyterian who is endeavouring to hobble into Parliament under old light colours, leaning upon two stilts, the one Popery and the other Infidelity'.[26]

In spite of the volume of theological ammunition hurled against them, the combined strength of the Donegall faction and the Liberals carried the day and for the first (and only) time two professed Liberals were elected for Belfast.[27]

Tennent at once complained that his five-year connection with Belfast as an M.P. had been severed through bribery of the poorest voters by the Liberals.[28] Dr Cooke made a similar complaint. But the petition when presented was based on two separate grounds – bribery of the voters who had polled for the Liberal candidates, a special charge of personal bribery (afterwards dropped) against Lord Belfast, and the alleged disqualification of Gibson inasmuch as he had failed when taking his seat to declare property which had come into his possession in the previous three years (as required of members by an obscure standing order of 1717).[29]

The petition went, as was customary, to a Grenville Committee (a Select Committee chosen by lot), and when it was seen that the composition of the Committee was ten Conservatives and one Liberal, the Belfast Liberals gave up the struggle, conceded the case against Gibson, and allowed the Committee to strike off a sufficient number of votes from Lord Belfast to put Dunbar in a majority of one. So Tennent and Dunbar were once more returned as members for the borough.[30]

In the same year a Select Committee of the Commons, under Daniel O'Connell's chairmanship and enquiring into the manufacture of fictitious votes in Ireland, heard disquieting evidence of the state of the register in Belfast. The assistant barristers who had served since 1832, including the egregious O'Dwyer, admitted to divergent standards for admission to the register of £10 householders.

Although one barrister took the police rate as his criterion, the others registered as £10 householders people valued at considerably less (in some cases as low as £5) by the police committee, and even the methods of assessment by the latter were too casual for the select committee's taste. It was clear also that any duplicate entries in the original register would remain for eight years. Bates was examined for five consecutive days and asked nearly 1,500 questions; but although the committee believed that the registration process in Belfast left much to be desired, they were unable to extract from him an admission that corrupt practices were widespread.[31]

Further evidence was provided in February 1841 by Solomon Darcus, Clerk of the Peace for Antrim and returning officer for Belfast, who appended to an official return giving the numbers of voters in Belfast in the years 1835, 1837 and 1841 respectively the note: 'the total number on the Register at February 1841 is 6,086; and there are not 2,000 actual voters who could be polled at any election taking place within six months'.[32]

Darcus's prediction was put to the test in July 1841 when the general election was held. At the outset Emerson Tennent and Dunbar appeared as the likely Tory candidates, but Dunbar soon withdrew and was replaced by William G. Johnston, while the Liberal candidates were Lord Belfast and David Robert Ross. At an early stage in the campaign a Liberal supporter wrote a public letter suggesting that to avoid the now inevitable concomitants of a contested election 'falsehood, drunkenness, anger, wrath, malice, bribery and perjury', the two parties should put up first one candidate apiece and share the representation.[33] To this letter John Bates replied promptly, saying that he had looked at the books and found that of 4,116 voters only 1,850 are good, thus leaving 2,266 to be manipulated and 'since (he) abhors this system of public corruption' he would be willing to divide the seats without a contest.[34] This offer was turned down by Grimshaw, who said that the Liberals could not stand the prospect of continuing with one of the M.P.s who had voted against the true welfare of the country.

So it was war *à outrance*. The campaign went on openly with great emphasis on free trade and less on religion than usual.[35] A small committee of eight members was occasionally consulted by Bates, but apart from the treasurer the management of the election was entirely in his hands.[36] £3,000 was disbursed on the Tory side, including £750 for (illegal) car hire. A list of Conservative voters, previously registered but who had lost their qualifications through removal, was privately printed on Bates's instructions for circulation to his assistants. A copy unfortunately fell into the hands of 'Pop' Mulholland, a ginger-beer manufacturer, who gave it to McBrair, the Liberal agent, but refused to disclose more about its provenance than that he had secured it from a prostitute. Finally, four poor men, small farmers or labourers, were imported from Monaghan through the efforts of a clerk in John Bates' office, given £5 and a good suit of clothes apiece and an injunction to eat, drink and be merry. They spent the whole of polling day engaged in personation and even took the oath, which the clerk afterwards claimed they were urged not to do. Unfortunately one of them on his way home, when his tongue was loosened with whiskey, bragged about his achievement, and the Liberals were duly informed. Personation was, however, not confined to these four – almost sixty men were subsequently alleged to have been engaged in that malpractice.

The results showed Emerson Tennent and Johnston comfortably ahead of Belfast and Ross.[36] But the air was thick with allegations of Tory personation. The Liberals duly filed a petition on four grounds – personation, bribery, non-age of certain deputy assessors and systematic and fraudulent delay in taking the poll, of which there was evidence at a number of booths.[37] The volume of evidence they accumulated was quite formidable, but so were the prospective costs.[38] Before the petition came up for trial an influential Conservative, John McNeill, director of the Northern Bank (and father-in-law of the future Lord Cairns), approached James Campbell, a Liberal flax spinner, and offered to make good the £600 that he had heard the Liberals still owed after the election and a further £400 to cover the initial costs of the petition provided that (i) the sitting members would admit the least opprobrious charge – the delay in taking the poll – and concede the petition; (ii) the petitioners would not produce further evidence to the committee; (iii) at the next election both sides would 'exert themselves' to secure the return of one Liberal and one Tory.

After some haggling over the sum involved, they secured the agreement of Grimshaw who then communicated the decision to the local agent, McBrair, and the national agent, James Coppock. Lord Belfast wished to go ahead with the petition but Coppock secured his 'very reluctant' consent, and on the very morning of the hearing the respondents conceded the petition and the election was declared void.[39]

The by-election was held in August 1842. The Liberals put up one candidate (Ross) and the Tories two. Lord Donegall insisted (despite a joint deputation of Tories and Liberals) in putting up another son, Lord Hamilton Chichester; but the two main parties kept their bargain and for the first time in Belfast a Chichester came at the botton of the poll.[40]

Meanwhile, however, several Liberals, indignant at the compromise, sent a long account of the compromise to O'Connell whom they thought to be 'the most prompt and energetic

M.P. to act'.[41] O'Connell's feelings towards the Belfast Tories
were not very favourable since he had had to receive police
protection during a speech-making tour of the city in January
1841.[42] O'Connell at once raised the question in the Commons
and a select committee was quickly set up under his chairmanship (June 1842).

The Committee heard several witnesses[43] testify to the
objectionable state of the Belfast register and to the propensities
of the electors for bribery and cheating. A frank Conservative
doctor said that he believed that perhaps five to six hundred
'of very low class' could be bought either by hard cash or by
hiring cars or paying taxes – the Catholics, however, 'having
more determination and stronger political feeling were not so
fond of bribery'. Much evidence was given of personation,
apart from the full tale of the Monaghan labourers; one witness
pointed out that a 'very strong Liberal' who had died in 1837
was personated in the Conservative interest. McNeill said that
the only reason why he had taken the initiative (without
consulting his party) in the compromise arrangements was
that he thought it was a great waste to have an election going
on for a week in a city of 100,000 since 'everybody who is not a
temperance or a teetotal man is drunk'.

Bates' former clerk, John Rowland (now a water rate collector), threw himself upon the mercy of the committee and
admitted to hiring the four personators (but claimed that he
had no authority from anyone for that decision). A surveyor
who claimed to be the 'Commander-in-Chief' of the personators said that there were about sixty altogether. John Bates,
however, did not submit himself, as he had four years earlier, to
an exhaustive examination by O'Connell. He pleaded professional privilege.[44] Coppock in his turn did not wish to examine
Bates unless the latter offered himself as a witness.[45]

The report of the committee stated that the 1841 election
had been characterised by 'extensive corruption' and 'gross
and corrupt personation of voters'; that the compromise had
the effect of excluding from the investigating Committee evidence of bribery, personation and perjury; that there was no
evidence to connect the sitting members or defeated candidates
with bribery; that the state of the registry was 'most objectionable' – not more than 1,800 actual electors, the rest having

lost their qualifications 'by death, removal or otherwise'.[46]

Had the Select Committee's report with its strong rebuke of Belfast electioneering been published twelve years later a Royal Commission might have been set up to investigate further. But in 1842 no further machinery existed for a more extensive inquiry (the *ad hoc* Sudbury Commission was the first of its kind) and no penalties were incurred by any of the Belfast bribers or personators. The by-election results were upheld.

2

While these exciting developments were going on the structure of local government in Ireland generally was being quietly transformed. There were two main statutes. The Irish Poor Law Act of 1838[47] established poor law unions, mainly on a parochial basis, administered by boards of guardians elected triennially by £10 householders. At first their duties were merely to levy the poor rate and apply the revenue for the construction of workhouses. But within ten years they had been entrusted with responsibility for outdoor relief, fever and other state-aided hospitals[48] and the peculiarly Irish institution of 'dispensaries' – and until the Public Health Act of 1878 were the main sanitary authority in boroughs. By the Local Government Act (1898) the guardians lost the power to levy the poor rate and their public health functions were gradually taken over by the borough councils. Although abolished in England in 1939 they survived in Belfast (and in Northern Ireland generally) until 1946.[49]

The Belfast guardians were rarely involved in disputatious politics, although later in the century some politicians (e.g. Joe Devlin and William Walker) used an election for poor law guardians as the first step in their political careers.

A much more sweeping reform was the Irish Municipal Corporations Act (1840)[50] which implemented the report of the Commissioners on Municipal Corporations in Ireland, 1835. Under the Act fifty-eight decaying Corporations were abolished and in the remaining ten, including Belfast, the £10 voting qualification was established (in contrast to England where after the municipal reforms of 1835 all ratepayers were admitted to the vote). The new borough councils were vested with general powers to make by-laws for good rule and government, watching and lighting and suppression of nuisances, and were empowered to carry out existing trusts. Their accounts were to be sent annually to the Lord Lieutenant and their funds were consolidated.

While the Commons and Lords were wrangling about the details of the new system of municipal government – several abortive Bills were introduced between 1836 and 1840 – several teams of commissioners were travelling around the country, dividing the preserved boroughs up into wards. The Belfast Commissioners, reporting in 1837,[51] recommended the preservation of the parliamentary boundary of 1832 plus the suburb of Ballymacarret on the east side of the Lagan. They recommended that the new municipal area be divided into five wards – Dock, St Anne's, Smithfield, St George's and Cromac, the last two to extend on both sides of the river.

These provisions were incorporated into the Act of 1840. Each ward was to elect two aldermen and six councillors – one third of the councillors was to be re-elected annually and half the aldermen every third year. The Town Clerk was to be responsible for drawing up the register and the prospective voter, in order to qualify, had to be rated as a £10 householder for twelve months before the last day of August in the relevant year and had to have previously paid all poor rates and grand jury and municipal cesses.

The passing of the Act attracted little attention in Belfast[52] (although the M.P.s Tennent and Dunbar had opposed it). When it was operative there was speculation that the Liberals would win a reasonable proportion of the seats. The Catholic journal, *The Vindicator*, fondly predicting a Liberal majority, said that the 30,000 Catholics would not be content with less than eight councillors and two aldermen.[53] The *Whig* was also optimistic about the Liberals' chances.[54] But Liberal ineptness ruined their chances. At the revision sessions the agent, McBrair, objected to many Tory claimants, but his objections were all set aside because the notice of objection stated the number of his house incorrectly.[55] Also, unaccountably, the tax offices had closed down during the month of August, effectively disfranchising any claimants whose rates had not been paid before, and the Town Clerk of the old Corporation failed to

produce lists of taxes paid.[56] While the Liberals were caught in
the trammels of procedure, John Bates had established in each
ward a committee to ensure that trustworthy Protestants were
being registered. By 20 October the Liberals were virtually out
of the contest. Only two wards were contested – Cromac,
where the Donegall faction tried to secure a footing by nominating the outgoing Sovereign, Thomas Verner, and St Anne's
where three Liberals stood. But on polling day the Conservatives swept all the wards and, at a doleful meeting to protest
against Verner's defeat, Lord Donegall burst into tears at
'this most dishonourable transaction'.[57]

The result – 40 Conservatives for five wards – marked the
apogee of Bates' career. He had in the newly formed Belfast
Conservative Society[58] a pliant tool. The ward associations
were dominated by him and even before the first meeting of
the new Corporation it was clear that he would be elected Town
Clerk.[59] From then until his fall in 1855 Bates held an ascendancy in Belfast politics greater than any of his successors (or
indeed any comparable top administrator in any British city).
The Council was all of the same political colour. The political
homogeneity of the Council facilitated control and it is clear that
in all the complexities of private bill legislation through which
Bates was to lead them in the following thirteen years, the bulk
of the members relied on his expertise and good sense.

The new Council assembled on 4 November 1842, appointed
John Bates as Town Clerk – his predecessor allowing himself to
express publicly his regret that they had not reappointed him!
– and elected as mayor George Dunbar, the former M.P.
Dunbar's opening speech made slighting references to the
Municipal Corporations Act which he had opposed at the time
of its introduction, and regarding which he said he had no
reason to change his mind since its effects were 'injurious
rather than salutary'. However, now that it was law, they had
to make the best of it, he said.

The Corporation quickly got down to business, undisturbed
by internal dissensions. Six committees were established –
Finance, Audit, By-Laws, Parliamentary Bills, Property and
General Purposes, two of which – the first and last – still exist.

The politico-religious homogeneity of the new town council,
assured by the ingenuity of John Bates, facilitated its efforts to

control the life of the town and take over the powers of the
unreformed authorities. The Police Commissioners refused to
hand over, and the Town Clerk had to call a meeting, to
which all two thousand people on the burgess roll were invited
and which about five hundred attended, to convince them that
under the Municipal Corporations Act there was no place for
the Police Commissioners in the government of the city. The
ex-Sovereign, Thomas Verner, vainly attempted to declare the
meeting illegal and was laughed to scorn. Dunbar, the mayor,
pointed out that the old Police Commissioners did not always
agree with the elected Police Committee and this was not
challenged. By the Municipal Corporations Act, he pointed out,
every burgess was a commissioner of police; but it would be
necessary to appoint a Committee which would be part of the
structure of the new Corporation. Dunbar's arguments were
not seriously answered and the meeting passed by a majority
of 391 votes to two a resolution to transfer the powers of the
Police Commissioners to the Corporation.[60] But the Commissioners subsequently challenged the validity of this procedure[61]
and an action in the Queen's Bench division was necessary
before they finally conceded defeat (January 1844).[62]

The early business of the Corporation was rather trivial –
striking the new police rate, attending to small works and
arguing with Dublin Castle as to whether they had to foot the
bill for the extra police rushed into the city to cope with the
riots of 1843.[63] Most of their energies, however, were directed
to promoting a series of private Bills which afterwards became
the Belfast Improvement Acts of 1845, 1846 and 1847, and set
the future course of development of the rapidly expanding
borough.

The first Bill, apart from prescribing a minimum width for
streets, sought permission to borrow £150,000, of which
£100,000 was earmarked for widening old streets and making
new ones. This was granted, but a clause extending the borough
boundary was struck out owing to opposition by Lord Donegall
and some millowners who did not wish to be encumbered with
borough taxes. The Act of 1846 authorised the Corporation
to borrow £50,000 to establish a gasworks, and the Act of 1847
authorised them to borrow £15,000 to drain the Blackstaff
river,[64] between the Linen Hall and the present Bradbury Place.

However, the Corporation under the guidance of the Town Clerk adopted a high-handed attitude to its Enabling Acts. The sums allowed were exceeded by £84,000 and the money appropriated to other purposes. The gasworks, which since 1821 had been operated by a private company,[65] remained outside municipal control. A large site was bought to extend the markets; the evil-smelling docks at the foot of Waring Street and Corporation Street were filled in and two new wide streets, Victoria Street and Corporation Street, were built and a new Court House and Custom House planned.

But the Blackstaff project was delayed, allegedly through the opposition of millowners and iron masters who did not wish to be deprived of their source of water, and fresh mills were built during this period, drawing their water from the Pound Burn – a tributary of the river.

It is hard to blame the Corporation for using the money authorised by statute for modernising the town, although not in the manner originally planned. During the 1840s people were flocking into the town from the neighbouring counties – the population increased by 32·2 per cent from 1831 to 1841, and 23·6 per cent in the next decade.

Flax-spinning mills were increasing in number from two in 1830 to eighteen in 1840, and twenty-four in 1846. Iron foundries were also being built for the manufacture of textile machinery as well as steam engines and boilers[66] – although marine engineering was yet to come. The port authorities, with expanded powers from two Acts of Parliament, were now following the imaginative policy of connecting the port with the waters of the lough two miles away by a deep channel or 'cut' – the first stage, completed between 1839 and 1841, cut off one bend of the river, and the second stage was completed by 1849.[67] The private docks and quays were also purchased and Belfast, already the first port in Ireland (although Dublin's population was four times as large) was set for further commercial expansion. The first railway line had been constructed as far as Lisburn in 1839, and after the 1847 Railway Act the provision of public funds for railway development enabled the construction of the main lines connecting Belfast with Londonderry and Dublin, as well as the nearer market towns.

But such rapid industrial and commercial expansion was

bound to impose a severe strain on the public services previously adequate for a provincial market town. The markets themselves were held in the streets, obstructing the traffic – potatoes were sold all over the town, grain in Cromac Street, and calves in Police Place. The construction of a central market was an obvious need and this the Corporation did by buying a perfectly adequate site. Moreover, building speculators would have had a free hand after the death of the second Marquis of Donegall in 1844 and the dispersal of his estate through fee-farm grants, large and small, particularly after 1850 when the remainder of the estate came into the hands of the Commissioners of Encumbered Estates. But the Act of 1847 ensured that all new buildings conformed to certain minimum standards, and houses built thereafter were regarded as a great improvement on the mean structures of earlier decades, erected in courts and alleyways with dozens of families sharing a single privy. Although back access was not required until the passing of the Belfast Improvement Act of 1878, the houses built in the 1840s had at least a small yard with a lavatory and ash-pit.[68] Many of them are still occupied.

Another consequence of rapid industrialisation – overcrowding, poor sanitation and endemic disease – was less effectively dealt with by the Town Council.[69] A special sanitary committee was set up in 1847 to deal with cholera, the dread concomitant of the potato famine, but this was a short-lived body and it was not until 1865 that a proper sanitary authority was set up.[70]

What the Corporation could have done was to drain the river Blackstaff which was virtually an open sewer into which the effluvia from factories, ash-pits and privies was discharged; but, as indicated above, the opposition from millowners was probably responsible for its failure.

This failure apart, the Corporation during its first ten years managed to secure a number of important social reforms and to modernise the city. Illustrative of its social concern was the maximum ten-hour day for women and children in the textile factories prescribed by the Act of 1847.[71] Nor is there much room for doubting that the Corporation regarded itself as enlightened and socially progressive. When Andrew Mulholland, one of the founders of Mulholland's Mill, was elected mayor in 1844, his speech in returning thanks promised 'to ameliorate the condition of the operatives'. Belfast, he said, should not fall behind the large manufacturing towns of England in coping with rapid population growth; and he suggested public walks, gardens, baths and washhouses, free fountains of pure water, free libraries and reading rooms, and coffee shops, which would 'promote their health and cleanliness and give them better tastes'.[72] Compared with Dublin of the 1840s, Belfast's Tory-dominated Corporation was very advanced indeed.

But in the eyes of the Liberals the socially ameliorative policies of the Corporation did not compensate for their political sharp practices. During general election years the *Whig* continually lamented the disadvantages affecting the Liberals – failure of Tory rate collectors to collect all the rates from Liberal voters so that the latter would afterwards fail to qualify as voters;[73] partiality by revising barristers;[74] eviction of Liberal electors whose houses were to be demolished to make new streets.[75] Throughout this period they failed to get a single Liberal elected to the Town Council, and at parliamentary elections they did not fare much better. After the 1842 result was upset both parties in the subsequent by-election honoured the earlier compromise by nominating just one candidate apiece (Emerson Tennent and David Ross, a radical merchant who simultaneously made overtures to Presbyterians and Catholics). Lord Donegall, however, who would face three months later the elimination of his interest on the Corporation, insisted on putting up another of his sons, Lord Hamilton Chichester, and although waited on by a mixed group, refused to withdraw Lord Hamilton's nomination unless R. J. Tennent were put in the field as the sole Liberal candidate. At the poll, however, Ross and Tennent were easily elected.[76] In 1845 Emerson Tennent was appointed Secretary to the Government of Ceylon and accepted the Chiltern Hundreds. The Liberals did not contest the by-election and allowed Lord John Chichester, brother to Lord Hamilton, an unopposed return as a Conservative. Lord John was the last of the Chichester family to represent the town of Belfast in Parliament. The spendthrift second Marquis died in 1844 and the Donegall interest was liquidated with the family estate. In 1847, however,

the Tories went back on the 1842 agreement and put up a
leading landowner, George Suffern,[77] together with Chichester.
R. J. Tennent again stood – his election address reproducing
verbatim his address of fifteen years before – as the sole Liberal
candidate, and Chichester merely appealed to the memory of
his father. With one candidate in the field the Liberals secured
a great victory, beating Chichester into second place by over
two hundred votes, and they rejoiced that Bates' hegemony
was overthrown.[78]

Their rejoicing was premature. During his five years in
Parliament R. J. Tennent tried hard to please his socially and
religiously mixed following. But the Catholics were affronted
by his 'lukewarmness' concerning the Ecclesiastical Titles Bill;
the Presbyterians regarded him as ambivalent on the repeal
issue, which came to a head again with the insurrection of
1848; the linen merchants' shipping interests were antagonised
by his support of free trade, and the *Whig* denounced him as
'a senatorial mute', linking him and Chichester in the following
scathing passage: 'Ask an arithmetician to add up two nega-
tives, and tell what is the result, then you may get an idea of the
value of the two men.'[79]

As the 1852 election approached the *Whig* made no secret
of its desire for a more efficient Liberal representative. It
reported that Sir James Graham had been approached by some
local Liberals and dilated on his excellent qualities, both as a
member of the Cabinet and his knowledge of the trade and of
the town of Belfast.[80] However, in March 1852 Graham decided
to stand for Carlisle and Belfast lost its only chance of having a
Liberal front-bencher as M.P. The *Whig* continued, however,
to inveigh against the 'stuffed puppets', and as the campaign
gathered momentum it strongly supported efforts to find
alternative candidates – first a shipping magnate, then Lord
Castlereagh (who declined 'because of unwillingness to face the
exertions of a personal canvass').[81] Both failed, however, and
with a very bad grace the *Whig* reported that there was nothing
for it but to support Tennent again. Lukewarmness on the part
of the Catholics in addition to the *Whig's* hostility combined
to produce a resounding victory for the two new Conservative candidates – Hugh McCalmont Cairns, originally from
County Down, then practising at the English bar and married

to a Belfast banker's daughter, and Richard Davison, a *rentier* of rather refined tastes.[82] Chichester had been quietly dropped.

The 1852 election showed an obvious falling off in Liberal support, which cannot simply be explained away by disillusionment with the candidate. In fact, the Liberal ranks had already been split over the fourth Belfast Improvement Act (1850). This sought permission to spend a further £100,000, widening the mouth of the Blackstaff to prevent flooding, building a new street over it, and extending two further streets (Oxford Street and East Bridge Street). At once, the Liberals, Grimshaw and Dunville, together with James Simms, editor of the *Northern Whig*, the ex-Sovereign, Verner, and an ex-mayor, John Clarke, organised a town meeting to protest against the Bill and to present a petition to the Select Committee. The evidence of Grimshaw was the most interesting. Some of it was directed to the technicalities of the Bill. Grimshaw rightly predicted that the two streets in question would never become useful traffic routes in Belfast. But the main burden of his argument was a complaint that the Liberals, who had in the past controlled the Police Commissioners, were totally excluded from the Town Council. However, as solicitor for the petition, John Bates was joined by an unexpected ally, Edward O'Rorke, one of the leading Catholic professional men, whose speech was virtually a diatribe against the old Police Commissioners, contrasting their record with that of the present hard-working Town Council, whose meetings had never – but once when the Queen visited the city – been postponed through lack of a quorum. O'Rorke seemed to have been needled by the Rev. Henry Montgomery's taunts that his role as town advocate was dishonourable and part of his speech was concerned to repudiate this charge and to display an indifference to the Liberal cause (which he had promoted for twenty years), far in excess of the requirements of professional neutrality.[83]

Opposition to the Bill was successful inasmuch as it was dropped, but the Corporation was not easily foiled. They petitioned the Lord Lieutenant for an extension of the town boundary to increase the area of taxation, and Captain F. Y. Gilbert of Sligo was duly appointed to hold a commission of inquiry in the town.

Gilbert duly reported[84] that the existing boundary had been fixed in 1836 (actually 1837) when the population of the town was some 68,000. It was now 115,294, of which 18,000 lived outside the boundary and these required proper municipal services. Though critical of the quality of houses built in the suburbs, Gilbert praised the improvements made by the Town Council. The Gilbert report recommended that the borough area be increased from 970 acres ($1\frac{1}{2}$ square miles) to 6,421 acres (10 square miles) and that the five existing wards be reconstructed, but called by the same names – only one (Smithfield) would be significantly larger than the others.[85]

A new statute was required to implement the Gilbert report and this was duly passed, with only minor amendments, as the Belfast Extension Act, 1852–3. It was noted that the Liberal Party in the city neither opposed the Bill nor troubled to give evidence before the commission of inquiry.

The Corporation appeared to have won again, since the new municipal area had a poor law valuation of nearly £250,000 compared with £156,645 in 1852. However, within a year a disaffected solicitor, John Rea (who had fought in the insurrection of 1848), filed a suit in the Court of Chancery in Dublin against the mayor and Corporation, citing several leading Tories including John Bates as special respondents. Rea's allegations covered a wide field.[86] He asked the court to declare that the Corporation had violated the provisions of several local Acts – they had exceeded by over £15,000 the borrowing limit of £150,000 set by the Act of 1845; they had misapplied the £50,000 allowed by the Act of 1846 by purchasing May's Fields instead of the gasworks; furthermore, when refused the £100,000 requested in the bill of 1850, they had illegally borrowed £84,000 on certificates issued through fraudulently representing the police rate of 1851 to show a profit when in fact it should have shown a deficit. There were several further charges against Bates himself – of cooking the accounts and charging exorbitant fees in his capacity as Town Solicitor – £32,000 in all in addition to his salary.

The action lasted from 11 to 19 June 1855 and was heard by the Lord Chancellor of Ireland, Mazière Brady, who twenty years earlier had been one of the Commissioners on Municipal Corporations. In his judgement the Chancellor said that the case appeared to be 'about as free from legal difficulties as almost any case he had had to consider'. He found all the main allegations proved. The Corporation had borrowed in excess; it had misapplied funds; it had borrowed illegally. Interestingly, he found that of the £84,000 allegedly borrowed on certificates only £48,000 had been so obtained – the rest had been overdrawn on the account of the Borough Treasurer, John Thompson, in the Belfast Bank of which he was also a director!

The Lord Chancellor expressed himself with great delicacy on the subject of Bates' costs. He would neither settle nor unsettle them, but submitted them again to a Taxing Master to determine whether the bill was drawn up on a very exorbitant scale. He also refrained from imputing blame to Bates, except in so far as he had tried to defend himself by producing recriminatory charges against John Rea. Nevertheless, the general tenor of the judgement could not but have a staggering effect on the Corporation, since the special respondents were held personally liable for a total of £273,000 misapplied or illegally raised since 1845.[87]

The consequences were immediately evident. John Rea, on his return from the Dublin hearing, received the traditional Irish hero's welcome – bonfires and a torchlight procession. John Bates, the discredited Town Clerk, resigned both his posts and was dead within three months. Thompson, the Borough Treasurer, also resigned. At the annual elections for one third of the Council later in 1855, six Liberals were returned, including the prosperous baker, Bernard Hughes, the first Catholic ever to hold municipal office in Belfast. The Conservatives then attempted to secure Liberal agreement to an Indemnity Bill to clear the special respondents. But in spite of their appeals, the Liberals proved obdurate and opposed the Bill so vehemently that the Private Bill Committee, in 1857,[88] threw it out.

Another proposal was that 10 Conservative councillors would retire and allow the Liberals unopposed returns: but Rea also objected to this – he wanted 17 Liberals out of 40 – so the scheme was dropped, although the Tory councillors had already retired and the names of the 'acceptable' Liberals had been published in the newspapers.[89]

A further Indemnity Bill was presented to the House later

in 1858 and was again the object of vehement Liberal opposition. (Their temper had not been improved by their failure to win back one of the parliamentary seats at the general election of 1857 in spite of the cloud of obloquy surrounding the Conservatives. With typical misjudgement they put up *three* candidates, and two Tories were returned on a split vote). For a second time the Select Committee turned down the indemnity measure, just after the advent to power of the second Derby Government.

In August 1858 the new Government appointed a Royal Commission to inquire into the state of the borough. Their terms of reference were to see how the money borrowed by the earlier Acts had been spent; whether the existing litigation should be continued, and whether the municipal taxes should be consolidated.

The conclusions of the Royal Commission were more favourable than the Chancery verdict had been to the Corporation. They absolved the Council from blame in taking the whole of May's Fields, since they had obtained a better bargain than if they had bought a portion; they held that the £50,000 allocated for the gasworks was not misapplied since it was 'wiser' to continue the existing arrangements; that the improvements effected by the Corporation in demolishing old streets and building new ones was 'very great'; that the building of the new market was a considerable advantage to the town; and that Bates' costs were not excessive.

The Commissioners recommended that the £84,000 be legalised and charged to the rates; that the special respondents should pay the costs of the suit and that some agreement should be reached on the remaining points since the continued litigation was injurious to the town. They also advised the consolidation of the four main rates – police rate, washhouses rate, poor rate and water rate. But they also deplored the fact that in spite of the provisions of earlier Acts, the Blackstaff had not yet been drained and improved. They recommended that the Corporation be not allowed to borrow further until they had reduced their existing debt (£269,958) to below £200,000.[90]

The Liberals had refused as a party to adopt a policy on the Royal Commission and they reacted with the usual bad grace when the award was made. Most of the proceedings before the

Commissioners were taken up by acrimonious wrangling between John Rea[91] and the Conservative witnesses as to the former's responsibility for exacerbating the bad feeling in the town.[92] Dr Cooke in particular testified that the suit had prevented valuable building ground from being utilised.[93]

After the report of the Royal Commission the Conservatives appeared to capitulate and 17 prominent Liberals were nominated without opposition to serve on the Council. There were not enough annual vacancies to accommodate them all, but it was understood that any casual vacancies would be filled from their number. The new members included such prestigious names as Thomas Sinclair, the bacon exporter and a leading Presbyterian elder, William Dunville, the distiller, a member of the Grimshaw family, and another Catholic, William Hamill.[94]

At the next mayoral election in 1861 the Liberals secured twenty members on the Council and were able to elect Sir Edward Coey, the first (and last) Liberal mayor of the town, in place of the millowner, William Ewart (Dunville and Sinclair having declined the honour). In the meantime, the vexed question of the indemnity was referred to arbitration, and the terms of an award were eventually incorporated in the Belfast Award Act, which stipulated that no Corporation funds were to be used in paying the costs of either party. The special respondents' costs were believed to be as high as £50,000.[95]

One may close this survey of the era of John Bates with a glance at the characteristic failure of the Liberals to maintain the advantage they had achieved in 1860. Coey was succeeded as mayor by the Liberal-Conservative architect, Sir Charles Lanyon; but in the following year John Lytle, a typical narrow Conservative, was elected. The Liberal representation on the Council dwindled partly through apathy (absence for more than six months from the borough constituted a disqualification under the 1842 Act), and partly through organisational weakness. After 1861 the Conservatives reverted to normal party politics. By 1864 there were a mere five Liberals left on the Council, including Bernard Hughes. The poor organisational state of the Liberals was further evinced by their failure to find a single candidate to contest the parliamentary election of 1859, thus giving Cairns and Davison a clear run. In spite of

all the jeremiads of the *Whig* and Durham Dunlop, it is plain
that the Belfast Liberals were either too indolent or apathetic
to attend to the register, and allowed the Conservatives to
achieve an almost insuperable lead over them. Dunville admitted in 1865 that on the ratepayers' roll, as it stood, the Liberals
could not secure election.

That this electoral advantage could not have been perpetuated except by fraudulent means (after all, the Liberals had won
parliamentary elections in the town) was stoutly maintained by
some Liberals, and before the Select Committee of 1858 the
Town Clerk was compelled to hand in a return showing the
number of candidates for the burgess roll disqualified by non-
payment of rates.[96] It showed that from 1843 to 1857 inclusive
the number of those rejected for non-payment of the various
municipal imposts ranged from *twice* the total electorate in
1843 to nearly half the number registered in 1857. The Liberals
loudly claimed that this was due to the failure of Tory-appointed
rate collectors to collect the rate at due time rather than
carelessness by would-be electors.[97]

This brings us to sum up the character of Belfast town
politics in the first years after municipal reform. The general
impression is an unpleasant one – of one party securing control
over the Corporation by questionable means and maintaining
itself in power without scruple, while the opposing party's
respectability is matched by its impotence. The aura of corruption with which Belfast Corporation was suffused at intervals
throughout its history was apparent from the beginning of this
period.[98] Nor can the rapid expansion of the population –
approaching 100,000 in 1850 – be readily pleaded in extenua-
tion of its actions. Another municipal body, the Harbour Board,
managed to organise as elaborate a programme of expansion
as the Corporation and to do so with perfect decorum and
scarcely any controversy.[99]

Indeed, after the Chancery suit there is considerable evidence[100] that the leading industrialists, merchant princes and
professional men looked on the Council with some contempt
and preferred to serve in the Chamber of Commerce, or (those
with specialised interests) on the Harbour Board. Sinclair and
Dunville had to be enticed from the Harbour Board to the
Corporation. Nor did they last long – Sinclair was back again

to serve a term as chairman of the Harbour Board from 1863 to 1867. And it was noted that in 1865 there was no representative of the shipping interest on the Council.

Apart from one-party dominance and a penchant for corrupt practices, the Council of the era of John Bates exhibited another unpraiseworthy characteristic, sectarianism. In every election of the period, with increasing emphasis, the close connection between civic prosperity and Protestantism was loudly proclaimed. This point will be developed in the next chapter when the sectarian riots are considered. But one might end here with a cautionary tale, illustrating the different attitudes of Council and Harbour Board. The second mayor of the reformed Corporation was John Clarke, a large property owner, who had previously supported the Donegall interest.[101] In his speech of acceptance he promised to show no partiality to any party or sect.[102] In 1844 the third Catholic Church in the city, St Malachy's was dedicated and Mr Clarke on that day assisted in the collection and personally subscribed £10. He was at once attacked by the *Banner of Ulster* as 'an open promoter of popery, the deadly enemy of all civil and religious liberty'.

Two months later Clarke was succeeded as mayor by Andrew Mulholland and was dropped from the Council in 1845.[103] He never stood again but in 1849 found refuge in the Harbour Board, where he served as chairman from July 1855 until his death in April 1863. In 1859, when giving evidence to the Royal Commission on Municipal Affairs, he was unfortunately not allowed to reply when John Rea claimed that the reason for his demotion was that a meeting of the Cromac Conservative Association held 'in Mr Bates' office' had resolved that 'having acted as collector in a Roman Catholic chapel [he] had lost their confidence and they could not give [him] their support'.[104]

NOTES

1. Cf. J. H. Whyte, *Irish Historical Studies*, XI (September 1959), pp. 33–40.
2. Four Irish boroughs (Belfast, Galway, Waterford and Limerick) and Trinity College, Dublin, each received a second seat under the Irish Reform Act.

3. James Emerson Tennent was the third son of William Emerson, a tobacco merchant. He had accompanied Byron in the struggle for Greek independence and had already published a *History of Greece*.
4. *B.N.L.*, 7 September 1832. This is Emerson's account. It is true, however, that he had previously inserted a notice in the *Whig* (30 August), repudiating a requisition emanating from a number of voters and published in the *B.N.L.* (28 August) on the ground that the two candidates supported the same cause as himself. At the outset of the campaign the Reform Society published a declaration of principle binding on all candidates, included further parliamentary reform, abolition of grand juries, slavery and tithes, and of the East India Company's monopoly.
5. *B.N.L.*, 14 September 1832. He had referred to it as 'the insidious remnant of the superstition of a darker age, a pampered Prelacy and a domineering Church'.
6. *B.N.L.*, 7 December 1832.
7. *B.N.L.*, 13 November 1832.
8. Printed notice in Cordukes' Papers, *PRONI*, DOD, 861/1. This must not be confused with the Belfast Loyal Protestant Constitutional Society 'representing the wealth, the respectability, the influence of the people of Belfast', which was apparently founded earlier in the month. *B.N.L.*, 5 November 1832. This was a much more obscure body, but it was still extant in 1844. See below, p. 53.
9. Chichester, 848; J. E. Tennent, 737; R. J. Tennent, 613; Crawford, 597.
10. Colonel Coulson, the commander of the Belfast militia, told the inquest that he was very indignant when he saw the procession going down Hercules Street and tried to divert it by blocking the entry; cf. *B.N.L.*, 28 December 1832.
11. *N.W.*, 24 December 1832.
12. *B.N.L.*, 25 December 1832.
13. *Electors of the Borough of Belfast and How They Voted at the First Election* (Belfast, 1833).
14. *B.N.L.*, 21 September 1832.
15. *P.P. 1837*, XI, Pt I, 60 ff.
16. *Brief Historical Sketch of Parliamentary Elections in Belfast* (Belfast, 1865), p. 11.
17. *N.W.*, 12 January, 15 January, 19 January 1835.
A crowd assembled daily opposite Emerson's committee rooms and on their way home smashed the windows of almost every Roman Catholic, whose house they passed, and the windows of not a few Protestants whose political sentiments were supposed to differ from theirs, while another mob attacked the houses of some Orangemen. (*B.N.L.*, 20 January 1835.)
18. The voting figures were: Tennent, 772; McCance, 719; Chichester, 713; French, 3.
19. *B.N.L.*, 28 August 1835.
20. It was agreed on all sides that more shopkeepers living over their

premises would be expected to vote Liberal rather than Conservative.

21. George Hamilton Chichester, third Marquis of Donegall (1797–1883), succeeded his father in 1844, having been given a U.K. peerage in 1841.
22. *N.W.*, 15 July 1837.
23. *B.N.L.*, 25 July 1837.
24. *N.W.*, 27 July 1837.
25. *B.N.L.*, 22 August 1837.
26. *N.W.*, 27 July 1837.
27. The voting figures were: Gibson, 941; Belfast, 922; Tennent, 901; Dunbar, 869.
28. *B.N.L.*, 11 August 1837.
29. *Brief Sketch*, pp. 9–10.
30. The costs of the petition were estimated at £10,000. *P.P. 1842*, V, 279.
31. *P.P. 1837*, XI, Pt 1, 1–19, 25–37, 43–53, 53–156 (Bates' evidence).
32. *P.P. 1841*, XX, 599.
33. *B.N.L.*, 14 June 1841.
34. *B.N.L.*, 17 June 1841.
35. Though clashes between Catholics and Orangemen were not entirely absent they were less noticeable than in the previous elections, possibly because the Catholics seemed anxious to avoid trouble. On polling day a barrier, twelve feet high, was erected 'to keep the parties apart' but this did not prevent the two groups from throwing stones at each other. (*N.W.*, 6 July 1841.)
36. The main source for the account of the election of 1841 and its aftermath is the report of the Select Committee on the Belfast election compromise, *P.P. 1842*, V (Report) 265–6, (Minutes of Evidence) 269–414.
37. *N.W.*, 13–17 July 1841. A satirical advertisement also appeared stating that a meeting of 'spirits of departed electors of the Burough of Belfast' was held in Shankill graveyard in consequence of the usual statutory notice signed by John Bates asking for submission of claims against the Conservative candidates appearing in the newspapers (*N.W.*, 17 July 1841).
38. Full costs were not awarded to successful petitioners until after the transfer of jurisdiction from the Commons to the Courts in 1868. At this period even successful petitioners were liable to payment of fees to the Clerk of the House, to shorthand writers and other officials which might run to several hundred pounds. Generally the (non-recoverable) fees amounted to one sixth or one eighth of the total cost of petitioning, cf. *P.P. 1837–8*, X, 25–99.
39. 2 June 1842. See the brief report, *P.P. 1842*, V, 69–70.
40. Cf. *N.W.*, 9–23 August and *B.N.L.*, 23 August 1842. See above, p. 57.
41. *Brief Sketch*, pp. 15–16.
42. For a racy account of the O'Connell visit and the challenge (refused) to debate with Rev. Henry Cooke, see a contemporary pamphlet, *The Repealer Repulsed* (Belfast, 1841).
43. Cf. *P.P. 1842*, V, 271–86, 288–92, 298–312, 320–82.

44. Ibid., 412–14.
45. Coppock made the same plea (professional privilege) to avoid examination by the Special Commission on the Sudbury election of 1841. Unlike Bates, his claim was refused. (*P.P. 1844*, XVIII, 247–561.)
46. *P.P. 1842*, V, 265–6.
47. 1 & 2 Vict., c. 56.
48. The Belfast Charitable Society managed to secure the exemption of its funds and property from control of the poor law authority. Henceforth, however, it played a much more restricted role, being virtually confined to the management of the poorhouse (later Clifton House) with about one hundred and forty elderly inmates. See R. W. M. Strain, *Belfast and Its Charitable Society* (Oxford, 1961), pp. 294–314.
49. From the beginning Belfast Poor Law union comprised in addition to the borough a considerable part of Counties Antrim and Down – later the Belfast rural district, the Castlereagh rural district and the Holywood urban district, amounting to 51,196 acres in all.
50. 3 & 4 Vict., c. 108.
51. *P.P. 1837*, XXIX, 46–9.
52. Practically the only comment was by the *Whig*, which thought the franchise too restricted. (*N.W.*, 8 August 1840.)
53. *Vindicator*, March 1840. (Founded by Gavan Duffy, of Young Ireland fame, it lasted from 1839 to 1852.)
54. *N.W.*, 15 September 1842. But *contra*, the *Ulster Times* admonished their readers 'to resist the common enemy'. 'We would, therefore, impress on the mind of every Conservative elector the *absolute*, the *stern necessity*, which exists for their being united in their exertions to keep their antagonists from possessing municipal honours.' (Quoted in *N.W.*, 30 August 1842).
55. *N.W.*, 8 October 1842.
56. Also a certain poor-rate collector had failed to collect all his rates in 1841. The Tories knew this but did not produce the evidence until the revision sessions. (*N.W.*, 15 October and 20 October 1842.)
57. *N.W.*, 25 October 1842.
58. A twenty-four man committee was appointed including Bates, Dr Cooke, George Dunbar, the first mayor, his successor John Clarke, the future M.P., Richard Davison, and eight other members of the reformed Corporation. (*N.W.*, 1 October 1842.)
59. For the first year Bates served without a salary. In 1843 a special Committee of the Council recommended a salary of £350. *Minute Books of Belfast Town Council*, C.H. 43, (1 November 1842 – 1 April 1847).
60. *B.N.L.*, 20 January 1843.
61. The fact that a majority of the Commissioners, headed by Richard Grimshaw, were Liberal may have helped to stiffen their opposition to the Town Council.
62. The Council were less successful in their efforts to get Lord Donegall to hand over the Town Book (the Corporation minute book going back

to 1613). Donegall just simply refused to hand it over (*B.N.L.*, 2 January 1844), and the Town Book passed through a number of private hands before being bought by the Corporation.

63. See below, p. 76.
64. 'Low-lying in unpleasant sleech as disease-ridden as it was dull.' E. Jones in Beckett and Glasscock, *Belfast*, p. 113.
65. One of the first of its kind in the United Kingdom. See below, p. 116.
66. In 1852 six firms employing 1,000 men and boys were manufacturing flax spinning machinery in Belfast. W. E. Coe, *The Engineering Industry of the North of Ireland* (Newton Abbot, 1967), p. 63.
67. The slob land, excavated through cutting the new Channel, was used to construct an artificial island which, originally called Dargan's Island (after the contractor), was renamed the Queen's Island after Queen Victoria's visit to the town in 1849. This later became the site of the shipyard of Harland and Wolff.
68. E. Jones in Beckett and Glasscock, *Belfast*, p. 112. Most houses built at this time had a large living-room with a small scullery on the ground floor and three bedrooms (two very small) above. The average number of children per family was about eight.
69. Cf. *Report on the Sanitary State of Belfast*, a rare pamphlet published in 1848, containing a mass of social statistics which have found their way into the works of Emrys Jones and Beckett and Glasscock, viz. the average age of death in Belfast was nine years, in all Ireland, 23; half the population of Belfast was under 20 years of age; 1,800 houses were in courts (i.e. accessible only by a covered archway); over 3,000 houses had no yards; perhaps 25,000 people had no privies at all; 331 of 579 streets were less than 20 feet wide and suburbs were unpaved and without sewers.
70. From 1820, in addition to temporary bodies set up to deal with emergencies (like the cholera epidemic), 'a general permanent board of health' had existed in Dublin with power to advise the Lord Lieutenant on the establishment of local boards. Cf. R. B. McDowell, *The Irish Administration, 1801–1914* (London, 1964), pp. 168–9.
71. Similar provisions applicable to men were included in the Belfast Improvement Act of 1850 – fifty-five years before *Lochner* v. *New York*.
72. *B.N.L.*, 3 December 1844. Mulholland admitted that it was not the business of the Council to provide such amenities, but hoped it could be done by 'a combination of the benevolent individuals of every sect and party'. The only concrete result was a clause in the 1845 Improvement Bill providing public baths and washhouses financed by a special rate. But at least one member of the Council (Councillor S. Thomson) thought that this was a work of supererogation – 'They might as well insert a clause to enable the Council to rent dairies in the neighbourhood, in order to see that the poor of the town get pure milk.' *B.N.L.*, 4 April 1845.
73. *N.W.*, 20 October 1842.
74. *N.W.*, 8 October 1842.
75. *N.W.*, 20 July 1847.

76. The figures were: Ross, 886; Tennent, 859; Chichester, 500.
77. As a member of the Council – and fourth mayor – Suffern was regarded as Bates' nominee, *Brief Sketch*, p. 29.
78. *N.W.*, 10 August 1847.
79. *N.W.*, 18 March 1852. See *Brief Sketch*, pp. 31–9 for a more favourable assessment of Tennent.
80. *N.W.*, 30 September 1851. Graham had been guardian to a Belfast nobleman.
81. *N.W.*, 6 March 1852. See also 24 April and 15 and 24 June 1852.
82. The *Whig* poked fun at his 'quiet domestic circle, his friends, his books and his rare collection of shells (6 April 1852).
    The final result was: Davison, 1,259; Cairns, 1,202; Tennent, 904.
83. O'Rorke's evidence was afterwards printed as a pamphlet, cf. *Speech of Edward O'Rorke, Esquire, . . . as delivered by him in the town hall of the said borough on Monday and Tuesday, the 15th and 16th days of April 1850 . . .* (Belfast, 1850).
84. *P.P. 1852–3*, XCIV, 23–43.
85. The old boundary was drawn as follows: the Milewater river (north), Donegall Pass (south), the river Lagan (east), and on the west a line running slightly to the west of Sandy Row. The new boundary was drawn roughly from the Northern Counties railway terminus (north) to Adelaide Park (south), the Rope Works (east), and Crumlin Road/Ardoyne on the west.
86. Although Irish law reports of this period are sometimes maddeningly uninformative, the best account of the action is to be found in *Irish Chancery Reports*, IV (1856), 119–72. See also D. J. Owen, *History of Belfast*, (Belfast, 1920), pp. 279–81 and *Brief Sketch*, Appendix D. The *Northern Whig* published the complete transcript of the case – *The Town Council in Chancery. The Case of the Attorney-General at the Relation of John Rea, Esq., v. The Belfast Municipal Corporation* (Belfast, 1855).
87. The only defence entered, and that half-heartedly, was the pre-1835 doctrine that municipal corporations dealt with their affairs without reference to the ratepayers. This had been superseded by the trusteeship doctrine (corporations hold their funds as trustees for the ratepayers).
88. The records of the Chamber of Commerce reveal that they were also approached for assistance in promoting the Indemnity Bill of 1856, and disdainfully refused on the ground that the responsibility rested with the Town Council, but that they wished to see an end to the affair. Their half-yearly report went further: the Bill was highly objectionable and likely to arouse opposition in Parliament and in the town. The Chamber was then largely Liberal in composition. (PRONI – Chamber of Commerce Records – D. 1857/1, No. 3.)
89. *P.P. 1859* (Sess. 1), XII, 268.
90. *P.P. 1859* (Sess. 1), XII, 1–19.
91. Rea admitted that his special respondents were chosen on the basis of long service to the Council – those who had been continuously on the Council from 1846 to 1854. (Ibid., p. 350.)
92. A typical speech in favour of the Corporation was made by John

Thompson, the ex-borough treasurer, who testified that in the forty-two years during which he had know the town it had progressed greatly, and that the Corporation and Harbour Board between them had spent half a million pounds in far-sighted improvements. (Ibid., p. 284.)

93. Ibid., p. 318.

94. It was reported that when some Catholic gentlemen attended a meeting to protest against the 1859 Indemnity Bill, the proceedings were suspended until their departure.

95. When this deal was reported to the Commission on the Belfast riots of 1864, one of the Commissioners (Richard Dowse) asked how the ratepayers had reacted to it and a witness, William Mullen, a leading Conservative (mayor, 1866–7), replied that the Conservative leaders had 'influence' over the ratepayers. Dowse then asked: 'There are some men in Belfast, it appears, who can manage the ratepayers?' Witness: 'I daresay the ratepayers can be managed.' (*P.P. 1865*, XXVIII, 278.)

96. *Brief Sketch*, p. 104. Unfortunately the minutes of evidence taken before Committees on private Bills were not preserved at this time.

97. It is interesting to note that O'Connell made precisely the same complaint against the Dublin Corporation in 1835. See *Five Letters to the Precursor Society* (Dublin, 1835).

98. Even as late as 1864 a millowner, Robert Lepper, admitted that the sale of May's Fields benefited him more than Sir Stephen May since he, Lepper, held a mortgage on the property. He was at the time of the transaction (1847) a member of the Council, and also of the Improvement Committee which recommended the purchase. (*P.P. 1864*, VI, 320.)

Before the same inquiry (see below, p. 82) William Ewart, one of the largest millowners and a former mayor (1859–61) admitted that he had his mill (and the mills of some Tory friends) exempted from police rate and in consequence the Crumlin Road district was neither watched nor lighted. (*P.P. 1864*, VI, 143–7.)

99. To summarise briefly the harbour developments. The first stage of the channel linking the Lagan with Belfast Lough was completed in 1841. In 1847 the Belfast Harbour Act was successfully promoted, replacing the Harbour Corporation by a new body, the Belfast Harbour Commissioners. The first were named in the Act and included *ex officio*, the mayor, the Lord of the Castle (Donegall), and his son (later the fourth Marquis), the Very Reverend Lord Edward Chichester, Dean of Raphoe. One third of the Commissioners were to retire annually and their places be filled by election – the franchise being based on shipping ownership, property ownership and rating (a £20 valuation). The other named members were mainly Liberals, e.g. Robert Grimshaw, William Pirrie, Hugh Magill (a Catholic), George MacTier, and the subsequent elections maintained a slight Liberal majority. In the years immediately afterwards the Commissioners took a number of highly important decisions – extending the new deep

water channel to Garmoyle, the mouth of the Lough, so that liners could enter the harbour, and tie up at the town quays; providing a site for the new iron shipyard of Hickson on the Queen's Island; and building a graving dock for ship repairs on the Down side of the river (near the shipyard, while trade and passenger traffic remained on the Antrim side). These decisions, which ensured the opening of the port to the largest passenger and cargo liners and the development of the greatest of Belfast's sources of wealth, were more important for the economic life of the city than any taken by the Town Council.

During the first twenty years of Victoria's reign the number of ships using the port more than doubled, and the harbour revenue quadrupled, (from £9,000 to £37,000). (Owen, *A Short History of the Port of Belfast*, p. 48. For the subsequent development of the port, see R. E. Glasscock in Beckett and Glasscock, *Belfast*, pp. 98–108.)

100. Cf. *P.P. 1859*, XII, 318; cf. *P.P. 1864*, VI, *N.W.*, 12 January 1859.
101. *B.N.L.*, 5 December 1843. See also *Brief Sketch*, p. 52.
102. Clarke appears to have been as good as his word. In addition to visiting St Malachy's he was also reported as attending the Primitive Wesleyan Missions (a tiny sect). (*B.N.L.*, 23 January 1844.)
103. The *B.N.L.* made no reference to Clarke's demotion at the time. But in 1847 they wrote: '[He] thought fit to compromise the Council in his own person by an act of political partisanship.' (*B.N.L.*, 29 October 1847.)
104. *P.P. 1859* (Sess. 1), XII, 141.

3 The Age of Riots: 1855–74

AT the beginning of his chapter[1] entitled 'Late Victorian Belfast' in Beckett and Glasscock's compilation, Professor Emrys Jones cites from an unnamed newspaper of 1853 a remarkable piece of Belfast self-congratulation: 'this great emporium of trade, manufacturing and commerce now exciting the attention and claiming the admiration of every community whose good example we have been following, and of every community to which, in our turn, we present a model of imitation'. But this effusion was not untypical. The *Belfast News Letter* in the late 1850s and early 1860s waxed lyrical about the boom town, e.g. 'warehouses of large dimensions and great beauty'; 'the steam-hammer and steam-punch cease not from morning till night'.[2]

The cause of this increasing prosperity, the greatest that any Irish city has known, was twofold. First, the expansion of the linen industry which became fully mechanised between 1852 and 1862 with the rapid acceptance of the power loom.[3] With the coming of the American Civil War Lancashire mills were starved of raw cotton and the Belfast mills soon found a new market for their high quality finished goods.[4] The linen trade continued to expand until the 1870s,[5] but while the labour force trebled between 1850 and 1875 (from 16,000 to 50,000), the proportion represented by adult male workers never exceeded one third.

The other major development has sometimes been referred to as an industrial miracle – a large shipbuilding industry in an area with no native supplies of coal or iron. The story has frequently been told and need only be summarised here. A wooden shipbuilding industry had been established in 1791 by one William Ritchie, who transferred his business from Saltcoats in Ayrshire to the Lagan. He was followed by two other firms, one of which, Ritchie and MacLaine, made one of the first steamships[6] in Ireland, the *Belfast*. But this industry never really flourished – Cork was a much more important Irish centre for wooden shipbuilding.

In 1838 the first iron[7] sailing ship was constructed by a firm of boilermakers, Victor Coates, which had made the engines for the earlier wooden steamships. But progress was slow and by the time (1853) that the Belfast Harbour Commissioners obligingly laid out a yard on the Queen's Island for another boilermaker, Robert Hickson[8] (who turned to shipbuilding because of stiff competition from England and Scotland), there was little evidence that Belfast would become a major centre of the craft.

Hickson, however, though deficient in ability as a ship-builder, was able to recognise talent in others and in 1854 appointed as his yard manager Edward Harland, a young Glaswegian who had been trained in Newcastle. His ability in this field soon proved outstanding and within four years of his arrival he was able to find enough money to buy out Hickson. The purchase money (£5,000) was provided by a Liverpool financier of German origin, G. C. Schwabe, whose nephew, Gustav W. Wolff, was working under Harland. Whether as a condition of the agreement or not, Wolff became a partner in the firm and through his uncle's connections they were able to make contact with a Liverpool line (the Bibby Line) and later with the White Star Line, with which they established a long working relationship.[9] Harland and Wolff right from the beginning specialised in ocean-going liners.

Since Harland and Wolff insisted on top quality work, it is not surprising that some of their early labour force should have been imported – though from the Tyne, it would appear, rather than the Clyde. But it remained a fixed policy of Harland to reduce the possibility of unrest by relying to an increasing extent on local labour. The labour force grew very rapidly – 500 in 1861, 900 in 1865, 2,400 in 1870, 3,000 in 1886, 9,000 in 1900, and by the end of the century the shipyard area had increased from three and a half to seventy-six acres, all leased from the Harbour Board. Two smaller shipbuilding firms were established in the 1860s, but never really competed with the 'Big Yard'.[10]

The triumph of the Belfast shipbuilders brought a number of ancillary industries in their train – marine engine works were

established in 1880.[11] Likewise the fantastic development of the
linen industry soon resulted in a native textile engineering
industry. Ropemaking, vehicle building, heating and ventila-
tion machine-making and armaments followed in rapid
succession, together with food and drink manufacturing, and
the service industries. Belfast population continued to expand,
from 87,062 in the 1851 census to 121,602 in 1861 (40 per cent),
and 174,412 in 1871 (43·4 per cent) – the highest decennial
increase ever recorded. Most happy augury of all, in these
two censuses nearly half the population was under twenty, and
the birth rate was high. During this period (1850–70) the
English- and Scottish-born share of the population came to
double that of the non-Ulster Irish-born; but then, as always,
three quarters of the population were born in the city itself and
the counties of Antrim and Down.[12]

But this great increase in population and prosperity which soon
brought Belfast close to Dublin in numbers, while greatly
exceeding it in valuation, did not serve to knit together a stable
community. During the very period that its economic growth was
at its highest Belfast came to be characterised by recurrent,
communal rioting of a sectarian nature to a much greater
extent than ever before.

Sectarian rioting was not unknown in England and Scotland
in the first half of the nineteenth century, although never
reaching the frenzied pitch of the Gordon riots. Glasgow,
Liverpool, Manchester and Newcastle were all afflicted by it
from time to time; but although the presence of two strata of
Irish labourers, from the Protestant north and the Catholic
south, frequently led to friction, especially where job competition was keen,[13] it could not be said that sectarian rioting
became endemic in any large urban centre in Great Britain.
It is particularly noteworthy that while rioting at elections was
quite frequent while open voting persisted, it was hardly ever
based on sectarianism.[14]

Although the first riot[15] in Belfast was not associated with an
election but with an Orange and Green fracas on 12 July 1813,
those immediately following were. Two mobs stoned each other
during the chairing of Emerson Tennent in 1832 and four people
were killed.[16] After the declaration of the result in 1835

several Orange lodges assembled in the hope of celebrating the victory of Tennent were so outraged by the unexpected Liberal victory that they rampaged through the city smashing the windows of almost every Catholic whose house they passed and recognised.[17] It was noted that in the court proceedings following this disturbance the two factions were for the first time given a specific location – the 'Sandy Row boys' and the 'Pound Street boys'. A similar fracas occurred after the election of 1841.[18]

The Orange Order (as described above)[19] was formally dissolved by its Imperial Grand Master, the Duke of Cumberland, in February 1836. But the Irish Orangemen were not put down so easily. Professing not to see in the King's reply to the address of the Commons an absolute command, they decided to hold themselves in readiness for the reconstitution of the Grand Lodge of Ireland.[20] Orangemen continued to parade under slightly different names, as 'Loyalists' or simply as 'Protestants'.

After the customary July celebrations in Belfast in 1843 a pitched battle took place between the Pound Street boys and the Sandy Row boys in a field behind a large mill, while rival effigies of King William and O'Connell blazed. The riot continued for days, culminating with a great display of force by the 'Repealers' at the funeral of an old man whose house had been wrecked at the beginning of the disturbances, and another bout of fighting followed the funeral. Many houses were wrecked and 18 people, equally balanced religiously, were sent for trial.[21]

Meanwhile, the former dignitaries of the Irish Grand Lodge were quietly preparing to re-establish it. But they were very anxious not to overstep the law. In 1845 the Party Processions Act[22] expired and in that year the *Belfast News Letter* reported that the gentry and nobility were opposed to marches commemorating the Twelfth and itself urged that all 'loyal and constitutional men' should voluntarily abstain from public processions and celebrations which might produce a disturbance.[23] (None in fact occurred.) On 3 August 1846 the Grand Lodge of Ireland was reconstituted with the Earl of Enniskillen as Grand Master; earlier, the ordinances of the revived institution had been prudently sent to an eminent Queen's

Counsel for vetting.[24] During the remaining years of the decade Orange processions, though held in increasing numbers, passed off quietly. In 1857 there were about thirty lodges in Belfast with an average of forty men in each.[25]

The next riot in Belfast occurred after the election of 1852 (held inappropriately enough on 12 July) when R. J. Tennent lost his seat and the representation was again monopolised by the Conservatives. According to the *Northern Whig*, it was not clear whether it was 'the Orangemen' or 'the Catholics' who began it,[26] but at any rate shots were fired both in Durham Street (Orange) and the Pound (Catholic), and one man (a Catholic) 'made himself very conspicuous by the almost unremitting fusillade he kept up from the windows of his house'.[27] At least one person was killed, the wounded were carried away and it was not until a troop of dragoons and two companies of the 46th Regiment arrived on the scene that order was restored. A new feature of this riot was that large numbers of Catholics and some Protestants fled their homes, carrying their furniture with them.

Apart from sporadic rioting by sectarian mobs, two other proofs that Belfast was religiously polarised in the late 1840s and early 1850s may be quoted. Municipal elections passed completely without excitement, even in the crucial year 1855. But during parliamentary election campaigns the sectarian motif was increasingly obtruded. The columns of the *News Letter* during the election of 1847 were redolent of anti-Catholic propaganda to a much greater extent than in previous campaigns.[28] In 1852 Messrs Cairns and Davison came out for free trade (in contrast with their earlier attitude) but counterbalanced this drift towards liberalism by 'abusing Maynooth and Romanism'.[29]

By the election of 1857 the *News Letter* had lost its earlier defensiveness about mixing religion and politics and openly ran articles on 'Romish Intolerance'. It also strongly opposed the Presbyterian tobacco manufacturer, Thomas McClure,[30] who was competing for the Liberal nomination.[31] Unfortunately for the *News Letter* its attempt to prevent Presbyterian voters from leaving their Tory fold to vote for a fellow-Presbyterian[32] nearly came unstuck when the evangelical *Banner of Ulster* denounced the Conservative candidate, Davison, as a Puseyite!

However, Cairns, the senior member, made a number of speeches
on the theme 'the Protestant religion and the liberties of England', and Davison was able to demonstrate that he had kept a
pew for several years in Dr Cooke's church and abhorred
Puseyism.

Although McClure was nominated by William Pirrie and
Thomas Sinclair, two of the leading members of the Harbour
Board who were also Presbyterian, it availed him nothing and
the Conservative majority was higher in fact than in 1852. This
result may not have been unconnected with a peculiarly
partisan action of the mayor, Samuel Gibson Getty,[33] helped
by the police in allowing a mob of ship-carpenters into the Court
House on polling day so that the Protestant party got possession
of the place.[34]

The other development was the increasingly important role
of anti-Catholic clergymen of both the Episcopalian and
Presbyterian communions in Conservative politics. Dr Henry
Cooke has been mentioned already. For nearly forty years,
from 1830 until his death in 1868, he was not only the most
formidable preacher in the Presbyterian Church but also one
of the leading Conservatives in the city. He was active in
attempts to settle the election dispute of 1842 and the Corporation dispute in the 1850s. Perhaps his most celebrated achievement was to bring to nothing Daniel O'Connell's visit to Belfast
in 1841 which the Repealers hoped would be the occasion of
a triumphal procession, but was nearly converted into a riot.

Although Cooke was strongly anti-Catholic (though never
an Orangeman), and saw a necessary connection between
schemes for Irish political autonomy and the designs of the
Vatican, his speeches and sermons were generally in an intel-
lectual vein based on fundamentalist theology. The same could
not be said of the next militant cleric, the Rev. Thomas Drew,
Rector of Christ Church.

Drew was a Dubliner who came to Belfast in 1833 to take
charge of the new 'Free Church', which had been built to
attract the poorer Anglicans, repelled by the exclusiveness of the
two existing churches.[35] Combining a strongly evangelical bent
with a social conscience far more developed than in most
clergymen of his time, Drew quickly built up one of the largest
congregations in Ireland. He also established Sunday schools,

pioneered Sunday excursions for school children, and an early
form of credit union known as a 'parochial loan office'. He was
extremely active in relief work during the famine.[36] Culturally
he was a philistine. He campaigned against the stage and
drama as polluting the actors and weakening Protestantism. He
forced, by a press campaign, his bishop, Dr Mant, to drop some
'advanced' schemes for church architecture. But as the years
passed Drew's sermons became increasingly imbued with anti-
Catholicism. It is not clear when he joined the Orange Order,
but the Grand Lodge of Antrim met in his parochial hall in
1849 and Drew is listed as a Grand Chaplain in 1852. He adver-
tised courses of lectures on the errors of the Church of Rome, to
which Roman Catholics were 'cordially invited'. In 1854 he
founded the Christ Church Protestant Association – one of the
founder members being the M.P., Richard Davison – whose
main objectives were to recover the ground lost in the struggle
for Protestant ascendancy, to protest against the unscriptural
Queen's Colleges and National Schools, to press for the withdrawal of *all* grants from Maynooth, and especially to aim at
the repeal of the Act of 1829 which allowed Catholics to sit in
Parliament. In 1856 it was decided to preach an open-air
mission. Drew used the steps of the Albert Clock (erected in
1853) as his pulpit, and throughout the summer of 1857
preached regularly on Sundays. Some of the sermons have been
printed and are quite Paisleyite in character. To give a typical
extract: 'You possess your churches and your meeting-houses,
and your churchyards only *until popery has gained sufficient power*
to nail up the one and to rob you of the other.'[37]

Nor was Drew the only open-air anti-Catholic preacher.
The Rev. Thomas McIlwaine (Church of Ireland) and the
Rev. Hugh Hanna of Clifton Presbyterian Church were also
publicising the evils of Romanism throughout the summer of
1857.

The stage was now set for the most violent outburst of rioting
Belfast had hitherto experienced. It began on 12 July 1857,
shortly after a stirring oration by Dr Drew[38] to the assembled
Orangemen. Once again it was largely confined to the Pound
and Sandy Row. But unlike previous riots, after ten continuous
days of fighting, it went on intermittently until 6 September.

During the riots the Pound district founded a 'Gun Club',
which provoked a counter blast, 'the Protestant Defence
Association'.[39] Street preaching continued for a time during
the riots but eventually Drew and McIlwaine ceased. Hanna
however continued, offering to leave a narrow passageway for
Catholics to pass through his crowds, which he christened 'the
Pope's Pad'.[40] Another feature was the prominent part played
by three hundred ship's carpenters, Protestant to a man, who
were armed with thick staves sharpened to a fine point. By
early September the troops had once again come to the aid of
the hard-pressed police and the riots petered out. But not until
11 September did the city magistrates, under the chairmanship
of the mayor, Samuel Getty, issue a proclamation forbidding
assemblies in the streets.[41]

After the riot a number of Liberals signed a requisition for a
public inquiry and this was granted in the form of a Royal
Commission. The Commissioners[42] heard a good deal of evidence
from both political parties, the magistracy and the police.
Their conclusions may be summarised as follows. The proximate
cause of the riots was the inflammatory preaching of Drew;
but a more fundamental cause was the persistent 'incitement'
occasioned to the Catholics by the Orange Order, which the
Commissioners believed to be unnecessary in a city where
Protestants predominated. The 160 police and ten magistrates
were too few to deal with civil disturbances. Moreover, the
police were (with six or seven exceptions) all Protestants and a
'great many' were known to be Orangemen and hence to
sympathise with the Sandy Row mob. The two areas, both
exclusively of one religion, had developed a tradition of rioting
in July, although they lived in peace and friendship for the
rest of the year; and it must be realised that future riots could
get further out of hand and so it behoved the clergy and the
'educated members of society' to try to cure this sectarian evil.

The riots and their aftermath attracted much attention. The
Whig and *News Letter* took up their predictable positions. The
Catholic mass circulation *Morning News* took great care not to
antagonise any section of its readers and reported both the
riots and the inquiry virtually with no editorial comment.
The *Irish Presbyterian*, however, the leading religious journal in
that community, blamed both factions in the affected districts,

but also interestingly blamed the long management of the city by one party and the exploitation of bigotry by some politicians. It did not hesitate to censure Dr Drew for his 'high toned and bitter political partisanship'.[43]

It is also significant that throughout the proceedings of the Commission of Inquiry there was scarcely any reference to the city council and the mayor was referred to only in his magisterial capacity.

The next year, 1858, passed without incident, although 50 extra constabulary were brought into the city at the time when the Town Improvement Bill (i.e. the Indemnity Bill) was going through the Commons and feeling ran high among both the partisans and the opponents of John Rea. When the news that the Bill had been rejected in committee reached Belfast tar barrels burned for three nights. In 1859, apart from the investigation into Belfast local government, the only noteworthy happening was the trial of 17 men for membership of the Ribbon Society,[44] a Catholic equivalent of the Orange Order, but much more secret and less organised and resolute than the former. The accused were acquitted, largely through a spirited defence by the irrepressible John Rea, and the *Whig* pointed out that if Orangeism was controlled Ribbonism would go too.[45] An interesting non-event was the failure of the Belfast Liberals to nominate a candidate for the parliamentary election. The *Whig*[46] at the start of the campaign made a plea for unity among the scattered Liberals, and alleged that the failure to win one seat in 1857 was due to the defection of the Presbyterians to the Tories. It suggested William Kirk, Liberal M.P. for Newry (a Presbyterian); but Kirk's electors would not release him and Cairns and Davison secured a walk-over. There was surprisingly no mention during the campaign of the riots of 1857.[47]

The next major riot, in 1864, was not sparked off by the 12 July celebrations but by an event in a city one hundred miles away. On 5 August 1864 the O'Connell monument was formally unveiled by the Lord Mayor of Dublin, attended by a vast crowd. On 8 August a crowd of 4,000 in Sandy Row burnt an effigy of O'Connell. On the following day a crowd of similar dimensions tried to march to the Catholic cemetery carrying a

mock coffin but were turned back. Two days later the Sandy
Row boys once again attacked the Pound Street boys, and the
latter retaliated by attacking a Methodist Church in the Falls
Road. In the following week prominent institutions of one side
or the other were attacked, and shots were fired through their
windows – a Presbyterian school, a Catholic female peniten-
tiary, St Malachy's Catholic Church, and Dr Cooke's house.
While in the 1857 riots the muscle power had been contributed
chiefly by ship's carpenters, in 1864 they were nearly, but not
quite, matched by Catholic navvies who 'seem to have given
to the Roman Catholic party an accession of physical strength
that rendered them more ready than at former periods to
encounter adversaries with whom they felt themselves thus
placed on a par'.[48]

This unexpected aggressiveness served to provoke the ship's
carpenters who left their work and armed with the tools of
their trade won a pitched battle with the navvies (on 16 August).
The rioting continued for another week until the arrival of
troops from Dublin and 500 extra police urgently sent for by
the mayor, John Lytle. By then a dozen people had been
killed and hundreds injured.

As in 1857, the 1864 riots were followed by a formal investigation – this time a public inquiry headed by Serjeant Barry,
Q.C. The evidence was less diffuse than in 1857 and the inquiry
was shorter. But the conclusions were unmistakably the same.
'The tenor of nearly all the evidence given before us, bearing
on this point, (the cause of the rioting) has left us painfully
impressed with the belief that the elements of contention were
never more rife amongst the population than at present.'[49] The
Commissioners anticipated even bloodier conflicts in the future
and as an 'absolutely necessary' remedy they recommended a
new police force of four to five thousand men under a Commissioner appointed by the Government, and two resident
magistrates, one Catholic and one Protestant.[50] They gloomily
predicted that . . . 'the Town Council is, and is likely to continue, of the exclusive character above described', i.e. not
merely Protestant, but anti-Roman Catholic and anti-Liberal.[51]
The Liberal element infused in the early 1860s had been spent,
and Conservative magistrates had displayed little zeal in trying
to curb Protestant rioters. The Commissioners were unfavour-

ably impressed by the Chairman of the Police Committee, Samuel Black, who in speaking of the methods by which police were selected said: 'In some cases I could tell a man's religion by his face, but not always.'[52] Black also asserted that there should be a Conservative-dominated Council, since the wealth and property of Belfast was Protestant and a great number of the lower classes of Catholics were 'disloyal'.

The recommendation of the 1864 Commissioners was quickly acted upon by the Government. The Chief Secretary, Sir Robert Peel, introduced a Bill, which quickly passed into law, abolishing Belfast's local police force and putting in their place 450 of the new national police force – the Royal Irish Constabulary. To counteract the Orange/Protestant influence on the old force, the new force was mainly Catholic. 'A green badge of disgrace', the *News Letter* grumbled.[53]

Once again the general election of that year was held in July and once again the mayor fixed the twelfth as polling day. The Conservative M.P.s Cairns and the former mayor, Samuel Gibson Getty (who had replaced Davison on his retirement in 1860), were renominated. The Liberals for the first time went outside Ulster and selected a single candidate, Lord John Hay (brother-in-law of Peel). He had no previous connection with the city and could not be accused of religious partnership. But this did not prevent the *News Letter* from playing its familiar tune – 'What have the Presbyterians of Belfast and Ulster in common with the Roman Catholics?' 'All Protestants must stand together in their own defence.' 'Dr Dorrian (the Catholic bishop) is supporting Hay.' Dr Cooke's organisation, the United Protestant Association, pledged its support to Cairns and Getty.[54] There was little or no discussion of Conservative policy.

On polling day, as in 1857, the Protestant party gained control of the Court House and shouted down Lord John Hay and his supporters, Sinclair and Dunville, while outside a Catholic mob did their utmost to provoke a conflict, 'wrecking Protestant houses, and stoning the constabulary'.[55] According to the *News Letter*, the Catholics to a man voted for Hay: the result, however, was disappointing.[56] Even with a single candidate of impeccable, aristocratic lineage, the Liberals seemed unable to detach enough Presbyterians from their Conservative moorings.

After 1865 there was a brief Liberal revival. An Ulster Liberal Society was founded with the intention of smartening up the inefficient registration societies and of achieving the 'signal utility' of bringing Liberal Protestants and Roman Catholics together. The prospectus of the Society admitted that the two components of the Liberal force were becoming increasingly isolated and thereby prone to social persecution, from which only a strong party organisation extending over several counties and boroughs might protect them.

The founder members of the Society included Thomas Sinclair, Durham Dunlop, and a young solicitor, Charles Brett, who, unlike most of his colleagues, was to remain unswerving in his Liberal allegiance after 1886. Brett took over responsibility for registration in Belfast and appears to have managed it quite efficiently.[57]

By the time of the 1868 election the efforts of the new Liberal organisation had borne fruit to such an extent that they had agreed on a single candidate, Thomas McClure, whose efforts had been unavailing eleven years before. At the same time, a serious split occurred in the Conservative ranks. The official candidates were both new. Cairns had gone to the Woolsack on the formation of Disraeli's Government, and Getty died in 1866 and had been replaced by the ex-mayor architect, Sir Charles Lanyon. Lanyon's running-mate, selected by the Belfast Conservative Association, was the mill owner John Mulholland. However, a public meeting, said to amount to four thousand working men, passed a resolution denouncing 'clique dictation' and nominated William Johnston, a small landowner and leading Orangeman as a fourth candidate. During the campaign the *News Letter* refrained from attacking the good Orangeman, Johnston, while urging Protestant voters not to desert Lanyon, who was not an Orangeman. An added complication was that the electorate of Belfast had been increased by about seven thousand, mainly working-class voters, through the Irish Reform Act of 1868;[58] but although candidates on both sides held meetings in factories it soon became clear that Mulholland lacked popularity among the working class and was not infrequently booed.

An interesting feature of the 1868 election was the intrusion of municipal issues into the grand discourse about disestablishment and foreign policy. A Ratepayers' Protection Society had been formed by owners of small house property originally to complain about the failure of the Corporation to honour a promise not to raise the rates of houses valued below £20. But they managed during the campaign to articulate a number of grievances against the 'Town Council clique' – the failure to drain the Blackstaff, to pave numerous alleys and entries, to build wash-houses and baths when a tax had been levied for them, to appoint a Collector General of Taxes.[59] They also asked pointedly why the mayor received £1,000 a year 'when Glasgow gave nothing and Edinburgh £500'. Pleading the necessity of electing to the Town Council 'men of independence who would do their duty', the Ratepayers' Chairman urged his supporters to vote for McClure and Johnston.

In vain did the dying Dr Cooke issue a manifesto warning his 'dear friends and brethren' that 'the Established Church and all the Protestant institutions of the land, are now in danger',[60] and did the *News Letter* point out that Dr Dorrian was voting for McClure. The result showed that Johnston had effectively split the Protestant vote and Belfast had in Thomas McClure its last Liberal M.P.[61]

Nor did the last election before the ballot pass without its usual concomitant of mob violence at the hustings and a farcical intrusion by the former terror of the Council, John Rea, who, now far gone in eccentricity, tried to nominate a fictitious candidate, 'Colonel Chambers of the Italian Army', and was savagely assaulted.[62]

The next major riot of this period occurred in August 1872 and is remarkable on a number of counts. It was the first to be sparked off by a Catholic, not an Orange, procession. Secondly, it was the only one where an inquiry was demanded by the Corporation and refused by Dublin Castle.

It started on 15 August, the feast of the Assumption of the Blessed Virgin, when Catholics (who normally took the day off) organised a procession, armed themselves with banners carrying slogans, both religious and political, including support for the new Home Rule Association, assembled in north Belfast and tried to walk through Carlisle Circus, where the redoubtable Rev. Hugh Hanna had his church. In spite of protection from the new police force the procession was attacked several

times. On the next evening rivetters from the Queen's Island
tried to march into a Catholic area and mill workers broke
up into sectarian groups. Shooting broke out and the rioting
quickly became general. Although the police received reinforcements of over one thousand men and the garrison of
320 men was trebled almost immediately it took the combined
force nine days to restore order, and the toll included one
policeman dead and 73 wounded, 170 civilians injured and 837
families forced to leave their houses. The Corporation later
estimated the damage to property as amounting to £17,500.[63]

After the riots were over the Town Council asked the Lord
Lieutenant to set up a commission of inquiry, as in 1857 and
1864, to ascertain the causes. The Chief Secretary, Lord
Hartington, replied on 6 January 1873 in the negative. It was
felt in Dublin Castle, he wrote, that such an inquiry would
revive and perpetuate ill feeling in the city. However, he
enclosed a ten-page memorandum, based on the reports of
various Government officials in the city, in which neither the
mayor nor the city magistrates were spared. The report pointed
out that while the reinforcements asked for were sent immediately, the magistrates seemed incapable of utilising the
force under their command either speedily or effectively and
although regular meetings were held during the disturbances to
coordinate plans for their suppression, the magistrates who
actually appeared on the streets were very slow in assuming
responsibility.[64]

The Chief Secretary made a number of suggestions for the
better prevention of rioting – that a new functionary, a Commissioner of Police for the city, be appointed, and that all
police dispositions be made by him; that whenever disturbances
were apprehended the magistrates should meet under the
presidency of the mayor together with the G.O.C. and the
senior officer of the R.I.C.; and that they should hold continuous sittings in a convenient place until order was restored;
that resident magistrates and police should be drafted into the
city from the adjoining counties; and that the militia be called
on only if the police proved unable to cope. He ended by tartly
reminding the magistrates that although the Party Processions
Act had been repealed[65] the common law enjoined on them the
duty of dispersing dangerous assemblies and that the perform-

ance of this duty should not be delayed until a breach of the peace had actually occurred, 'especially in Belfast where such fiierce animosity exists between the rival factions'.[66]

The Corporation discussed the Hartington report at a special meeting on 10 January 1873 and virtually refused to consider its implications. Instead, they passed a resolution, afterwards incorporated in a letter to the Chief Secretary, 'respectfully' repeating their request for an inquiry, and pointing out that although the 'Government police force' was costing the rate-payers upwards of £9,000 a year, nevertheless 'the lives and property of the inhabitants have been most improperly left quite unprotected'. Their animus against the R.I.C. was also evident in the statement: 'The recent riots show that it is not an in-crease in the police force of the Borough that is required so much as a complete change in the semi-military character in arms, discipline, organisation and management of the present force.'

In reply Hartington refused to consider holding an inquiry but said he was open to any practical suggestions about improv-ing the efficiency of the R.I.C. in Belfast. But since the Corpora-tion's real desire was the restoration of the old Belfast police force, which was much more amenable to their control, this closed the issue.

In 1880 there was a small-scale repeat of the 1872 riot. The 'Lady day' procession of Catholics on 15 August was set upon by a Protestant crowd on its return journey at Boundary Street and Dover Street (between the Falls and Shankill Roads). Although not less than three hundred R.I.C. men were on duty, two people were killed and eight detained in hospital after a bout of stone-throwing. On the next three days the shipyard workers were attacked (also with stones) on their way home through the Catholic areas, but on 19 August they were given strong police protection and the trouble ended. In 1884, on 13 July, a Catholic crowd at Carrick Hill (overlooking the Shankill) flung stones at an Orange procession and then were embroiled in a struggle with the police. Thirty were arrested and eight injured (including two policemen).

These disturbances, however, were a mere curtain-raiser for the riots of 1886. Although these and subsequent riots lie outside the time limits of this chapter, they may profitably be considered at this point, both to appreciate the contrasts and also the enduring similarities between them and their predecessors. The riots began on 3 June 1886, the day after the defeat, on the second reading, of Gladstone's Home Rule Bill. It started through the overwhelmingly Protestant shipwrights of the 'Big Yard' marching *en masse* to attack the predominantly Catholic dock labourers[67] because the latter had expelled a few Protestant fellow-workers. The dockers got very much the worse of the battle; some sought refuge in the Lagan and one was drowned. The next day the 'island men' were attacked as they marched to work through Catholic districts. Then the usual cycle of attacks by people of one religion on the houses and property of the other continued until 10 June, when there ensued an uneasy peace which lasted until 12 July. Further outbursts were sporadic until 25 October. Thirty-two people were killed, 371 injured, and property valued at £90,000 destroyed. The Riot Commissioners (duly appointed, as in 1857 and 1864), found that almost from the beginning the riots assumed the aspect of a determined attack by the Protestant mobs upon the police as well as the Catholics:[68] at one stage the magistrates had to urge that the police be entirely withdrawn from the Shankill Road.[69] Although Catholic mobs also attacked the police, the Commissioners had no doubt that there was a widespread belief among humbler Protestants that the Glad-stone Government had been packing the town of Belfast with Catholic policemen from the south of Ireland,[70] and they concluded: 'We are not aware of any other period at which the animosity of a vast number of the Protestant community of Belfast, many of them persons in a respectable walk of life, was so fiercely directed against the Constabulary.'[71] Like their pre-decessors, the Commissioners marvelled at the intensity of feel-ing in the city and the extraordinary persistence of rioting, which, in their view, was not unconnected with such manifesta-tions as processions, marches and bonfires. Unlike previous riots, the 1886 disturbances closely followed an extremely in-tense political conflict in which more than one Conservative leader spoke rashly of an appeal to arms should the hated Home Rule measure become law.[72] As in 1864 and 1872, the Church militant was represented by Dr R. R. Kane, the first clergyman to become Grand Master of the Orange Institution,[73] and Dr Hugh Hanna, in whose evidence the Royal Irish Constabulary

TABLE 3.1

Religious Riots in Belfast 1813–1912

Date	Precipitating event	Extent	Results	Duration
12 July 1813	Orange procession	40 Orangemen; Catholics of Hercules St	2 deaths; 4 injured	1 evening
12 July 1832	Parliamentary election	Protestant and Catholic riots at polling place	4 deaths	1 day
12 July 1835	Parliamentary election and Orange gathering	Sandy Row, Pound St	Extensive window smashing	1 day
8–10 July 1841	Parliamentary election	Sandy Row, Pound St	Property damage	2 days
12 July 1843	Customary Protestant procession	Pound St, Sandy Row	Home wrecking, 18 tried	5–7 days
12 July 1852	Parliamentary election	Durham St, the Pound	1 death; shift of Catholics and Protestants	5–7 days
12 July 1857	Orange procession	Pound, Sandy Row	Indefinite number injured; extensive property damage	56 days (sporadically)
8 August 1864	Protestant protests at unveiling of O'Connell monument	Pound, Sandy Row, Falls Rd	12 deaths; 100 injured	18 days
15–22 August 1872	Nationalist procession	Sandy Row, Falls, Shankill	5 deaths; 243 injured	9 days
15–19 August 1880	Catholic procession	Boundary St, Dover St	2 killed; 10 injured	4 days
13 July 1884	Orange procession	Carrick Hill	8 injured	1 day
3 June–25 October 1886	Defeat of Home Rule Bill	Shankill, Falls, Donegall St	32 killed; 371 injured; £90,000 damage to property	4 months (sporadically)
7–8 June 1898	Nationalist procession	Falls, Shankill	16 injured	2 days
11–14 August 1907	?	Divis St, Falls Rd	2 killed; 23 injured	4 days
13–14 July 1909	Orange procession	Grosvenor Rd	6 injured	2 days

were indicated as 'incarnations of official pride'.[74] A statement
by the Commissioners that in their view the semi-military
character of the R.I.C. was well suited to Belfast did not allay
the resentment felt by the Corporation against the military
force in their midst.

The table above gives in succinct form the most important
features of the religious riots during the century between 1813
and 1912. The riots occurring after the setting up of Northern
Ireland are discussed in a subsequent chapter (Chapter 5).
Three 'minor' riots occurred between 1886 and 1912. In
June 1898 the Irish Nationalist Party organised celebrations
all over the country for the centenary of '98. In Belfast an
elaborate procession, to some extent emulatory of the Orange
processions, with ''98 Clubs', named after the leading republican heroes (McCracken, Orr, etc.) and duly equipped with
banners and sashes, marched to Hannahstown, where it was
commended by a Nationalist leader, John Dillon, M.P., as the
most magnificent demonstration he had ever seen.On its return
it suffered the same fate as the processions of 1872 and 1880, a
fusillade of stones from a crowd on the Shankill Road. The
police baton-charged the crowd, but not before one of their
number was knocked off his horse and seriously injured. The
following day the 'island men' were attacked on their way home
and altogether 15 people were injured, two seriously.

The 1898 riot may be regarded as a small-scale replica of the
riots of 1880. For the next riot, however, in 1907, no precipitating event can easily be assigned. In that year some regiments
of the line were stationed in Belfast, as a precaution against
labour disputes, and on 10 August, in a manner similar to
what their successors experienced sixty-three years later, the
troops were stoned and jeered at by youths in the Falls Road.
On the first night eleven police and troops were injured. The
next day the troops were greeted by stones, trip wires, chains
and road metal, the Riot Act was read, the mob fired at, and
two people killed. On the third day, a number of Catholic
priests and laymen requested the Lord Mayor (Lord Shaftesbury) to have the troops and police temporarily withdrawn from
the Falls. This was done, the Catholic priests (and magistrates)
effectively controlled the area and, apart from an isolated attack
on a soldier in uniform, there was no further disorder.

The 1909 riot lasted a mere two days, having been precipitated by the old familiar cause – an attack on an Orange procession in the Grosvenor Road. Three policemen were badly
injured.

Table 3.1 shows that the riots, almost always restricted to the
same area of Belfast, increased both in intensity and frequency
as the century progressed. In the first half of the century the
precipitating event was almost invariably a parliamentary
election, but all elections after 1857 passed without disturbance,
and Orange (or, more rarely, Nationalist) processions provided
the *casus belli*. The riot of 1907 is unique in that there was no
easily assigned cause, just a general antipathy to the troops in
the Catholic area. It is also noticeable that the Catholic antipathy to the old Belfast police, on account of their Orange
associations, was not replaced by friendly feelings towards
the Royal Irish Constabulary. Although the latter bore the
brunt of Protestant hostility during the 1886 riots, by 1898
they were equally disliked in the Falls and in 1907 troops and
police were attacked indiscriminately.

Viewing the riots as a whole, one may reasonably seek for
causes, especially since Belfast is the one city of the British Isles
to be periodically convulsed by disturbances of that magnitude.
There can be little doubt that as the century progressed the
pattern of rioting developed into the form that is so familiar
today – attacks by Catholics on Protestant processions (or
vice versa) followed by street fighting, burning of houses and
schools, and conflicts with the police. Especially after 1864 it
was noticeable that the districts were becoming religiously
homogeneous and in times of trouble the 'wrong sort' would be
summarily ejected from their homes. The police too always
played a major role. These features gave the riots a momentum
of their own – the residential and social apartheid which they
encouraged in turn fostered prejudices and hostilities which
rendered the next riot more likely.

It is easy to postulate economic factors as the underlying
cause. Certainly Table 3.1 shows a regular cyclical pattern in
rioting as well as a secular upswing but this cycle was political
not economic. All but one riot can be associated with some
definite political event – usually a regular parliamentary election or political procession. Moreover the general economic

facts in respect of the years when major riots occurred do not
support an interpretation in terms of job-competition, particularly in times of depression.[75] In 1857 there was in the United
Kingdom as a whole a financial panic and in consequence
there was some unemployment in the linen industry. This, however, occurred in the last quarter of the year – after the riots.
1864 was one of the most prosperous years of the century, with
constant employment at high wages in the linen trade, a boom
in shipbuilding, and the port scarcely able to handle the
amount of tonnage available. 1872 was a normal year. In 1886
there was a depression throughout the country in which agriculture particularly and linen had shared; but by all accounts
the shipyards were kept occupied by new Government contracts and the docks continued to handle a very heavy volume
of trade. Another fact worth mentioning is that the few contemporary pamphlets[76] dealing with the riots, e.g. the polemical
pro-Orange *History of the Belfast Riots* (1864) by Thomas Henry,
never mention economic rivalry;[77] it is all the fault of the
British Government in indulgently allowing 'Fenians' to hold
processions in Dublin while refusing similar favours to loyal
Protestants. The newspapers, too, concentrate exclusively on
politico-religious causes, the *Whig* forever fulminating against
Orange provocation, while the *Morning News*,[78] which,
remarkably enough, had a circulation greatly exceeding its
neighbours, became more vehemently sectarian as the years
passed. Its comments on the 1857 riots were careful and guarded,
in 1864 slightly less guarded; in 1872 the editorials were just
as vitriolic as the *News Letter's*. The following is typical: 'If
they (the Catholics) are to live under the ascendancy of an
Orange mob, they will shed the last drop of their blood.'[79]

It is impossible, when studying the riots, to get away from
the Orange Order and its rapidly increasing membership.
Since the formal re-establishment of the Irish Institution in
1847 its growth in Belfast had been phenomenal.[80] In 1851
there were thirty-five lodges in Belfast with a total membership
of 1,335. At that time Belfast still had no distinct representation
in the Grand Lodge of Ireland, although Dr Drew was one of the
Grand Chaplains. As the 1850s progressed several Belfast
Orangemen were added to the Grand Committee – Hutchison
Posnett in 1850, James Henderson of the *News Letter* in 1853,

and the linen merchant, Crommelin Irwin, in 1855. By 1858 Belfast had the largest number of lodges in County Antrim. As early as 1860 a resolution was passed to establish the District Lodge of Belfast as a County Grand Lodge, but this, which involved the separation of Belfast from Antrim, was not implemented until December 1864. The first County Grand Master was William Johnston of Ballykilbeg and the officers were highly respectable – travellers, woollen drapers, Episcopalian clergy. By 1868 there were four districts in Belfast, a fifth was established in 1869, a sixth in 1870, when the Order had 4,000 members, and a seventh in 1871.

The Order appears in its private deliberations to have been sensitive to allegations that the riots of 1857 and 1864 were instigated by Orangemen. In 1857 the Grand Lodge of Ireland set up a special committee to investigate the charge. Their report completely exonerated the Order, and censured the Lord Chancellor for suggesting that the 'gracious enterprise' of street preaching was unlawful.[81] The Grand Lodge resolved that the Inquiry Commissioners' Report was a 'perversion of justice'. The Grand Lodge did not openly concern itself with the 1864 riots until three years later, 5 June 1867,[82] when a grand Protestant demonstration was held in the Ulster Hall at which denunciations of Gladstone's pro-Roman policies were mingled with anathemas against Serjeant Barry, and firm resolutions were passed to stand together against their insidious enemies. By 1886 their position was so firmly established that criticism was no longer a cause for concern. There were then no less than five Orange Halls in Belfast (only one until 1853) and a contemporary pamphlet could write (inaccurately) that 'Belfast has ever been the home of Orangeism'.[83]

One particular group, the craft workers in the shipyard, played a very prominent part in the riots of 1864 and after.[84] It has sometimes been suggested that militant anti-Catholic feeling in the yard was not an indigenous growth but had been imported into Belfast by Harland's immigrant labourers from Clydeside. This contention is difficult to prove. Harland did import a considerable quantity of labour in the 1850s, but it is not possible to assess what proportion of the total labour force they represented, and in line with his policy of relying on local labour, the proportion was continually diminishing. Most of these workers in fact came from Tyneside, where Harland had previously worked, rather than Glasgow.

Unquestionably, the number of Orangemen in the shipyards was so large that the seventh Belfast district, established in 1871, was entirely confined to the Queen's Island. Nevertheless, there is no evidence from the records of the Orange Order that the shipyard Orangemen were not native Ulstermen. Sir Edward Harland,[85] in evidence before the 1887 Commission, said that of his 3,000 operatives only 225 were Catholic, but they were not segregated and worked in identical jobs with their fellow-workers. Replying to allegations that he had not sufficiently exerted himself to prevent victimisation of the small Catholic minority (of whom 190 had fled during the riots), Harland pointed out that during the 1864 riots, when attempts were made in the Yard to drive out every Catholic worker, he had posted a notice threatening to close the Yard until the Catholics were permitted to return. However, in 1886, as a worker told the Commissioners, Harland, in spite of urging from a deputation of Catholic workers, did not threaten similar sanctions[86] and the Inspector-General of the R.I.C. reported that the partners had resignedly told him that it would take 1,000 soldiers to protect the Catholics on the Island.[87] It would appear that although the shipyard (and docks) were particularly virulent areas of infection, the same symptoms were found throughout Belfast industry, certainly by 1886. Copious details of Catholics being forced to leave their work, especially in Ewart's mill, the Ropeworks and Agnes Street weaving factory, were provided for the 1886 Commission, and an even more sinister development, religious discrimination in employment by certain firms, was also alleged – for the first time.[88]

It must be said, therefore, that the economic hypothesis, job competition between Catholics and Protestants as a continuing cause of the disturbances in mid-century Belfast is not sustained by the evidence. The growth of religious *apartheid* through the development of Orangeism with its deliberate policy of segregation[89] and the official Catholic policy (general in Ireland since the 1830s) of separate schools for Catholic children, and lastly the incendiary preaching of clergymen such as Hanna, Drew, MacIlwaine and Kane, is an obvious cause. But another politico-religious cause which unfortunately cannot be developed here is the growing nationalisation of Irish politics. If the newspapers are an accurate guide there can be little doubt that Belfast people were more aware of events in Dublin and elsewhere in Ireland in the second half of the century than in the first. The connection between the riot of 1864 and the unveiling of the O'Connell monument in Dublin, the widespread fear of the revolutionary Fenian movement,[90] and subsequently of the Home Rule Party, are all amply demonstrated.

NOTES

1. *Belfast*, p. 109.
2. *B.N.L.*, 1 January 1864.
3. 'In 1852 there was only one power loom in Belfast. Ten years later there were 6,000.' (Jones in *Belfast*, p. 109.)
4. The number of new buildings constructed annually between 1861 and 1864 ranged from 730 to 1,400 – thereby increasing the total valuation by about 20 per cent. (*B.N.L.*, 2 January 1865.)
5. The number of flax spindles in Ireland increased from 300,000 in 1850 to nearly 600,000 in 1860, and nearly one million by the end of the 1870s. This peak figure was never equalled – too much machinery had been installed for normal output, cf. W. E. Coe, *The Engineering Industry of the North of Ireland*, pp. 60–61. In 1870 80 per cent of spindles and 70 per cent of power looms in the whole of Ireland were to be found in Belfast and its environs. D. L. Armstrong, 'Social and Economic Conditions in the Belfast Linen Industry, 1850–1900', *Irish Historical Studies* VII (September 1951), 238.
6. Not, as has sometimes been claimed, *the* first. That was built in Cork in 1816. (Coe, op. cit., p. 78.)
7. Iron shipbuilding is not an extension of wooden shipbuilding, but a different craft: a development of boilermaking. (Ibid.)
8. Hickson was not the first shipbuilder to be provided with a site by the Harbour Board. In 1851 the wooden shipbuilding firm, Thompson and Kirwan, moved their yard from the site of a new dock to the Queen's Island. But this shipyard soon declined.
9. It lasted from 1870 until 1934 when the White Star Line merged with Cunard.
10. For the details of the Belfast shipbuilding boom see W. E. Coe, *The Engineering Industry of the North of Ireland*; S. Pollard, 'British and World Shipbuilding, 1890–1914: A study in Comparative Costs', *Journal of Economic History*, XVII (1957), 426–44; R. W. Kelly and F. J. Allen, *The Shipbuilding Industry*, and most detailed of all, D. Rebbeck, *The history*

of iron shipbuilding on the Queen's Island up to July 1874 (unpublished
Ph.D. thesis, Queen's University, Belfast, 1950).

11. The technical innovations of Harland and Wolff in the field of marine
engineering are described in D. Rebbeck, *The History of iron shipbuilding
on the Queen's Island up to July 1874*, and more briefly, W. E. Coe, op.
cit., pp. 82–4.
Harland himself, it is often forgotten, retired from the active control
of his firm when still quite young, in 1877. He had already secured
election to the Harbour Board of which he was Chairman from 1875
to 1887 and indulged a taste for politics by becoming a member of
the City Council, serving as mayor 1885 to 1887, and as Conser-
vative/Unionist M.P. for North Belfast from 1892 till his death in 1895.
Wolff also entered the House in 1892 as M.P. for East Belfast and
served till 1910. But his contribution to debates within the Palace of
Westminster was made in the smoking room rather than the Chamber.
See H. Jefferson, *Viscount Pirrie of Belfast* (Belfast, 1947). The man who
above all shaped the future of Belfast's leading shipyard was William
James Pirrie (afterwards Lord Pirrie), who was controlling director of
the firm for 45 years. See below, p. 108.

12. See above, Chapter 1 Appendix.

13. Cf. J. Handley, *The Irish in Modern Scotland* (Cork, 1947), pp. 113–20,
and J. A. Jackson, *The Irish in Britain* (London, 1963), pp. 154–6.

14. Cf. C. O'Leary, *The Elimination of Corrupt Practices in British Elections
1868–1911* (Oxford, 1962), pp. 46, 61. It might have been thought
that the incidence of sectarian rioting in Belfast would have been a
natural subject for study by political historians and sociologists. To date,
however, apart from polemical works, only one study has appeared –
Andrew Boyd's *Holy War in Belfast* (Tralee, 1969). See also O. Dudley
Edwards, *The Sins of Our Fathers* (Dublin, 1970), Chapter 3.

15. See above, p. 50.

16. *B.N.L.*, 25, 28 December 1832.

17. *B.N.L.*, 20 January 1835; *N.W.*, 19 January 1835.

18. *N.W.*, 8–10 July 1841.

19. See above, p. 24.

20. R. M. Sibbett, *A History of Orangeism in Ireland and throughout the Empire*
(London, n.d.), II, 219–27.

21. *B.N.L.*, 18 July, 15 September 1843. Professor McCracken in Beckett
and Glasscock, *Belfast*, p. 96, refers to a serious riot in 1845. This is
probably a misprint for 1843. The 1845 processions passed off without
incident (except in Armagh).

22. Renewed at five-yearly intervals since 1832.

23. *B.N.L.*, 20 June, 8 July 1845.

24. Sibbett, op. cit., pp. 308–18.

25. *P.P.*, 1857–8, XXVI. By 1850 there were in Ireland, according to
the Earl of Enniskillen, 1,800 lodges. Sibbett, op. cit., p. 395.

26. *N.W.*, 15 July 1852.

27. Ibid. The writer continues: 'the horrors of the scene almost transcend
description. At the moment of the savage conflict the peals of thunder

which had been heard at intervals during the day increased in loudness, the lightning flashed vividly and in quick succession, while the screams of women, and the savage shouts of the insane wretches engaged in the deadly contest, joined with the crash of breaking windows and smashing doors, completed a scene which few who beheld can ever cease to remember.'

28. Cf. *B.N.L.*, 27 July, 3 August 1847.

29. *N.W.*, 27 May 1852. The increased Government grant to Maynooth in 1845 had exercised many strongly Protestant M.P.s throughout the United Kingdon.

30. Their opposition was based partly on the assumption that McClure was not 'a man of any mental power', but more importantly, because he supported 'the anti-Protestant' Palmerstonian Government who in the last year had appointed eight Roman Catholics and only one Protestant to bar appointments. (*B.N.L.*, 7 March 1857; see also 11 March 1857.)

31. Three Liberals entered the field: John Francis Ferguson (chairman of the executive committee of the Liberal Party), John McClean and McClure, but the highest vote secured by any of them was McClean's – 973 (to Davison's 1,369). The importance of McClure's candidature was that he was the first Presbyterian to seek parliamentary honours in Belfast.

32. *B.N.L.*, 24 March 1857.

33. Conservative M.P. for Belfast, 1860–68.

34. *P.P., 1857–58*, XXVI. Riot Commission Report, 1857–58, 210

35. They could hold about 2,300 people, but pews were bought for £100 and bequeathed, and only six seats allocated for the poor. In 1831 Belfast had 16,388 Church of Ireland members. See above, p. 32.

36. *The Annals of Christ Church*, PRONI, T1075/11/150–237. These parochial records, preserved in the PRONI, give a vivid picture of numerous charitable and social works undertaken by Drew in his early years in the parish.

37. *The Christians and the Churchmen – The Protestant, an address delivered at the Christ Church Mission Rooms, Belfast, to the Church of Ireland Young Men's Society on Monday evening, July 5, 1852*, by Thomas Drew, D.D. (Belfast, 1852). See also, *Thoughtful Protestantism. A sermon preached before the the twenty-third anniversary of the opening of the Church*, by Thomas Drew, D.D., L.B. (Downpatrick, 1856).

38. *Sermon preached in Christ Church, Belfast, on Sunday evening, Feb. 21, 1858*, by the Rev. Thomas Drew, D.D. (Belfast and Dublin, 1858). This was a deliberate repetition of the sermon before the 1857 riots.

39. *Riot Commission Report, P.P.* 1857–58, XXVI, p. 10.

40. Ibid., p. 13.

41. Ibid., p. 12.

42. One of the two Commissioners was a Catholic. For the report and minutes of evidence see *P.P.*, 1857–58, XXVI, 1–249.

43. *The Irish Presbyterian*, V. No. 58 (October 1857), 253–4. It tried to soften the denunciation by referring thus to Drew: 'there is no man

from whom we differ so often that we love so much' and suggesting that the Government should confer on him a benefice 'where his past services would be in some measure rewarded and his intense political sympathies not brought into play'. In 1859 Drew was made Rector of Loughinisland (a rural benefice). He died in 1871, having maintained his connection with the Orange Order until his death.

44. Like the Orange Order, the Ribbon men had their roots in the agrarian secret societies of the eighteenth century. About 1880 they were given a more respectable persona as the Ancient Order of Hibernians.

45. Cf. *N.W.*, 15–17 January, 8–9 April 1859.

46. *N.W.*, 13 April 1859. The *Whig* used a singular metaphor when proffering advice to the Liberals. Belfast liberalism, it said, was like a bundle of sticks – 'the sturdy Presbyterian staff – the elegant gold-tipped clouded cane of the Established Churchmen – the sturdy cudgel of the Roman Catholic party – the silver-mounted malacca of the Unitarians – the Quakers' sober ebony support'. Of the bundle the two strongest sticks were the Presbyterian and the Catholic. The implication of all this was that no Liberal could win unless he got all the Catholic vote and a sizeable share of the Protestant.

47. Durham Dunlop succinctly describes the state of the Liberals in 1859: 'no unity, no spirit, no organisation'. (*Brief Sketch*, p. 62.)

48. Report of Commissioners of Inquiry 1864. *P.P.*, 1865, XXVIII, 11.

49. Ibid., 17.

50. They referred to the religious disparity in the force – only five Catholics out of one hundred, while the Chief of Police was an ex-master of an Orange Lodge and there was 'a strong general suspicion' that many policemen were in the Order, although this was not proved. Ibid., 5–10. The 1857 inquiry had come to the same conclusion.

51. Ibid., 6.

52. Ibid., 152.

53. *B.N.L.*, 5 July 1865.

54. Ibid., 8, 10 July 1865.

55. *B.N.L.*, 15 July 1865. Durham Dunlop's account gravely censured the mayor (John Lytle) for selecting a 'notoriously partisan' barrister from Dublin to act as his assessor, for appointing 'insolvent and dubious' people as deputies and for allowing 'a gang of ferocious Orange ruffians armed with bludgeons of a most formidable character' to take possession of the Court House. (*Brief Sketch*, p. 68.) The election of 1865 was the last to be covered by Dunlop's pamphlet.

56. Cairns, 1,822; Getty, 1,728; Hay, 991.

57. The Brett Papers in the PRONI contain much evidence of Brett's assiduity in 'attending to the register'.

58. After the Act, which reduced the borough franchise qualification from £8 to 'over £4', Belfast had 12,168 parliamentary and 3,243 municipal voters; Dublin had 12,894 parliamentary and 5,112 municipal voters The Act also extended the boundaries of the parliamentary constituency to the municipal boundaries of 1853. The real increase was probably about 7,000 voters.

59. *B.N.L.*, 28 October 1868, for report of a meeting in the Ulster Hall where these complaints were voiced.

60. *B.N.L.*, 26 October 1868. At the beginning of the campaign the *B.N.L.* (13 October 1868) produced a detailed analysis of the electorate over the five wards, concluding that Roman Catholics numbered 1,953, Whigs and Radicals 1,736, and Conservatives 9,219; and that therefore McClure had no chance. After the election the paper adhered to its estimates, but claimed that the 10,000 Conservatives were lulled by their strength and did not recognise the danger. (Ibid., 21 November 1868.)

61. The voting figures were: Johnston, 5,975; McClure, 4,202; Lanyon, 3,540; Mulholland, 1,580.

62. Ibid., 18 November 1868.

63. The account by Andrew Boyd of the 1872 riots (pp. 89–119) is the most comprehensive given in *Holy War in Belfast*.

64. See above p. 82 for similar adverse comments on the Belfast magistrates in 1864.

65. In 1870.

66. The Hartington report, though circulated to the magistrates, was never published. It reposes in the strong room of the City Hall, and was consulted by courtesy of the Town Clerk.

67. They were working on the new Alexandra graving dock – the biggest in the world.

68. *Report of the Riot Commissioners* (1887) *P.P.*, 1887, XVIII, p. 11. Unlike the previous Commissions, this one was headed by a judge, Mr Justice Day.

69. Ibid., p. 14. The Commissioners also censured the police for weakness in parlying with the mob.

70. Ibid., p. 17. Even Sir Edward Harland appeared to believe this, judging by his evidence (p. 291).

71. Ibid., p. 14.

72. *P.P.*, 1887, XVIII, p. 556; 535 (Dr Tohill's evidence).

73. Kane told the executive committee of the J.P.s (the only reform arising out of the Hartington report of 1873) that if they tried to put up a police barrack in a loyal locality, he would arm 4,000 Orangemen to drive them out. (Ibid., p. 326.)

74. Ibid., p. 379.

75. For 1857 see *The Mercantile Journal and Statistical Register*, 12 January 1858. The Chamber of Commerce *Records*, PRONI, D/1857, contain reports on the state of trade from 1857.

76. T. Henry, *History of the Belfast Riots* (London and Belfast, 1864). In this rather racy account the Sandy Row boys are always 'fearless and resolute', while the Pound Street boys are a 'crowd of desperadoes'.

77. The same is true of the numerous Orange song-books.

78. The first Catholic newspaper in Belfast, the *Belfast Vindicator*, edited by Charles Gavan Duffy, the Young Irelander, lasted from 1839 to 1852 (Duffy emigrated to Australia, later becoming Premier of Victoria). The *Belfast Morning News* started in 1855 as Belfast's first penny news-

paper. Its circulation within a year was 7,080 copies, compared with 1,795 for the *Whig* and 916 for the *News Letter*. By 1872 the *Morning News* had 12,500 issues and became a daily paper.

79. *Belfast Morning News*, 20 August 1872. See also *Belfast Morning News*, 20 July and 11 September 1857; 26 August 1864. It is noteworthy that in 1872 a new editor, J. P. Swann, an English Catholic, had been appointed.

80. This information is mainly derived from the unpublished *Minutes of the Grand Lodge of Ireland* 1848–86, and the *Annual Reports of the Grand Lodge of Antrim* 1848–64, consulted by courtesy of Mr J. A. McClelland. These are far more useful than Sibbett's *Orangeism in Ireland and throughout the Empire*, cf. II, 453–78. It is remarkable that no mention of the riots appears in the Minutes of the Presbyterian General Assembly for the years 1858, 1865, 1873 or 1887.

81. *Grand Lodge of Ireland Minutes*, November 1857, p. 24; May 1858, p. 10. Mazière Brady, Lord Chancellor of Ireland (who had adjudicated in the Chancery suit of 1854) after the 1857 riots, wrote to Lord Londonderry, Lord Lieutenant of Co. Down, announcing that in future applicants for the Commission of the Peace would have to pledge themselves that they were not and would not become Orangemen. The letter was published in the *Whig*, 8 October 1857.

82. Cf. *Grand Lodge of Ireland Minutes*, 1867, Appendix.

83. Cf. *Clifton Bazaar* (a Bicentenary Pamphlet), Belfast, 1888.

84. In 1886 Harland and Wolff employed 3,000 men. (See above p. 74.) In the same year the smaller shipyards would have accounted for another five hundred.

85. *P.P.*, 1887, XVIII, 295–6.

86. *Ibid.*, 520–21.

87. *Ibid.*, 253.

88. *Ibid.*, 535–40. According to the evidence of the Rev. John Tohill, Professor at St Malachy's College, later Bishop of Down and Connor, (1914–18), Ewart's Mill was the main culprit. On the other hand, in a minority report, one of the Commissioners, Commander McHardy, basing himself on the 1881 census, concluded that the Catholics 'took their full share in all the occupations of the people to which their number and education entitle them'.

89. The records of the Grand Lodge show that 'marrying a Papist' was the most frequent cause of expulsion from the Institution.

90. The term 'fenian' passed into ordinary conversational usage in Ulster as a pejorative synonym for Catholic. It is still used.

4 The Age of Consolidation: 1874–1920

'Arise! Advance!'
And we have risen, and advanced, and never
Thro' change or chance,
Swerved from the path of earnest endeavour!
A little town
Hath grown a mighty city, thro' the thrift
That stamps Wrong down,
And thro' those thews of Truth, that never drift
From Creed and Crown!

SAMUEL K. COWAN, *Ode on the Opening of the City Hall* (1906)

I. PARTY DEVELOPMENTS

'It is just as bad as bad could be. There is scarcely a town in the United Kingdom, except Belfast, in which a Liberal candidate could not count on polling a very considerable number of votes.'[1] This lament in a *Northern Whig* editorial after the general election result of 1874 had been declared marks the recognition by the Belfast Liberals that Belfast was incontrovertibly a Conservative city, and might well serve as the keynote for the developments of the next fifty years.

The unexpected loss of one seat to the Liberals in 1868 forced the Belfast Conservative Association to come to terms with the newly formed Orange and Protestant Working Men's Association. After two meetings originally held to promote a joint list of candidates for the next election, the Conservative Association adopted a new set of rules, the most important of which prescribed that all the ward committees should meet to select a candidate and that their choice be ratified by a general meeting of Conservative electors.[2] It was clear that the Orange influence was directed to getting away from the old country-house or grand jury meeting system of nomination, to give the newly enfranchised working classes a share in the process.

The new arrangement worked most smoothly in 1874. Johnston,[3] who had supported a number of Liberal policies in the previous parliament – he had supported disestablishment and the ballot and had promoted for the Belfast Liberals a motion to assimilate the Irish municipal franchise to the parliamentary – was duly nominated by the Conservative ward committees and approved by a public meeting, his running-mate being J. P. Corry,[4] a leading shipper whose disadvantages were that he was a master, of previous Liberal leanings, and a non-Orangeman, but who was also a Presbyterian and thus able to compete on equal terms with McClure. A scurrilous eve-of-election poster on the union of 'Romish priests and radical Presbyterian parsons' for MacClure aptly sums up the tone of the campaign.[5]

The fact that the Irish Home Rule Association had been founded four years previously to revive formally the demand for a separate Irish legislature did not help the Liberal cause.[6] In a very high poll Corry and Johnston both doubled McClure's vote.

However, the alliance between upper-class Tories and working-class Orangemen in Belfast was not without its growing pains. In 1878 Johnston applied for the Chiltern Hundreds following his appointment as Inspector of Fisheries. A hurried meeting called at a time when workers could not conveniently attend put up for nomination William Ewart, owner of one of Belfast's largest spinning mills. Affronted by this breach of the understanding of 1873, the Orange and Protestant Working Men's Association decided to contest the by-election and nominated Dr William Seeds, Q.C., a prominent member of the Order who was of Ulster background, though practising in Dublin. Seeds was little known in Belfast and Ewart easily won the by-election. However, when the general election came up Seeds was again nominated and the combined efforts of Dr Hanna's Presbyterian Constitutionalists, the *News Letter* and the newly founded *Belfast Evening Telegraph*, were required to secure the election of Ewart and Corry.[7] The class motif was much more evident than in former contests. The official Conservatives were among the leading employers in the city and came under fire for reducing wages and opposing workmen's compensation. Seeds showed himself a Disraelian Tory democrat, claiming adequate representation for the working classes – 'the overwhelming majority of the electors of the United Kingdom.[8] Though unsuccessful in this election the Orange Institution[9] had established the precedent of putting up its own candidates, irrespective of the wishes of the Conservative Association. But this did not imply a split between the Orange Order and the official Conservative body. On the contrary, the policy appeared to be to work through the Association and to nominate separate candidates only as a last resort.[10]

From the elections of 1885 to 1920 the politics and parties of Belfast are inextricably bound up with the politics and parties of Ireland as a whole. The nationalisation of politics was greatly advanced by the trio of reformist measures, the Corrupt and Illegal Practices Act of 1883 (although that was less effective in Ireland than in Great Britain), the Franchise Act of 1884, which quadrupled the Irish electorate, and the Redistribution of Seats Act of 1885, which abolished the old decaying boroughs and transferred their seats to the growing cities of Dublin, Belfast and Cork.[11]

Long before polling day it was clear that the election of 1885 would provide the first major test of the strength of the Irish Home Rule party which had secured more than 60 of the 103 Irish seats in 1880, and had shortly afterwards elected as leader the militant nationalist, Charles Stewart Parnell. The Home Rulers were vigorously opposed by the Irish Liberals and Conservatives and a newly formed organisation led by three Ulster Conservatives, the Loyal Irish Union, decided to promote 'loyalist' candidates in every constituency against the Home Rulers.[12] For his part Parnell carried the war into the enemy's camp and several of his followers with no Ulster connection whatever were nominated for Ulster constituencies.[13]

One of these was the new constituency of Belfast West, centred on the Falls Road which was by now a Catholic ghetto, but also containing Sandy Row and the Shankill Road. It was the only constituency in the city where the Catholics and Protestants were evenly balanced and Sexton, who was a Cork barrister, and one of the most eloquent of Parnell's lieutenants obviously expected to get the Catholic vote, on Nationalist grounds.[14]

Elsewhere in Belfast the situation was confused. The Orange County Grand Lodge demanded the right to nominate two of

the four Conservative candidates. But since the Redistribution
Act the Belfast Conservative Association had split into four
divisions and Sir James Corry was selected by the divisional
association of East Belfast. Promptly E. S. de Cobain was put
up against him as an 'Orange Conservative Working Men's'
candidate. South Belfast was left to the Orangemen, and Seeds
(standing for the third time) found himself opposed by William
Johnston, who had tired of administrative life and wished to
return to the House. Ewart in North Belfast was opposed by
Alexander Bowman, Secretary of the Belfast Trades Council
(standing as a Liberal), and the Conservative candidate in
West Belfast was J. H. Haslett, another prominent Orangeman.
The Belfast Liberals, though counting such well-known shippers, stockbrokers and linen merchants as William Pirrie,
Jaffé, Adam Duffin and J. S. Brown, put up two other candidates, R. W. Murray (a tobacco manufacturer), and Workman
(of the minor shipbuilding firm), but with apparently little hope
of success.

The election results of 1885 established a pattern of party
distribution which persisted in Ireland for the next forty years,
and in Belfast almost to the present day. West Belfast emerged
as a marginal seat, Haslett beating Sexton by 37 votes in a poll
of 7,500. Johnston won South easily, defeating Workman and
Seeds. In North, Ewart secured three times the vote of Bowman,
and in East the Orangeman defeated the non-Orangeman,
Corry, by 104 votes.

But the overall result in Belfast, a three to one victory for
Conservative-cum-Orange candidates, was strikingly different
from that of the rest of Ireland. Parnell's Home Rule party
secured the greatest electoral victory in Irish history. They won
every seat in the three provinces of Munster, Leinster and
Connaught[15] and a majority of seats in Ulster (17 to 16).
Their victory was highlighted by the ignominious defeat of the
Loyalist candidates, who in many cases secured a few hundred
votes, and in some even less than a hundred. Though not a
single Liberal candidate was returned in the whole country
no less than ten of the Ulster seats were won by Orange/
Conservative candidates.

At once the Home Rule issue was pushed to the forefront
of British politics, since the Home Rule party held the balance

of power. The formation of Gladstone's third administration with its commitment to introduce an Irish Home Rule Bill produced an instant reaction in Belfast. Already (22 December 1885) the Grand Lodge of Ireland had taken the initiative in summoning a meeting of the Ulster Conservative members together with three Irish-born Conservatives returned for English constituencies. They decided to meet regularly to formulate policy, and out of these informal arrangements developed the Unionist parliamentary party.[16] The announcement of Gladstone's conversion was followed by a flood of resolutions from the municipal bodies, the Chamber of Commerce, and even the Presbyterian General Assembly. In Belfast Orange and loyalist meetings were held by the score throughout 1886[17] but it was not until May that the Belfast Liberals took the decisive step. A meeting in the Ulster Hall, attended by several hundred people, passed by a large majority a resolution condemning with deep regret the abandonment of past Liberal policy for one which 'in their judgement (was) fraught with danger to the industrial, social and moral welfare of the country'. A new committee was set up containing such Liberal stalwarts as Thomas Andrews, Thomas Sinclair and David Lindsay. The Belfast Liberal organisation, such as it was, had gone over to the Liberal-Unionists (the title was formally adopted later in the year), and the only prominent Gladstonian Liberal left was the former secretary, Charles Brett, who, like the majority of Liberal activists in England, remained true to Mr Gladstone. A counter-move to form a Protestant Home Rule Association in Belfast misfired[18] and one of its founder-members, Alexander Bowman, was ejected from his office in the Belfast T.U.C.[19]

In January 1886 the Irish Loyal and Patriotic Union, the mass organisation which later developed into the Ulster Unionist Alliance, was reconstituted[20] under the leadership of the Conservative aristocrat, the Duke of Abercorn and the ex-Liberal M.P., Colonel Saunderson, a leading Orangeman, who later became the official leader of the Ulster Unionist M.P.s. By the time of the general election in July 1886, the marriage between the Irish Conservatives and the Orange Order had been consummated and the new movement, for the first time designated 'Unionist', was a formidable combination of the parliamentary skills and resources of the Conservatives with the grass-roots appeal of the Orangemen. It was from this time that local lodges took it on themselves to do registration work for the new party. Local Unionist associations were not, however, set up until 1893 when Lord Templeton established Unionist Clubs which spread rapidly all over Ulster. Finally in 1905 the Ulster Unionist Council was set up based on the Unionist Clubs, but the Orange Order was given 100 seats on the Council and the Derry Apprentice Boys were also represented.

The year 1886 marks the dividing line between two eras in Irish politics – the era of unorganised, upper-class politics in which party associations were virtually autonomous and elections were contests for power between local interests, and the era of mass parties in which the party associations, even in the largest cities, were subject to some control by a national organisation. The Unionists had their mass party in the I.L.P.U.; The Nationalists in the National League; the Liberal Unionists had a small organisation (mainly centred in Belfast) which maintained a formal independence until the foundation of the Ulster Unionist Council in 1905; the Gladstonian Liberals no longer counted. The transformation of party structure and electioneering which Ostrogorski notes as having occurred in Great Britain between 1879 and 1885 occurred in Ireland in 1886. Henceforth, even in Belfast, the party organisations had no independent existence of the national organisations. Apart from the short-lived Catholic Association of 1897–1905 and the Ratepayers' and Citizens' Association of the 1900s, the only addition to the two-party system was the formation of the Belfast Labour Party in 1908.[21]

The polarisation of politics in Belfast, three seats being solidly Protestant/Unionist and the fourth a Catholic/Nationalist marginal, led to a decline of interest in parliamentary elections. In the elections of 1892 and 1900 three seats were uncontested; in 1895 all four. In the elections of 1906 and 1910 some opposition was offered by an independent Orangeman, T. H. Sloan[22] (who won South Belfast in 1906 but was easily beaten by an orthodox Unionist in both elections of 1910), and by Labour candidates in the Northern division.

But the result was never seriously in doubt and no Labour

candidate appeared in the December 1910 election. Joseph Devlin (Nationalist), however, won West Belfast in 1906 in a three-cornered contest in which J. A. M. Carlisle (brother-in-law of Lord Pirrie) stood as an 'Independent Liberal Unionist' (winning by 15 votes out of 8,000), but kept it with increasing majorities in the two contests of 1910. Devlin, a Catholic publican, had already made a name for himself in Belfast municipal politics and soon became a leading figure in the United Irish League, which replaced the National League as the mass Home Rule organisation after the Parnellite split.[23]

II. ECONOMIC AND SOCIAL

(i) General

The Liberal-Unionist case against Home Rule, adumbrated by Thomas Sinclair with increasing cogency from 1886,[24] was quite simply that *Belfast* had done very well under the Union: her population had quadrupled in fifty years; her wage rates were higher than anywhere in Ireland and in some cases up to British standards; as to customs revenue she ranked as the third port in the United Kingdom, being exceeded only by London and Liverpool; she had the largest weaving factory, the largest shipping output, the largest tobacco factory, and the largest ropeworks in the world.[25] The basis of her prosperity was the economic link with Britain, and she was not prepared to come under the rule of a Dublin Parliament dominated by impoverished small farmers from Munster and Connaught.

The developments referred to in Sinclair's speeches were by and large predictable consequences of the basic technological innovations of the first half of the century. But there were considerable variations.[26] The linen industry experienced a continuing boom between 1850 and 1875, followed by a period of stagnation with slack demand and prices generally trailing downwards. The overall employment figures and the percentage of adult male workers (never more than one third) remained virtually constant from 1875 to the end of the century. Average wages, however, doubled between 1850 and 1900 and the real value in a period of falling prices went up by 200 per cent.

In the case of shipbuilding and its ancillary marine engineering
there was a record of unbroken success. Harland and Wolff's
first ocean liner, the *Oceanic*, built for the White Star Line in
1870, was the most advanced of its day, and that firm continued
to have all its ships built by Harland's until its merger with
Cunard in 1934. The firm also made marine engines not only
for its own ships but also for naval ships. The 'wee yard' of
Workman and Clark by 1900 was also among the top half-
dozen shipbuilders in the British Isles. The period of most
rapid, indeed fantastic, growth occurred, however, after 1880,[27]
five years after Harland had handed over control of his shipyard to his third partner, William Pirrie, who differed strongly
in politics from both the original partners but nevertheless was
the controlling director of the firm for nearly fifty years (1874–
1924).

In addition to the twin giants of linen and shipbuilding,
Belfast rapidly developed other industries, agricultural (especially flax-spinning) machinery, brewing, distilling, flour
milling, tobacco and ropemaking being the most important.[28]
The Ropeworks Company was founded in 1873 and by 1900
was the largest in the world (40 acres). The same was true of
tobacco. Gallaher's factory, opened in 1867, by 1896 covered
14 acres, while Dunville's original enterprise (tea blending) was
replaced by distilling after 1860, and by the end of the century
that firm was one of the largest distillers in Ulster.

The tremendous industrial expansion was facilitated by a
number of causes. A plentiful supply of cheap labour from the
neighbouring counties,[29] a flexible system of banking, operating the Scottish 'cash credit' system, and lastly, a continuing
boom in the construction industry. To keep pace with the
population movement into the city, speculative builders
constructed street after street of identical, red-brick artisans'
houses in the neighbourhood of the linen mills and factories
and engineering plants in the north and west (Falls-Crumlin-
Shankill triangle), and on the east side of the river near the
shipyards and ropeworks. The building boom was facilitated
by the dismemberment of the Donegall estate after 1850 into
numerous fee-farm grants and also by the availability of cheap,
durable bricks. Since the boom largely came after the middle
of the century, the houses put up in Belfast were governed by

Corporation by-laws requiring a small yard, with lavatory, ashpit and (after 1878) back access – and they compared favourably with working-class housing in most industrial cities in Great Britain. Indeed, one of the attractions for Clydeside workers coming to the Belfast shipyard was that they would have better living conditions there than in Glasgow.[30]

Side by side with the provision of houses for the rapidly growing working-class population, came the development of the rural areas to north and south as middle-class suburbs.[31] The move from the centre of the city began about mid-century southwards towards Malone, northwards towards Antrim, and eastwards in the direction of Bangor. Scarcely a single public or institutional building existing in Belfast today antedates this period.[32]

The rapid population growth to which the building boom was an immediate response also posed a challenge for the municipal authorities to provide at least the same standard of services in the new areas as in the rest of the town. How they met this challenge is discussed below under a number of sub-headings.

(ii) *Public Health*

In the beginning of this period the main concern of the Town Council was to widen existing streets and construct new ones in the areas where demands for housing space was greatest. In the 1850s they built Victoria Street, and some twenty years later Royal Avenue, Belfast's main shopping centre, was constructed on the site of Hercules Street, a narrow, very unsanitary thoroughfare full of butchers' shops. Three bridges and seven parks were also constructed.

But the Corporation lagged behind other growing British cities in the provision of sewerage. In 1848, the year when the famine fever, cholera, hit Ireland, it was estimated that 331 of the 579 streets were less than twenty feet wide, 232 houses had no yards at all, the new suburbs were unpaved and without sewers (the all-purpose Blackstaff river being the only available substitute), and that perhaps 25,000 people did not even have privies in their houses. In such crowded and unsanitary conditions it is not surprising that Belfast had, next to Dublin, the highest incidence of cholera and typhoid in the whole country

(62,000 cases in the previous thirty years of which 6,000 were fatalities).[33]

The municipal authorities – like their counterparts elsewhere in Ireland – were not adequately organised to deal with health problems. Parochial officers of health existed under the Acts of George III, but these were short-lived and did not survive the 1820s. The local Acts of 1845 and 1847 gave the mayor and Town Council some sanitary powers. But they were not put immediately to effective use. In 1848 a voluntary committee of clergymen and businessmen was set up to deal with the cholera problem. It was fondly hoped that this might become a permanent body, but with the decline of the epidemic public interest also declined, and the Belfast Sanitary Committee was moribund by 1850.

One suggested solution was a permanent borough authority to supervise health. But in spite of prompting from Dr Malcolm and other social reformers like the brilliant but eccentric Dr Henry McCormac,[34] the Corporation was prepared to let well alone. The Blackstaff continued to be a 'large, open sewer' until it was finally culverted in the 1880s, and a municipal sanitary committee was not established until 1865.

When it was set up, its first task was connected not with sewerage but with slaughterhouse conditions. Belfast slaughter-houses (mainly in the old Hercules Street) were highly un-sanitary – in the previous century blood and garbage used to be flung into the streets. Following the report of a deputation sent to Paris in 1869, a public abattoir was built on what were then the most modern lines.

The next Corporation had to turn its attention to the sewerage problem, which by then was particularly acute, with the growth of new suburbs with non-existent sewerage, the dry closets and ashpits in the older parts of the town, and the river Lagan (and Blackstaff) as the main repository of sewage.

However, it took twenty-five years to devise the main drainage system.[35] Under a private Act of 1887 (the Main Drainage Act) intercepting sewers were constructed and a large tract of land on the Antrim side of the river purchased for purification and outfall works. The scheme was completed in 1894, while by 1902 the old houses with dry closets and ashpits were converted to water closets. Even then, major health problems remained. The disposal of the city's sewage ultimately into Belfast Lough created a continuing risk of typhoid, both through direct infection and through shellfish mainly gathered by the poor on the shores of the Lough. Unlike other industrial cities (e.g. Glasgow) Belfast had no adequate drop to low water and no strong ebb tide; and these natural disadvantages were extremely difficult to counter. Another symptom of the inadequate drainage was flooding, which occurred regularly, as it happened, in mainly Catholic areas.

The inadequate sewerage system was an issue mainly brought up by Nationalist and Labour councillors and especially by the Citizens' Association (1905–10), during the last decade of the nineteenth century and the first decade of the twentieth. Their chief weapon was the death rate from tuberculosis and typhoid which had not appreciably diminished in spite of the advances in medical science. In 1893 another voluntary society, the Belfast Health Society, was set up, and in 1896, after much controversy, the Corporation appointed a special committee, under the chairmanship of Councillor Thomas Harrison, to investigate the city's health. The report of the Harrison Committee severely castigated the Corporation for not making better use of the sanitary powers under the public Acts of 1878 and 1891 (providing for inspection of workshops). However,[36] when the report came up for discussion the combined weight of estate agents and landlord interests on the Council was sufficient to have its main recommendations – more stringent by-laws – rejected.

By 1906 the opposition members of the Corporation managed to persuade Dublin Castle to appoint a Vice-Regal Commission to examine the city's sanitary state. The Health Commission compared the overall death rate in Belfast with that of ten major British and Irish cities, and discovered that it was better than Dublin's, about the same as Manchester's and Liverpool's, but not as good as Birmingham's or Sheffield's. The death rate from typhoid, however, over the previous twenty-five years was such that 'no other city or town of the United Kingdom equals or even approaches it in this respect',[37] while the annual death rate from tuberculosis was more than double that of England and Wales and higher even than that of Dublin. The causes assigned by the Commissioners were the prevalence of

infected shellfish and the insanitary condition of parts of the
town 'the result of inefficient sanitary administration extending
over many years'.[38]

However, the new medical officer of health appointed in
1906, together with a new chairman of the Health Committee,
bludgeoned the more reactionary members of the Council into
modernising the city's health administration. By 1911 the
superintendent of Purdysburn Fever Hospital could report that
enteric fever (typhoid) which used to provide their main work
in the Fever Hospital was by then 'quite rare'.[39] From that time
onwards few complaints were made about the sanitary state of
Belfast. (Another incidental cause of delay in the reforms was
the intransigent attitude of neighbouring rural district councils
who discharged their sewage into the Lough and resolutely
refused to share responsibility for cleaning it. They also very
unreasonably opposed the attempts to impose uniform standards
for milk production.)

(iii) *Water*

As might be expected, the provision of fresh water for a rapidly
growing industrial population, though essential, was not
accomplished without many difficulties. The first supply of
water in wooden pipes from a source near the present Boyne
Bridge dated from the mid-seventeenth century, but a century
later the wooden pipes were rotten. The next public provision
of water was made by the Charitable Society,[40] who set up a
Committee called the Spring Water Commissioners, and
promoted a private Bill compelling every occupier of a dwelling
house who wished to have piped water to pay their rate. The
appropriate statutory provision was, in fact, made in the
Belfast Police Act 1800.

The new Commissioners were unable to find a new source of
supply for the growing population without incurring responsibility for heavy compensation. The rapid growth of the population and the demands of industry on water required heavy
capital outlay which the Charitable Society was unable to
provide, nor were they either able or willing to extract water
rate from traders dissatisfied with the poor supply. In 1840
another private Bill transferred the water powers of the Charitable Society to a new body, the Belfast Water Commissioners,

to be elected by those paying water rate, and the boundary of its jurisdiction was fixed approximately half-way between the municipal and parliamentary boundaries.

The new Commissioners[41] set to work constructing a large new reservoir in Carr's Glen and two clear water basins, and fought several actions against recalcitrant millowners. The new supply was carried by cast iron distributing pipes. However, by 1851 a survey commissioned by the Water Board predicted that the population, then 100,000, would have reached 150,000 by 1861, that their needs, excluding the requirements of industry, would be two million gallons daily. The entire water output of Belfast was then less than one million gallons.[42] However, the Bill empowering the Board to extend their catchment scheme was not presented to Parliament until the spring of 1865.[43] Almost immediately after it became law Belfast experienced its worst water famine. All the reservoirs ran dry during the hot summer of 1865 and only the Cromac springs, where water sold at prohibitive prices, remained unexhausted. Tap water was green in colour, and a single glass could contain 'tens of thousands of minute insects, many of them an inch in length'.[44]

With its enhanced powers, the Water Board proceeded to set up a permanent staff including a (very much overdue) engineer. Another upland catchment was built at Stoneyford (ten miles south-west of Belfast) in 1884, and by 1889 storage facilities for nearly 1,000 million gallons were available.

But soon again the demand was greater than the supply. By 1890 the city was using nine and a half million gallons per day, twice the amount of 1880.

In 1891 the Commissioners found an adequate supply of water at a sufficiently high altitude to flow by gravity into Belfast – two rivers (Annalong and Kilkeel) in the Mourne Mountains, forty miles from Belfast, unencumbered by riparian rights, and providing water so pure that filtration was unnecessary. In 1893, the Board put through another Bill enabling them to acquire the 9,000 acres in the Mourne country. By 1901 the first Mourne water was being piped to Belfast from Annalong and later from Kilkeel. But the major task of constructing a reservoir with a capacity of 9,000 million gallons in the Silent Valley, drained by the Kilkeel river, posed formidable engineering problems, and work was not finished until 1929. In the interval the Boundary Commission set up pursuant to the 1921 Anglo-Irish Treaty had to hear evidence affecting the Silent Valley. The entire area of South Down surrounding Kilkeel was Catholic/Nationalist and the Irish Free State Government argued that it ought to be transferred. However, the Water Commissioners argued that it would be extremely inconvenient for them if the water supply of Belfast were under the control of another State. This argument convinced the Boundary Commissioners[45] who in 1925 voted to keep the Silent Valley within the jurisdiction of Northern Ireland.

The last stage was the building of a tunnel through the mountains to replenish the Silent Valley (1945–52), and the construction of another reservoir nearby (1954–7). By the early sixties, however, the peak demand was beginning to outrun the forty-two million gallons a day available from the existing resources, and since 1966 a major scheme to utilise the water of Lough Neagh (the largest lake in the British Isles, with a surface area of 150 square miles) has been under construction.

In their lengthy history the Belfast and District Water Commissioners have rarely been involved in controversy. In composition they were more Conservative than the Harbour Board, but less so than the Town Council. Since 1889 when the water boundary was extended to include parts of Antrim and Down (when 'and District' was added to the title) the electorate has been the same as the local government electorate. Members serve for three years and elections for five wards occur annually. But contests are very rare: there have been only two since 1960. The area of the Board's jurisdiction was again extended in 1938 and now covers 64 square miles, or roughly double the former area. It supplies one third of the population of Northern Ireland and a high proportion of its industry.[46] It managed successfully to resist takeover bids by the City Council – the last serious one was in 1896–7 – and at the time of writing is the only water authority of its kind in the United Kingdom, although under the forthcoming reorganisation of local government, following the Macrory Report, its powers will be handed over to central authorities.[47]

(iv) *Transport Undertakings*

Under the Belfast Tramways Act of 1872 a private company run by William Norris and Jorgen Daniel Larsden was empowered to operate a tramway system on condition that the Corporation could buy it over within twenty-one years. The company laid many miles of tramlines and bought the most modern vehicles. By 1892 it was a flourishing concern, but in that year the Corporation decided not to exercise its option to buy the company for another fourteen years, partly through pressure from the ex-mayor, Sir William Ewart, a director of the company, on consideration of an annual payment ranging from £4,000 to £5,000.

But by 1897, with the extension of the boundary and election of a new Corporation with Labour members, pressure for municipalisation was renewed. Eventually in 1904 the Corporation promoted a private bill authorising purchase of the undertaking. But the Corporation had to pay a heavy price, not only in compensation, and for electrifying the whole system (almost £1,000,000), but also in having inserted in the Bill a clause obliging the city transport system to pay its way. Unlike most English cities, Belfast would henceforth be unable to subsidise road transport from the rates.

Initially the undertaking prospered. Revenue in 1911 was nearly double that of 1905 and in 1912[48] the Corporation began the first major extension of the system, which was carried further after 1921. Further landmarks were the inauguration of omnibuses in 1926, the establishment of a Corporation monopoly over public transport in 1928, after a brief and near disastrous period of free competition (June to December 1928), the first trolleybus service in 1938 followed by a gradual conversion from tramcar to trolleybus which was effected by the end of 1944, and the decision in August 1959 to replace trolleybuses by omnibuses.

In recent years public transport has suffered a continuous decline in the numbers of passengers, from 258 million a year in 1944–5 to 150 million in 1964–5.[49] Various attempts have been made to cope, ranging from steep increases in fares to the employment of one-man buses; but a solution here – as in other cities in the British Isles – is not yet in sight. The Macrory

Report (1970) suggested that road passenger transport be centralised, but no firm decision has yet been taken.

(v) *Gas and Electricity*

The Belfast Gas Company, incorporated by Act of Parliament in 1822, following a contract with the old Police Commissioners, was one of the earliest in the British Isles. It was immediately successful and the 'mild radiance flowing from the (street) lamps' was in startling contrast to 'the gloomy twilight, or rather darkness visible, which formerly issued from our dull and sombrous globes'.[50] In 1846, as previously recounted, the Corporation, under John Bates' management, secured £50,000 to buy out the Gas Company, but spent the money otherwise and it was not until 1874 that another Bill was passed which attained this end. The Act of 1912, referred to above, also extended the Corporation's powers to purchase fresh land and build new gasholders. From the beginning the Belfast gas works ran on coal, but from May 1964 it has been gradually replaced by oil.

The provision of electricity has always been a municipal responsibility in Belfast. Having successfully opposed several applications by private companies, the Corporation secured a provisional order in 1890 authorising it to supply electricity within the city. The first generating station was erected in 1895 (in Chapel Lane) and other stations were erected in 1898, 1923 and 1955, increasing the capacity from 430 to 414,750 kilowatts. The last two stations, which are still in use, feed into a grid system affording supplies to all parts of Northern Ireland.

III. BOUNDARY EXTENSION

During the last quarter of the nineteenth century the powers of Belfast Corporation increased in proportion to the growing importance of the town. By the Act of 1865 they were entitled to levy a single general purposes rate (for maintaining and paving streets, roads and bridges, and for providing police). The Irish Public Health Act (1878) made them a sanitary authority with power to make by-laws, governing streets and houses, and to construct sewers.[51] In 1879 they secured from the Lord Lieutenant a public inquiry into the need for boundary extension.[52]

The Council argued the necessity of extending the boundary to bring in the new suburbs of Strandtown, Ballyhackamore and Knock (on the east), Malone (south) and Ballymurphy (west), on the ground that under the lazy regime of Antrim grand jury and the various boards of guardians, the sewerage facilities were virtually non-existent; and also claimed that since they shared many of the town's amenities the suburbs should also share in the rate burden. The Commissioners accepted the Corporation argument (which would have more than doubled their area), and also the desired increase in the number of wards – from five to eight.[53]

Nothing happened after the report, but in 1885 the parliamentary boundary was extended to bring in about 15,000 acres; so the Corporation were encouraged to try again. But before they could do so, they sponsored another private Bill, the Main Drainage Bill of 1887.[54]

This, however, ran into unexpected opposition. Thomas Sexton, the Nationalist member for West Belfast, insisted on tacking on to the Main Drainage Bill an amendment reducing the Belfast municipal franchise from a £10 qualification to household suffrage. When it appeared that the Drainage Bill might not get through, a compromise was reached – the Nationalists withdrew their opposition to the Drainage Bill, on condition that another Bill be introduced establishing household suffrage in Belfast. This was done by two Belfast members (Corry and de Cobain), and Belfast therefore had household suffrage for local elections twelve years before the rest of Ireland.[55]

This incident showed how powerful the Nationalist block at Westminster could be, at least in relation to private Bills. The Corporation held its fire until 1895. In the meantime the status of Belfast had been enhanced by a Royal Charter conferring the title of 'city' in 1888, and a further Charter of 1892 elevated the mayor to the rank of 'Lord Mayor'. In that year (1895) a sub-committee of the Council prepared a Bill, which, broadly speaking, would extend the municipal to the parliamentary boundary.[56] The sub-committee instructed the city surveyor to draw up a scheme for fifteen wards, radiating from the city centre, the boundaries of which were to be determined according to the twin criteria of population and valuation.

The scheme that emerged from the sub-committee was approved by the City Council in the autumn of 1895. Almost immediately, the Catholics of Belfast reacted against it. At a meeting of Catholic ratepayers presided over by the bishop, Dr Henry, it was decided to set up a Catholic Representation Association to promote opposition to the Bill and to act as the guardian of Catholic interests.[57] In the meantime an executive committee was to prepare its case. The brief was drawn up by Joseph Devlin, then in his twenty-fifth year.[58] The plan to divide the borough into fifteen wards was denounced as calculated to continue the exclusion of Belfast Catholics from the government of the city.[59] Moreover, the principle of valuation was condemned as anti-democratic. The counter-proposal involved four wards, roughly based on the parliamentary divisions. Though Devlin's proposals were accepted by a meeting on 13 January 1896, in spite of his objections[60] the bishop persuaded the meeting to entrust its case in the Commons to Vesey Knox, Protestant Nationalist M.P. for Londonderry.

The Belfast Corporation Bill was referred to a Select Committee on 6 March 1896, four members of which were nominated by the House of Commons (including John Dillon and Vesey Knox), and four by the Committee of Selection. The eminent landowner, Sir William Houldsworth, was elected chairman of the Committee.[61]

Apart from minor objections,[62] the main case against the Bill was the Catholic case – that they had only had three councillors elected in fifty years in spite of their constituting a quarter of the population; that the new wards would all have a Protestant majority; that experience had shown that Protestants just would not vote for Catholics and that Catholics were deliberately excluded from Council employment.

The Catholic members of the Committee and their Counsel were particularly hard on Sir Samuel Black,[63] the Town Clerk, who was not allowed to forget his indiscreet remark before the 1864 riot commission that he could recognise a Catholic by his face! He was also reminded that on 16 April 1896 Father Laverty (administrator of St Peter's parish) wrote on behalf of the Catholic Committee to ask him to furnish the names and addresses of Catholics in the employment of the Corporation and the wages they earned. Black replied by return to the effect that the only particulars he could furnish were those of wages paid to Catholics, amounting to £18,764 2s 2d. Laverty wrote back immediately, doubting the accuracy of this figure and asking for further particulars, to which Black replied: 'all the hands employed by the corporation are taken on without reference to their religious belief'.[64]

In the witness box Black was unable to square this statement with the precise financial information cited above. Nor was he helped by an admission wrung out of the Lord Mayor (Pirrie) that the Catholics would not be assured of getting a single councillor elected under the new scheme, and that there was not, to his knowledge, a single Catholic contractor employed by the Council. The Catholic lay witnesses (mainly solicitors) claimed that they should have at least two of the fifteen wards.

Eventually, on 19 May 1896, by majority decision, the Select committee suggested to the parties that they would come to an agreement on the question of wards, either by actual division or by instruction to the (Boundary) Commissioners, which would be self-effecting.[65] They were prepared, if necessary, to increase the number of wards to twenty.

The Corporation with alacrity decided to meet a deputation from the Catholic Committee. The latter, on 24 May, selected a deputation of ten persons (excluding Devlin). By 1 June it was clear that the Corporation had capitulated to the Catholic demands. Two wards (Falls and Smithfield) were to be carved out so as to ensure, as far as was possible, a permanent Catholic majority; while in the others they were to have 'considerable influence'.[66] So the Catholic Committee had its way, although more far-sighted observers, such as Devlin[67] regarded their solution as the worst possible arrangement – certain to perpetuate sectarian feeling in the city.

IV. MUNICIPAL POLITICS (1897–1920)

The Belfast Corporation Act of 1896[68] extended the area of the borough from 6,800 to 16,500 acres. The electorate was similarly increased from 39,603 to 47,294. The laborious task of carving out the thirteen new 'Protestant' and two new 'Catholic' wards could not be completed in time to hold fresh elections in the same year. So the first general municipal election since 1887 was held in November 1897.

As the election approached, a distinctly sectarian pattern was discernible in the candidatures. Only Catholic candidates appeared in Falls and Smithfield, and only Protestants in the rest. But the Catholics were sharply divided. In October 1896 the Catholic Association made plans to contest the next municipal election as an independent group, strongly backed by the bishop, Dr Henry, and turned a deaf ear to the protests of Devlin and the older and more prestigious Nationalist leaders that they were in effect playing the Orange game by totally identifying Nationalist politics with Catholicism.[69] The Catholic Association blandly replied that it was concerned with local and municipal issues, which did not at all concern Home Rulers from elsewhere in Ireland, and Dr Henry claimed that the establishment of the Association would avert the 'disgrace' of having the Catholic and Nationalist body represented by 'incompetent men who would make a mess of municipal government'.[70] However, the Association's published programme contained little that was original, apart from a staunch protestation of loyalty to the Church and especially the local bishop.[71]

It soon became clear that the Irish National Federation (the central Nationalist organisation), if only to save its face, would have to nominate candidates for Falls and Smithfield, which it did to a chorus of abuse from the *Irish News* for introducing 'anti-clericalism' and 'factionalism' into the campaign.

The internecine warfare between the Catholic/Nationalists was confined to the wards they had been instrumental in creating. Elsewhere in the city three main groups competed: the Belfast Conservative Association; the Liberal-Unionists, who put up five candidates, including the Lord Mayor, the shipbuilder W. J. Pirrie, and the furrier Otto Jaffé, later to become Belfast's only Jewish Lord Mayor; and the Trades Council which put up six candidates described as 'Labour'.[72] There was also a sprinkling of independent candidatures. The final results were surprising. Nineteen of the 60 seats were uncontested (two independent, two Liberal-Unionist and 16 Conservative), involving three entire wards (Cromac, St Anne's and Windsor) and seven aldermanships. The six Labour and five Liberal-Unionist candidates were all successful, while in Falls and Smithfield the Catholic Association made a clean sweep of the eight seats. The *Irish News*, while rejoicing in the Falls-Smithfield result, claimed also that the six Labour candidates had received solid backing from Catholic voters in their wards.[73] In all the Conservative Association won 33 seats, Liberal-Unionists five, Labour six, Catholic Association eight, and there were eight independents.

If Dr Henry really expected the Catholic representatives of Falls and Smithfield to be given the opportunity to make a mess of local government, he was doomed to disappointment. In the new Corporation the Catholic Association members, allied with Labour, tried to make some impact; but the corporate offices, Lord Mayor, High Sheriff and chairmanships of committees remained firmly in the hands of the Conservatives. Five years after the Catholics were first elected, a candidate in Dock was able to claim that 'they had got a few members on the Corporation, but their wishes were practically ignored, and every proposal they put forward was voted down by the huge majority against them'.[74] Apart from the occasional cooption of a parish priest to the Education Committee, the only concession made to the new groups on the Council was the election, in 1907, of Dr Peter O'Connell, a councillor for Smithfield, to the High Shrievalty – the first and only time a Catholic held this office.[75]

Belfast's municipal history in the early 1900s presents a bizarre contrast between the external trappings of extreme prosperity and damaging allegations of inadequate services and municipal graft. On the one hand, the growing prosperity of the city which the newspapers never ceased to proclaim and which generated a sense of civic pride[76] (in which the Catholics shared as well as their fellow-citizens) was signalised by lavish municipal entertainments by three Lord Mayors, Pirrie (1896–8), Sir Daniel Dixon (1892–4, 1901–4, 1905–7), and the ninth Earl of Shaftesbury (1907–8). But the most important outward sign of Belfast's prosperity was to be the City Hall, 'the great quadrangle of Portland stone, with its corner domelets and soaring dome',[77] decorated with the choicest marbles and alabaster and costing not less than £320,000.

The excessive cost (eventually twice the original estimate)[78] of the City Hall provoked a good deal of hostile criticism, from the auditor from the Local Government Board at Dublin Castle[79] and, less enthusiastically, from the Catholic and Labour councillors. The latter indeed helped to increase the expense by pressing for local contractors for furnishing the City Hall rather than English contractors who submitted lower tenders. Backed by the Trades Council, the Labour councillors helped to keep the rates escalating by pressing for annual increases in the wages of Corporation workers,[80] while the Catholic councillors were less concerned with the size of the municipal cake than the share available for Catholic consumption. In 1911 the Liberal Chief Secretary for Ireland, Augustine Birrell, charged in a public speech that there was only one Catholic in Corporation employment, and he a scavenger. The then Lord Mayor, R. J. McMordie, M.P. for East Belfast, complained in the House of Commons that Birrell's utterance was not only prejudiced but unfair: there were 900 Catholic employees out of 3,700.[81]

The rows over municipal extravagance and defaulting rate-collectors were not, however, the most serious that the Corporation had to experience during those years. The Vice Regal Health Inquiry of 1906 was another grave blow to Belfast's pride. Since Belfast's sanitary history has been dealt with above it should be sufficient to mention here that the 1907 inquiry was visited on the city through representations made to the Chief Secretary, John Bryce, by the leading Liberal, Charles Brett, and Professor Byers of Queen's College, and was also due to the efforts of the Citizens' Association. The latter, an overtly 'non-sectarian and non-political' group, was established in March 1905 by a number of large ratepayers, businessmen and professionals alarmed by the apparent extravagance of the City Council and its inability to provide adequate sanitary services. Dedicated to the goals of competence and economy in administration and merit[82] as the criterion for public appointments, the Association prepared to put up not less than ten candidates for the municipal election of 1907.

This election marked another watershed in Belfast politics

with the collapse of the Catholic Association. This was partly due to the persistent refusal of the new Nationalist leader at Westminster, John Redmond, to recognise it (on the ground that political sectarianism was incompatible with nationalism), partly to a quiet but persistent opposition to Dr Henry by some of his own priests, who continued, in spite of episcopal disapproval, to subscribe to the funds of the United Irish League. The waning popularity of the Association was demonstrated during the municipal election of 1904, when after a narrow victory in Smithfield over a United Irish League (official Nationalist) candidate, a crowd shouted against clerical intimidation and Bishop Henry 'was consigned to a place to which, on the Falls Road at least, King William is supposed to have a prior claim'.[83]

After the Catholic Association agreed to dissolve in May 1905, the ward machinery in Falls and Smithfield was available to the official Nationalist, and Devlin became the 'boss' of the Catholic section of the city.[84]

In the 1907 election the five Citizens' Association candidates succeeded, a result which considerably pleased the *News Letter*,[85] as did the defeat of the two 'Labour Socialists', Walker (who had represented Duncairn since 1904), and Murphy (Dock).[86] The United Irish League made a clean sweep in Falls and Smithfield, and henceforth rather vindictively refused to support the remaining Catholic Association councillors when their term of office expired. The leading casualty was Dr Peter O'Connell, Catholic Association councillor for Smithfield since 1897 and alderman since 1901, who had earlier in the year been elected the first and only Catholic High Sheriff of Belfast. By 1909 the entire representation of the two Catholic wards was in the hands of the followers of Redmond, Dillon and Devlin (now Secretary of the Party).

By 1907, therefore, the Belfast Conservatives had beaten off a challenge from the growing Labour movement and had managed to contain the Catholic/Nationalists within their two carefully constructed wards. A Temperance Party which had put up candidates in 1902 and 1904 had likewise been demolished[87] and the Belfast Protestant Association of Arthur Trew and Tom Sloan sporadically contested elections between 1903 and 1910 but never won any seats.

Apart from the occasional independent councillor, the Citizens' Association appeared to be the only group capable of winning seats from the Conservatives during this period. At their first attempt in 1907 they won five seats; in 1908, seven; in 1909, three, and in 1910 their original five were re-elected. But apart from the fact that they were the only rival group to secure the support of the strongly Unionist *Belfast News Letter*, it is difficult to regard the Citizens as other than a variant of the Conservatives. Even in 1907 two of their successful candidates stood under the joint aegis of the Conservative Association and the Citizens' Association, and in 1908 all but one of the candidatures were joint. In the troubled year, 1911, the group was virtually absorbed by the Conservatives in the new Belfast Unionist Municipal Association, although it maintained a notional independence until 1922 and its representatives (though never opposed by official Unionists) preserved their distinctive label. The best known members of the group were R. J. McMordie, who was elected Unionist M.P. for East Belfast and served as Lord Mayor from 1910 until his death in 1914; Frank Workman of the shipbuilding firm; and W. F. Coates, afterwards Lord Mayor. So completely had they become identified with the Unionist cause that in 1912 McMordie was able to advertise for a non-political and non-sectarian volunteer force, which would plainly be able to take over the policing of the city from the suspect R.I.C., if and when the provisional government should sound the tocsin.[88]

From 1912 to the end of the First World War Belfast Corporation receded from the public eye. The dramatic events centred on the city – the signing of the Ulster Covenant, the formation of the Ulster Volunteer Force, the gun-running from Larne to Belfast, the formation of the Provisional Government under the chairmanship of Lord Carson – all captured the public imagination and municipal affairs were dull by comparison. Annual elections were held for the Corporation until 1916, when local elections were suspended throughout the United kingdom, but Unionist hegemony was virtually unchallenged. The Belfast Labour Party seemed temporarily to disintegrate. After 1911 Labour candidates stood only in the Catholic wards. The only exception was James Connolly (then Belfast organiser of the Irish Transport and General Workers' Union and soon to win a permanent place in the pantheon of Irish heroes by leading the Citizens' Army during the 1916 rising in Dublin), who in 1913 unsuccessfully contested Dock Ward as 'a Labour candidate totally independent of any political party'.[89]

CONCLUSION

Two general observations must be made before passing from the subject of Belfast municipal politics between the reforms of 1897 and the end of the First World War.

(i) The surprising failure of organised labour to make a significant impact on municipal politics. Industrially, labour was quite well organised with 57 unions in 1900 comprising 19,000 members[90] – more than in any other Irish city – yet it never succeeded in improving on the ten per cent of the councillors which were secured at the very first election for the enlarged Corporation. This may have been due partly to the emergence even at this early stage of the divisive tendencies, which on several subsequent occasions nearly wrecked Labour as a political force in Ulster. As early as 1904, when Walker was President of the Irish T.U.C. and the formation of an Irish Labour Party was proposed by Connolly at the annual Congress, Walker successfully proposed an amendment that such an organisation, when founded, would not be autonomous but affiliated to the Labour Representation Committee and a similar resolution was carried (though by a much smaller majority) at the annual Congress of 1911. Walker's attitude was not just that of a cautious Ulster Protestant, anxious not to weaken the ties between the Labour movement in Ulster and its progenitor in Britain; he also argued on grounds of efficiency – the Scottish Labour Party had been singularly unsuccessful until it affiliated to the British Labour Party.[91] But as the decade progressed the tide of nationalism engulfed the Labour movement in the rest of Ireland. The Independent Labour Party of Ireland was founded in spite of Walker in 1912, and four of the five Belfast branches of the Independent Labour Party participated in its formation. Although, as Harbinson says, the Belfast Independent Labour Party was 'broadly, if unofficially in favour of Home Rule', it was highly sensitive to the unpopularity of that policy and Connolly's open-air speeches had to be discontinued after 1912.[92]

So, even under conditions which elsewhere helped to secure direct working-class representation, like the slump of 1908 (caused by a recession in the building and linen trades which involved 15,000 unemployed), it did not work to Labour's advantage in Belfast. Instead, the trade union movement itself, for long immune to the sectarian virus, was affected at that very time with separate unions for Catholic and Protestant female mill-workers.[93]

(ii) Another point worth noting is the number of issues which elsewhere agitated municipal governments during this period, but seemed dormant in Belfast. Education was a particularly glaring example.[94] In the first decade of the century there was considerable controversy as to whether Catholics should attend the new technical college established in 1901, in which there were no Catholic teachers, and the Bishop eventually set up a rival institution in Hardinge Street. Intermediate education aroused little discussion; but primary education was in dire need of local control, partly because nine tenths of the city schools were under church control and the churches, both Protestant and Catholic, had insufficient funds to equip the schools properly and still less to build fresh schools in the greatly overcrowded working-class sectors of the city. Year after year the reports of inspectors from the Board of Education in Dublin complained about gross overcrowding and insanitary conditions in Belfast primary schools – '401 children in a school in Ballymacarrett with proper accommodation for only 209';[95] '70 children packed into a room 17 feet by 9 feet';[96] '65 to 70 per cent of the larger schools in Dublin and Belfast must have conditions which have almost disappeared in England in the last twenty years'.[97]

The remedy was for the Corporation to take the initiative in building new schools, but the Council, dominated by estate agents and apprehensive of a possible increase of as much as 30 per cent on the rates did nothing, and a new generation of the poorest children grew up with education acquired in conditions of maximum discomfort. Although individual councillors like Dr Henry O'Neill, Otto Jaffé and R. J. McConnell, were so disturbed by the social injustice perpetuated by the existing system as to build schools out of their own resources, the only remedy the Corporation could collectively propose was that Belfast be regarded as a congested district which would enable the Council to recoup the full cost of buildings. This would put the proud city of Belfast on a par with the poorest areas of the West of Ireland, and may not have been seriously intended. Not until the end of the First World War did the Corporation propose a Bill to levy an education rate.

Another example of apathy was provided by the failure of the Corporation to anticipate the housing problem which was to bedevil their successors in subsequent decades. This problem came to Belfast later than to most large British cities, because of late industrialisation, cheap land and a plentiful supply of cheap local bricks. During the 1890s and early 1900s speculative builders built even more houses than could be absorbed by the rising population, and by the early 1900s a building slump followed, bankrupting many small builders. Rising wages and prices caused the price of housing to increase sharply, so that by 1910 the Corporation should have been building municipal houses. This, however, was strongly opposed by the great builders and property owners on the Corporation, Sir Daniel Dixon and Sir R. J. McConnell, to whom the idea of municipal competition was most unwelcome. Only one scheme[98] was attempted, and this a scheme of slum clearance – demolishing some 700 houses in the most crowded areas bounded by the Falls, Shankill and York Street areas, and rehousing their occupants. However, the Nationalist councillors, doubtless with electoral considerations in mind, strongly objected to their people being rehoused elsewhere, and the controversy dragged on until the outbreak of war. This controversy revealed the effectiveness of Nationalist opposition to private Bills promoted by Belfast Corporation, since they could call on their parliamentary colleagues at Westminster to defeat legislation of which they disapproved.[99]

NOTES

1. *N.W.*, 6 February 1874.

2. A similar primary-type arrangement existed in some English cities in the 1880s, e.g. Bristol.

3. Johnston resigned from the Orange Order because of its opposition to secret voting (May 1871). However, he returned to the Order and his offices therein within six months.

4. Corry's nomination was strenuously opposed by the Rev. Hugh Hanna, who had founded a Presbyterian Constitutional Association. A rival association (the Belfast Presbyterian Association) in spite of the presence of the then Moderator and his description of true liberalism as 'the application of Christian ethics to secular politics' attracted very few clergymen. (See *N.W.*, 4 February 1874.)

5. *B.N.L.*, 5 February 1874.

6. *B.N.L.*, 6 February 1874.

7. The result was Ewart, 8,132; Corry, 7,683; Seeds, 6,119; J. S. Brown, Liberal (a linen manufacturer, nominated at the last minute), 5,122. For the campaign see especially *N.W.*, 20 March–23 March and *B.N.L.*, 12, 15, 19, 27 March 1880.

8. *N.W.*, 13 March 1880.

9. The direct involvement of the Institution in electioneering may be traced to a Grand Lodge resolution of December 1865, which noted 'with deep concern the continued encroachments of Popery upon our Protestant Constitution' and resolved to bring the full weight of their organisational influence to bear on the constituencies so that 'as many thoroughly Protestant representatives as possible' be elected to the Imperial Parliament. There followed detailed plans to attend to the register, circularise candidates, issue voting instructions to the Brethren, etc. (*Grand Lodge of Ireland Minutes*, 7 December 1865.)

10. Apart from Johnston, many of the leading Belfast Conservatives in this period were also leading Orangemen. Alexander Wilson, Secretary of the Conservative Association in 1880, was also Secretary to the Grand Lodge of Ireland, the most important executive post in the Institution. Prominent councillors, John Lindsay and James Haslett, were also members of the Grand Committee, in 1880 and 1882 respectively.

11. The electorate of Belfast was increased from 21,000 to 30,368. The city was divided into four single-seat constituencies, North, South, East and West.

12. See *B.N.L.*, 23, 26 October 1885.

13. T. M. Healy (South Derry), William Redmond (Fermanagh), William O'Brien (Tyrone), Justin McCarthy (Newry), Thomas Sexton (Belfast West). For a description of the national campaign, see D. C. Savage, 'The Origins of the Ulster Unionist Party, 1885–6', *Irish Historical Studies*, XII (March 1961), 185–208.

14. *B.N.L.*, 23 November 1885.

15. Apart from the two university seats in Dublin. The 86 seats won in 1886 may seem more spectacular, but one seat (Londonderry) was won on petition.

16. See Savage, op. cit.

17. The famous meeting at which Lord Randolph Churchill predicted that 'Ulster will fight and Ulster will be right' and delivered the less memorable quatrain: 'Sail on, O Ship of State, Sail on O Union great. Shall Ulster from Britain sever? By the God Who made us – never!' was held in the Ulster Hall, 22 February 1886. It was an exclusively Conservative/Orange occasion.

18. *N.W.*, 27 May 1886.

19. Cf. David Bleakley, 'Trade union beginnings in Belfast and district, with special reference to 1881–1900' (unpublished M.A. thesis, Queen's University, Belfast, 1956) pp. 85–6 for the background to this dispute.

20. It had been founded secretly in May 1885. Several attempts were made in this year (1886) to create a mass organisation for Irish Unionists. The Loyal Irish Union had disappeared soon after its electoral débâcle in December 1885. But in addition to the Irish Loyal and Patriotic Union there was also the Ulster Loyal Anti-Repeal Committee and the North-west Loyal Registration and Electoral Association. All these were afterwards subsumed in the Ulster Unionist Council.

21. Although Labour candidates stood in municipal elections as early as 1897. For the Catholic and Ratepayers' Associations see below, pp. 120–4.

22. Sloan first won the seat in a by-election after William Johnston's death in 1902 – his official Unionist opponent was a Fellow of All Souls, C. W. Dunbar-Buller.

23. Professor J. W. Boyle in Beckett and Glasscock, *Belfast*, pp. 132–43, argues that the general election of 1906, in which the founder of the Belfast Labour Party, William Walker (with Ramsay MacDonald as election agent), reduced his Unionist opponent's majority to 300 and Sloan won South by a majority of 800 was 'the strongest challenge to official Unionism in Belfast's political history' (p. 135). But Boyle overstates his case. The Labour support quickly evaporated in East; and Sloan was a political freak, an extreme Orangeman who left the Order because it was not sufficiently anti-Catholic and then teamed up in the 'Independent Orange Order' with Lindsay Crawford, a landowner with Home Rule leanings. However, by 1908 Crawford was expelled from the Independent Order and Sloan, succeeding him as Imperial Grand Master, in Boyle's admission, 'soon reverted to his original sectarian policy' (p. 137). It is worth noting, however, that Walker in his first attempt at Parliamentary honours (a by-election in North Belfast in 1905) felt constrained to answer in the affirmative a number of anti-Catholic questions put to him by the Belfast Protestant Association (Sloan's organisation), including the crucial question whether he would place the interests of Protestantism before those of the political party to which he belonged. See O. Dudley Edwards, *The Sins of Our Fathers*, pp. 156–9.

24. See his speech at a banquet in honour of Joseph Chamberlain at the National Liberal Club, 8 March 1892. (*B.N.L.*, 9 March 1892.)

25. All these facts were beyond question and the only difficulty in interpreting them came when Belfast chose to speak for the whole province of

Ulster, in which there was a small Catholic majority, supporters of Parnell and his successor, John Redmond.

26. There were slight recessions in 1854, 1857 and 1867. See D. L. Armstrong, 'Social and Economic Conditions in the Belfast Linen Industry, 1850–1900', *Irish Historical Studies*, VII (September 1951), 235–69.

27. 'From just over 1,000 tons in 1850, and less than 14,000 tons in 1880, output had reached 100,000 gross tons per annum in the 1890s and 150,000 tons per annum in the first decade of the twentieth century.' W. E. Coe, *The Engineering Industry of the North of Ireland*, p. 91. The labour force increased from 900 in 1865 to 9,000 in 1900 (see above, p. 74). By 1900 Workman and Clark had 4,000 men employed.

28. Owen, *History of Belfast*, p. 403, lists 83 separate industries existing in Belfast at the time of writing (1920).

29. Up to 1914 there was a much greater differential between the wage rates for skilled men and labourers in Belfast (and Ireland generally) than in Britain. The influx of cheap labour from the rural areas forced down labourers' wages in the towns, but skilled labour was always scarce. Wages for semi-skilled workers approximated to those of labourers rather than skilled workers. The differential between labourers' and skilled workers' wages was sometimes as high as 300 per cent. Cf. Coe, *The Engineering Industry of the North of Ireland*, p. 178.

30. Coe, op. cit., p. 173. The annual rate of construction increased from 1,000 (1850) to 4,000 (1900).

31. Cf. E. Jones and C. E. Brett in Beckett and Glasscock, *Belfast*, pp. 113–15, and 120–29, for details of Belfast housing developments, 1850–1900.

32. The list given by Brett, op. cit., pp. 121–2, includes the Courthouse (1850), Queen's Bridge (1843), Custom House (1857), Water Office (1869), Ulster Hall (1865), and the town halls (1871 and 1906).

33. Two pamphlets, *Report on the Sanitary State of Belfast* (1848), and Dr A. G. Malcolm, *The Sanitary State of Belfast, with suggestions for its improvement* (1852). Almost the only item on the credit side, in Malcolm's opinion, was the establishment of public baths and washhouses in 1847. But these, although the first in Ireland, owed more to pressure from the Society for the Amelioration of the Conditions of the Working Classes (another short-lived group) than to the initiative of the Corporation. See above, p. 69, nn. 69, 72.

34. Ibid., p. 17. McCormac pioneered some techniques in the treatment of tuberculosis. His pamphlet *Moral-Sanatory (sic) Economy* (1853) gives a harrowing picture of living conditions in the poorest quarters of Belfast. For a brief biographical account, see Sir Ian Fraser, 'Father and Son – A Tale of Two Cities', *Ulster Medical Journal*, XXXVII (Winter 1968), pp. 1–12.

35. Much expert advice was sought by the Corporation. Professor Letts Smith of Queen's College, Belfast, was brought in as a consultant, but took ten years to give an opinion!

36. In *Truth* (November 1896), Labouchère wrote of the *Report*: 'The

whole document constitutes about the most damning indictment of a municipal body that I have ever read.' See *Report of the Special Committee appointed by the Corporation on the 1st August, 1896* (reprinted by Belfast Citizens' Association, 1896).

37. The Commissioners found that in contrast to most other towns the mean annual mortality from typhoid actually increased – by 50 per cent – between 1891 and 1900, and reached its peak, two per 1,000, in 1898. *Report of Belfast Health Commission* (1908).

38. Ibid. This was partly due to the appointment in 1890 of a medical officer who was not only inadequately qualified but also elderly. When the post fell vacant in 1906 another local man, Dr H. Baillie, was appointed in preference to several better-qualified candidates. But in spite of (or perhaps because of) the public furore over his appointment Dr Baillie proved a competent and energetic administrator. See below, p. 133, n. 82.

39. *City Hall Records. L.G.B. Inquiry into Purdysburn Fever Hospital and operation of small dwellings Acts* (22 March 1911).

40. Cf. R. M. W. Strain, *Belfast and Its Charitable Society*, Chapters XI–XIV, for a detailed account of the Charitable Society's role in providing a water supply between 1800 and 1840.

41. The first ten Commissioners were (according to the usual custom) nominated. Thenceforward two Commissioners retired annually and elections, when contested, were settled by those paying water rate within the rated area. The only significant qualifications for membership of the Board were residence in Belfast and annual payment of not less than thirty shillings in water rate. (In 1885 the number was increased from ten to fifteen, and two *ex-officio* Commissioners were added.) Incidentally, the Charitable Society was allowed £5,000 to cover any debts arising out of the water supply and also given an annuity of £800 and free water 'for ever'. For the history of the Belfast Water Board see J. Loudan, *In Search of Water* (Belfast, 1940).

42. At this time Manchester was constructing a waterworks to supply 30 million gallons daily, and in Glasgow a similar project with a daily output of 50 million gallons was being undertaken.

43. One of its provisions was that the mayor and Chairman of the Harbour Board were to serve on the Water Board *ex officio*.

44. Cf. Loudan, *In Search of Water*, p. 57.

45. Cf. *Report of the Irish Boundary Commission, 1925*, edited by G. J. Hand, (Shannon, 1969), Chapter 5, p. 133.

46. Cf. R. J. Lawrence, *Water Supply in Northern Ireland: Organisation and Administration* (The British Waterworks Association, 1969).

47. See below, Chapter 5.

48. A note in the private papers of the Transport manager reveals some interesting facts concerning the religious distribution of the tramway employees in 1912. The following are the Catholic proportions: 1 in 20 clerks, 1 in 9 traffic inspectors, 46 of 255 motormen, 59 of 262 conductors, 1 in 5 shop foremen, 28 of 288 engine shop workmen. (We owe this information to Mrs Sybil Baker.)

49. Cf. *Municipal Year Book, 1965–1966*, p. 121.
50. Owen, *History of Belfast*, p. 246.
51. Between 1878 and 1896, 857 previously private streets were handed over to the Corporation and 'sewered and paved'. *P.P., 1896*, VIII, 459. The Act of 1865 had empowered the Council to subsidise the construction of sewers by private landlords.
52. The Commissioners' report is called the Exham Report, although he died before it was completed.
53. Cf. *N.W.*, 3 July 1882, for hostile criticism of the alleged partiality of the Commissioners towards the Town Council.
54. See above, p. 110.
55. The local electorate was quadrupled – from about 5,700.
56. With the addition of the Deramore estate (about 700 acres), making a total of 15,815 acres.
57. See *I.N.*, 31 October 1895.
58. Devlin was then manager of a public house, owned by Sam Young, a Protestant Home Ruler and M.P. for East Cavan.
59. The last Catholic councillor (the third) had died in 1878.
60. Devlin's objection to Knox was related to the current internal struggle within the Home Rule party. Devlin was an ardent Redmondite, Knox a supporter of Healy.
61. For Minutes of Evidence, see *P.P., 1896*, VIII, pp. 301–597.
62. Such as the objection of Lord Deramore (whose demesne had been exempted from police tax by the Act of 1847) and the Harbour Commissioners, who enjoyed a similar exemption and, in fact, paved and lighted two streets.
63. 1830–1910: probably more important than any member of the Council after 1850. Articled to John Bates in 1848, Councillor for St George's, 1859–71, appointed Town Solicitor in 1871 and Town Clerk in 1878, retired 1909. See above, p. 83.
64. *P.P., 1896*, VIII, pp. 332–3.
65. *P.P., 1896*, VIII, p. 291.
66. *I.N.*, 2 June 1896.
67. Cf. *Joseph Devlin and the Catholic Representation Association of Belfast, 1895–1905* (unpublished paper by F. J. Whitford, Queen's University, Belfast, Library).
68. The fifteen wards were each to elect three councillors and an alderman. One third of the councillors were to be re-elected annually and half the aldermen every three years.
    By the Irish Local Government Act (1898) Belfast was constituted a County Borough and the Council became entitled to appoint a High Sheriff, a post which came to rank next to Lord Mayor in the municipal hierarchy.
69. In a letter to John Dillon (see above, p. 90) Devlin wrote: 'If we are beaten in this fight, it practically means the extinction of nationality in Belfast, if not in Ulster. If we triumph, it will be a great blow for civil and religious liberty, as well as a powerful argument in favour of Home Rule.' (Devlin to Dillon, 26 July 1897.) We owe this to the kindness

of Mr F. J. Whitford. The standard biography of Dillon, by Professor
F. S. L. Lyons, is silent on this matter.

70. *I.N.*, 11, 23 November 1897.
71. *I.N.*, 11 November 1897.
72. The Belfast Trades Council was established in 1881 (affiliated to the
T.U.C. in 1882), and tried to avoid politics generally, especially sectarian
politics, in the post-1886 period. Alexander Bowman, its first Secretary,
was forced to resign for actively espousing Home Rule (see above, p.
105). In 1891 a branch of the I.L.P. was founded by William Walker,
Belfast's first socialist, and after some initial reluctance the Trades
Council agreed to join forces and in 1897 'United Trades and Labour
Council' candidates were backed by both groups.
73. *I.N.*, 26 November 1897. These wards were: Court, Shankill, St
George's, Victoria, Duncairn and Pottinger. The successful candidate
in St George's also stood unsuccessfully in Dock – where, incidentally,
two Catholic Association candidates were badly beaten in separate
contests.
74. *B.N.L.*, 16 January 1902.
75. Labour councillors (apart from Robert Gageby, the Shankill representative) were frequently the objects of ridicule by the Conservative press –
one because he attended Corporation meetings in dungarees.
76. Cf. *B.N.L.*, 12 September 1899: 'We Belfast people are proud of our
city and its many activities. We are in the very front in the race of civic
development and industrial progress, and we have a laudable ambition
to keep there, and make our mark as it were.'
77. C. E. Brett in Beckett and Glasscock, *Belfast*, pp. 129–30.
78. The first Act, passed in 1890, authorised £30,000 for the site and £180,000
for the building: a second Act in 1899 granted another £30,000; a
third in 1902, £50,000, and a fourth in 1905, £40,000.
79. At a special inquiry into the cost of City Hall, the inspector, on learning
that the foundation stone cost £500, said sardonically: 'It is a precious
stone, I suppose?' *City Hall Records: L.G.B. Inquiry (1905)*.
80. In the 1900s Corporation labourers were paid on average three shillings
a week more than their counterparts in private employment. The tram
and gas managers were paid £500 more than in any other British
city.
81. The official Unionist reply, however, helped to bear out the original
Catholic contention. Of the total wage bill £292,430 went to Protestant
employees, £53,728 to Catholic.
82. In 1906 the City Council appointed Dr H. W. Baillie as Medical
Officer of Health (see above, p. 131). This aroused great feeling in the
city, since Baillie was a Conservative alderman who resigned to be
eligible for the post and was poorly qualified besides. The Irish Local
Government Board deplored the appointment, and the *Lancet* wrote
scornfully (13 October 1906) that Belfast needed 'a school of ethics
at which all would-be councillors, and we must add, aldermen, should
be compelled to procure a diploma before practising on the public as
members of the Council'.

83. *B.N.L.*, 16 January 1904.
84. A disgruntled remnant of the Catholic Association established in 1905 a new body, the Catholic Defence Society, which vainly contested the municipal elections of 1907, 1908 and 1909. It received the *coup de grâce* in the Westminster election of December 1910, when its Secretary, P. J. Magee, stood and secured 75 votes to Devlin's 4,651.
85. *B.N.L.*, 16 January 1907. 'We look forward with confidence now to a healthier spirit altogether inside the City Council.'
86. Walker had been leading a frontal attack on Nance, the manager of the Tramways Company, on account of his refusal to employ union labour). Subsequently Walker failed, in spite of several attempts, to return to the Council.
87. In spite of strong support from Presbyterian clergymen, one of whom said that he would vote for a Home Ruler if he were a temperance man. However, the influence of the temperance movement was indirectly felt in that receptions at City Hall were sometimes strictly teetotal.
88. It is worth mentioning that G. R. Black, a Citizens' candidate, stood unsuccessfully in 1910 against a Conservative in St Anne's. Thirty-two years later the same Mr Black, then an alderman for Duncairn, was elected Lord Mayor for the year when the Corporation was superseded by Commissioners (see below, p. 154).
89. Connolly (1864–1916) founded the Socialist Republican Party of Ireland (never exceeding 200 members) in 1896, and from 1901 consistently advocated the formation of an All-Ireland Labour Party. In 1909 he became the Belfast organiser of the newly formed I.T.G.W.U. and until 1914 frequently held public meetings advocating the unpopular cause of socialism and the still more unpopular cause, Home Rule. Cf. J. F. Harbinson, 'A History of the Northern Ireland Labour Party, 1891–1949', (unpublished M.Sc.Econ. thesis, Queen's University, Belfast), p. 30.
90. Cf. J. D. Clarkson, *Labour and Nationalism in Ireland* (New York, 1925), pp. 207 ff.
91. A controversy between Walker and Connolly on the merits of national and international approaches to socialism ran in the issues of *Forward* (May–June 1911). Walker's consistent support of the British connection was rewarded by a seat on the National Executive of the Labour Party and an invitation to contest Leith Burghs in the first general election of 1910. At the polls Walker secured 2,724 votes to the Conservative's 4,540 and the Liberal's 7,146.
92. Harbinson, op. cit., p. 31. In 1912 Walker was appointed an insurance inspector and played no further part in politics.
93. Another complication was that after the dock workers' strike (engineered by Connolly in 1907), the unskilled labourers began to form unions and seek representation on the Trades Council, and immediately the traditional hostility of the skilled craftsman for the labourer was reinforced by the religious cleavage.
94. The controversy about the incorporation of Queen's College, Belfast, as a separate University following the abolition of the Royal University

of Ireland in 1908 is not discussed here, since it was a national rather than a local issue. See T. W. Moody and J. C. Beckett, *Queen's Belfast, 1845–1949: the History of a University* (London, 1959), Vol. 1.

95. *72nd Report of the Commissioners of National Education in Ireland* 1905–6 (Cd. 3154), p. 16.

96. *1st Report of the Vice-Regal Committee of Enquiry into Primary Education in Ireland*, 1913 (Cd. 6829), Minutes of Evidence, p. 35.

97. *Report of H.M. Inspector of Schools on Primary Education in Ireland*, 1904 (Cd. 1901), p. 2.

98. The first houses actually erected at ratepayers' expense were not put up until 1917.

99. Similarly, between 1908 and 1910, to the intense annoyance of the Unionists, Devlin was able to insist on the purchase price of the Cavehill tramway being reduced and a new recreation ground thrown in as the conditions for allowing the Belfast Corporation (Tramways) Bill through the Commons. (See *I.N.*, 13 February 1908; *B.N.L.*, 4 March 1908.)

5 1920 and After

On 11 March 1919 the British Government, through its law
officers for Ireland, formally introduced in the Commons a
bill entitled the Local Government (Ireland) Bill. Its proximate
cause was the fact that the suspensory Acts of 1916, 1917 and
1918, prolonging the lives of the existing local authorities, were
shortly due to expire. The local authorities were either four or
five years old and were in grave need of renewal.[1] To hold
fresh elections under the existing system would not, of course,
require new legislation, but as the Attorney-General for
Ireland[2] indicated in his speech opening the second reading
debate, the Government was taking advantage of this opportunity to introduce proportional representation as the mode of
election for Irish local authorities 'in view of the dissatisfaction
which largely prevails in the country'.[3]

This was indeed an understatement. The election of December 1918 had resulted in a complete polarisation of the Irish
representation, with the 73 Sinn Fein members constituting
themselves a separate parliament in Dublin (the first Dáil) and
the 26 Ulster Unionists, plus a few survivors of the old Nationalist Party (of which Joe Devlin became the effective leader)
remaining at Westminster.[4] The Government was vacillating
between 'ineffective repression and half-hearted attempts at
conciliation',[5] of which the Black and Tan incursion later
in the year exemplified the first and the Local Government
Bill the second.

The ostensible reason given for the electoral innovation was
the success of the Hare method of P.R. in securing adequate
minority representation in the Sligo borough[6] election of 1918
at almost the same time as the Sinn Fein landslide. The *Irish
Times*, the organ of minority opinion, pronounced it a complete
success. It was hoped that the application of the same principle

to local elections would blunt the edge of Sinn Fein success in the three provinces and Unionist success in Ulster.[7]

The Bill was one of the least debated major constitutional measures ever introduced for Ireland. A brief second reading debate, an unreported committee stage, two fresh amendments and a third reading, all on the same day; and that was all.[8] English members did not bother to attend (to Devlin's intense annoyance), except to rush in whenever the division bells rang. But in spite of its brevity, the debate clearly shows that the proposed change was not to the liking of the Ulster Unionists. On the second reading Major Hugh O'Neill[9] proposed an amendment excluding P.R. from the Bill, since the system was not in use in England, and he saw no reason why Ireland should be made the subject of an experiment. Sir Edward Carson also opposed it, partly because he claimed it was unintelligible, partly because the Unionists were not consulted.[10] On both the second and the third readings the entire Ulster Unionist complement in the House voted against the Bill. The Bill speedily passed through the Lords and became law on 3 June 1919.

The Act provided that the Irish Local Government Board be required by order to divide the boroughs into wards containing not less than six members apiece and equal in population. However, borough councils were enabled within three months of the passing of the Act to submit schemes of their own for the

TABLE 5.1

Distribution of Seats between New Wards for the Belfast Municipal Election 1920 (P.R.)

Ward	Aldermen	Councillors	Total
Cromac	2	5	7
Duncairn	2	5	7
Falls	1	5	6
Ormeau	1	5	6
Pottinger	1	5	6
St Anne's	2	4	6
Shankill	2	6	8
Victoria	2	5	7
Woodvale	2	5	7
	15	45	60

approval of the Local Government Board. In spite of the tur-
moil which gripped the whole of Ireland during this year, only
three of the six county borough councils and five borough
councils subject to the order failed to submit a scheme within
the prescribed time.[11]

Belfast Corporation submitted a scheme dividing the city
into nine wards, co-extensive with the nine parliamentary
divisions established by the Representation of the People Act,
1918. The allocation of seats is shown in Table 5.1.

The Act also repealed the provisions of the Municipal
Corporations (Ireland) Act 1840, prescribing that one half of
the aldermen should go out of office every third year and one
third of the councillors annually. Henceforth aldermen and
councillors would serve for an equal term (three years) and the
aldermen would be those candidates who were first elected in
every ward.[12]

The campaign in Belfast did not get under way until after
Christmas 1919; but by 6 January not less than 147 candidates
were nominated for the 60 seats. Apart from Unionists and
Nationalists, the Belfast Labour Party (which mounted 22
candidates), Sinn Fein, Labour Unionists,[13] independent
Unionists and Independent Labour candidates appeared. The
newspapers paid far more attention to the campaign than had
been their wont during the pre-war elections, and candidates'
speeches and manifestoes were prominently reported. The main
Unionist concern as voiced by the *News Letter*, was to ensure that
'The Unionists and Protestants of Belfast' . . . would 'vote the
party ticket straight'[14] and not waste their lower preferences
on any but Unionist Labour candidates (whose loyalty,
unlike that of their more Socialist colleagues, was already
proved). Apart from the dangers of the new electoral system –
the *News Letter* hinted darkly at an electoral deal between
Sinn Fein and the B.L.P. – the issues raised were the familiar
ones of sound businesslike management of the city's affairs,
the provision of new schools, and the 1910 housing scheme
which was still hanging fire.[15] The women's vote was very much
wooed during this election and half a dozen women candidates
appeared.

Polling day was on 15 January but the results were not
available until three days later. Out of 135,548 voters on the

register, 89,031 polled, a turnout of 65·7 per cent, well above the norm for local elections. The results in detail are given in Table 5.2.

TABLE 5.2

Distribution of First Preference Votes and of Seats Won for the Belfast Municipal Election 1920 (P.R.)

	1st Pref.	Percentage	Seats in Proportion	Seats Won
Official Unionists	40,907	45·95	27·6	29
Off. Lab. Un.	4,699	5·28	3·1	6
Ind. Unionist	4,167	4·68	2·8	2
B.L.P.	12,768	14·34	8·6	10
Nat. Amalgamated Union of Labour	1,138	1·28	0·8	0
Ind. Lab.	3,007	3·37	2·0	2
Nat.	10,758	12·08	7·3	5
Sinn Fein	7,120	8·00	4·8	5
Ind.*	4,467	5·02	3·0	1
TOTAL:	89,031	100·00	60·0	60

* The Independent was an Independent Labour candidate in St Anne's

Faced with these results in which a Unionist block of 52 councillors was reduced to 29 – apart from the six Labour Unionists and the two independent Unionists, it was not surprising that the partisan newspapers drew different conclusions. To the *Irish News* the results were a 'death-blow to the Unionist clique',[16] while the *News Letter* ascribed these 'frankly disappointing results'[17] to a combination of apathy among Unionist voters, successful socialist propaganda against a Council that had served overlong, and the pernicious effects of the new electoral system.[18]

The results produced a council more balanced politically and socially than before or since. A Unionist councillor was returned for the Falls Ward (together with two Sinn Fein, two Nationalists, and one Labour), a Nationalist alderman in Victoria, and only in Cromac, Ormeau, St Anne's and Woodvale did the official Unionists secure a majority of seats. The background characteristics of councillors were much more diversified than on pre-war councils. In 1901, 55 out of 60 were upper middle or middle class (Classes I and II), and a

mere five from the working classes. In 1914 the proportions
were slightly altered (50 to 10). In 1920, however, the upper
classes could mount only 31, and the 19 from Classes III and
IV included the largest single occupational group on the
Council – 10 trade union officials.[19] The long interval since the
previous election, more than the new system of voting, had
removed the great names of the past, McConnell, Jaffé,
Pirrie. The new Council, however, had some well-known figures
– Sir James Johnston (St Anne's), (Lord Mayor 1917–19), Sir
Crawford McCullagh (Cromac), (Lord Mayor 1914–16),
W. F. Coates (Ormeau), Patrick Dempsey (Duncairn), and
Mrs McMordie (Pottinger).[20] Among the new members were
Denis McCullough, Sinn Fein councillor for Falls and the leader
of the Irish Republican Brotherhood, Sam Kyle, Labour
alderman for Shankill, the future leader of the N.I.L.P. in the
House of Commons, and Thomas Gibson Henderson, indepen-
dent Unionist councillor for Shankill, who was to serve for
longer on the Council than any one in its history – 50 years.[21]

It is worth examining the voting statistics to see whether the
charge of cross-voting alleged by the *News Letter* and frequently
repeated by their spokesmen can be sustained. Very little
contemporary analysis is to be found, apart from the P.R.
Society pamphlets produced mainly by John H. Humphreys.
Nor were the details of the counts reproduced by the local
press.[22] A glance at Table 5.2 will show, however, that all the
Unionist groups secured a premium of seats, that the Belfast
Labour Party did likewise, and that the official Nationalists
(who were rarely the recipients of lower preferences) fared
worst.[23]

II. THE ESTABLISHMENT OF NORTHERN IRELAND

The Hare method of Proportional Representation had indeed
secured one of the objectives – well-balanced local authorities –
which its parliamentary sponsors had envisaged, but only in
Ulster. While Londonderry Corporation and Tyrone and
Fermanagh County Councils were returned with Nationalist
majorities, Sinn Fein had virtually a clean sweep of the
authorities in the rest of the country. The polarisation was as
great as ever.

Once again municipal politics were submerged by great national events. The guerrilla tactics of the I.R.A. in the three provinces during the spring and summer of 1920 showed that, backed by a sympathetic population they could wreck the administration of the country. The policy of repression by the auxiliary forces (or 'Black and Tans') was effective only in deepening the hostility of the ordinary population. But the I.R.A. could not hope for such favourable conditions in Ulster. Instead they relied upon daring but sporadic sorties on police and military barracks and an ill-fated boycott of Belfast goods operative from the summer of 1920. To these moves the British Government retaliated by setting up a new force for the defence of Ulster, the armed special constabulary[24] (established in November 1920), who were predictably almost entirely Protestant, and by accepting the principle of separating the six northern counties from the rest of Ireland. They decided in September 1920 to set up two regional governments with identical powers, greater in substance than earlier Home Rule Acts had conferred. However, Irish nationalist aspirations would no longer be satisfied with such qualified autonomy. The Parliament of Northern Ireland did come into existence in May 1921; the Parliament of Southern Ireland was still-born; the Truce of July 1921 was followed by the Anglo-Irish Treaty of December 1921, which conferred dominion status on the whole of Ireland but allowed the Northern Ireland Parliament to opt out within one month of April 1922 – a right which was duly exercised. Partition was complete.

Even before the establishment of the new semi-autonomous state, sectarian violence had made an unwelcome return to Belfast. The Sinn Fein representatives on the City Council made no attempt to participate in its activities, the I.R.A. raids grew more daring, and inevitably strong speeches were made during the 12 July processions against the 'disloyal' and 'rebellious' element in their midst. Starting with the victimisation of Catholic workers in the shipyard an intermittent campaign of arson and intimidation of Belfast Catholics lasted from the summer of 1920 until the spring of 1922 when the new Unionist Government was able to exert its control.[25] The cause of the minority was scarcely helped by a boycott of Belfast goods elsewhere in Ireland, with which the I.R.A. retaliated to the riots. On their part, the Catholics firmly believed that a number of murders of their coreligionists were committed by the new forces of law and order, the B Specials.

In such an environment the P.R. system failed to exercise its normally fissiparous effects. At the elections for the new House of Commons in May 1921 the Unionists secured 40 seats (their highest total) and the remaining 12 seats were divided between Nationalists and Sinn Fein[26] who, though violently disagreeing on political objectives, agreed on taking no part in the proceedings of the new subordinate Parliament.

The new Government, unhampered by opposition, proceeded energetically with its task of setting up a viable political system. Housed in the City Hall, which Belfast Corporation immediately offered for its use, the Government passed three measures which ensured its control over the local authorities and the peace preserving forces – apart from the British armed forces. A Special Powers Act virtually enabled the Minister of Home Affairs to suspend the right to *habeas corpus* and arrest and detain without trial. A new regular police force, the Royal Ulster Constabulary, was set up, the Special Constabulary was brought under its control, and the local government electoral law was altered again – P.R. was to be replaced by the majority system, boroughs were to revert to the pre-1919 wards, and counties were to present fresh schemes. Urban local elections were to take place in 1923 and rural elections in 1924.

There can be little doubt that this last measure was in breach of the spirit, if not the letter, of the Government of Ireland Act and it is interesting that it was the only Act passed by the Northern Ireland Parliament from which the royal assent was withheld – between July and September 1922 – just before the fall of the Lloyd George Government. However, from the Unionist point of view it was essential to regain control of the authorities of West Ulster, three of which – Londonderry, Tyrone and Fermanagh – had already opted to join the Irish Free State.

The draconian measures soon resulted in the restoration of comparative peace. In March 1922 the heads of the two new Irish Governments met for the first time, in London. Michael Collins, chairman of the Provisional Government[27] of the Irish Free State, arranged with Sir James Craig, Prime Minister of

Northern Ireland, to call off the Belfast boycott in return for a guarantee that the Northern Ireland Government would protect the interests of the Catholic/Nationalist minority. The Ulster Government used the special powers ruthlessly, and by summer 1922 the rioting had ended in Belfast, although peace was not generally restored until the following year.

These riots differed from the earlier (though not the most recent) riots in being sporadic and individually of short duration, but extending over a period of two years. The overwhelmingly Protestant shipyard and the largely Catholic docks were the focal point of the disturbances; but they were liable to occur in any area of East or West Belfast where the two religious groups were found in uneasy proximity. Sometimes they were sparked off by an isolated incident, like the shooting of an Ulster Unionist M.P., W. J. Twaddell (in June 1922)[28] or by a fusillade of bullets at a funeral procession. The objective, however, was in some respects similar to 1886 – to drive the Catholics more and more into the Falls Road ghetto. There is no reliable estimate of the number of houses burnt or the number of householders forced to flee, but the total number of deaths was 544, of whom nearly 232 occurred in 1922.

The riots of 1920–22, a sustained attack on the Catholic population of Belfast, have been described as 'far more terrifying than all the disturbances of the nineteenth century'.[29]

III. 1923–45

After 1923, when the Northern Ireland Government showed itself strong enough to repel attacks from beyond the border, and still more after 1925, when the Boundary Commission report recommending minimal territorial adjustments was suppressed and an agreement signed between the Governments in London, Dublin and Belfast recognising the *status quo*, it became clear that the new political system would be more durable than its framers dared to hope. This marked a notable change in the role of the city. Belfast was no longer merely the second city in Ireland: it was the capital of a self-governing province with some of the trappings of sovereignty. A palladian Parliament building was constructed at Stormont on the

Castlereagh Hills just outside the city boundary and lavishly decorated with marble and alabaster, as the City Hall had been thirty years before. The Parliament Building was intended to house both legislature and executive, but before long extra buildings had to be erected to accommodate the growing ministerial departments. Stormont Castle became the official residence of the Prime Minister, and Hillsborough Castle, ten miles outside Belfast, the former residence of the Downshire family became the official residence of the Governor of Northern Ireland. A building was erected in Chichester Street to accommodate the new Supreme Court of Northern Ireland and the public records. The new functionaries, both elected and permanent, were all politically homogeneous. The Governor was a leading Unionist peer, the judges were also Unionists; the civil servants were either Ulster-born of Unionist leanings or new arrivals from Whitehall[30] ready to accept and work the system as best they could.

But the existence of an indigenous one-party system of government plus a complaisant civil service did not necessarily mean that Belfast was better off than in pre-war days. The economy had taken a sharp downward turn after the end of the World War. Indeed, a major strike in the shipbuilding and engineering industry had occurred in 1919, not long before the recrudescence of sectarian riots. The recession did not begin in earnest until 1931, when monetary difficulties substantially reduced the flow of international trade and the shipbuilding and engineering industries for the first time were unable to find export markets.

The fall in world trade caused a continual decline in the Belfast shipbuilding industry; the number of employees dwindled from 20,000 in 1924 to 2,000 in 1933. The linen industry enjoyed a temporary boom in the early 1920s, but this too petered out and by 1930 there were 20,000 *unemployed* linen workers in Belfast.

For the textile industry the late 1920s and 1930s were 'a succession of depressions followed by partial recoveries'.[31] By 1938 more than half the labour force was unemployed. Subsequently, it became clear that exactly a hundred years after linen had supplanted cotton in Belfast it would likewise succumb to competition from mass-produced cotton and synthetic fibres. The linen industry never regained its pre-war position.

The engineering industry made a slow recovery. Shipbuilding regained the 1929 level only at the very outbreak of war. But engineering became diversified. Heating and ventilating equipment, electric motors and boilers and (after 1937) aircraft construction, supplemented the traditional textile machinery, still the major source of output.

The first depression suffered by Belfast resulted in a spectacular increase in the number of unemployed, which continued at a high level right through the 1920s and 1930s. The peak years were 1925, 1931 and 1938, when nearly 25 per cent of the insured population were out of work.

The domestic policy of the first Unionist Government was largely conditioned by these harsh economic realities. Essentially it consisted in attempting to ensure parity of social services, particularly unemployment assistance, with the rest of the United Kingdom in spite of a much lower per capita yield of personal taxation – £3 4s. 0d. as against £7 5s. 0d. in Britain in 1924. After long and tortuous negotiations this principle was conceded in 1929.[32]

While attempting to extract from Whitehall the acceptance of the principle of parity with its implication that British subsidies would be available if the taxable capacity of the Province were unable to maintain the services up to the appropriate standards, the Northern Ireland Government also brought pressure to bear on the local authorities to do *their* part in bridging the gap between British and Irish social services. Two policy areas were of particular importance – housing and education – and in no area more so than in Belfast.

Belfast Corporation, its Unionist majority comfortably restored after the abolition of P.R. in 1922,[33] might have been expected to form much more friendly relations with the new Unionist establishment than in pre-war days with Dublin Castle remote and under Liberal-Nationalist influence. Ironically, however, the first major development after 1921 – the city housing scheme – was the occasion of a serious clash with the provincial government and the first major municipal scandal since 1855.

When the Local Government (Ireland) Act came into

operation in 1919 the Corporation was obliged to prepare its own housing scheme. They accordingly set up a Housing Committee of fourteen under the chairmanship of Sir Crawford McCullagh, ex-Lord Mayor; with Councillor T. E. McConnell, a member of the well-known family of estate agents, vice-chairman. A Housing department was established in the Town Solicitor's office and the usual staff of valuers and agents appointed. When the scheme[34] was eventually prepared, the Corporation decided to construct most of the houses by direct labour under the city surveyor's department, and the rest by outside contractors.

The scheme proceeded without attracting public attention until March 1925 when the auditor of the new Ministry of Local Government wrote to the Corporation, complaining that they were purchasing building materials, without advertising for tenders as required by the Acts. After a certain amount of wrangling the Council then asked two independent accountants to report on the purchase of building materials for the first six months of 1925. The report showed deficiences in quality and quantity in respect of the timber charged for in the accounts and also found that out of £13,977 paid in that period, £5,171 10s was overpaid. The investigators stated their opinion that overcharging was not confined to one site (the Whiterock Road) nor to the year in question, but was much more extensive.[35]

The Housing Committee fought a rearguard action against the reports (and two independent Unionists were severely castigated for demanding an inquiry), but an inquiry was inevitable. On 1 September the Corporation formally petitioned the Governor to appoint a commission of inquiry into the whole question of the Belfast Corporation Housing Scheme. A single commissioner, Robert Dick Megaw, K.C.,[36] was appointed by the Minister of Home Affairs. His public investigation lasted from October 1925 to January 1926, but the report was not available until October 1926.

The Megaw report disclosed considerable negligence in the affairs of the City Housing department: inadequate checking of accounts, poor and inferior materials being passed, and unexplained discrepancies both in quality[37] and quantity[38] of building materials submitted. Apart from irregularities in accounting, other serious charges were sustained. Certain firms had received contracts without tender and some members and officials of the Housing Committee, and even the city solicitor, had a financial interest in the sites. 'I believe it to be the truth,' Megaw wrote, 'that there was an undertaking, lubricated with an amount of give and take, between certain members of the Housing Committee, the City Surveyor and [an official] as to the allocation of some of the contracts.'[39] The commissioner also pointed out that the allocation of the sites for the new houses was dictated by the consideration of 'profit to the vendor and not suitability for working-class housing'.[40]

Megaw concluded his report by complaining of the 'disinclination of everyone concerned' to help the Inquiry, the Housing Committee's failure to produce documents, unwillingness to give testimony by some members, a quite unjustifiable air of complacency on the part of the Chairman (Sir Crawford McCullagh) and, most ominous for the reformers: 'a feeling akin to fatalism as regards the chances of effecting any reforms in the Corporation's management of its public duties'.[41]

The severe strictures of the Megaw report, echoing the Chancery decision of 1855, both in proof of maladministration and of pessimism concerning the possibility of reform, caused the Council considerable initial embarrassment. The city solicitor and surveyor resigned, and some of the persons implicated in the housing contracts were prosecuted.

In November 1927 the Lord Mayor, Alderman W. G. Turner, persuaded the Council to set up a special committee (five Unionists and one Nationalist) to look over the whole field of municipal administration and recommend accordingly. The Committee of Six engaged the services of a London accountant with municipal experience, Arthur Collins, F.S.A.A., to conduct an inquiry for them.[42] Its tone is indicated by the patronising remark that Belfast was trying to manage the town's affairs on lines suitable for a village and for that alone.

Collins' complaints covered both structure and functions. There were too many committees; they were encroaching on work that should properly be done by officials;[44] there was undue participation by council members in the engagement and firing of staff; and worst of all, the council was still operating the 1840 procedure[45] of reviewing all the decisions of committees

instead of delegating authority to them after the manner of
English county boroughs under the Act of 1888, and as a
result of the volume of work 'its present system of control of the
departmental activities is (in my opinion) nominal rather than
real'.[46]

Mr Collins made over thirty recommendations intended to
assimilate Belfast government to that of Birmingham, which
he considered to be a particularly well-run borough. Many of
them were purely technical (methods of accounting and
presenting estimates), some were purely for the sake of uni-
formity with British practice (election of aldermen by the
Corporation, not the people). But the main burden of the
recommendations would ensure closer financial control by the
City Treasurer's department and greater oversight by the Town
Clerk over the other departments, a simplification of the
committee system and the replacement of patronage by a
competitive system of staff appointments.[47] Finally, Collins
urged the Council to convert itself into a deliberative body
for the settling of policy, the execution of which should be left
to officials.

The Committee of Six accepted all Collins's recommendations. The majority could be implemented by resolution of the
Council. However, a change in the mode of election of aldermen
would require legislation by Stormont and for good measure
they urged that such a private bill would also incorporate a
provision debarring councillors from acting professionally in
any way on behalf of the council, in addition to the existing
legal prohibition on contracts.

On receiving the Collins report plus the recommendations
of the special committee, the Council listened to a plea by
Alderman Turner, the Lord Mayor, for an end to the 'baneful
influence and dry rot' of patronage for which he distributed
blame between the members of the Council and the weakness
and acquiescence of the officials.[48] However, after a confused
and disorderly meeting, all the main recommendations were
carried, except the suggestion of indirect election of aldermen,
and that a chief financial officer be appointed.[49]

The Town Clerk was instructed to prepare a new private
bill which incorporated these changes and passed into law
without question in 1930.[50]

That the Council incurred some public odium during these years is unquestionable. Many dark hints were dropped that temporary rule by Commissioners would be the only remedy (as Dublin was experiencing at the very same time for similar reasons).[51] Moreover, an attempt to establish a corporation monopoly over omnibuses within the city boundary was rebuffed at a plebiscite of ratepayers.[52]

But these contemporary outbursts, reinforced by the sardonic comments of local journalists,[53] do not provide an adequate test of the impact of the 1926 scandals on the Corporation. It is necessary to consider electoral shifts of fortune and especially those of the leading characters in that episode.

First, it is necessary to look at electoral developments after the reintroduction of the old electoral system operating within the old wards. The election of 1923 more than satisfied the Unionists. Labour representation was reduced from eleven to two (Sam Kyle being among the casualties), the Nationalist monopoly was restored in Falls and Smithfield and the Unionists and Independent Unionists took the rest of the seats. In 1924 (a year of high unemployment), Labour won two more seats (Dock and Court); in 1925 there was another Labour victory in Dock (Harry Midgley, the future Party leader), and in 1926, the trend in Dock was continued with the return of Dawson Gordon, who had served in the P.R. Council. These victories might be attributed to the gradual increase in Labour strength in Belfast as a whole (as evidenced by the election of three Labour M.P.s in the Stormont election of 1925), and the corresponding decline in Nationalist effort and propaganda. In 1927, moreover, the N.I.L.P. won a seat in St George's[54] (a ward that had never previously fallen to them) and also in the Catholic ward, Smithfield.[55]

In the election of 1928 there was no further change. In 1929, however, occurred the only major reverse to the Unionists during this period. Sir Crawford McCullagh stood again for his aldermanic seat in Cromac, and he was opposed by W. H. Alexander, a leading manufacturer and member of the reform group in the Chamber of Commerce, standing as an independent Unionist. Alexander was dissatisfied with the Collins proposals and campaigned on the slogan 'immediate reform or commissioners'. As chairman of the Housing Committee, McCullagh had to take the blame for the 1926 fiasco and his campaign was not helped by the fact that the General Purposes Committee had already designated him as the next Lord Mayor, in succession to Sir William Turner, then approaching the end of his sixth term. The other leading figure in the Housing Committee, T. E. McConnell, also coming up for re-election, was similarly opposed.

By an *argumentum ad misericordiam*, pleading ill health, McConnell persuaded his opponent to withdraw.[56] But Alexander went on to defeat McCullagh by a comfortable majority,[57] while Midgley won the Dock aldermanship from an official Unionist.

In its post mortem on the election results the *News Letter* said that McCullagh had only himself to blame for his defeat.[58] Events were to show, however, that the reforming zeal was quickly spent and the Unionists reverse very temporary. In the elections of 1930 there were few contests, the Unionists not bothering to put up a candidate for Dock. Sir Crawford McCullagh stood for the vacant councillorship in Woodvale and was returned. In 1931 there were a mere two contests. The newspapers, for the first time since 1920, did not comment on the speeches or even the results, although the *News Letter* averred that there was reasonable satisfaction with the retiring councillors.[59]

Following the election, one of the last survivors of the Citizens Association, Sir William Coates, who had been elected Lord Mayor for 1929 and 1930, retired and Sir Crawford McCullagh was elected to succeed him. He was to hold office – with a short break in 1942 – for sixteen continuous years, a record in the history of Belfast.

During McCullagh's long tenure of office the Corporation again faded from public controversy. The number of contests dropped to three in 1932 and two in 1934.[60] By 1934 the newspapers were lamenting the apathy with which the electorate was affected.

It was indeed surprising, in view of the bad unemployment situation in the early 1930s that the N.I.L.P. candidates did not fare better in municipal elections during these years.

After the abolition of P.R. for Stormont elections in 1929 the

Nationalists appear to have opted out of the political system at all levels – Westminster, Stormont and local government. They contested merely their own seats and sometimes not even those, especially after the death of Joe Devlin in 1934 and the accession to the leadership of a prosperous barrister, T. J. Campbell. Devlin was the last Nationalist to sit for West Belfast; hence forth it alternated between Unionist and Labour.

The electoral malaise[61] experienced in Belfast did not mean complete or general satisfaction with social and economic conditions. In 1932 a non-sectarian riot occurred in the city. A hunger march of the unemployed on Stormont was banned by the Minister of Home Affairs under the convenient Special Powers Act. Nevertheless crowds of unemployed workers gathered both in the Falls and the Shankill. When the police baton charged and fired over the heads of the crowd in the Falls Road, for the first time in history the Shankill crowd rioted in their support. The result was two deaths and many shops destroyed.[62]

Three years later, however, Belfast reverted to type. The Ulster Protestant League,[63] founded in 1932 and resembling, both in name and objectives, so many previous organisations since the days of Cooke and Drew, publicly agitated against any social or economic intercourse with Catholics. With continuing unemployment, tension gradually mounted until the inevitable flashpoint, 12 July 1935.

The Minister of Home Affairs, Sir Dawson Bates, first banned *all* processions, then capitulated to a demand by the Orange Order to exempt their procession. Rioting broke out in the Falls–Shankill area and lasted for three weeks. Twelve people were killed and about 400, mainly Catholics, rendered homeless. The Belfast Catholics, dispirited by the pogrom of 1920–22, appeared to have lost the will to resist and were readily prevented from retaliating by the exhortations of their Bishop. An attempt by a number of Catholics, led by a young priest, Monsignor A. H. Ryan, to induce the British Government to intervene came to nothing. Although some 100 Westminster M.P.s, led by J. R. Clynes, agreed to support a demand for an inquiry, the Prime Minister (Baldwin) replied that the matter lay within the jurisdiction of the Government of Northern Ireland.

Sir Crawford McCullagh and his Unionist-dominated Corporation played no significant part in the Belfast riots which they allowed the police to deal with. Nor, apart from a few 'relief works' did they help the Belfast Board[64] of Guardians to increase the amount of outdoor relief in 1933 when soup kitchens were opened in East Belfast.[65] The relief of distress was rather left to private charity and the policy of the Council was determined by conservative orthodoxy.[66] In 1935 occurred the second major clash with the provincial parliament, arising out of another new responsibility of the Council – education. In 1923 primary education which hitherto, as in the rest of Ireland had been provided mainly by denominational schools, was entrusted to local authorities – the six county and two county borough boards. At that time the legacy of pre-war neglect was estimated to be 12,000 school places too few in Belfast alone. Almost immediately the sectarian issue was raised again. The Catholic hierarchy refused to hand over their schools to the new local education Committees. The Orange Order and some Protestant schools also bitterly opposed the principle of non-denominational education. A long controversy followed involving the resignation of the Minister of Education, but since it belongs to the field of national rather than municipal politics it would be out of place to recount it here.[67] By 1930 a compromise was reached. The voluntary schools were allowed to remain under the existing clerical managers and half the cost of fresh buildings was to be met by the Ministry of Education and the other half loaned by them.[68]

While the controversy was still raging, Belfast Corporation with its new education committee found itself obliged to build new schools to replace the decaying buildings of the previous century.[69] In Dr Lawrence's words, 'the volume of new building, though impressive at a time when money was scarce, fell far short of what was needed'; and the standard of school equipment and amenities was 'a generation or more behind most of England and Wales'. Nevertheless, in 1935 the Corporation challenged the new Finance (N.I.) Act, which required local authorities to levy a rate so as to produce a lump sum payment towards central expenditure upon education.[70] This legislation was determined by the then policy of the British Government to distribute more evenly the burden of taxation.

Belfast Corporation, however, objected strongly to doubling its existing expenditure on education[71] and challenged the validity of the Act by a petition to the Governor, asking for a reference to the Judicial Committee of the Privy Council, on the ground that the legislation imposed a tax substantially the same in character as an income tax and, if so, was *ultra vires*, since only Westminster could levy income tax under the Government of Ireland Act.[72]

The Stormont Government was so incensed by this reaction that for a time it suspended all grants to the Corporation.[73] However, the decision of the Judicial Committee was unfavourable. It was the 'essential character' of a tax that mattered, they said, and the essential character of the education levy was that it was imposed irrespective of income. In the words of one law lord 'Income tax, if I may say so, is a tax upon income'.[74]

The Corporation accepted the decision quietly and proceeded to increase its ordinary education expenditure as well as to pay the levy.

As in 1914, the outbreak of war in 1939 meant that municipal politics and local government generally faded into the background in the United Kingdom. The same was true of Belfast. Elections were suspended and virtually the only municipal affairs to arouse general interest were the proposals to modify Belfast's strict sabbatarianism to the extent of opening a cinema on Sundays to which only uniformed members of the armed forces would be allowed access,[75] and the Whiteabbey inquiry, which bore an astonishingly close resemblance to the Megaw inquiry of 1926. Following a row between senior members of the staff of Whiteabbey sanatorium, the Corporation asked the Minister of Home Affairs for an inquiry into the entire administration of the hospital.[76] The Inquiry was set up under two inspectors, one of whom was Mr John Dunlop of the Ministry of Home Affairs.

Then the Council decided not to tender any evidence (apart from the officials) which considerably hampered the inspectors. The Inquiry lasted 34 days and its report was issued on 15 June 1941. As in 1926, it went far beyond the immediate issue (in respect of which the medical superintendent was censured). It asserted that the City Treasurer's Department had displayed 'complete laxity' and 'gross neglect' in the management of the sanatorium accounts; that the T.B. committee had made a determined effort to force the purchase of a site for the sanatorium 'without any regard to its obvious unsuitability and extravagant price'. The T.B. committee had made many wrong decisions and 'improvident bargains', including the purchase of 'totally unsuitable' blackout material. The inspectors recommended the dissolution of the T.B. committee and that the corporation be relieved of its powers under the Tuberculosis Prevention Acts.[77]

Immediately after the publication of the Dunlop Report, the Council on 19 June set up another 'Big Six' committee, consisting of the Lord Mayor, three Unionists, one Labour and one Nationalist councillor, to look into the entire affairs of the council. The 'Big Six' quickly recommended that they be allowed to control future appointments.[78] Then they traced the 'totally unsuitable' blackout material to a firm in which four councillors were involved and asked them to resign. (At the same time, the Town Clerk and Town Solicitor, John Archer, retired on reaching the age limit.)[79] At the next meeting of the council (7 August 1941) the Special Committee was itself dissolved, a decision which by exerting his personal influence Sir Crawford McCullagh managed to get rescinded at the following meeting (13 August). The Big Six then proceeded to appoint a new town clerk and throughout the winter prepared their report. Eventually, they recommended the establishment of a special committee to control appointments; a return to direct instead of contract employment of semi-skilled and unskilled workers, legislation providing more stringent definitions of 'interest' and requiring anyone tendering for a corporation contract to disclose the names of Council members who might have helped him. The Council reacted by rejecting all these recommendations (by a majority of 18 votes to 14) at a meeting on 2 April 1942.

Then the Ministry of Home Affairs stepped in, giving the Council a deadline of two months to put their house in order. McCullagh having retired, the new Lord Mayor, G. R. Black, could only suggest lame expedients – for example a fresh committee – and early in June the ministry produced a bill to appoint three administrators for a $3\frac{1}{2}$-year period who would make all appointments, purchases, contracts and rates and municipal taxes. The Bill passed through Stormont by 23 votes to 10 (including four Unionists) and became law on 1 October 1942.[80] The administrators comprised one full-time commissioner (Mr C. W. Grant, a senior civil servant from the Ministry of Home Affairs) and two part-time Commissioners, well-known businessmen who had held the office of President of the Belfast Chamber of Commerce.[81]

The change-over from Council to Commission government did not attract quite as much public attention as a libel action[82] brought by 10 councillors, including the new Lord Mayor, against the *Northern Whig* for writing on 7 August 1941 that the names of the 21 councillors (including the ten above mentioned) who had voted for the dismissal of the Big Six should never be forgotten. The plaintiffs demanded £5,000 damages apiece; the editor of the *Whig* pleaded justification, since these men had refused to clean up their own city, and the jury found for the plaintiffs, but merely awarded them £50 damages each – a scarcely satisfactory result.[83]

Black retired from the Lord Mayoralty at the end of 1942 and McCullagh, whose record throughout this crisis appears to have been thoroughly pro-reform,[84] was elected once again and served until 1946, when he retired from public life. In the meantime the Commissioners had been governing the city with quiet efficiency and from 1943 had the help of Mr John Dunlop, who was brought over from the civil service to become Town Clerk.

To sum up the era of Crawford McCullagh, one must begin by asking for an explanation of his extraordinary hold over the Unionists on the Corporation for a decade and a half. It has been remarked[85] that he was extremely hospitable, both in a public and private capacity, and in the former brought back nostalgic memories of the era of Pirrie, Jaffé and Shaftesbury. And on this point his few contemporaries, still serving on the Council in the late 1960s, concur. But that was not all. It is to be noted that during the 1930s the Unionist councillors developed a permanent structure, the 'City Hall party', with leader, secretary, treasurer and regular meetings. The consequence was a more intensive control of the Council by the ruling party. Apart from appointments, in respect of which the Chairmen of Committees formed an 'advisory' committee, all

offices within the council itself were monopolised by the
Unionists.[86] No longer did they feel, as in the period immediately before the First World War, the need to placate the Nationalists, who, though meagre in Belfast, were powerful at Westminster and disagreeably inclined to interfere in local legislation.
The setting up of the Northern Parliament obviated this
difficulty. The City Hall party developed without any encouragement from Unionist headquarters in Glengall Street which
discerned in it an alternative focus of power.[87] In 1936 there
was an outright clash between them when two candidates
were nominated for the same ward (Clifton) – one an 'official'
Unionist, the other a nominee of the City Hall party.[88] It
would appear that after an initial false start in the late 1920s
Sir Crawford McCullagh controlled the Corporation through
building up a highly disciplined party machine, which only an
extreme crisis, such as the Whiteabbey scandal, could put out of
action.

The conclusion to be drawn, then, at the end of the war is
that the corporation had to its credit a modest record of social
reform, but, more significantly, was demonstrating, as a
century earlier, the effects of non-competitive one-party rule –
control of all offices by one party and the 'ancient and festering
tradition'[89] of municipal corruption.

IV. 1945–66

The elections for Stormont and Westminster immediately
after the end of the war showed a marked swing to Labour –
though not as devastating as in Great Britain. The first election
for Belfast County borough in 1946 at the end of the statutory
3½-year period of commission government was eagerly awaited.
The N.I.L.P. nominated 30 candidates, and Commonwealth
Labour and Communists also ran.

The election was governed by new legislation. The Elections
and Franchise (Northern Ireland) Act 1946 consolidated the
laws concerning local government voting qualifications[90] and
elections. Henceforth all the councillors in every borough
council would be subject to re-election every third year and the
aldermen every sixth. In Belfast a special provision required
half the aldermen to be elected every third year.

The campaign was fought vigorously. Housing was the main issue, and Belfast was compared unfavourably to other British cities (especially Liverpool and Manchester) which had coped with the problem of building fresh houses, on the two main counts of war damage and slum clearance.

The results showed that Labour had doubled its strength from four to eight councillors. Harry Midgley, the veteran leader, who had formed his own 'Commonwealth Labour' party was also elected as alderman for Ormeau, although he was then Minister of Labour. The Nationalists, however, seemed to be on the decline. Only the four Smithfield seats went to them while the three Falls councillorships went unopposed to 'Independent Labour' candidates, i.e. Labour with a republican tinge.

The slight swing to Labour was not maintained, however, at the next triennial election in May 1949. This was shortly after the sweeping Unionist victory in the Stormont election held on account of the establishment of the Republic of Ireland outside the Commonwealth. A similar victory was scored at the local election. Six wards went to the Unionists without a contest. The N.I.L.P. strength was reduced from eight seats to one and the Nationalists to the aldermanic seat for Smithfield.[91] The gainers, apart from the Unionists who increased from 43 seats to 48, were a new party, inaccurately called 'Eire Labour',[92] a splinter group from the N.I.L.P. formed when that party at last (in February 1949) committed itself to the Northern Ireland Constitution. 'Eire Labour' candidates claimed to be members of and were backed by the Irish Labour party in Dublin. They won all four seats in Falls and three in Smithfield.

After 1949 Belfast municipal elections appear to have excited no more interest then in the late 1930s. The next three elections were reported with the utmost brevity. Not that there seemed much likelihood of any significant alteration in the party distribution on the Council.

Occasionally there was a surprise. In 1952 an independent Unionist in Court easily defeated Alderman Malcolm Mercer, who had spent thirty years on the Council. In the same election Alderman J. A. McGlade, the last Nationalist, was defeated by an Irish Labour candidate. In 1955, in spite of a vigorous challenge, the N.I.L.P. managed to get only one out of 19 candidates elected. In 1958 Irish Labour and Independent Labour fought against each other in Falls and Smithfield and the latter won all seven contests – the notion of a party affiliated to Dublin seemed no longer attractive. In the same election Sir John Harcourt, Lord Mayor 1955–7, was defeated for the aldermanic seat in Court by a young N.I.L.P. candidate[93]; Gerry Fitt, soon to be celebrated in another context, won a seat in Dock through his own machine which bore the name 'Dock Eire Labour'; and two Protestant Unionists were elected – one had sat on the Council since 1946 as an official Unionist.[94] In 1961 the election was held at a time when the Government had announced yet another inquiry into allegations that councillors were involved in contracts with the Corporation.[95] Mrs Florence Breakie, who had already been chosen by the City Hall Party as Lord Mayor for the coming year, stood for the aldermanic seat in St Anne's against Sir Cecil McKee, who was not renominated by his local association. Sir Cecil fought back vigorously and defeated Mrs Breakie. In the same election the N.I.L.P. established a firm foothold in Court ward with two out of four councillorships. In 1964 the Rev. Ian Paisley for the first time played a prominent part in local politics. His wife stood in Windsor against the outgoing Lord Mayor, Sir Martin Wallace, who had actually lowered the City Hall flag to half-mast when Pope John XXIII died in May 1963. The Protestant Unionists made the flag issue the focal point of their campaign.

In the upshot the Protestant Unionists retained their two seats in St George's but failed elsewhere, Mrs Paisley being beaten two to one by Sir Martin Wallace. A more simplified pattern was discernible in the 'Nationalist' wards. Republican Labour, a party established by Mr Gerry Fitt after his election to Stormont in 1962,[96] took three seats in Dock and two in Falls. Independent Labour was left with two seats in Smithfield and two in Falls and was clearly on the way out. (Mr Fitt's party differed from the Irish Labour party of the early 1950s in having a local base and local leaders.) The N.I.L.P. polled well, and though losing a seat in Court,[97] gained two in Clifton There were now two wards which Labour might regard as its own. 1967, however, saw another pro-Unionist reaction. Mrs Paisley

won a seat in St George's – but from a fellow Protestant Union-
ist. However, the N.I.L.P. lost two seats in Court and two in
Clifton. It was left merely with the aldermanic seat in Court
which would not come up until 1970 and a new seat in Falls.
Republican Labour had a clear sweep in Dock – all four seats,
Mr Fitt now becoming an alderman – and two seats in both
Smithfield and Falls. Independent Labour kept the Falls
aldermanship and one seat in Smithfield.

Unionist control (apart from the first year, 1946) appeared
to be beyond question even as in the 1930s. However, there was
no successor to Sir Crawford McCullagh. The convention arose
that the Lord Mayor was eligible for election for three years and
no more. The Unionist City Hall Party played a more obvious
role in policy-making and the election of a new Lord Mayor
came to be announced as a matter of course after a meeting
of the party, not, as in the early 1930s, after a meeting of the
General Purposes Committee. Members of the City Hall
Party were bound to accept majority decisions. That these
precluded nomination of any non-Unionist to a post in the
Council became clear in 1968 when Alderman George Kelso
and Councillor Ben Horan were censured by the City Hall
Party for proposing the Independent Labour member for Falls,
Alderman Daley, for the not very prestigious post of vice-
chairman of the Parks and Cemeteries Committee[98]. Councillor
Horan has refused to sign an undertaking to accept majority
party decisions and has since then been excluded from the
City Hall Party.

However, the Unionists on the Corporation have not always
manifested monolithic solidarity. Some issues in fact have cut
across party divisions. Three such issues were among those
chosen for our questionnaire in 1966 – a long-term issue, a
short-term issue and a once-for-all issue.

I. THE MATER HOSPITAL ISSUE

The Mater Hospital was founded by the Catholic Church and
staffed by nuns (the sisters of Mercy) in 1833. It was completely
rebuilt in 1900 and put under the control of a board of management of Catholic clergy and laity. Thus it was an archetypal

voluntary hospital, financed by church collections, street collections and later lotteries.[99] Since 1909 it was a centre for
clinical teaching recognised by Queen's University, Belfast.

In 1947, following the acceptance by the then Labour
Government at Westminster of the principle that social services
in Northern Ireland should not fall below the national level, the
Northern Ireland Government introduced the Health Act,
1947. In its general terms, it followed the English and Scottish
acts, but with a significant difference concerning the voluntary
hospitals: whereas the English and Scottish Acts provided that
'where the Character and Associations of any hospital transferred . . . are such as to link it with a particular religious
denomination regard shall be had in the making of appointments to the Board of Management to the preservation of the
character and associations of the hospital', the Stormont
legislation omitted this clause. Opposition members protested
in vain. The Mater and its chairman, the Bishop of Down and
Connor, refused to come into the scheme unless a similar clause
were enacted. Deadlock followed. Then the hospital authorities
asked to be reimbursed for the out-patient services which they
were willing to provide freely as if they were a state hospital.[100]
The Minister of Health refused: they should either be fully in
the service or completely outside. The Mater decided to opt
out and relied on a football pool scheme for the necessary funds.

Subsequently various tentative steps were taken to resume
negotiations. During the Stormont election of 1962 the then
Minister of Health denied that negotiations were under way.
Then in 1968 legislation was passed enabling voluntary hospitals to claim from the state in respect of free services. During
the Stormont election of 1969, the then Minister of Health
said that negotiations with the Mater were almost completed.
Nothing further has been heard, although the drying up of the
main source of funds – the YP football pools were terminated
in December 1970 – will soon mean that state subvention will
be a necessity. (It was conceded in 1971.)

The Mater hospital issue, while primarily connected with
government policy, was of particular interest to Belfast people,
since its services were almost wholly used by people in the city.
It cut across party loyalties – the free services provided were a
tangible benefit and it was obvious that if the Mater did not

exist the Government would have been obliged to build a
hospital in North Belfast. From time to time Unionist spokesmen at Westminster, Stormont and Belfast City Council
spoke in favour of a settlement of the Mater's claim. The Labour
Party and needless to say, the various Nationalist groups
consistently supported the hospital.

II. THE SUNDAY SWINGS ISSUE

Like the wartime issue of Sunday films for troops the Sunday
swings issue of the 1960s cut across party lines. In the early
1960s the licensed trade, the hotel interest and trades unions
generally, supported by all the newspapers, occasionally
bewailed the rigours of the Ulster Sunday with its complete
absence of normal amenities. The economic argument – the
adverse effect on tourism – was the one most frequently used,
but social arguments were also proffered – especially the lack
of amenities for children in Belfast's crowded streets.[101] However, reformist arguments generally broke on the rock of
sabbatarianism – some orthodox Presbyterian ministers, the
Reformed Presbyterians, Mr Paisley's Free Presbyterians and
the Orange Order were always certain to oppose every relaxa-
tion. In the municipal elections of 1964 the N.I.L.P. pledged
itself to agitate for the Sunday opening of the play centres
and also for the provision of children's amenities on Sundays in
the eleven parks in the city.

Action came perhaps sooner than they expected. On 15 June
1964 the Education Committee headed by a liberal Unionist,
Mrs Hilda Hawnt, undertook a survey of youth organisations,
trade unions and the churches on the issue. Following their
investigation they recommended (by a majority of one) at their
October meeting that the play centres be opened.[102]

Meanwhile Orange and Paisleyite opposition was mounting[103]
and when the Council met on 2 November to debate the
Education Committee's recommendation they turned it down
by a majority of two – 25 voting for (12 Unionists, 2 N.I.L.P.
and 11 from the Nationalist groups) and 27 against (24 Unionists, 1 Independent Unionist and 2 N.I.L.P.) while another
N.I.L.P. councillor abstained.

Newspaper reaction even from the *News Letter* was very

unfavourable to the Council decision, but the issue nearly broke the N.I.L.P. The two councillors who voted against opening were backed by their local association but refused to give an assurance to the Executive that in future they would 'accept and uphold party policy'. Then the situation became farcical. The two councillors who voted against (and the third who abstained) were expelled from the party on 30 November and readmitted on 10 December, without giving any assurances.[104] They were all evangelical Protestants and represented strongly Protestant wards – Woodvale and Court.

However, the 1964 agitation proved to be the thin end of the wedge. On 1 March 1965 the council passed by 30 votes to 24 a Parks and Cemeteries Committee recommendation to open swings on Sundays in the eleven parks. But the play centres remained locked. In the municipal elections of 1967 Mrs Hawnt and the two Woodvale Unionist councillors who voted for Sunday opening were refused renomination by their local association[105] while all Labour councillors up for election lost their seats, irrespective of whether they voted for or against.

In 1968 the City Hall administration took a hand. They organised a referendum of ratepayers within 200 yards of each play centre on the question of Sunday opening. In 17 cases a majority favoured opening, in four (in Woodvale and Court wards) a majority opposed – the aggregate majority being about two thirds. At the July Council meeting it was decided by a majority of 30 votes to eight, in spite of vociferous opposition from Protestant Unionists, to allow local option in respect of Sunday swings.[106]

On the Sunday swings issue, the Unionist Party was divided, a majority originally being against; Nationalist-type councillors were consistently for and the N.I.L.P. were equally divided. In the last case clearly, and also in respect of many Unionists, strong religious conviction cut across party loyalty.

III. THE CARSON BRIDGE ISSUE

A new bridge over the river Lagan was constructed between 1963 and 1965 to ease the pressure of the traffic, mainly from the shipyard, along the existing Queen's Bridge. While it was under construction it was generally referred to as the Lagan Bridge. Early in 1965 it was reported that the favourite name among councillors was 'Churchill'.[107] Exactly a year later, it was announced that Queen Elizabeth II would visit Ulster to commemorate the 50th anniversary of the Battle of the Somme and would open the new bridge. Then speculation centred on 'Somme' as the most likely name.[108] At a meeting of the City Hall Party, on 14 February 1966, Alderman W. D. Geddes, after a ballot, won the nomination for the Lord Mayoralty and by a '3 or 4 votes' majority the party decided on 'Carson' as the name for the new bridge.[109]

As expected, the decision provoked a loud outcry among the pro-Nationalists and complaints that the liberal efforts of the then Lord Mayor, Sir William Jenkins, who had been completely in tune with the O'Neillite policy of conciliation, were being brought to nothing. However, on the following day the Governor, Lord Erskine, phoned the City Hall and informed the Town Clerk that 'he was perturbed at the effect on Her Majesty of possible controversy over the name of the bridge'.[110] This intervention was sufficient to turn the minds of a majority of the Unionists on the Improvement Committee, which technically had the right to chose the name; and with the eager support of Republican Labour councillors they voted to call the bridge 'Queen Elizabeth' bridge.[111] On 21 February the City Hall Party sullenly accepted the decision:[112] shortly afterwards, the chairman, Councillor Charles McCullough resigned, partly because of the volte-face over the bridge; but also because the City Hall Party had refused to discipline a councillor who had earlier voted against a party decision.[113]

There followed a threat (soon to be called off) of intervention by Lord Carson's son in the Westminster election (March 1966); then the Paisleyite protest march when Lord Erskine opened the Presbyterian general assembly (June 1966) and the Queen's visit (the last to be made by the Queen to Ulster) marred by the hurling of a block of concrete on the royal car. From the point of view of Belfast municipal politics this case provided an example both of the pretensions of the governing party and the conditions under which they could be hopelessly divided.

Apart from contentious issues, the Belfast City Council

during these years displayed a good deal of unanimity. After the war the three major policy areas as in the case of similar municipalities were education, housing and overall planning. The Education Act, 1947, applying to Northern Ireland the provisions of the Butler Act, 1944, made the City Council responsible for secondary as well as primary education. The latter was already well in hand and the former was dealt with by ignoring the thorny religious issue and constructing between 1946 and 1966 three new grammar schools and sixteen county intermediate schools. In 1961 the council committed itself to awarding a university scholarship to anyone with the appropriate entry qualification and by 1962 they were awarding annually 1,000 scholarships tenable at Queen's University (nearly a quarter of the entire University population).[114] The educational policy of the council both in these respects and also in regard to specialist and ancillary services was far more enlightened than in the pre-war period. Housing and overall planning have briefly to be considered together. At the end of the war Belfast had had 3,200 houses destroyed by enemy action; but more important, 18,440 houses (out of a total of 114,995) were either in serious disrepair, or lacking standard amenities. The city council, responsible after 1956 for slum clearance as well as building new houses, prepared a number of schemes which between 1944 and 1968 provided 11,600 houses in thirty development areas apart from 21,000 constructed by the Housing trust.[115] One of these opened in 1966 was the celebrated Unity Flats, a Catholic enclave at the end of the Shankill Road. It must also be mentioned that the Estates Department, where possible, mixed tenants of both religious groups – Ballymurphy, now almost entirely Catholic, was originally 50 per cent Protestant. But the housing needs of Belfast Corporation were not to be met by more boundary extension – although this was requested – and rejected – in 1947. In 1944 a (temporary) Planning Advisory Board drew attention to the population imbalance in the province with two fifths of the whole population living in the Belfast area. A similar body in 1945 recommended a gradual reduction of the population of inner Belfast to 300,000 people, plus 27,000 new dwellings as an immediate priority. However, until the 1960s no further planning was undertaken.

In 1962 Sir Robert Matthew was invited to produce a plan for the whole conurbation and produced two outstanding recommendations – alternative areas for housing and industrial development,[116] and a 'stop-line' for Belfast – the open areas on the present edge of building (the Antrim and Down hills) to be preserved as visual and recreational amenities.

The Matthew 'stop-line' (which in one part of West Belfast went inside the County borough boundary) was grudgingly accepted by the Corporation.[117] In 1962, however, they did not have a planning committee. In the following year they divided the planning functions into transport and architectural planning and through lack of qualified staff entrusted (in 1966) to two sets of consultants – Building Design Partnership and Travers Morgan & Co. – the task of planning housing and road development within the city.[118]

The *Belfast Central Area Plan* did not appear until June 1969.[119] It recommended development on both banks of the river and three main commercial areas and an increase in the number of areas in the city centre to be returned to housing use. But city centre renewal was to be accompanied by relocation of industry outside the city boundary in the North and East.[120] The *Belfast Transportation Plan* recommended the construction of a ring road to link to the existing motorways, which they hoped could be constructed by 1976 – they calculated that within the plan period (1966–86) the demand for private vehicular traffic would increase to two and a half times the 1966 level.

The two plans were accepted by the Corporation in May and August 1970. By then, however, there had occurred the riots of August 1969, resulting in six dead and 200 houses (mainly Catholic) destroyed and a British military presence, which, two years later, has all the signs of permanence. Neither plan has got off the ground – even the housing schemes have been disrupted by squatters, and tenants from mixed areas are fleeing to their own coreligionists. The acceptance by Stormont of the Macrory Report means that shortly housing and planning together with other major local government services will be entrusted to central authorities.

NOTES

1. Between 1916 and 1920 Belfast City Council experienced 20 vacancies, all of which were filled by co-opting fresh Unionists, including Mrs R. J. McMordie, the first woman to serve on the Corporation.
2. A. W. Samuels, K.C., Unionist M.P. for Dublin University.
3. *Parl. Deb.*, Vol. 114 (24 March 1919) 99.
4. The Nationalists won six seats altogether, five in Ulster. As to Devlin's role in the Commons after 1918 see F. S. L. Lyons, *John Dillon*, pp. 459–60.
5. Beckett, *The Making of Modern Ireland*, p. 446.
6. See C. O'Leary, *The Irish Republic and Its Experiment with Proportional Representation* (Notre Dame, 1961), Chapter 1.
7. It must be remembered, however, that this was not the first Irish Bill (apart from the Sligo Improvement Bill) to incorporate the principles of P.R. The Irish Home Rule Act of 1914, which never came into operation, prescribed P.R. for the election of members of the Irish Legislative Body.
   The voting was 240 to 27 on the second reading; 244 to 42 on the third. On both divisions the Irish Nationalists abstained, and in the debates Devlin exhibited little enthusiasm for the Bill and constantly harped on the tendency of 'English' members to legislate for the Irish people, without even undergoing the formality of consulting the Irish members.
8. For the debates see *Parl. Deb.*, Vol. 114 (24 March 1919) 99–182; Vol. 116 (27 May 1919), 1064–1104.
9. Father of the House of Commons, 1945–51, now Lord Rathcavan.
10. On the third reading Carson said: 'I really regard the whole of this Bill with the greatest contempt. It is the most wretched, miserable Bill and nobody wants it.' (Ibid., p. 1968.)
11. The authorities had to act with unprecedented speed. The order of the Local Government Board, issued on 24 June, prescribed that the borough schemes be submitted before 1 October 1919. Only Wexford and Sligo Borough and Waterford County Borough councils failed to submit schemes and the Local Government Board acted on their behalf. Cf. *48th Annual Report of the Local Government Board for Ireland*, Cmnd. 1432, pp. v–vii. (This, incidentaly, was the last report of the Irish Local Government Board.)
12. This practice still persists in the Republic of Ireland.
13. Afterwards called Unionist Labour – the organisation founded by Lord Carson to keep the loyalist working class away from the Labour movement proper. It has had one minister (Mr William Grant, Minister of Labour 1943–53) and a small number of senators.
14. *B.N.L.*, 6 January 1920.
15. However the attractiveness of P.R. to small pressure groups was manifested by the U.S.P.C.A. which lobbied candidates for their views on humane slaughtering and published the names of those who agreed

or declined to promote their views, and the Temperance Union published similar lists.

16. *I.N.*, 19 January 1920.
17. *B.N.L.*, 19 January 1920.
18. *B.N.L.*, 17 January 1920 (this was the day before the results were announced, but when the Unionist losses were already expected).

    'We fear, however, that the danger which was foreseen and of which we warned the Unionist electors repeatedly, has come about . . . We fear that the block plan of campaign is not advantageous to one Party majority; that good Unionists decline to vote rigidly to order on a Party block.'
19. In 1901 there were six solicitors, nine doctors, three shipbuilders and five associated with the building trade (architects or estate agents). In 1914 the comparable figures were eight, seven, one and three. In 1920, four, one, none and two.
20. The outgoing Lord Mayor, John C. White (a solicitor), was also re-elected.
21. Alderman Henderson died in July 1970.
22. Nor are any records kept in the Ministry of Home Affairs.
23. The Nationalists were similarly discriminated against in the general election of 1921.
24. The 'A', 'B' and 'C' Specials of whom only the second survived. See the *Cameron Report* (Cmd. 532) Appendix V, and L. de Paor, *Divided Ulster*, (London, 1970), pp. 107–10.
25. Belfast was under curfew continuously from July 1920 to December 1924.
26. Among the newly elected Sinn Fein M.P.s were Eamon de Valera, Michael Collins and Arthur Griffith. One member (Devlin) was elected for two constituencies.
27. The new Constitution did not come into operation until December 1922.
28. The only assassination of a Member of Parliament in the history of Northern Ireland. Senator J. E. N. Barnhill was killed by the I.R.A. in December 1971.
29. A. Boyd, *Holy War in Belfast*, p. 176.
30. Apart from two very senior civil servants transferred from Dublin Castle to help set up the Ministries of Education and Agriculture. They were both Catholic – one, Mr J. N. Bonaparte Wyse, a distant connection of Napoleon.
31. W. Black, in Beckett and Glasscock, *Belfast*, p. 163.
32. The highly complex story of the dealings between the British and Northern Ireland Governments on the issue of parity of social services is excellently recounted in R. J. Lawrence, *The Government of Northern Ireland* (Oxford, 1965), especially Chapters 3 and 4.
33. See below.
34. The total number of houses built by the Corporation between 1919 and 1939 was 2,562. But they were all erected before 1930. Subsequently local speculative builders were given the benefit of this government subsidy. See Lawrence, op. cit., p. 147–51.

35. See *Interim Report to the Chairman and members of the Housing Committee of the Belfast Corporation, on questions arising in connection with the timber contracts relative to the housing schemes by A. H. Muir and Addy, chartered accountants (Belfast, 1925).*

36. Megaw had been a parliamentary secretary in the government of Lord Craigavon, but lost his seat in the (P.R.) election of 1925. He was created a High Court judge in 1932. He died in 1947. See *Report of the Enquiry into the housing schemes of the Belfast Corporation, held by Mr R. D. Megaw, K.C.* (Belfast, 1926).

37. One contractor alleged that the Corporation were paying 25 per cent more than the market price for inferior quality timber. (Ibid., p. 16.)

38. Out of one million bricks delivered by one firm, 66,000 were unaccounted for. (Ibid., p. 97.) Belfast folklore has it that those bricks were used to build a cinema owned by a member of the Housing Committee.

39. Ibid., p. 135.

40. Ibid., p. 60.

41. Ibid., p. 137. Megaw also pointed out that the high cost of Belfast housing was due to the practice of direct instead of contract labour. This practice, in fairness to the Housing Committee, had been introduced at the behest of the Labour members of the Corporation.

42. He was a past president of the Institute of Municipal Treasurers and Accountants.

43. See *City of Belfast: Enquiry into Administration, July 1928. Report of Mr A. Collins, F.S.A.A.* (Belfast, 1928).

44. In an appendix to his report (p. 83) Mr Collins showed that five whole (Education) Committee or Sub-Committee meetings were taken up with the business of appointing a hall porter and sifting the 1,460 application forms.

45. Under Section 102 of the Municipal Corporations (Ireland) Act, 1840.

46. *Collins Report*, p. 7. The monthly volumes of Corporation minutes sometimes ran to 400 pages.

47. And the provision of a proper superannuation scheme for the 40 salaried officials aged between 65 and 83.

48. *B.N.L.*, 20 September 1928.

49. and the proposal that the Rates department be incorporated with the Finance (Treasurer's) Department.

50. The Committees were reduced from 21 to 14, Law, Markets, Public Parks and Playgrounds, Improvements, Blind Persons, Employee's Provident, Maternity and Child Welfare, Children's Act, Tuberculosis, Baths and Lodging Houses, and Housing being suppressed and the following new committees created: Estates, Parks, Cleansing and Public Works.

51. The Belfast Chamber of Commerce and Belfast Rotary Club felt so strongly that they decided to initiate discussions with other civic bodies to see whether they should apply for a City Manager and/or commission government. *B.N.L.*, 6 January 1928.

52. By 64,859 votes to 30,901 votes. (*B.N.L.*, 13 January 1928.) The Corporation was then driven to dealing with individual proprietors

and the monopoly was not finally established until December 1928. See Chapter 4, above.

53. See especially *I.N.*, 24 September 1928, and *N.W.*, 11 September 1928.
54. Paradoxically they lost a seat in Dock in 1927.
55. A Labour candidate (William McMullen) had also won in Smithfield in 1925.
56. *B.N.L.*, 8 January 1929.
57. 4,301 to 2,870.
58. 'Having regard to the past, into which we do not wish to delve unnecessarily, his candidature for the Lord Mayoralty was a mistake.' *B.N.L.*, 16 January 1929. The average turnout in the eight contested wards was 65 per cent; in Cromac, 74·5 per cent.
59. *B.N.L.*, 6 January 1931.
60. *B.N.L.*, 5 January 1934.
61. After 1930 Belfast newspapers ceased to report speeches in municipal campaigns, and as the decade wore on they even declined to comment editorially. Cf. *B.N.L.*, in 1937 and 1939.

    The Local Government Act (N.I.), 1934, prescribed that borough elections be held on 15 May instead of 15 January. In 1937 on account of the coronation of George VI elections were deferred until November.
62. For a graphic account of this almost forgotten riot see J. J. Campbell in Beckett and Glasscock, *Belfast*, pp. 150–51.
63. This organisation faded out of the picture after 1936. Its leaders were very obscure, but they appear to have expressed sympathy with Nazism. Cf. A. Boyd, *Holy War in Belfast*, p. 178.
64. The Guardians reported a deficit of £127,000 for 1932. *B.N.L.*, 14 January 1933.
65. The Belfast City Mission served thousands of dinners daily in 1933.
66. In 1933 a Unionist Councillor suggested that the City hall administration could bulk-buy coal and sell it to poor householders at cut price, but his proposal met with no support.
67. The story is succinctly told in R. J. Lawrence, *The Government of Northern Ireland*, pp. 109–17. See also R. H. Semple in *Belfast in Its Regional Setting* (Belfast, 1952), pp. 179–84.
68. Or met in full where the schools were transferred, i.e. operated by 'four and two' committees.
69. Between 1924 and 1944 230 new elementary schools were built in Belfast. See also Lawrence, op. cit., p. 114.
70. Mainly on teachers' salaries. Grants from central funds towards education expanded from £51,529 in 1921 to £194,608 in 1938 (op. cit., p. 116).
71. The summary of Belfast City estimates for 1936–7 allocates £72,705 for education in 1936–7 and £201,665 for the aggregate contribution to the N.I. exchequer under Finance Act (NI), 1934, for the three years 1934–7. See *Memoranda as to Meetings of the Council*, etc. 1936–7, p. 171.
72. For details see H. G. Calvert, *Constitutional Law in Northern Ireland*, pp. 243, 298–301.
73. *B.N.L.*, 11 January 1935.

74. Lord Thankerton. This was the only occasion in which a Northern Ireland statute was challenged in this way. Otherwise the High Court decides the validity, or otherwise, of Stormont legislation by the normal process of judicial review.
75. Having been turned down several times between 1940 and 1942, the proposal eventually passed, by a small majority, in 1943. The arguments were very similar to those advanced on the Sunday swings issue twenty years later. See below, p. 161.
76. At the initiative of the T.B. Committee – originally set up in 1914, when the Abbey sanitorium was handed over to the Council by agreement with the Belfast Board of Guardians.
77. *Dunlop Report* (Belfast, 1941), p. 23.
78. *N.W.*, 31 July 1941.
79. He had been in the service of the Council since 1905 and in 1935 had succeeded Sir Robert Meyer, who had held the post of Town Clerk since Sir Samuel Black's retirement in 1909.
80. Belfast County Borough Administration Act 1942. The remaining six of the ten were opposition M.P.s.
81. Mr W. Robinson and Mr C. S. Neill.
82. For details see *B.N.L.* and *N.W.*, *Belfast Telegraph*, 3–22 June 1942.
83. Three of the ten plaintiffs resigned from the Council before the judgement in the libel case was announced.
84. The Dunlop Report went out of its way to express appreciation of the Lord Mayor's 'fearless and impartial leadership of the best elements in the Council'.
85. *B.N.L.*, 14 April 1948 (obituary notice).
86. Very occasionally an independent Unionist was appointed to a committee chairmanship. Otherwise the only exception is Ald. Thomas Henderson, (Ind. Un.) who in the year of the Dunlop Report was elected High Sheriff.
87. To this day Glengall Street takes no official cognisance of the existence of the City Hall Party, to the great annoyance of its leaders.
88. The Glengall Street nominee (Dr H. P. Lowe) was beaten. The *B.N.L.* wailed: 'Belfast citizenship has lost its sense of responsibility' (16 May 1936).
89. St John Ervine in a letter to the *Belfast Telegraph* (23 June 1941) on the Whiteabbey affair.
90. The local government franchise was restricted to Northern Ireland parliamentary electors who either (a) reside as owner or tenant in a dwelling-house for three months ending on the qualifying date or (b) occupy other land or premises valued at not less than £10. The spouse of a resident qualified under (a). In addition a company might nominate up to six electors, one for every £10 of the valuation of its premises, who must be British subjects. This system which disfranchised about a quarter of the parliamentary electorate continued until 1969. For an examination of its effects see Chapter six and Tables 6.1, 6.2 and 6.3, below.
91. Which did not come up for election in that year.

92. 'Irish Labour' was the official name of this party: it claimed to be a branch of the Irish Labour Party: but was invariably referred to in the Belfast press as 'Eire Labour'. It was their claim to affiliate to Dublin not any matter of policy that distinguished them from Independent Labour.

93. W. R. Boyd, afterwards one of the two Labour councillors to oppose the opening of swings on Sundays.

94. A. H. Duff. He sat as a Protestant Unionist until his death in 1970.

95. The inquiry by R. E. Lowry (afterwards Lord Chief Justice Lowry) was to show that several members of the Corporation were present at meetings when contracts with firms with which they were involved were under discussion. Mr Lowry recommended that there should be (as in England since 1933) no disqualification affecting members concerned with contracts; but that the interest should be declared beforehand. He recommended that councillors who were professionally connected with outside interests (e.g. estate agents, solicitors) should be precluded from making use for professional purposes of information gained in the course of their official duties.

96. Shortly after the election, he joined with Mr Harry Diamond, hitherto Socialist Republican M.P. for Falls.

97. To Mr John McQuade, later well-known as an extreme Unionist in Stormont.

98. Cf. Budge and O'Leary, *New Society* (December 1968).

99. *The Belfast Protestant Record* (June 1901), p. 7, noted with approval that a recent street collection had raised less money than expected.

100. As the Health Act, 1947, allowed voluntary hospitals in England and Scotland unwilling to enter the national scheme to claim.

101. A curious anomaly was provided by Dixon Park (four miles from Belfast) presented to the Corporation in 1959 by the widow of the linen magnate, Sir Daniel Dixon, on the strict understanding that any swings erected for children there would be available on Sundays. The Corporation accepted the gift. Opposition councillors were not slow to contrast the free swings of Dixon Park with the chained swings of the city play centres.

102. *B.N.L.*, 22 September 1964, carried fifteen letters on the subject – most (including one from Paisley) in support of the *status quo*.

103. On the day of the debate the council received a deputation representing the sabbath schools, the Belfast County Grand Orange Lodge and the Sunday Observance Vigilance Committee.

104. Because of his insistence on applying the rule book, Mr Sam Napier, Secretary of the Labour Party, was deprived of his post as Secretary to the *Parliamentary* Labour Party, two of whose members Mr Bleakley and Mr W. R. Boyd were opposed to Sunday swings.

105. *B.N.L.*, 22 February 1967. 'It would be hard to convince anyone that it (this decision) is not related to Sunday swings.'

106. See *Irish Times*, 2 July 1968. Some Unionists, however, left the Chamber before the vote was taken.

107. *B.N.L.*, 29 January 1965.

108. *B.N.L.*, 10 February 1966.
109. *B.N.L.*, 15 February 1966. The deliberations of the City Hall Party are held in secret and only very occasionally are voting figures issued. Likewise, the party records were not made available for this study.
110. *B.N.L.*, 16 February 1966.
111. *B.N.L.*, 17 February 1966.
112. *B.N.L.*, 22 February 1966.
113. *B.N.L.*, 29 April 1966.
114. In the same year Dublin County Borough awarded 100 university scholarships.
115. Set up in 1945, financed by the Exchequer, to supplement the efforts of local authorities some of which 'lacked the resources . . . and energy' to build the requisite number of houses; cf. R. J. Lawrence, *The Government of Northern Ireland*, p. 152.
116. Larne, Carrickfergus, Ballymena, Antrim, Lurgan, Portadown, Bangor, Newtownards and Downpatrick.
117. F. W. Boal in Beckett and Glasscock, *Belfast*, p. 175.
118. The Improvement Committee henceforth concerned itself mainly with roads, the rest being left to a new Planning Committee of the council. A Planning Officer was not appointed, however, until 1968.
119. *See Belfast Central Area: A report to Belfast Corporation on planning policy in the city centre* (Belfast, 1969).
120. B.D.P. were also charged with drawing up a plan for the whole urban area. See *Belfast Urban Area Plan*, Vol. I (Belfast, 1969). They calculated that 74,500 new houses would be necessary in the conurbation, ibid., p. 33.

6 Local Elections and Party Competition: 1897–1967

MODERN social and institutional developments in Belfast are entangled with politics to an even greater extent than in other cities. It is to the political severance of the North from the rest of Ireland that Belfast owes its present role as an administrative and, in a modest sense, cultural centre. It is the political link with Britain that has provided financial aid for the post-war restructuring of the economy, and technological assistance for the ailing shipbuilding and aircraft industry. The British link has also provided a political and financial stimulus to the development of welfare services and housing (far more extensive than in the Republic) which as we have seen became one of the main preoccupations of the Council and its committees.

While the latter channel services which are generally regarded as necessary and non-controversial, they also serve as a major base (along with the Stormont Parliament) for Unionist hegemony in the city. It is in fact the Unionist hegemony in local government which has been a major focus for the disturbances which began in 1968 and which persist.

Given the circumstances from which it emerged and the religious hostilities which have supported it, Unionist predominance in local government could hardly fail to be criticised. The major concern of this chapter is to examine the conditions under which the Unionist hegemony described in the last two chapters continued after the political reforms of 1896, and the constitution of the Province in 1920, and under which it existed at the time of our survey. In the course of analysis we shall try to answer the question of how far Unionist predominance was secured through such institutional arrangements as the drawing of ward boundaries, methods of voting and the continued restriction of the local government franchise after 1945, and how far it genuinely reflected the political preferences of the majority of the population.

In Belfast as in most other large cities these preferences are channelled through votes for political parties. Accordingly, we shall in this chapter examine the electoral fortunes of the parties which have emerged and regrouped over the seventy years since 1897. In Chapter 7, on the basis of survey responses, we turn to the related question of what factors influenced party voters – at least under the one-party dominant system of the mid-1960s.

The context of party competition in any relatively demo-cratic system is the extent and intensity of popular participation. As a preliminary to discussion of parties we have to consider the development of the Belfast local franchise from 1897 to 1967 and estimate the degree to which any section of the population could be said to be involuntarily excluded from voting at the latter date. We then use turnout in local elections as a further measure of the effects of involuntary exclusion and as an indicator of voluntary withdrawal from normal political activity. Turning to party competition itself, we con-sider how far various parties have benefited or lost by existing electoral arrangements. Our analysis of these points is based mainly on electoral and census statistics. These not only reveal the grass roots of political developments previously described but provide a further historical perspective within which to view the survey findings presented in subsequent discussion.

THE BELFAST FRANCHISE 1897–1967

The disfranchisement of persons not holding property (and not the spouse of a property owner) from local government elections has been a main grievance that the Civil Rights movement in Northern Ireland has sought to redress. The slogan 'one man, one vote' has also been aimed at the plural votes enjoyed by business proprietors and landlords in virtue of their multiple property holdings in the city. A comparison of the proportions of adults excluded from the local franchise in Belfast and comparable British cities shows however that for almost the first half of the twentieth century a limited local franchise was neither unique to Belfast nor peculiarly restrictive there. The third of all adults enfranchised before the First World

TABLE 6.1

Proportion of Adults Enfranchised in Belfast and
Comparable British Cities 1901–66

(Percentage of registered local electors out of total population over 20, various
dates)

	1901	1911	1921	1931	1951	1961	1966
Belfast	35	31	65*	70*	65	73	79
Glasgow	31	32	75	81	99	100	100
Edinburgh	27	29	73	79	97	99	99
Liverpool	27	26	61	70	100	100	100
Manchester	29	36	63	61	99	99	99
Birmingham	35	28	50	60	98	95	96

Sources for figures on qualified electors are Registers of Electors for the cities for
appropriate years and compilations such as *Facts and Figures* (Glasgow), the *Liverpool Red Book*, *Municipal Year Book* and newspapers. Figures for the population
aged 20 and above can be obtained from relevant census figures. The starred
entries for Belfast are for the census years of 1926 and 1937, corresponding to the
British census years of 1921 and 1931, respectively.

War and the general admission of qualified women to the vote,
actually compares favourably with the average for British
cities. Nor did creation of the Province affect this comparability:
during the whole inter-war period Belfast assumes a median
position among the other cities. Only after the retention of
property as the basis of the franchise in 1946 and the recognition
in Britain of the local vote as a right inhering in the individual
does a difference appear between the proportions qualified to
vote in Belfast and in comparable cities.[1]

While the retention of property qualifications appears as the
result of conservatism rather than deliberate restrictiveness on
the part of the Northern Irish authorities it is of course possible
that conservatism was strengthened by a belief in the party
advantages that would accrue from inaction. To put the matter
crudely, the groups excluded from the franchise may have been
the ones who were most likely to vote against the dominant
Unionists – Catholics in particular and possibly also the
working classes. We can examine this question directly – at
least for the limited period of the 1960s – by comparing the
background characteristics and policy views of ordinary
electors and non-electors whom we interviewed in our survey
in 1966.

TABLE 6.2

Belfast Local Electors and Non-Electors Compared on
Background Characteristics

(Percentages of electors and non-electors)

	One-vote electors	Non-electors
Occupational class		
I Professional, managerial	3	4
II Semi-Professional	11	20
III(1) Clerical, supervisory	12	4
III(2) Skilled manual, service	40	31
IV Semi-skilled manual	16	20
V Unskilled manual	14	13
Other	4	7
Subjective class		
Middle class	39	24
No class	9	18
Working class	53	58
Religious affiliation		
Church of Ireland	21	18
Presbyterian	37	22
Other Protestant	13	13
Catholic	21	31
Non-believer	8	16
Party identification		
Unionist	51	38
N.I. Labour	35	38
Liberal	3	7
Nationalist Labour	4	4
Other	7	13
N	173	45

Tables 6.2 and 6.3 are based on responses from our survey of
residents in the summer of 1966. Seven electors had more than one
vote: they are not included in Tables 6.2 or 6.3. Percentages in this
and subsequent Tables may not add exactly to 100 because of
rounding.

In Table 6.2 certain differences do emerge between the
characteristics of electors and non-electors. There are 15 per
cent more Presbyterians among the former than among the
latter, 10 per cent fewer Catholics and eight per cent fewer non-
believers. Unionist electors also outnumber Unionist non-
electors by 13 per cent. On the other hand there are roughly
equal proportions of electors and non-electors supporting

Northern Ireland Labour and Nationalists, and Protestant denominations other than the Presbyterian are not unduly favoured by the franchise. There is a mixed pattern of class differences between electors and non-electors: manual occupations are not under-represented among electors but those residents who describe themselves as middle class are over-represented.

Certain of the differences between electors and non-electors which might be expected on the hypothesis of Unionist manipulation of the franchise do therefore appear. But the absence of other differences which might equally be expected on that hypothesis suggests that the bias is so unsystematic as not to be the result of any concerted plan. More importantly, the result of a further comparison shows that the social differences appearing between electors and non-electors do not result in a distortion of the popular preferences which are fed into the electoral process. Table 6.3 contains the results of a comparison

TABLE 6.3

Belfast Local Electors and Non-Electors Compared on Reactions to Current Issues and Perception of Most Important Problem Facing Belfast Corporation

(Percentages of electors and non-electors)

	Electors %	Non-electors %
Agree with:		
Opening swings on Sundays	70	73
Naming Lagan Bridge after Carson	25	16
Giving State aid to Mater Hospital	79	76
Raising rates	10	11
Mixing Catholics and Protestants on Corporation housing estates	55	60
Desire change in Belfast local government	45	31
Most important problem facing Corporation is housing	35	33
Very or quite likely to succeed in action on issues	20	13

The form of the questions used to ascertain preference on issues is generally: Have you heard about the proposal to . . .? (If Yes) Do you agree or disagree with this proposal? How strongly do you agree with this proposal – very strongly, fairly strongly or not very strongly? Respondents who said they had not heard of the proposal were given a brief standard review of its salient points and then asked their reactions. Only total percentages for agreement are given in Table 6.3.

between electors' and non electors' preferences on a number of local issues current at the time of our survey. No difference appears that could be regarded as substantively important. On the question of naming a new bridge after the Protestant-Unionist hero Carson, fewer non-electors agree: but only a small minority of electors agree also. On the question of state aid to the Catholic Mater Hospital and integration of religiously segregated council housing – issues with similar politico-religious overtones – differences are minimal. A more substantial difference of 14 per cent opens between the proportions expressing some desire for change in local government, but those underprivileged by the existent system mention change less than the electors who enjoy its benefits. Non-electors feel less likely to suceed in any action taken on issues – naturally, since they lack the backing of a vote. But a comparably small proportion of ordinary electors display confidence in their prospects of success in spite of their admission to the franchise. Possession of an individual vote is hardly a major source of political influence.

PARTICIPATION IN ELECTIONS 1897–1967

Opportunities for participation can be measured partly through the proportion of adults enfranchised. But participation can

TABLE 6.4

Participation in Belfast Municipal Elections 1897–1967

(Number of seats contested out of all involved in election and percentage voting out of (i) electors in contested wards, (ii) electors in city and (iii) all adults in city)

Date	No. seats contested out of all seats for election	% Turnout of electors in contested wards	% Turnout of electors in whole city	% Turnout of all adults in city
1897	41/60	55	52	15
1899	8/16	52	33	10
1900	5/16	39	13	5
1901	8/22	38	17	7
1902	12/16	37	27	11
1903	9/15	45	24	9
1904	9/23	58	23	8
1905	8/15	48	21	8
1906	8/16	42	20	7
1907	16/22	64	47	16

TABLE 6.4—*continued*

Date	No. seats contested out of all seats for election	% Turnout of electors in contested wards	% Turnout of electors in whole city	% Turnout of all adults in city
1908	14/15	55	47	16
1909	9/16	46	24	8
1910	9/23	60	31	10
1911	7/15	63	26	8
1912	15/15	39	39	12
1913	16/22	22	19	6
1914	15/15	23	23	7
1915	4/16	58	9	3
1920	60/60	66	66	35
1923	37/60	66	56	32
1924	10/15	52	39	25
1925	4/15	56	11	7
1926	12/22	60	45	29
1927	8/14	61	28	19
1928	6/16	63	21	14
1929	7/23	63	24	16
1930	4/15	42	9	6
1931	2/15	51	6	4
1932	3/22	43	7	5
1933	5/15	47	15	11
1934	2/15	50	7	5
1936	6/23	44	13	9
1937	3/15	39	8	6
1938	3/15	37	8	6
1939	1/22	52	4	3
1946	48/60	58	46	32
1949	32/52	45	31	19
1952	40/53	31	27	17
1955	38/52	40	32	21
1958	42/53	40	33	23
1961	25/52	34	21	15
1964	38/53	42	34	27
1967	52/53	50	50	39

Notes on Table 6.4. Sources for Tables 6.4–6.9 are the annual Corporation handbooks, the booklet *Local Government Services 1923–32* (Northern Ireland Ministry of Home Affairs), newspaper reports of elections, municipal voting returns and statistics from relevant census. All municipal elections for the period are reported: during the two World Wars normal elections were suspended, as was normal municipal government on the occasions mentioned in Chapter 5. All elections from 1897 to 1967 were conducted within the ward boundaries drafted in 1896, with the exception of the election of 1920 when party lists competed under the Hare system of Proportional Representation in eight large wards. Throughout the remainder of the period the wards of 1896 were each represented by three councillors, who each served for three years, and a directly elected alderman who served for six. From 1897 to 1939 a third of all councillors were elected annually, aldermen standing as their term expired. From 1946 to 1967 councillors stood *en bloc* at triennial elections, along with half the aldermen.

also be reduced through the absence of competition in some of the seats at stake. The nomination of only one candidate for a ward implies his automatic selection without electors exercising any choice through the vote. Thus our estimate of the degree of voluntary participation in local elections must take into account involuntary exclusion through residence in an uncontested ward as well as the lack of property qualifications. Accordingly Table 6.4, as well as reporting the number of contested seats out of all those at stake, calculates turnout percentages (the percentages of those voting at each election) on three distinct bases.

One base is the total number of enfranchised adults living in contested wards – the only persons with the opportunity to vote. The percentage of non-voters among this group represents the extent of voluntary withdrawal from elections. The second base is the total number of enfranchised adults in the city as a whole, whether living in contested or uncontested wards. When most seats are contested this percentage approaches the first: when many seats are not contested the difference between this second percentage and the first gives an indication of the extent of one type of involuntary exclusion. Comparison of the second percentage with the third – turnout among all adults, enfranchised and unenfranchised in the city as a whole – shows the influence of franchise restrictions in directly reducing election participation.

All these measures of turnout reflect not only the general historical influences of the pre-war, inter-war and post-war periods but also the particular influence of the institutional arrangements which initiated each – the 1896 Act, the general admission of property-owners' spouses after the First World War and the change from annual to triennial elections after the Second World War. In all three periods there is a tendency for the first election to produce a higher turnout which then declines in subsequent elections. This is clearest for the inter-war period for reasons we shall examine in detail later, but is also apparent in the post-war period: pre-war, the peak of 15 per cent total turnout in 1897 was surpassed in 1907–8. This decline from higher to lower participation in the inter-war and post-war periods appears not only in total turnout, but in the turnout of electors in contested wards, as well as in the numbers of seats contested. There is thus a tendency for all the indicators of participation and competition to move in line with each other: when party competition (i.e. numbers of contested seats) is subdued so is popular interest as reflected in the figures for voluntary turnout.

Fluctuations in total turnout thus reflect both voluntary and involuntary abstention. When franchise restrictions and general political conditions were similar in Belfast and comparable

TABLE 6.5

Average Participation in Municipal Elections in Belfast and Comparable British Cities, for the Pre-war, Inter-war and Post-War Periods

	Belfast average %	Comparable British cities: average %
Pre-war – 1897–1915		
Seats contested	60	48
Turnout of electors in contested wards	47	52
Turnout of electors in whole city	27	25
Turnout of all adults in city	9	8
Inter-war – 1920–39		
Seats contested	45	77
Turnout of electors in contested wards	53	48
Turnout of electors in whole city	19	35
Turnout of all adults in city	12	22
Post-war – 1945–67		
Seats contested	70	96
Turnout of electors in contested wards	41	38
Turnout of electors in whole city	32	39
Turnout of all adults in city	22	36

Notes on Table 6.5. Belfast averages are calculated from figures collected from the sources mentioned in notes to Table 6.4. Data for other cities come from *Political Development*, Chapter 6.

British cities[2] – i.e. in the pre-war period – average percentages of adults voting also approached each other: the average turnout of 9 per cent for Belfast compares with an average of 8 per cent for the other British cities. In the inter-war period the Belfast franchise, as we have seen, was not more restrictive than other local franchises in Britain. However political conditions increasingly diverged as local party competition became more vigorous in Britain – thus greatly boosting the number of contested seats – while in Belfast the consolidation of Unionist rule progressively reduced competition. This development emerges graphically from a comparison of the average percentage of contested seats in Belfast and in comparable British cities: 60 per cent to 48 per cent pre-war: 45 per cent to 77 per cent inter-war: 70 per cent to 96 per cent post-war. As a result the inter-war average of 12 per cent for total turnout in Belfast fell markedly below the average, in comparable cities, of 22 per cent. In the post-war triennial elections more Belfast seats were contested, but still substantially less than the total at stake; combined with the more restricted franchise this meant that even the higher total average turnout of 22 per cent in Belfast fell well below the 36 per cent of other cities.

Is this lower total participation caused mainly by voluntary abstention or by involuntary exclusion? The contrast which appears between turnout in Belfast and the other cities where institutional conditions began to diverge after the First World War certainly suggests that involuntary exclusion is more important. We can directly check this inference by comparing the inter-city turnout of electors in contested wards: this comparison controls for the effects of the franchise and of seats left uncontested since it focuses only on those able to vote free from these institutional restrictions.

Average turnout of electors in contested seats, for Belfast compared with the other cities, is: 47 per cent to 52 per cent pre-war: 53 per cent to 48 per cent inter-war: 41 per cent to 38 per cent post-war. The proportions of those able to vote who actually did vote thus show a rough correspondence in all periods. We infer that Belfast residents have been just as active (or apathetic) as the residents of comparable cities in utilising the channels of political activity normally open to them.

Institutional constraints, then, depressed total turnout in Belfast compared to other cities after the First World War. But which constraints? – restrictive franchise, limited party competition, or both? Here we can utilise the third turnout percentage given in Table 6.4, based on all electors in the city. If the percentage voting out of all those not debarred by the franchise falls in Belfast markedly below the average percentage for comparable cities, then the limitations on party competition must exert substantial effects. If, on the other hand, the percentages correspond, the depression of total turnout must be an effect of the restricted franchise. As between Belfast and the other cities the average turnout for all electors was: 27 per cent to 25 per cent pre-war; 19 per cent to 35 per cent inter-war; 32 per cent to 39 per cent post-war. The placing of the greatest difference between these percentages in the inter-war period is significant, for it was then that the widest difference existed in the proportions of seats contested. A difference exists for both the inter-war and post-war periods when party competition was more limited in Belfast than in the other cities, whereas pre-war, when it was not, the difference is reversed. These findings indicate that limited party competition does depress turnout in Belfast: however the inter-war and post-war differences just cited are less than would be anticipated if party competition were the sole cause of depressed turnout and indicate that franchise restrictions exert some influence.

Whatever long-term influences are at work, the immediate determinants of what we have termed total turnout in Belfast – the percentage of all adults voting – are the franchise, number of contested seats and the percentage of electors voting in contested wards. At the extreme total turnout would be 100 per cent if all adults were enfranchised, all seats contested and all able to vote did vote. Equally the actual percentage for total turnout in each of the years listed in Table 6.4 depends on the values of these other factors listed in Table 6.4 and in Table 6.1. We can take advantage of the relationship between these factors, through the procedures described in the notes to Table 6.6, to estimate the relative and mutually independent effects of franchise, contested seats and voluntary turnout on total turnout in Belfast.

The figures presented in Table 6.6 are partial correlation

TABLE 6.6

Mutually Independent Effects of Franchise Restrictions, Numbers of Seats Contested, and Voluntary Turnout, on Percentage of Adults Voting in Belfast Municipal Elections 1897–1967

Partial correlation with per cent of adults voting (total turnout)	Franchise	Per cent no. of contests	Per cent of electors voting in contested wards (voluntary turnout)
1897–1915	0·495	0·893	0·862
1920–1939	−0·649	0·310	0·473
1946–1967	0·879	0·910	0·966

The figures in the table are partial correlation coefficients. These are derived from the formal statement of the relationship between per cent of adults voting and the other factors listed in the Table, which can be written as follows:

$$X_1 = b_2X_2 + b_3X_3 + b_4X_4 + \epsilon$$

X_1 =	b_2X_2 +	b_3X_3 +	b_4X_4 +	ϵ
Per cent Adults Voting	Per cent enfranchised	Per cent contests	Per cent of electors voting in contested wards	error

The extent to which all three factors acting together account for variation in the per cent of adults voting in a given set of elections is expressed by the multiple correlation coefficient (R) which assumes in this case a value of 0·914 pre-war, 0·829 inter-war and 0·984 post-war. Most variation is therefore accounted for by these three factors. The extent to which the per cent enfranchised affects variation in per cent of adults voting, independently of the per cent of contests and voluntary turnout, is given by the correlation between per cent adults voting and per cent enfranchised, controlling for per cent contests and voluntary turnout – symbolically expressed by $\gamma13·34$. Relationships between per cent adults voting – and per cent contests ($\gamma13·24$) and per cent electors voting ($\gamma14·23$) can be estimated by similar partial correlation coefficients, which all vary in value between − 1·00 and + 1·00. See H. M. Blalock, *Social Statistics* (New York, 1960), Chapters 17–19.

coefficients: each gives the strength of relationship between the factor named in the column heading and total turnout, i.e. percentage of adults voting. The correlation coefficients vary in value between +1 and − 1, depending on whether their effect is to boost or depress total turnout. They are calculated separately for the pre-war, inter-war and post-war periods.

Since the correlations in Table 6.6 are based on the extent to which values for total turnout fluctuated for each election in accordance with values of the factor under consideration, they can only be estimates of the factor's influence and are subject to error. This point is dramatically illustrated by the negative correlation between franchise and total turnout in the inter-war period. Taken literally, it indicates that an extended franchise operated to reduce total turnout! This spurious conclusion nevertheless reflects the statistical fact that as the franchise was extended in the 1930s total turnout fell. Common sense tells us that at worst extensions to the franchise could only have zero effects on turnout, and that the fall during the inter-war period was due to other factors operating concurrently with franchise extensions.

However, the other estimates of effect reported in Table 6.6 are consonant with commonsense. In the pre-war period a more extended franchise did increase total turnout, but only to half the extent that party contests did: the effect of voluntary turnout in contested wards was almost equal to that of party contests. Inter-war, as we have seen, extensions to the franchise failed to inhibit the decline in total turnout. The effect of party contests was also diminished compared with the pre-war period. The effects of voluntary turnout (strongest of all factors interwar) are produced by the general inertia that engulfed the politics of both city and Province in the 1930s, with the sub-sidence of political passions under the debilitating effects of Depression. The post-war period saw franchise extensions, party contests and voluntary turnout all contributing strongly and relatively equally to higher total turnout. Still at the present time, as more markedly in the earlier periods, the institutional constraints on turnout exercised by the restricted franchise and more particularly by the limitations on party competition, affected total turnout equally with popular apathy. The reformers who in the late 1960s focused their propaganda on franchise restrictions might well pause to reflect that, in the Province as well as in Belfast, the more important constraint on popular participation is the informal regulation of party con-tests rather than constitutional limitations on the electorate. To this central question of party competition we now turn.

PARTY COMPETITION AND VOTING TRENDS 1897–1967

Table 6.7 states the end results of party competition in local elections in terms of the distribution of Council seats and the control they gave of the Corporation. The end percentages clearly reveal the rootedness of Unionist control. In every

TABLE 6.7

Council Seats Gained by Local Parties in Belfast 1897–1967

Year	No. Uncontested seats gained by:				No. Contested seats gained by:				Per cent total seats gained by:			
	Unionist N	N.I.L.P. N	Nat. N	Other N	Unionist N	N.I.L.P. N	Nat. N	Other N	Unionist %	N.I.L.P. %	Nat. %	Other %
1897	17	0	0	2	19	6	8	8	60	10	13	17
1899	6	0	2	0	6	1	0	1	75	6	12	6
1900	8	1	2	2	4	0	0	1	75	6	12	6
1901	7	1	2	0	4	2	0	2	50	14	18	18
1902	2	1	4	2	10	0	1	1	75	6	12	6
1903	4	0	1	0	7	0	0	2	72	0	13	13
1904	9	2	2	2	5	1	2	0	64	14	9	14
1905	6	1	0	0	4	2	2	0	66	20	13	0
1906	7	0	0	0	6	0	1	1	81	0	12	6
1907	3	0	1	3	12	0	4	0	68	0	18	14
1908	0	1	0	0	11	1	1	1	73	13	7	7
1909	7	0	0	0	7	0	2	0	87	0	13	0
1910	13	0	0	1	7	0	2	0	87	0	9	4
1911	6	0	2	0	7	0	0	0	87	0	13	0
1912	0	0	0	0	13	0	2	0	87	0	13	0
1913	6	0	0	0	11	0	4	1	77	0	18	5
1914	0	0	0	0	13	0	2	0	87	0	13	0
1915	10	0	1	1	2	0	2	0	75	0	19	6
1920	0	0	0	0	37	13	10	0	62	22	17	0
1923	23	0	0	0	27	2	8	0	83	3	13	0
1924	3	0	2	0	7	2	0	1	66	13	13	7
1925	11	0	0	0	1	2	1	0	80	13	7	0
1926	9	0	1	0	9	1	2	0	82	4	14	0

TABLE 6.7 —continued

Year	No. Uncontested seats gained by: Unionist	N.I.L.P.	Nat.	Other	No. Contested seats gained by: Unionist	N.I.L.P.	Nat.	Other	Per cent total seats gained by: Unionist	N.I.L.P.	Nat.	Other
	N	N	N	N	N	N	N	N	%	%	%	%
1927	5	0	1	0	7	1	0	0	86	7	7	0
1928	10	0	0	0	2	2	2	0	75	12	12	0
1929	15	0	1	0	2	3	1	1	74	13	9	4
1930	10	1	0	0	1	1	2	0	73	13	13	0
1931	10	1	2	0	2	0	0	0	80	7	13	0
1932	16	0	3	0	3	0	0	0	81	0	14	0
1933	7	1	2	0	4	0	0	1	73	7	13	7
1934	10	0	2	0	1	2	0	0	73	13	13	0
1936	15	2	0	0	3	0	2	1	78	9	9	4
1937	10	0	2	0	3	0	0	0	87	0	13	0
1938	9	1	2	0	3	0	0	0	80	6	13	0
1939	18	0	3	0	1	0	0	0	86	0	14	0
1946	5	3	4	0	41	5	2	0	77	13	11	0
1949	19	1	0	0	25	0	7	0	85	2	13	0
1952	12	0	7	0	31	1	9	0	81	2	17	0
1955	7	1	7	0	37	0	0	0	85	2	13	0
1958	11	0	0	0	32	1	9	0	81	2	17	0
1961	20	0	7	0	21	2	2	0	79	4	17	0
1964	15	0	0	0	23	6	8	1	72	11	16	2
1967	1	0	0	0	41	10	10	0	79	2	19	0

Notes to Table 6.7. In this and subsequent Tables in the chapter the votes gained by allies, associates and forerunners of the three leading groups are aggregated. For example, the votes gained by the Citizens' Association pre-war are added to those of mainline Unionists, as are those of Protestant Unionists later. Similarly, Trades council and unemployed votes are assigned to the N.I.L.P., and Sinn Fein to the Nationalists. The justification for aggregating votes in this way is that whatever personal differences exist between groupings, they all represent a broad *tendence*, whose fortunes should be reviewed as a whole.

election reviewed the Unionist and their allies gained a plurality
of the seats at stake, and in all years except 1901 they gained an
absolute majority of over 60 per cent of the seats. While they
always gained heavily in terms of seats left uncontested they
also – save for a few exceptional years – secured a swinging
majority of contested seats.

The Nationalist groupings also gained disproportionately
from uncontested seats. The extraordinary stability of the
percentage of seats gained by Nationalists over the whole
seventy years should be noted: pre-war, inter-war and post-
war it remained fairly constantly within the range of 13 to
17 per cent. The other main political group – Northern Ireland Labour and its allies – shows much more fluctuation in its
final share of the seats. Nor – important in a party which set
out to challenge the existing denominational parties – is there
any sign of a steady upward climb in its proportion of seats.
The 20 per cent of 1905 is unsurpassed: by the mid-1950s its
share was a mere two per cent, although this rose to 11 per
cent in 1964. Most Labour gains have been contested.

Council seats are only one aspect of election performance.
Perhaps more important as an indicator of popularity are the
percentages of votes cast for each party, which appear in Table
6.8. An initial qualification to interpretation of these figures
is, however, that they relate only to votes cast in the contested
seats. Where many are left uncontested this is for the good
reason that a particular party (usually Unionist or Nationalist)
is judged to be so popular in certain wards that its position is
unassailable. Only wards where these parties are less popular
are often contested. Thus percentages of votes cast often under-
estimate Unionist and Nationalist support.

In spite of this the Unionists gained a plurality of popular
votes, and usually an absolute majority, in every year examined.
They always gained a majority in years when most seats were
contested (in every post-war election, for example). Because of
fluctuation in numbers of contested seats it is difficult to
interpret the marked variation in the Nationalist share of the
vote. Certainly it was generally higher pre-war than either
inter-war or post-war. But in the two latter periods it has
sporadically hit 20 per cent. Owing to greater competition
post-war it has never declined to zero, the nearest being the

TABLE 6.8

Percentage of Votes Cast for Local Parties in Belfast 1897–1967

	Unionist	N.I.L.P.	Nat.	Other
	%	%	%	%
1897	39	12	24	25
1899	56	11	6	27
1900	69	0	14	16
1901	50	8	8	34
1902	61	5	25	9
1903	70	0	0	30
1904	43	15	24	19
1905	38	30	32	0
1906	66	6	11	16
1907	46	18	23	12
1908	59	19	5	16
1909	65	0	28	7
1910	60	0	16	23
1911	67	17	2	13
1912	76	0	7	17
1913	57	11	28	4
1914	68	0	16	15
1915	60	5	25	10
1920	56	19	20	5
1923	71	9	11	9
1924	59	29	0	13
1925	30	47	23	0
1926	59	33	8	1
1927	56	40	3	0
1928	42	41	17	0
1929	37	31	11	21
1930	18	46	36	0
1931	61	39	0	0
1932	79	21	0	0
1933	49	24	0	26
1934	60	40	0	0
1936	55	14	16	14
1937	94	6	0	0
1938	56	0	0	44
1939	100	0	0	0
1946	64	26	9	1
1949	69	10	20	1
1952	66	23	11	1
1955	82	14	4	0
1958	64	21	16	0
1961	81	16	3	0
1964	60	28	9	3
1967	60	24	15	1

three per cent of 1961, when seven out of nine Nationalist victories were uncontested.

Northern Ireland Labour also shows fluctuations in its share of the vote. Since most of its victories have been contested, such fluctuations run parallel with those noted earlier in its share of the seats. Thus there is no consistent upward trend in popularity, although its very minor share of seats in the 1950s does not fairly reflect its substantial share of the popular vote. In terms of votes although not seats the N.I.L.P. outruns the combined Nationalist groupings.

In discussing the discrepancy between a party's votes and its share of council seats a useful summary measure is the difference between the percentage of seats gained in the election and the percentage of votes. Where the percentage of seats is larger the difference is treated as positive, and where it is smaller the difference is considered negative. On the point already made about interpretations of the popular vote the measure must be treated with caution. For any party gaining a fair number of uncontested seats will always have a substantial positive difference in its favour, i.e. it will gain a larger proportion of seats than of votes. But of course, had an election been held in the uncontested seats, that party would have received a large proportion of the votes cast, which would have brought its share of the seats and of the voters into closer correspondence. This consideration must be borne in mind particularly when interpreting results from the late 1920s and 1930s, when the proportion of uncontested seats was high. Obviously in 1939 when only one seat was contested the voting statistics are of less value as an indication of city electors' preferences than the final distribution of seats. Nevertheless the very fact that the system produces large numbers of uncontested seats, i.e. constituencies where one party enjoys unquestioned predominance, points to an institutional bias favouring that party regardless of changes in electoral preferences, so that with due caution the discrepancy between seats and votes gained can be employed as a useful analytic tool. The sum of the largest positive and negative discrepancies, termed the 'range of distortion', can then be used to estimate the degree of bias in the voting system as a whole.

The most striking feature of the discrepancies is the extent to which they constantly favour the Unionists. Only in the two inter-war elections of 1937 and 1939 and the one post-war election of 1961 was the Unionist discrepancy negative – reflecting a Unionist share of seats proportionately less than their share of votes. Usually the Unionists gain a higher percentage of seats than of votes. The discrepancy in their favour ranges from three to 50: in the post-war period it fluctuated from – 2 to + 16. While this partly reflects Unionist success in uncontested seats it underlines the extent to which the electoral system as a whole favours Unionism – a feature which will receive more detailed examination below.

No other party was so favoured by the system. However the Nationalists did on balance benefit from a higher share of seats – especially post-war. In contrast, Northern Ireland Labour consistently received less seats than votes – often very much less. Since their share of votes has rarely exceeded a quarter, their representation on the Council has never been substantial.

Besides estimating the extent to which individual parties gain or lose from the electoral system, we can examine the 'range of distortion' for different years to discover how biased the system is as a whole and how this varies over time. (The 'range of distortion' is calculated by adding the highest positive and the highest negative discrepancy between the percentage of votes cast for any party and the percentage of seats it gained, in each election. Independents of varying hues are not taken into account in this statistic, since they constitute such an amorphous and changing group.) Bias is greatest between the wars, being strongly affected by the number of seats left uncontested. It ranged from 9 in 1920 to 88 in 1930. Post-war bias is about the same as appeared before the First World War.

Looking at the range of distortion for Belfast alone the level appears fairly high. This impression is upheld by comparison with British cities, among which only the similarly one-party dominant system of Edinburgh shared the inter-war average of 41 per cent in Belfast. Average post-war distortion ranges from 10 to 15 for British cities compared with 28 for Belfast.

Confronted with a high level of bias in the electoral system, which we have already shown to favour the Unionists, there is a temptation to detect some kind of conspiracy by the dominant party to rig the system in their own favour. The existence of such a conspiracy is not inconceivable under Northern Irish conditions, but any assertion must be tempered by the historical evidence presented in previous chapters. In the seventy years under review only three major institutional changes have occurred. These are the reorganisation of boundaries in 1896, in the drawing of which the Catholics played a large part; the change between 1920 and 1923 from proportional representation in the eight large wards to the single constituency simple majority system of annual elections, with the wards of 1896;[3] the institution of triennial elections of all councillors in 1946. The latter change was non-controversial. Only the change from P.R. to the old system in the early 1920s seems open to the charge of Unionist manipulation, particularly since it was bitterly criticised at the time by minority parties as being aimed at reducing their representation. Since any allegation about Unionist manipulation of elections must rest heavily on their part in bringing about a return to the old system it behoves us to focus on the effects of this change, both on popular participation and on party competitiveness. The results of such statistical analysis must, of course, be qualified in the light of the historical circumstances already considered, and particularly by the fact that the change from P.R. was forced through by the Stormont Unionists for both Belfast and Derry rather than by the City Hall Unionists themselves.

THE CHANGE FROM P.R.: EFFECTS AND
CONSEQUENCES

Participation and competitiveness have already been examined through the statistics presented in Tables 6.4 to 6.8. By comparing figures for the election of 1920 with those for subsequent elections we can assess the effects of change, and perhaps make inferences about partisan motives behind it.

Comparing results for the election held under Proportional Representation (1920) with those emerging from the first election under the traditional ward system (1923), the most obvious finding is that the 'range of distortion' almost doubles (from 9 to 17), as does the Unionist advantage and the Labour disability. The Nationalists moved from a moderately unfavourable to a moderately favourable discrepancy. Taken in isolation, this finding might be taken as indicating more pro-

Unionist bias in the simple majority constituency system (although the Unionists improved their electoral majority between the two years and would have won anyway).

However, if we place the change from 1920 to 1923 in the context of later elections, the bias shown by the voting system as a whole as well as the Unionist and Nationalist increment, varies more between election and election held under the simple majority constituency system than it does between the election held under P.R. and many under the subsequent system. The range of distortion almost doubled between the elections of 1923 and 1924 and tripled between 1924 and 1925. Certainly the Unionists gained a much greater advantage between 1923 and 1924 or 1925 than between 1920 and 1923, in terms of the positive discrepancy between votes and seats gained. And in spite of some overlap in the range of distortion between the generally annual elections of the inter-war period and the triennial elections of the post-war period, the mean distortion of 41 for the former compared to 23 for the latter indicates a more consistent and sustained contrast than that which opens between the elections of 1920 and the following years.

The advantage accruing to the Unionists from the abolition of P.R. stemmed less from the discrepancy between their share of seats and the votes they gained (since they generally had a plurality of votes in any case) than from a consequent reduction in the number of contested seats. The reason for this reduction lies in the behaviour of parties in a situation where most wards contained solid Unionist or Nationalist majorities. Under a P.R. system inside extended wards there was every advantage in running a list of candidates for all seats, since every vote, no matter where electors lived, was utilised for a party candidate. From 1923 onwards the existence of rock-ribbed majorities in certain of the more restricted wards created in 1896 made it electorally unprofitable for any except the favoured party to contest them. The minority of votes which might be attracted in such areas would serve no purpose in increasing Council representation. It was a more paying strategy to concentrate resources and energy behind some candidate in marginal areas who might win the seat. Thus by virtue of their loyalty certain areas were left uncontested for years at a stretch and large sectors of the electorate were denied the opportunity to vote; this had the depressing effects already noted upon the turnout of enfranchised electors and of adults as a whole (Table 6.4).

Whereas in 1920 the Unionists had to electioneer for all their seats, from 1923 they gained from nearly half to nearly all their seats without a contest. (Again the proportion uncontested fell under another institutional change – to three-year 'general elections' from 1946.) The advantage of gaining some seats without a fight lay in the provision of a solid block of seats from which to dominate the returns, and in the ability to concentrate canvassers and resources on the reduced number of contested wards.

In this situation it was the Unionists' unchallenged dominance of certain old wards that produced their favourable discrepancy between votes and seats. The others favoured by the change from P.R., though not as consistently as the Unionists, were, curiously, the Nationalists, who with their support concentrated from 1896 into two or three wards could similarly count on a high proportion of uncontested returns. The party whose share of seats consistently lagged behind their share of votes was Northern Ireland Labour. Although the unfavourable discrepancy was present in 1920 and not spectacularly noticeable in 1923, it was consistently present at fairly high levels thereafter for all elections except that of 1938. This seems to have resulted from the fact that Labour seats were much more frequently contested than Unionist or Nationalist – probably due to the Unionists' tactical advantage in being able to funnel efforts away from their own uncontested wards to those liable to fall to Labour. If these interpretations are correct it was the Labour Party with its widely spread but thin support which lost most heavily from the change from P.R. Certainly it gained more seats in the election of 1920 than ever again in the period under review. It is ironical that Labour, which with reservations also accepted the constitutional status of Northern Ireland, should have lost in the Unionist-inspired changes more heavily than the Nationalists, who diametrically opposed them. On the other hand, Labour's attempt to change the main political cleavage from religion to class may have posed more of a long-term threat to the Unionists, in Belfast at least, than the disunited Nationalists' espousal of a cause on which there was a built-in Unionist majority.

To the question of who gained from the change from P.R. there can only be one answer in light of the foregoing discussion – the Unionists. The other parties were discouraged by the change and lost the will to compete. How far the system devised in 1896 produced further institutional biases towards the Unionists and might have strengthened the Conservatism of Stormont in this context is a question we consider further in the next section.

WARD BOUNDARIES: MALAPPORTIONMENT AND
GERRYMANDERING

We have seen that the simple return to a ward system secured to the Unionists large numbers of uncontested seats. The question considered here is whether it secured them further differential advantages in terms of population distribution over the old wards. Two kinds of advantage might have accrued. The population in Unionist wards might have been less than the population in non-Unionist wards (malapportionment). Or electors might have been so distributed as to ensure the Unionists small majorities in many wards, while their opponents piled up large majorities in a few wards (gerrymandering). Either situation would have ensured that Unionist votes weighed more in the selection of councillors than non-Unionist votes.

From our account of the circumstances surrounding the initial drawing of ward boundaries in 1896 it is apparent that if anyone was favoured then it was the Catholics and Nationalists. Certainly neither population nor electors were evenly distributed in 1896 – wards varying from 13,652 residents and 1,985 electors in Smithfield, the smallest, to 34,230 residents and 4,307 electors in Pottinger, the largest. Variation had increased in 1961, when the smallest ward (Smithfield) had 8,903 residents and 3,350 electors and the largest (Clifton) had 47,882 residents and 22,333 electors. Over time this uneven distribution of population might have shifted to favour the Unionists and might therefore account for the eagerness of Stormont to return to the old system in the 1920s.

We can test to see how far malapportionment or gerry-mandering favoured the Unionists over elections in our period. For malapportionment our interest focuses on the relationship between the proportion of Unionist councillors returned and ward population – whether this is measured as all residents, all adults, or simply enfranchised electors. If the relationship is negative – that is to say, that as population becomes less the proportion of successful Unionists goes up, then we can say that malapportionment favours the Unionists. If the relationship is strong then we can attribute to this institutional bias a fair influence on Unionist success. If, on the other hand, the relationship is positive this means that Unionists are more successful in wards with high populations: thus that a Unionist vote counts for less than a non-Unionist vote and that Unionist success was obtained in spite of institutional biases not because of them.

We can summarise the relationship between population and proportions of successful Unionists in terms of the bivariate or product-moment correlation, which is closely related to the partial used previously (Table 6.6).[4] The strength of the relationship is shown by its position in the range from zero (no relationship) to 1 (complete relationship). Positive or negative signs before the product-moment correlation indicate whether the relationship is positive or negative, and thus reveal whether the Unionists were helped or hindered by the distribution of ward population. For all the years examined – all those when at least eight wards were contested – there is only one negative correlation, and this is for the relation with enfranchised electors but not total population in 1927. Correlations for other years, ranging in value from ·106 to ·613 for the relationship between total ward population and number of Unionists returned, from ·147 to ·553 for the relationship with adult population, and from ·184 to ·582 for the relationship with enfranchised electors in the ward reveal that Unionists wards throughout the entire period were more heavily populated. This is supported by inspection of actual ward populations. The central wards of Falls, Smithfield and Dock, with a heavy Catholic population, have always been among the smallest, while such staunchly Protestant areas as Shankill have always had a larger population.

We can apply a similar type of analysis to the question of gerrymandering. Here the product-moment correlations reflect the relationship between the proportion of Unionists elected and the size of the winning party's majority, for each ward. If the Unionists enjoyed wafer-thin majorities in most wards while their opponents piled up huge wasted majorities in a few wards, this relationship should be negative. But in fact there are over the years only five negative correlations compared with fourteen positive. Obviously there is little consistency in the party advantages enjoyed under the boundaries of 1896. But the Unionists have more generally had votes pile up in useless superfluity than had them weighted in their favour.

These results suggest once more that the main advantage the Unionists secured from the abolition of P.R. was tactical – the ability to concentrate party resources in marginal seats, and thus to beat down the challenge of the N.I.L.P., while receiving enough undisputed returns for automatic domination of the Council. The fact that other institutional biases penalised the Unionists emphasises one important point which concentration entirely on discrepancies might cause one to overlook. Besides the strong support which they obviously enjoyed in uncontested seats, the Unionists did contrive to win a plurality and in most cases an absolute majority of votes actually cast at each election (Table 6.8). There can be no doubt that the Unionists' uninterrupted tenure of local office has rested on genuine majority support. Whatever its other quirks, the Belfast electoral system has responded to popular preferences in securing Unionist hegemony.

It is because of this responsiveness that post-war Belfast can be considered as a democracy in the sense of 'a polity in which power to make policy decisions is allocated basically as the result of free competitive elections in which every citizen's vote is weighted identically and all have relatively equal access to information about the competing alternatives'.[5] On a summary index of democracy based on this definition, combining the extent of the franchise with measures of party competition and information equality[6] Belfast scores 0·543. This is less than the post-war score achieved by Glasgow (0·692) and the post-war average for comparable British cities (0·746) but fairly high in a world context – greater for example than a score of 0·404 for the American city of Pittsburgh. These comparisons provide a justification for our treatment of Belfast as an unstable democracy rather than a stable oligarchy, a point which will be reviewed again in our conclusions.

NOTES

1. Figures for Belfast are slightly inflated by the continuance of plural voting there, through possession of multiple business property. Only three per cent of our 1966 sample of the population possessed plural votes, however, and we can infer that its incidence was equally limited throughout the whole post-war period.
2. Comparable cities are taken as those listed in Table 6.1.
3. See the discussion of the original changes in 1896 and of the changes in the 1920s in Chapters 4 and 5, above.
4. The product-moment, or bivariate, correlation describes the strength and direction of linear relationships between two factors, and is associated with the equation:

$$y = a + bX + \epsilon$$

where y represents the number of Unionist councillors returned, a is a constant, X is one of the measures of ward population (i.e. either total population or adult population or electors enfranchised, as the case may be) and ϵ is error. See H. Blalock, *Social Statistics*, Chapter 17.
5. This definition is a summary of the ten 'polyarchal' conditions specified by R. A. Dahl, *A Preface to Democratic Theory* (Chicago, 1956), p. 84.
6. For the original index see D. E. Neubauer, 'Some Conditions of Democracy', *A.P.S.R.* LXI 1002–1009 (hereafter the *American Political Science Review* is cited as *A.P.S.R.*). The index adopted here has the component measures suggested by Neubauer (per cent enfranchised, equality of representation, information equality, per cent of time – period during which the dominant party held office and average percentage vote received by dominant party) but these are modified so as to give scores ranging from 0 to 1.

7 Party Images and Voting Choice: 1966

THE fact that Unionist hegemony in Belfast rests on genuine majority support rather than electoral sharp practice shifts our explanatory concern one stage back from the distribution of votes cast to the motivations behind these votes. In turn this shift implies a change in the main type of evidence considered, from aggregate, historical voting statistics to contemporary survey responses. What we learn about motivations from the answers made to us in 1966 is of course strictly time-bound. We cannot extrapolate backwards to the reasons for voting Unionist in the Depression years between the wars, nor to the springs of Unionist support during the pre-war struggle for Irish independence. Nevertheless, the motivations which reveal themselves in the 1960s are affected by the historical developments reviewed in the foregoing chapters and may in turn provide insights to aid interpretation of these developments. And contemporary motivations do relate most immediately to the development of the contemporary crisis; for whatever historical influences are present can act only through their effects on current motivations.

POPULAR REACTIONS TO THE BELFAST PARTIES IN 1966

The relatively bare synopsis of party operations given in voting statistics can be fleshed out through views expressed by Belfast residents in 1966 in reply to queries about what they liked and disliked about Unionists, Nationalists and Northern Ireland Labour. The first interesting point is the somewhat greater inclination of Belfast compared to Glasgow respondents to express some opinion in spite of the greater possibilities of confusion inherent in the larger number of parties and limited

TABLE 7.1

Belfast Residents: Likes and Dislikes about Parties

	Pro-Unionist	Anti-Unionist	Pro-Labour	Anti-Labour	Pro-Nat.	Anti-Nat.
Total Sample N=229						
Substantive remarks	179	183	174	126	71	149
Nothing, D(on't) K(nows)	91	108	111	121	148	107
Nothing at all!	17	7	7	8	31	4
(Emphatic Negative)						
Total R(espondents) making substantive remarks	121	114	111	99	50	118
Percentage Rs making definite remarks (substantive remarks and emphatic negative)	60	53	52	47	35	53
Unionists N=109						
Substantive remarks	136	63	44	75	40	70
Nothing, D(on't) K(nows)	27	62	68	50	74	53
Nothing at all!	0	4	6	3	19	1
Total R(espondents) making substantive remarks	82	43	35	56	14	55
Percentage Rs making definite remarks	75	43	38	64	30	51
Labour N=81						
Substantive remarks	30	78	93	31	23	46
Nothing, D(on't) K(nows)	44	37	24	49	51	41
Nothing at all!	15	3	1	5	12	2
Total R(espondents) making substantive remarks	22	41	56	27	28	38
Percentage Rs making definite remarks	46	54	69	40	37	49
Nationalists N=11						
Substantive remarks	2	13	11	7	10	6
Nothing, D(on't) K(nows)	7	3	5	7	5	7
Nothing at all!	2	0	0	0	0	0
Total R(espondents) making substantive remarks	2	8	6	4	6	4
Percentage Rs making definite remarks	36	73	55	36	55	34
Total Non-Unionists N=120						
Substantive remarks	45	120	130	51	31	79
Nothing, D(on't) K(nows)	64	46	43	71	74	54
Nothing at all!	17	3	1	5	12	3
Total R(espondents) making substantive remarks	39	71	76	43	36	63
Percentage Rs making definite remarks	47	62	64	40	40	55

The source for this and most subsequent Tables in the book is the Belfast Survey conducted by the authors. Total numbers of residents in the total sample and sub-groups in subsequent Tables in the book are as reported here, unless specific mention is made to the contrary.

opportunities to affirm party support at local elections. Seventeen per cent of Glasgow residents professed to know nothing about the opposition Progressive Party there, compared with the 16 per cent of Belfast residents who confessed their ignorance about the Nationalists and the 8 per cent who said they had not heard of Northern Irish Labour. Only 4 per cent evaded any remark about the dominant Unionists, compared to 9 per cent in Glasgow who vented no like or dislike of the governing Labour Party. The Belfast population seems no more or less apathetic than the population of British cities generally.

The reply that respondents liked or disliked 'nothing' about a party might indicate lack of knowledge or reluctance to comment but on the other hand may also signify the existence of entirely negative and hostile feelings between partisans. We have attempted to distinguish between indifference and hostility by coding the latter type of reply under the strongly negative 'nothing at all!' It is remarkable, given the strong politico-religious cleavages underlying party competition in Belfast, that emphatically negative replies were no more numerous than they were in response to similar questions about the Glasgow parties. A range of 5 per cent to 11 per cent liked or disliked 'nothing at all' about one of the parties in Glasgow: in Belfast the range was 3 per cent to 13 per cent, much the highest number of strongly negative replies being given in answer to a question on likes about Nationalists. Negative feelings are more pronounced in the reactions of party adherents to questions about likes for other parties (especially by Unionists and Labour about Nationalists, and by Labour about Unionists). But the noticeable point is the low level of negative reaction throughout.

Besides examining views of the parties for evidence of apathy or strongly marked hostility, we also examined the tenor of substantive remarks passed, always bearing in mind that these were reactions of only a third to roughly two thirds of the population, depending on the party at which they were directed. The contrast between Labour's failure to establish itself firmly in Belfast and its success in other British cities, in addition to the existence of Nationalist groupings based in part on a different cleavage, raises the question of whether Labour and Unionists are perceived in the same way in Northern

TABLE 7.2

Belfast Residents: Images of the Local Parties

(Multiple percentages of all residents and Unionist and Labour residents endorsing various general comments about the local parties)

	Old religious political divisions	Attempts to overcome old religious-political divisions	Attitude on discrimination	Service to the whole community all the people	Uncompromising attitude towards opponents	Leadership qualities
All residents						
Likes about Unionists	9	0	0	12	0	31
Dislikes about Unionists	23	0	25	0	7	20
Likes about Labour	1	13	0	7	0	26
Dislikes about Labour	21	0	5	0	0	40
Likes about Nationalists	45	0	0	7	0	24
Dislikes about Nationalists	50	0	20	0	0	13
Unionists						
Likes about Unionists	9	0	0	13	0	24
Dislikes about Unionists	14	0	19	0	8	24
Likes about Labour	2	16	0	2	0	34
Dislikes about Labour	24	0	8	0	1	35
Likes about Nationalists	25	0	0	5	0	15
Dislikes about Nationalists	50	0	24	0	0	10
Labour						
Likes about Unionists	10	0	0	10	0	40
Dislikes about Unionists	24	0	18	0	7	18
Likes about Labour	0	10	0	9	0	18
Dislikes about Labour	18	0	6	0	0	48
Likes about Nationalists	32	0	0	8	0	20
Dislikes about Nationalists	44	0	12	0	0	18

TABLE 7.2—continued

	Handling of economic questions	Welfare policies	Attitude to working-class socialism	Other policies	General philosophy	Traditional family-related attitudes
All residents						
Likes about Unionists	15	7	0	2	6	18
Dislikes about Unionists	3	7	7	2	4	3
Likes about Labour	0	14	24	6	4	6
Dislikes about Labour	0	0	13	8	8	4
Likes about Nationalists	0	3	0	0	7	14
Dislikes about Nationalists	0	1	3	0	7	7
Unionists						
Likes about Unionists	13	7	0	2	5	23
Dislikes about Unionists	1	11	6	3	6	5
Likes about Labour	0	11	23	0	0	0
Dislikes about Labour	0	0	12	0	9	9
Likes about Nationalists	0	0	0	0	7	12
Dislikes about Nationalists	0	1	1	0	6	7
Labour						
Likes about Unionists	13	3	0	3	10	0
Dislikes about Unionists	0	6	7	1	7	3
Likes about Labour	0	15	23	7	6	8
Dislikes about Labour	0	0	6	3	6	3
Likes about Nationalists	0	4	0	0	4	4
Dislikes about Nationalists	0	2	4	0	10	2

Notes on Table 7.2: Responses in Tables 7.1 and 7.2 derived from a series of standard questions devised by the Survey Research Center, University of Michigan. Is there anything in particular you like about the (Unionist Party, Labour Party, Nationalists) in Belfast? Is there anything in particular you don't like about the (Unionist Party, Labour Party, Nationalists) in Belfast? Answers were taken verbatim, detailed categories common to all questions devised on the basis of the natural clusters into which responses fell, and answers coded into these categories. These categories are too detailed to use in any one analysis but facilitate recombination in secondary analysis by other investigators. For our own purposes the detailed substantive categories have been grouped into the 12 broad categories which appear in Table 7.2. Thus 'leadership' groups likes or dislikes of specific named leaders, national leaders (such as M.P.s, Harold Wilson, etc.), local leaders, party members and references to intra-party democracy, party fairness or justice, state of organisation, and performance in government. Percentages in the Table are based on the number of all responses to avoid double counting, since respondents were free to give more than one answer and hence could possibly be coded twice into one of the broader categories in the Table. Some responses are excluded from the Table, e.g. 'other' responses and ones mentioned only by a few respondents which did not fit into the broad grouping. Thus percentages do not always add up to 100; in some cases they add up to slightly more than 100 because of rounding.

Ireland as in Britain. British electors generally have been found
to characterise the Labour Party as standing for the working
class, the poor, the welfare state and socialism. Conservative-
Unionists, on the other hand, have been viewed as more
favourable to the middle class, business interests and individual
effort. The question is whether the existence of politico-religious
cleavages over partition and treatment of the minority in
Belfast completely altered these views, particularly under the
stimulus of Nationalist activity.

Some of the main party images obviously persisted in Belfast.
Thus a major cluster of favourable comment centred round
Labour's espousal of working-class interests and socialist
ideals (24 per cent of all responses) and its social welfare
policies (14 per cent with 6 per cent citing its other policies). A
specifically local note crept in when Labour's efforts to overcome religious divisions and introduce new issues were mentioned (13 per cent of responses). Another 7 per cent view Labour
as standing for all the people. A strong contrast with earlier
images of Labour in Britain appeared in comments made in
26 per cent of responses on the high quality of Labour leadership.

The Unionist leadership was also mentioned favourably in
31 per cent of replies and was seen as standing for all the people
in 12 per cent. However it was not perceived as seeking to
eliminate the old conflicts: on the contrary 9 per cent of
comments admired its stand in this area. Its conservative
stand on welfare policy attracted favourable mention from 7
per cent, but again a provincial feature was praise of its
efforts to attract industry and reduce unemployment (15 per
cent of responses).

A noteworthy contrast with Glasgow residents' views of their
own parties was the absence of any linkage between the
Unionists and the middle class in these comments. Labour's
connection with the working class and social welfare attracted
only a third of the remarks favourable to the party in contrast
to half in Glasgow. Positive qualities of leadership were
stressed very little in Glasgow in regard to either of the local
parties whereas they attracted the largest volume of praise for
both Labour and Unionists in Belfast. Thus Belfast contrasted
with Britain not only in the weaker stress on social welfare but

in the strong emphasis on leadership. The Nationalists attracted only half the number of positive remarks made about the other parties: 24 per cent of these, nevertheless, commented favourably on aspects of Nationalist leadership. The major positive comment came in the half of all replies which expressed approval of Nationalist stands on the politico-religious question.

Criticisms of the parties covered the same ground as favourable comments, but with some shift in emphasis. More comments (40 per cent) criticised Labour leadership than praised it. Criticism stemmed largely from its failure to attain power, and praise from the personal qualities of party members. Labour support for the working class and socialism and its welfare policies were disparaged in 29 per cent of replies. Its shifty stance on the border question was mentioned in 21 per cent.

The Unionists, like Labour, attracted much negative as well as positive comment on their leadership qualities (20 per cent of disliked qualities). Unionists were also considered intolerant of opposition by seven per cent, a characteristic linked with their tendency to regard criticism as disloyal in view of their rigid position on the politico-religious division (mentioned in 23 per cent). Linked again with this old division was their perceived tendency to discriminate in favour of their own supporters (25 per cent). There is less significance in the accusation that Unionists were against the working class and had negative social policies (both 7 per cent). The Nationalists, like their main opponents, were seen predominantly in terms of Irish divisions: 50 per cent of replies deplored their fostering of old hostilities and 20 per cent felt they complained too much of discrimination. Only 13 per cent deplored their leadership (mainly because it was unsuccessful). Much of the unfavourable comment stemmed from frustration at the rigid mould forced on politics by partition and religious hostility.

Supporters tended to praise their own party and criticise the opposition, as can be seen from the relative numbers of substantive remarks reported in Table 7.1. Labour supporters liked Labour primarily for its socialism and support of working-class interests (23 per cent of replies), welfare policies (15 per cent) and the personal calibre of its leaders (18 per cent). But its attack on religious conflict and stand against discrimination were mentioned by 10 and 9 per cent, respectively. The most sizeable cluster expressing discontent (48 per cent) focused on the failure of the leaders to win power, although 18 per cent were hostile to its compromise position on the politico-religious cleavage. This is a surprisingly large percentage to find among supporters and illustrates the loss of popularity suffered by any party trying to cross-cut the old cleavages.

Twenty-four per cent of Unionist replies criticised Labour on this point too, double the proportion which disliked its socialism and support of the working class. Thirty-five per cent of Unionist replies also criticised Labour leadership on various grounds. The major adverse comments made about the Unionist party by its own supporters were of the leadership, mainly for its internal divisions (24 per cent)[1] and tendency to favour its own political supporters (19 per cent). Labour responses echoed the same themes more strongly – 31 per cent mentioned intolerance and the unyielding Unionist position on the basic cleavage and 18 per cent discrimination in favour of its own supporters. The Unionist leadership attracted unfavourable comment in 18 per cent of Labour replies: 6 to 7 per cent respectively mentioned its general conservative philosophy, welfare policies and dissociation from the working class.

Twenty-four per cent of Unionist responses on the contrary favoured the leadership of their party, as in fact does the main cluster (40 per cent) of Labour replies favouring the Unionist Party. Unionist approval of their party leadership focused particularly on its conduct of government, and this is probably linked with its handling of the economy mentioned in 13 per cent of Unionist replies. Thirteen per cent saw the party as serving the interests of all the people, although a tenth of replies explicitly approved its resolute opposition to the severance of the link with Britain.

Neither Labour nor Unionist supporters offered strong endorsement of any positive Nationalist qualities, and the only sizeable cluster of Nationalist likings centred round the personal qualities of their leaders, as did their main adverse comment. Roughly half of Unionist and Labour replies concentrated on the same negative aspect of Nationalism – the extent to which it kept the old divisions in being. A quarter of Unionist replies (compared to 12 per cent of Labour) also resented Nationalist complaints about discrimination.

PARTY IDENTIFICATION AND VOTING

Attitudes to parties show that historical divisions based on Protestant and Catholic communalism continued up to 1966 to provide the main criteria by which the populace distinguished between Unionists, Labour and Nationalist groupings, although class themes did appear. The question is how far religion as opposed to class and other social characteristics influenced actual party support, as well as diffuse partisan attitudes. In view of the commonly accepted generalisation that British politics are essentially class politics it might be felt that class would exert a more powerful influence over voting choice than has appeared from the evidence presented up to this point, possibly because of a coincidence between class and religious divisions. We shall examine the direct relationship between class and religion in the next chapter. At this point, however, we can note the effects which various social characteristics, mainly related to class, exerted over party support. We can then pick out the class characteristic most closely related to support and discover how far its influence compares with that of religion.

TABLE 7.3

Party Identifications of Belfast Residents 1966

(Percentages of population)

	Strongly	Not very strongly	Total
Unionist	30	18	48
N.I. Labour	19	16	35
Liberal	3	1	4
Nationalist	4	1	5
Independent, Other	—	—	6
D(on't) K(nows)	—	—	2
N(ot) A(pplicable)			
			100

Questions on which the Table is based were in the standard form used by the Survey Research Center: Generally speaking, do you usually think of yourself as Unionist, Northern Ireland Labour, Liberal or Nationalist? (If party named) Well, how strongly (chosen party) do you feel? Strongly or not very strongly?

The initial problem is to identify party support. In the context of Belfast politics it is difficult to take this as coinciding with actual votes cast in the last election, since the ability to gain seats without a contest is a source of strength for the Unionists. Even though votes are not cast in uncontested wards, electors' feelings of identification and support for a party are as important in influencing politicians' strategies as 'objective' votes, and since we should expect, and shall confirm, that such feelings relate closely to actual votes in any case, they can be taken as the party support which we are interested in examining.[2]

The distribution of identifications over the Belfast population shows that over 90 per cent of Belfast residents gave definite support to a party: 87 per cent to either Unionists or Labour. The relatively low proportion of Nationalist identifiers (at 5 per cent) compared with their voting strength, leads to some question of how far residents identified with Northern Ireland Labour through its confusion with Irish Labour, Republican Labour or Independent Labour – three Nationalist groupings. Of course, Nationalist electoral strength was enhanced through the concentration of their supporters in certain central wards. The probable confusion of Nationalist Labour with Northern Ireland Labour also helps explain the gap between the impressive support felt for the latter and its miserable success in municipal elections. The tendency of its supporters to be confused by the appeals of Nationalist Labour as well as the bias of the electoral system explains the discrepancy between 35 per cent of identifiers in 1966 and 28 per cent of the vote in 1964 (Table 7.4).

From the distribution of identifications it appears that in 1966 the Unionists did not enjoy an absolute majority of support among residents (less for example than the Labour Party attracted in Glasgow at the same time). But the strength of that support as well as divisions among the other parties made it a solid basis for continued Unionist dominance.

The close connection between feelings of identification in 1966 and the vote in the previous municipal election is shown by the fact that the overwhelming majority of supporters of the Unionist and Northern Ireland Labour parties who voted in 1964 cast their votes for the appropriate party. Consistency was

TABLE 7.4

Belfast Residents: Party Identification in 1966 and Local Election Vote 1964

(Percentages of party identifiers)

Party Identification 1966	Non-voter	Unionist	N.I. Lab.	Liberal	Rep. Lab.	Ind. Lab.	%	N
Strong Unionist	28	69	—	1	—	—	100	68
Not Strong Unionist	56	42	—	2	—	—	100	41
Independent	54	15	15	8	—	—	100	13
Not strong N.I. Labour	54	11	33	—	—	2	100	37
Strong N.I. Labour	41	4	50	—	4	—	100	44
Nationalist	55	—	9	—	27	—	100	11
Liberal	44	—	22	11	11	—	100	9

Local Election Vote 1964

Total N = 223 for Tables 7.4 and 7.5 due to the failure of some residents to recall how they voted in 1964.

almost absolute among Unionists, although in the case of Labour 11 per cent of weaker identifiers and 4 per cent of stronger identifiers voted Unionist. The greater discrepancy between present identification and past voting for Labour might indicate an increase in Labour support from 1964 to 1966, but it most probably represents the usual 'breakage effect' accruing to the dominant party from the pull it exerts on the weaker minority (as in the case of choices forced upon Labour supporters in wards where no Labour candidate stood). A proportion of strong Labour identifiers equal to those voting Unionist voted Republican Labour in 1964, and Nationalists and Liberals voted Northern Ireland Labour where they did not cast a vote for their own candidate.

In view of the great obstacles to voting a more comprehensive picture of the correspondence between party identification and voting choice is gained by using both actual and intended vote in 1964 as the basis of the comparison (intended votes in the sense of those that would have been cast by non-voters). From this the carry-over between identification and voting choice becomes even clearer, and the defection of Labour supporters to Liberals and Nationalists slightly overbalanced defection to Unionists. Comparisons of party identification and actual and intended choice in the 1965 elections for the Northern Irish Parliament at Stormont also showed identifiers overwhelmingly endorsing their chosen party. In the case of Northern Ireland Labour (possibly because of the greater choice of candidates) nine tenths of the defecting Stormont votes went to Republican Labour and only a tenth to the Unionists.

As has been found in Glasgow and elsewhere[3] strong identifiers turned out to vote in greater numbers than weak identifiers: strong Unionists also turned out more than strong Labour identifiers (Table 7.4). This raises the possibility that besides benefiting from the limited number of contests, Unionists gained disproportionately in the local elections from the differential turnout of their own supporters. This has been found to be the case with the Progressives, the Glasgow party corresponding to the Unionists. Since General Elections rouse more interest than municipal elections a relevant comparison is between the distribution of party votes at the 1965 Stormont election and at the 1964 municipal election, to see whether

TABLE 7.5

Belfast Residents: Voting in the Stormont and Local Elections

(Percentages of the total population)

In 1964 Belfast Municipal Election voted:	In 1965 Stormont Election voted:				
	None	*Unionist*	*N.I. Labour*	*Liberal*	*Rep. Labour*
None	18	12	13	0	1
Unionist	3	27	3	0	0
N.I. Labour	1	0	16	0	1
Liberal	0	0	1	0	0
Rep. Labour	0	0	1	0	2
	23%	40%	33%	0	4%
N	50	89	74	0	10

Unionist turnout was more resistant to the decline of interest and concern than those of other parties. At the municipal election the Unionists had 3 per cent of total votes cast by those who did not vote in the Stormont election, and an equal proportion from those who voted for Labour at Stormont. Labour had 1 per cent of Stormont abstainers and 1 per cent who voted Republican Labour for Stormont, while losing 2 per cent of its votes for Stormont to Liberals and Republican Labour. The net advantage to Unionists from these changes was thus six per cent of the total population. As a result of supporters voting in 1965 and not voting in 1964 Unionists and Labour 'lost' 12 and 13 per cent of the total electorate respectively – a net gain to the Unionists over Labour of 1 per cent. While this is not as great as the 7 per cent net gain enjoyed by Glasgow Progressives over Labour, the fact that Labour was the smaller party meant that it lost a higher proportion of its potential votes through non-turnout at the municipal election than did the Unionists – four tenths compared to three tenths. As in Glasgow, the more conservative party gained locally from differential turnout, but the Unionists showed a further gain from other types of change.

CLASS AND OTHER DEMOGRAPHIC INFLUENCES ON PARTY SUPPORT

Basically, we conceive of class as the differentiation existing between members of a society in terms of their unequal prestige and resources, complicated by the sense of community between those at the same level of prestige and resources. The point has been made in some detail elsewhere that 'objective' differences in resources can equally well be tapped by income, education and occupation, which in any case correlate so highly that they can be used interchangeably. Since the prestige ranking of various occupations has been closely studied there are advantages in using occupation as our main 'objective' class indicator, although we shall also examine some of the political effects of education and home ownership. As well as depending on 'public' attributions of status and resources, class influences on voting also depend on 'private' feelings about which class one belongs to. Thus a manual worker who feels middle-class will tend to vote differently from a manual worker who feels working-class.[4] Subjective orientations towards class can also be tapped through the (largely voluntary) act of joining a work-related association, which is usually a trade union of some kind.

Table 7.6 shows the relationship between party identification and three class indicators – self-placement in a class and two different codings of occupational differences. Subjective class clearly influenced party support, more for Northern Ireland Labour than for Unionists. Thirty-eight per cent of association members compared with 55 per cent of non-members supported the Unionists, another differentiation produced by subjective feelings.

The two occupational rankings give an indication of the effect exerted by more objective class differences and are based on the standard classifications employed by the Registrar-General (listed in the *Classification of Occupations*, 1960). The only modification is in the Social Class, category III, which mixes clerical workers with skilled manual. In our categorisation these have been divided between non-manual (III (1)) and manual (III (2)). Generally speaking, the relationship of party preferences to the occupational codings supports the generalisation that the higher the class, the stronger the identification with the Unionist Party. But there are considerable discrepancies. Support of Northern Ireland Labour generally increases where Unionist strength declines, but was disproportionately great in Class III (1) because that group was strongly polarised between Unionists and Labour. Labour gained more

TABLE 7.6

Belfast Residents: Class and Party Identification

(Percentages)

	Unionist	N.I. Lab.	Liberal	Nat.	Ind. apolitical	Other N.A. refuse	N
Subjective class							
Middle	55	24	6	6	6	2	83
Working	45	41	2	2	10	4	122
No class	38	48	0	10	0	5	21
Tau$_a$	1·00	1·00	1·00	0·33			
Registrar-General: Social class							
I Professional, administrative	86	0	14	0	0	0	7
II Managerial, semi-professional	45	9	9	15	6	15	33
III(1) Lower non-manual	58	42	0	0	0	0	24
III(2) Skilled manual	48	38	4	1	5	3	86
IV Semi-skilled manual	50	31	3	6	8	3	36
V Unskilled manual	40	57	0	3	0	0	30
Tau$_a$	0·47	0·60	0·60	−0·33			

Socio-Economic Groups v. Party Identification

Registrar-General: Socio-Economic Group	Unionist	N.I. Lab.	Liberal	Nat.	Ind. and Other	N
1–4 Professional, employers and managerial	67	0	17	8	8	12
5–6 Non-manual	60	29	0	2	9	42
7–9 Service, skilled manual, foremen	44	40	4	3	9	108
10 Semi-skilled	83	0	8	0	8	12
11–15 Unskilled, students, unemployed	37	46	4	7	7	46
Tau$_a$	0·40	0·40	0·00	0·30		

Entries are percentages in each class group. 'Ind., apolitical' includes independents who do not feel close to any of the parties. Registrar-General's Class III is divided between manual and non-manual. Both occupational classifications are based on male and single females' own occupations and on spouses' occupation for married and widowed females. For social class and socio-economic grouping see the *Classification of Occupations* (London, H.M.S.O., 1960).

support than Unionists only in the lowest occupational group
in each case. This is a marked difference from Glasgow where
Labour attained a plurality in all predominantly manual groups.
Generally Unionist support was higher in all class groups than
Conservative support would be in Britain.

The discrepancies between occupational position and party
support are reflected in the middling values of the Tau_a
statistics[5] given in Table 7.6. Tau_a for the relationship between
social classes and the Glasgow Progressives was 0·53 compared
with 0·47 for Belfast Unionists, and for Labour 0·60 in Belfast
compared to 0·87 in Glasgow. In the case of socio-economic
groups values were 1·00 compared with 0·40 and 0·40 compared
with 0·74. There was obviously a stronger and more consistent
relationship between party support and occupational differences in Glasgow than existed in Belfast, although the relationship
was not absent there. With regard to subjective class, the
difference between the 55 per cent of middle-class identifiers
and the 45 per cent of working-class identifiers supporting the Unionists is miniscule compared with the difference between the 79 per cent of middle-class identifiers
and 28 per cent of working-class identifiers supporting the
Conservatives, in a British sample.[6] The Belfast Unionists were
much weaker among the middle class than the British Conservatives but counterbalanced this by winning almost half of the
numerically dominant working class.

Turning to the minor parties, class differences showed no
consistent connection with Nationalist support which from
previous evidence would seem to rest on religious divisions in
any case. Liberalism varied in the same way as Unionism in
attracting more support from the higher class groupings, but
showed no relationship with socio-economic groups.

Tendencies to Unionism showed little variation between
educational groups (a range of only 48–46 per cent) but there
was a substantial difference between the pro-Labour and pro-
Nationalist attitudes of those educated beyond the age of 15
(22 per cent N.I.L.P., 14 per cent Nationalist) and others (36
per cent N.I.L.P., 4 per cent Nationalist). The differences
involved were considerably less than in Glasgow.

A further class characteristic which in Glasgow related
closely to party loyalty was the type of housing occupied.

Owner-occupiers who bore the burden of the rates supported the 'economical' Progressives while council tenants benefiting from subsidised rentals inclined strongly to Labour. Little difference appeared in Belfast between the support given to Unionists by the different types of occupant, but in the case of Labour a neatly graduated difference opened up between occupiers (25 per cent N.I.L.P.), Private (36 per cent N.I.L.P.) and Corporation Tenants (50 per cent N.I.L.P.). Owner-occupiers who identified themselves as working-class were less likely than working-class tenants to support Labour, and the same was true of Catholic occupiers, whose loyalties were divided with Nationalists. The same contrast appeared among non-believers.

Sex is a further demographic characteristic which can affect voting choice. The difference between males and females is much more marked in Belfast than in Britain generally. Thirty-five per cent of men are Unionist compared with 59 per cent of women: 44 per cent of men are N.I.L.P. compared with 28 per cent of women. These differences merit further investigation, particularly in regard to the major influences of class and religion.

At all occupational levels except the top executive and

TABLE 7.7

Belfast Residents: Class and Religious Influences on Party Identification for Men and Women

Percentage Unionist among Registrar-General classes:	Men	Women
I Professionals, administrative	100	75
II Semi-professional	40	54
III (i) Lower non-manual	50	66
III (ii) Skilled manual	37	59
IV Semi-skilled manual	26	72
V Unskilled manual	10	55
Percentage Unionist among:		
Presbyterians	60	82
Other Protestants	55	74
Church of Ireland	42	69
Non-believers	31	50
Catholics	3	3

Total N for occupational table 217; total N for denominational table 223.

professional and in all denominations except the Catholic, women supported Unionists more than men. The Belfast findings reflect those made elsewhere in that differences in support are particularly marked among the lowest manual groups. Working-class women, whose lives centre on the family and children, tend to be more conservative in outlook than working-class men, whose experiences of the factory and union pushes them towards the working-class party. Middle-class experiences diverge less between men and women. Nevertheless, because of the consistent decline in Unionist support between male occupational groupings, work-related differences were only slightly less influential overall than differences between men and women. Denominational differences were consistent among both sexes so that denomination exerted a substantially greater push towards Unionist support than differences between men and women.

Age showed the same increase in Labour support and decline in Unionist sympathy among the younger age groups as appeared in Glasgow. Labour support was extremely apparent among the 21–36 group and almost disappeared among those aged over 66 (13 per cent). Unionist support remained the same among persons aged up to 56 (43 per cent) and jumped at that point to 58 and then 67 per cent. Persons aged 66 in 1966 had lived through the whole of the Irish troubles from 1912 to 1922: persons aged 57 and over had also experienced the conflicts which hastened the birth of the Northern Irish State. These groups might be expected to show a stronger attachment to Unionism than would be the case with individuals for whom it was an established fact of life. For the oldest age group at the time of their most formative political experience Labour could hardly have appeared as a serious contender for power. For the youngest generation, sheltered during youth and adolescence by the welfare achievements of the first post-war Labour Governments at Westminster, Labour must have appeared a more alluring political choice. An examination of class and religious influences on voting behaviour within the different age groups may thus give valuable indications of the main direction of change in Belfast politics.[7]

With the exception of the Church of Ireland, no denomination showed a marked decline in Unionist support among the

TABLE 7.8

*Belfast Residents: Class and Religious Influences on Party
Identification within Each Age Group*

(Percentage in each age group)

Percentage Unionist among Registrar-General class at each age:	21–36	37–46	47–56	57+
I Professional, administrative	100	100	50	100
II Semi-professional	33	22	37	80
III (1) Lower non-manual	50	100	55	62
III (2) Skilled manual	38	44	44	61
IV Semi-skilled manual	60	43	40	50
V Unskilled manual	0	50	45	50
Total N = 215				

Percentage Unionist among:				
Presbyterians	73	66	66	79
Other Protestants	70	100	63	66
Church of Ireland	30	73	46	75
Non-believers	25	33	25	50
Catholics	0	0	12	0
Total N = 221				

youngest age group. Even within the Church of Ireland the
decline with age was not consistent. The political relevance of
religion does not on this evidence show much of a secular
tendency to decline, in contrast with the situation existing
in Glasgow. On the other hand, age did consistently erode
Unionist sentiment among skilled manual workers, and among
younger groups of the semi-professionals and the manual
labourers. Class does seem to gain more relevance for politics
over time even although the influence of religion remains
constant.

CLASS PREDICTORS OF UNIONIST SUPPORT

We have investigated the relationship of various class characteristics, taken separately, to party support. For a comparison of
class and religious influences we need to select the class indicator
most closely linked to party identification. It is possible that
certain combinations of the characteristics examined above
might form better indicators than any one characteristic taken
in isolation. A practical limitation on the combination of
characteristics lies in the fact that we wish the resulting measure

to be reasonably compact and manageable, and thus to have no more than five categories at most. Since some of the occupational classifications have five or six categories already we can hardly use them in combination. Practically we are limited to combining dichotomies such as those formed on the basis of subjective class, the distinction between association members and non-members, and the manual-non-manual occupational divide.

A further question is what we wish to link these indicators with. For technical reasons connected with the estimation of mutually independent class and religious effects (Table 7.11,

TABLE 7.9

Belfast Residents: Relationship between Various Combined Class Characteristics and Support of the Unionist Party

(Percentage supporting the Unionists in each category)

	Percentage supporting Unionists
Subjective class	
Class-conscious middle class	48
Non-class-conscious middle class	58
Non-class-conscious working class	48
Class-conscious working class	39
Tau_a	0·33
Subjective class with manual-non-manual occupational distinction	
Non-manual middle class	65
Non-manual non-middle class	43
Manual non-working class	43
Manual working class	47
Tau_a	0·00
Subjective class with association membership	
Non-association middle class	64
Non-association non-middle class	45
Association non-working class	40
Association working class	38
Tau_a	1·00
Association membership with manual-non-manual occupational distinction	
Non-manual non-association member	62
Non-manual association member	35
Manual non-association member	57
Manual association member	39
Tau_a	0·33

below) we must convert the dependent characteristic, party identification, into a dichotomy. Unionist dominance makes it natural to conceive of the dichotomy as Unionist versus the other parties.

The best class indicators of Unionist support in terms of Tau_a values (reflecting the internal consistency of the ordering) are undoubtedly the combination of subjective class and association membership (Table 7.9) and subjective class identification by itself (Table 7.6). However, the range of Unionist support in the former case is 26 percentage points compared to only 17 in the case of subjective class alone. The range of both pure occupational codings in Table 7.6 is greater but their internal inconsistencies are too great to permit them to be used. The categories of manual-non-manual occupation with association membership (Table 7.9) could be re-ordered on the assumption of an interactive relationship between the influences of association membership and occupation, with non-manual association members coming at the bottom. In that case Tau_a would be 1.00 and the range one percentage point greater than the association-subjective class combination. However, these values are so close that one indicator will do as well as the other, and it seems on the face of it that the subjective class combination will have a closer relationship to some of the political attitudes we will later explore (Chapter 8, below) than the occupational combination.

RELIGIOUS INFLUENCE ON PARTY SUPPORT

The stronger and more consistent effect of religion compared with class upon party support in Belfast is shown both by higher Tau_a values (for both Unionist and Labour identifications) and a greater range between extreme categories. The Presbyterians show strongest support for Unionists, the other non-episcopal Protestant denominations (largely Methodist) next, then the episcopal Church of Ireland. The peculiar twists by which the dissenting and formerly penalised Presbyterians and Methodists came most strongly to favour the Unionists, have been described in Chapters 1 and 2. The coolness in the Church of Ireland towards the Unionists and the greater favour shown by its adherents to Labour perhaps stem from the fact that a

TABLE 7.10

Belfast Residents: Religious Affiliations, Church Attendance and Party Identification

(Percentages in each denomination)

	Unionist	N.I. Lab.	Lib.	Nat.	Indep. apolitical	NA DK refuse	N
'Prot.'	100	0	0	0	0	0	2
Presbyterian	73	23	0	0	4	0	75
Other named non-episcopal Prot.	65	23	0	0	12	0	26
Church of Ireland	55	32	2	0	7	4	47
Non-believer	33	47	7	0	0	13	22
Catholic	3	59	12	19	3	3	58
Tau$_a$	1·00	·87	—	—	—	—	—
		Church-attenders only					
'Prot.'	100	0	0	0	0	0	2
Presbyterian	82	16	0	0	2	0	44
Other named non-episcopal Prot.	76	12	0	0	12	0	17
Church of Ireland	67	13	7	0	7	7	15
Catholic	4	58	13	17	5	5	53
Tau$_a$	1·00	0·60	—	—	—	—	—

Tau$_a$ values have not been calculated for the Liberal and Nationalist parties since their support obviously does not vary across all religions but is based primarily upon Catholics. The category of 'Protestant' is applied to those who replied 'Protestant' instead of a specific denomination to the questions 'Do you regard yourself as belonging to any religious faith? (If yes) Which faith is that?

Church attendance is measured through the question 'Have you attended a church service during the last four weeks?'

considerable proportion of the Church's adherents are found in the South.

Avowed non-believers (who probably stem from both Catholic and Protestant backgrounds) were the first group to favour Labour more than Unionists. A majority of Catholics supported Labour (although there may be some confusion in their minds between the Northern Ireland and Nationalist varieties): otherwise they scattered between Nationalists and Liberals. Catholics spread their support more widely than any other sect, but wherever it went the Unionists were scarcely ever the beneficiaries.

The effect of stronger attachment to a denomination (as

measured by regular church attendance) was to increase the Unionism of Protestants. Church-attending Episcopalians were still, however, not very much more Unionist than non-Church-attending Presbyterians, so that the direction as well as the strength of affiliation continued to exert an effect.

In devising a measure of religious affiliation to compare with that already obtained for class, the relative Unionism of the groups distinguished by denomination and church attendance offers a useful criterion for the combination of various groups. Since their Unionist support is approximately the same, non-church attending Presbyterians can be joined with church-attending members of the Church of Ireland and other non-attending Protestants, and distinguished from non-church-attending adherents of the Church of Ireland, on the one hand, and church-attending Presbyterians and Methodists, on the other. With non-believers and Catholics these groups make up a convenient five-category ordering of religious groups by strength of Unionist support.

MUTUALLY INDEPENDENT EFFECTS OF CLASS AND
RELIGION UPON UNIONIST SUPPORT

Simply from the overall relationships between party support and religion, and party support and class, it is certain that religion exercises a greater effect than class. The question is, how far did class and religious divisions coincide and, additionally, how did the genuinely independent effects exerted by each compare?

By averaging the extent to which the proportion supporting Unionists within each cell of Table 7.11 differs between each (class or religious) gradation within the same (class or religious) category, and then, summing the average effects of all gradations, we can get an estimate of the mutually independent effects of both factors. (The procedure is detailed in the Notes to Table 7.11.) If either class or religion explained all proportional variation in the table its effect by this procedure would attain 1·00, and if neither exerted any effect the estimate for both would be 0·00.

In view of the possible values which 'effect parameters' could assume, the score of 0·65 attained by religion is impressive,

TABLE 7.11

Belfast Residents: Effects of Class and Religion upon Unionist Support

(Percentages of residents in each cell supporting Unionists)

Association membership	*Church attending Prot. – (except C. of I.)*	*Non-Church attending Prot. or Church attending C. of I.*	*Non-Church attending C. of I.*	*Non-believer*	*Catholic*
Subjective class					
Member					
Working	79	45	38	10	0
Non-working	73	20	25	67	7
Non-member					
Non-middle	75	65	64	50	4
Middle	100	80	75	40	0

Effect of being association member non-working class relative to association member working class $= c_1 = 0.04$.

Effect of being association non-member non-middle class relative to association member non-working class $= c_2 = 0.04$.

Effect of being association non-member middle class relative to association non-member non-middle class $= c_3 = 0.02$.

Summed influence of class independent of religion $= C = c_1 + c_2 + c_3 = 0.10$.

Effect of being church-attending Prot. (except C. of I.) relative to non-church attending Prot. or church-attending C. of I. $= r_1 = 0.21$.

Effect of being non-church attending Prot. or church-attending C. of I. relative to non-church-attending C. of I. $= r_2 = 0.18$.

Effect of being non-church attending C. of I. relative to non-believer $= r_3 = 0.03$.

Effect of being non-believer relative to Catholic $= r_4 = 0.23$.

Summed influence of religion independent of class $= R = r_1 + r_2 + r_3 + r_4 = 0.65$.

Notes to Table 7.11: Below we present the relationship between class, religion and Unionist support in the form used for calculating the mutually independent effects of class and religion on support. Religion is regarded as ordered in terms of decreasing support for Unionists, from church-attending Prot. (except C. of I.) to Catholic, class from non-association member middle class to association member working class. For each gradation of these ordered characteristics the average proportional difference in Unionist support is calculated in accordance with the formula:

$$\frac{1}{v} \sum_{c=1}^{v} (Pio - Pc)$$

where c is a gradation in the ordered characteristic associated with an increase in Unionist support and v is the total number of comparisons possible with that gradation. Because many of the cell numbers are small each proportional difference has been weighted by the inverse of its variance (J. Coleman, *An Introduction to Mathematical Sociology*, New York, 1963, pp. 203–4), before calculating parameters.

TABLE 7.11—*continued*

Church attending Prot.
(*except C. of I.*)

Non-member M.C.	Non-member Non M.C.	Member Non W.C.	Member W.C.
p	p1	p11	p111
1·00	0·75	0·73	0·79
N	N1	N11	N111
14	20	15	14

Non-church attending Prot.
or church going C. of I.

Non-member M.C.	Non-member Non M.C.	Member Non W.C.	Member W.C.
p2	p12	p112	p1112
0·80	0·65	0·20	0·45
N2	N12	N112	N1112
15	23	5	11

Non-church attending C. of I.

Non-member M.C.	Non-member Non M.C.	Member Non W.C.	Member W.C.
p3	p13	p113	p1113
0·75	0·64	0·25	0·38
N3	N13	N113	N1113
4	11	4	13

Non-believer

Non-member M.C.	Non-member Non M.C.	Member Non W.C.	Member W.C.
p4	p14	p114	p1114
0·40	0·50	0·67	0·10
N4	N14	N114	N1114
5	4	3	10

Catholic

Non-member M.C.	Non-member Non M.C.	Member Non W.C.	Member W.C.
p5	p15	p115	p1115
0·00	0·04	0·07	0·00
N5	N15	N115	N1115
10	24	14	10

In order to estimate the total effect of religion and class in increasing Unionist support the effects for each gradation can be added, as is done in Table 7.11. Generally effect parameters express the variation in the proportions of the dependent variable (Unionist support) which a given gradation accounts for, independently of other gradations, out of 1·00. The proportional variation remaining when the sum of effect parameters is subtracted from 1·00 is due to variables not explicitly considered in the Table. For an extended description of effect parameters see J. Coleman, *An Introduction to Mathematical Sociology* (New York, 1963), Chapter 6.

especially when contrasted with the score of 0·10 for class. Religion exerted more than six times the influence of class. Comparable values for Glasgow (where religious effects are stronger than they would be in most areas of Britain) are 0·30 for religion and 0·42 for class. Glasgow experienced a mixture of class and religious influences on party support, whereas in Belfast religious influences were almost totally dominant.

The strong relationship between religion and Unionist identification is eloquent testimony to its continuing influence in Belfast politics. Even if class was gradually emerging as more salient to the younger age groups (Table 7.8) such tendencies are now likely to have been undermined by the communal strife of 1968–70. We shall explore further aspects of class and religious influence in subsequent chapters.

The relationships between party identification and background characteristics are important, partly because of the party they serve to put in office, but also because the perceptions people have of these relationships can have a powerful effect on their other political reactions. If the connection between religion and voting choice was seen to be as important as it actually is, the Unionists would tend to be credited with a permanent tenure of office through their link with the religious majority, and Catholics would even in 1966 have felt a minority who could never win by electoral and parliamentary means. On the other hand, if class influences were given an exaggerated prominance and seen to favour Labour, the possibility of new voting alignments could have been foreseen, and Unionist dominance regarded as less than eternal. Findings on these points closely affect interpretations of the present crisis.

In actual fact, the working class was seen as predominantly favouring Labour by the population, although councillors (the elective politicians) overwhelmingly credited it with Unionist sympathies. This was true even of non-Unionist councillors. Both population and councillors gave Unionists the middle class.

Agreement on middle-class voting was nothing compared with unanimity on Protestant support for Unionists, which fell only once below 80 per cent even among opposition parties. The Catholic vote was seen by approximately equal proportions in all population groups to go to Northern Ireland Labour,

TABLE 7.12

Belfast Residents and Councillors: Perceptions of Class Voting

(Percentages of residents and councillors and of party groupings)

Working Class seen as voting by:	Unionist	N.I. Labour	Liberal	Nationalists mainly Rep. Labour	Splits, DK answer qualified	N
All residents	36	47	0	2	6	229
Unionist residents	47	48	1	1	1	109
N.I. Labour residents	26	57	0	2	12	81
Nationalist residents	9	55	0	18	18	11
All Non-Unionist residents	30	49	0	4	15	120
All councillors	87	2	0	0	11	45
Unionist councillors	93	0	0	0	7	31
N.I. Labour councillors	75	0	0	0	25	4
Nationalist-Labour councillors	70	10	0	0	20	10
All Non-Unionist councillors	73	7	0	0	20	14
Middle Class seen as voting by:						
All residents	65	12	3	1	17	229
Unionist residents	70	10	1	0	17	109
N.I. Labour residents	63	14	4	1	15	81
Nationalist residents	36	18	1	0	36	11
All Non-Unionist residents	61	14	1	1	17	120
All councillors	96	2	0	0	0	45
Unionist councillors	100	0	0	0	0	31
N.I. Labour councillors	50	25	0	0	0	4
Nationalist-Labour councillors	100	7	0	0	0	10
All Non-Unionist councillors	87	7	0	0	0	14

TABLE 7.13

Belfast Residents and Councillors: Perceptions of Religious Voting

(Percentages of residents and councillors and of party groupings)

	Unionist	N.I. Labour	Liberal	Nationalist mainly Rep. Labour	Split, DK answer qualified	N
Protestants seen as voting by:						
All residents	84	3	0	0	10	229
Unionist residents	81	4	0	0	11	109
N.I. Labour residents	89	2	0	0	6	81
Nationalist residents	91	0	0	0	9	11
All Non-Unionist residents	88	3	0	0	8	120
All councillors	98	0	0	0	2	45
Unionist councillors	100	0	0	0	0	31
N.I. Labour councillors	75	0	0	0	25	4
Nationalist-Labour councillors	100	0	0	0	0	10
All Non-Unionist councillors	93	0	0	0	7	14
Catholics seen as voting by:						
All residents	3	32	0	44	19	229
Unionist residents	5	28	0	49	17	109
N.I. Labour residents	2	35	0	42	20	81
Nationalist residents	0	45	9	9	36	11
All Non-Unionist residents	2	37	1	40	19	120
All councillors	0	13	0	35	47	45
Unionist councillors	0	17	0	27	47	31
N.I. Labour councillors	0	25	0	50	25	4
Nationalist-Labour councillors	0	0	0	60	40	10
All Non-Unionist councillors	0	7	0	53	33	14

Nationalists or to be split. A plurality of councillors settled for the most realistic perception – that it split. Hardly anyone saw Catholics voting Unionist.

Thus in regard to both class and religious voting clear perceptions emerged of the Unionist supporters, but ideas of who would attract opposition groups remained confused and contradictory. Episcopalian coolness towards Unionism might have encouraged the idea that Protestants as well as Catholics were internally divided. But instead of toning down religious cleavages the perceptions of politicians and residents exaggerated the divisions. Unionists were seen as more electorally entrenched than they actually were; opposition parties were dismissed as weak and divided. Such perceptions could only exacerbate Catholic frustration at their political impotence. This – more than ancient hostility – seems to have produced the extra constitutional actions of 1968–9. For if channels of electoral influence are seen as permanently closed, others will eventually be chosen.

NOTES

1. This was a realistic perception, even in 1966, as can be seen from Table 11.3, below.
2. Doubts have been increasingly expressed as to how far 'party identification' in Britain, ascertained on the question 'Do you usually think of yourself as (party)?', are anything more than expressions of current voting intention. On the argument advanced in the text this does not matter for our purposes. Cf. D. Butler and D. E. Stokes, *Political Change in Britain*, (London, 1969), pp. 40–43.
3. *Class, Religion*, Chapter 6.
4. Ibid., Chapter 2, for detailed discussion.
5. Given a rank-order on the independent variable (here the occupational rankings) Tau_a measures the extent to which ordering on the dependent variable (here party support) conforms. It can vary in value between -1 and $+1$ (cf. H. Blalock, *Social Statistics*, pp. 319–21).
6. *Political Change*, p. 76.
7. Nationalist support showed no consistent movement with age, fluctuating from 7 per cent of the oldest group to 2 per cent of the youngest.

8 Class and Religion in Belfast

THE perceived and actual influence of religion on party support provokes more extensive investigation of its effects, and of its relationship with other social characteristics in Belfast. However, it is also interesting to investigate class phenomena for the very reason that class does not exert as strong an influence as elsewhere in Britain. The most plausible explanation lies in the possibility that class distinctions and feelings assume a different guise in Northern Ireland. We are able to compare Belfast responses about class and religious affiliations with information obtained in Glasgow at exactly the same time and in the same way. The comparison shows whether the impact of religion and class differs from that encountered in at least one other city. Since in a modern industrialised community the absence of strong class effects is a more anomalous phenomenon than the presence of religious influence, we begin by considering occupational differences. We then link these to subjective class feeling, and consider the relationship of both factors to religious identifications.

OCCUPATIONAL DISTINCTIONS IN BELFAST

The distribution of the Belfast population over the Registrar-General's Classification of Occupations placed most members of the working population among the skilled and semi-skilled manual workers of Classes III (2) and IV and to a lesser extent among the lower white-collar strata of Class III (1). The only substantial difference from the occupational distribution in Glasgow occurred with the greater proportion of semi-skilled to skilled and service workers in Belfast, which may result from the even greater dependence of the city's economy on traditional heavy industry and the longer time-lag before its exposure to modern innovations.

Compared with Northern Ireland as a whole Belfast had roughly similar proportions in the business and professional

TABLE 8.1

Distribution of the Work Force over Occupational
Classes in Glasgow and Belfast in 1966

| | Percentage in | |
Occupational classes*	Glasgow	Belfast
I Professional, administrative	3	2
II Semi-professional	12	11
III (1) Inspectors, supervisors and other non-manual	15	17
III (2) Skilled manual	38	28
IV Semi-skilled manual	18	28
V Unskilled manual	14	14

* The classification of occupations is the Registrar-General's Social Classes, modified by the manual-non-manual distinction inside Class III, and further described in *Classification of Occupations*, 1960. Glasgow data is drawn from the survey and Belfast data from the Northern Ireland Census.

classes and more workers in clerical and lower supervisory positions. Comparisons of city and province in regard to these last groups are however distorted by the tendency to place farmers with lower non-manual workers. Comparisons of Belfast with Britain are also difficult since census figures for the latter do not split Class III. So far as the other classes are concerned it appears that professional, executive and managerial groups are under-represented in Belfast, while the lower manual workers are over-represented.

As between the parties, Labour appeared as having a greater proportion of manual workers among its adherents than the Unionists (86 per cent to 65 per cent), most noticeably among the unskilled of Class V. Skilled and semi-skilled workers formed as large a proportion of Unionist followers as they did of Labour (55 per cent). Forty-five per cent of Nationalists were in middle-class occupations.

It was to be anticipated that councillors' backgrounds would be considerably more exclusive than those of residents, as in Glasgow and in most other Western polities. What distinguished Belfast was the overwhelming extent to which councillors came from the semi-professionals and supervisors of occupational Class II. The 69 per cent who belonged to Class II contrasted with only 28 per cent in Glasgow, where 28 per cent also came

TABLE 8.2

Belfast Councillors: Distribution of Occupations by Party Identification

(Percentage of party groupings)

	Unionist	N.I. Labour	Nationalists	Total
I Professional, administrative	7	0	0	4
II Semi-professional	69	50	80	69
III (1) Inspectors, supervisors and other non-manual	17	0	20	13
III (2) Skilled manual	7	25	0	9
IV Semi-skilled manual	0	25	0	2
V Unskilled manual	0	0	0	0

For comparisons the Protestant Unionist councillor is grouped with the Unionists (of whom he was an ex-member) and Nationalist groups are combined.

from the professionals, employers and managers of Class I and 22 per cent from the lower non-manual workers of Class III (1). It is possible that the proximity of Stormont tempted those professionals and employers motivated to enter politics away from the City Council, while the weakness of the Labour Party diminished the representation of the white-collar workers of Class III (1). Because of the overwhelming preponderance of Class II few occupational differences of note were revealed between party groupings on the Council, although Labour councillors came equally from non-manual and manual classes.

CORRELATES OF OCCUPATIONAL DISTINCTIONS IN BELFAST

Bare comparisons of occupational background fail to penetrate the life-styles of the different classes. It is often assumed that the manual groups are less mobile – physically, socially and psychologically – than the non-manual groups, and hence are led to a more concrete and localised view of politics. In Glasgow the manual strata seemed to share many characteristics and experiences in contrast to the comparatively heterogeneous background of the non-manual groups (many members of which had emerged from a manual background). This pattern of characteristics contributed to the prevailing working-class identification of Glaswegians. Although Glasgow councillors emerged overwhelmingly from the non-manual strata their characteristics differed so widely from those of comparable classes among the population that they constituted a highly distinctive group.

Using similar indicators to those employed in Glasgow we can discover whether a comparable situation existed in Belfast. Taking geographical mobility first, it emerged that roughly the same proportions at each occupational level as in Glasgow had lived all their lives in the city, except that somewhat less of the lower non-manual and skilled manual workers (Classes III (1) and III (2)) had done so. As in Glasgow more in the non-manual than in the manual strata had moved into the city. Thus differences between occupational groupings were no greater in Belfast than in Glasgow. In all groupings there was a tendency to remain in the same house over a much longer period than in Glasgow, and while only 14 per cent of Class II had stayed in the same house all their lives, 50 per cent of Class IV had done so. This is a distinction which did not divide the Glasgow Classes, most of whom had moved house recently. In Glasgow three quarters of councillors on all occupational levels had lived in the city all their lives. In Belfast out of the two thirds of all councillors in Class II only 52 per cent had been born in the city, the same proportion as for members of Class II among the general population. Since only 50 per cent of the next largest group of councillors (lower non-manual workers of Class III (1)) had also stayed in the city all their lives it appeared that Belfast councillors had shallower local roots than Glasgow councillors.

Glasgow electors appeared residentially differentiated along the lines of their occupations. The two uppermost levels were dominated by owner-occupiers while manual workers lived predominantly in council housing. A majority of residents in all non-manual strata in Belfast were owner-occupiers and a third lived in private rentals. The situation reversed itself among the manual strata, where a majority lived in private rentals and a third to a fifth owned their own accommodation. The most divisive socio-political cleavage in British local governments between present or prospective council house tenants and owner-occupiers,[1] was thus absent from Belfast where at most only 15 per cent in any manual stratum occupied council houses compared with more than 50 per cent in Glasgow.

Education affects both life-style and related prospects of social mobility. Practically 95 per cent of Glasgow manual workers had left school at the minimum age, as had three quarters of the lowest non-manual workers and 60 per cent even of Class II. In contrast, this was true for only a quarter of employers and professionals in Class I.

Members of Class I in Belfast divided in a curiously sharp way between those who left school at the minimum age and

TABLE 8.3

Belfast Residents: Occupation and Length of Education

(Percentage of residents in each occupational class)

Occupational class	Left school					
	15−	15	16	17	18	18+
I Professional, administrative	43	—	—	14	—	43
II Semi-professional	48	9	9	12	9	12
III (1) Inspectors, supervisors and other non-manual	29	21	13	21	4	13
III (2) Skilled manual	78	12	6	3	1	—
IV Semi-skilled manual	75	19	6	—	—	—
V Unskilled manual	87	10	3	—	—	—

professionals who received an extensive education. The distribution of school-leaving ages in the other non-manual classes was broadly comparable with Glasgow except that the lower non-manual workers (Class III (1)) were somewhat better educated in Belfast. In both cities manual workers almost universally left school at the earliest possible age.

In Glasgow councillors were generally less well educated than corresponding electors. In Belfast councillors were undoubtedly better educated than residents of the same occupational grade, and were also better educated within each Class than Glasgow councillors.

Closely related to education is the occupational background of parents, which indicates both the resources available for maintenance during childhood and attitudes towards education. As in Glasgow, members of the manual strata originated either at that level or in other manual Classes. Only six to eleven per cent came from non-manual classes. On the other hand, many

TABLE 8.4

Belfast Councillors: Occupation and Length of Education

(Percentage of councillors in each occupational class)

Occupational class	Left school					
	15–	15	16	17	18	18+
I Professional, administrative	—	—	—	—	—	100
II Semi-professional	26	16	16	6	13	23
III (1) Inspectors, supervisors and other non-manual	17	33	17	17	17	—
III (2) Skilled manual	75	—	25	—	—	—
IV Semi-skilled manual	100	—	—	—	—	—

fathers of non-manual workers were manual workers (the range extending from 43 per cent in Class I to 46 per cent in Class III (1)). The manual origins of non-manual workers were even more marked in Glasgow (from 37 per cent in Class I to 67 per cent in Class III (1)). If one can take the comparison of respondents' own occupation and father's occupation as an imperfect indication of occupational mobility it is apparent that each Class recruited disproportionately from itself, the non-manual Classes disproportionately from each other, and Classes IV (semi-skilled manual) and V (unskilled manual) disproportionately from each other. Class III (2) recruited itself most as might be expected if parents' Class were not linked to membership of the present Class. Mobility seemed slightly less in Belfast than in Glasgow but on the whole few differences appeared between the two cities either in the distribution of fathers' class among members of present classes, or in the indication this gave of occupational mobility.

Of the two thirds of all Belfast councillors in Class II, 48 per cent had fathers in that Class, and 17 per cent respectively in Classes III (1) (lower non-manual) and III (2) (skilled manual). Half the present members of Class III (1) had fathers in that Class: otherwise it recruited equally from manual and non-manual Classes. Given the present strongly non-manual nature of councillors' occupations, there seemed no greater tendency for each occupational class to recruit from itself than among the population, but the fact remains that councillors in origin as in present occupation were drawn overwhelmingly not simply from non-manual occupations but from the professionals and supervisors of Class II.

In terms of style and quality of life, data reviewed in this section point to considerable homogeneity among manual workers. Most had originated in manual working-class families, had received minimal education, and moved little within or outside the City. On the other hand, members of each non-manual class had mixed occupational origins, many being sons of manual workers, had received varying amounts of education and were split between those born inside and outside Belfast. Differences between manual and non-manual workers on these indicators were slightly greater in Belfast than in Glasgow. But in housing – a central question in Glasgow politics – there is much less difference between the various Classes, particularly in regard to the occupancy of council housing which is in both cities (although with more inconsistency in Belfast) linked to Labour voting (Chapter 7). Overall, differences associated with occupational status appeared as great, if no greater, in Belfast compared with Glasgow.

In Glasgow the councillors, while overwhelmingly non-manual in origin, were very different in life-style from corresponding members of the population. In Belfast these differences seemed less marked: councillors were like other professionals and supervisors in Class II. However, the fact that they so overwhelmingly shared a single occupational status made them just as socially unrepresentative of the general population as Glasgow councillors, and their very similarity to other members of their Class rendered them less capable of acting as honest brokers between Classes.

OCCUPATIONAL CLASS AND SUBJECTIVE CLASS

Feelings and perceptions of class differences do not always follow occupational lines, and it is perhaps in these subjective reactions that Belfast differs most from Glasgow. Voluntary affiliation with a class through membership of work-related associations is still affected by employment status. Housewives are unlikely to join, although their political attitudes will be affected by their husband's membership. Thus the best estimate of the incidence of membership among the population are the proportions of the actual work force who are members. This also facilitates comparisons with the largely male councillors.

We have no working respondents in Class I but 60 per cent in Class II belonged to work-related associations – probably professional. Among manual workers the associations in question are likely to be trade unions. Membership was highest among the skilled and semi-skilled manual workers of Classes III (2) and IV. The white-collar workers of Class III (1) and the unskilled of Class V were less extensively unionised. Classes II, III (2) and IV had a higher proportion of association members than Glasgow, and Classes III (1) and V less. Little difference opened up between the membership of Belfast councillors and population within those classes that can be compared. However, the concentration of councillors in Class II implied that most belonged to professional and managerial associations as compared to the unions in which most of the population were grouped.

TABLE 8.5

Belfast Residents and Councillors: Occupation and Trade Union/Professional Organisations

(Percentage of work-related association members in each occupational group)

Occupational class	All Residents	Working Residents	Councillors
I Professional, administrative	14	0	100
II Semi-professional	42	60	65
III (1) Inspectors, supervisors and other non-manual	28	43	33
III (2) Skilled manual	52	82	100
IV Semi-skilled manual	61	74	100
V Unskilled manual	27	35	—

Table 8.6 reports class identifications of Belfast electors and councillors. The percentage in each cell gives the total proportions of those in the population or appropriate party grouping who indicated their placement in a particular class. The proportion reported in each cell is the proportion of those in the cell who spontaneously indicated their membership of that class without being forced to make the choice. These proportions can be taken as indicating the extent of class-consciousness among those in each cell.

Working-class identifiers substantially outnumbered the

TABLE 8.6

Belfast Residents and Councillors: Self-perceived Class

(Percentage of councillors and residents in each party: proportions of
class-conscious in middle- and working-class cells)

	Upper, capitalist class	Middle-class	Working-class	No class
All residents	2	35	53	9
	—	0·39	0·35	—
Unionist residents	2	40	51	7
	—	0·34	0·31	—
N.I.L.P. residents	1	23	62	12
	—	0·37	0·42	—
Liberal residents	—	63	37	—
	—	0·40	0·00	—
Nationalist residents	—	45	27	18
	—	0·80	0·67	—
All councillors	7	60	24	11
	—	0·35	0·27	—
Unionist councillors	6	74	3	16
	—	0·43	0·00	—
N.I.L.P. councillors	25	—	75	—
	—	0·00	0·33	—
Nationalist councillors	—	30	70	—
	—	0·00	0·28	—
All Non-Unionist councillors	7	21	71	—
	—	0·00	0·30	—

middle-class among the Belfast population, but the 18 percentage
points difference between them was much less than the 35
percentage points between middle-class and working-class
Glaswegians (28 per cent middle, 63 per cent working) and
between middle-class and working-class identifiers among the
British population as a whole (32 per cent and 67 per cent
respectively).[2] The 0·39 of middle-class residents of Belfast
who spontaneously identified with their class compared with
0·36 in Glasgow, and the 0·35 of spontaneous working-class
identifiers in Belfast was substantially less than the proportion
of 0·44 among working-class Glaswegians, reflecting a lower
level of working-class consciousness.

Naturally, Unionist residents were more strongly middle-
class than Labour residents. Among Labour indeed the ratio
of middle-class to working-class identifiers approached that of
the British party. Unionist supporters were almost evenly
divided between working-class and middle-class, and the latter

were somewhat more class conscious than the former. The minor parties had strongly middle-class support. Too much should not be made of this in the case of Nationalists in view of probable confusion of respondents between Nationalist Labour and Northern Irish Labour. Non-Unionists as a whole were much more working-class – and working-class conscious – than Unionists.

Belfast councillors placed themselves overwhelmingly in the middle class – 60 per cent compared with 35 per cent among the population, although the proportion of councillors who spontaneously identified with the middle class was less. Seven per cent of councillors compared to 2 per cent of the population placed themselves in the upper class. Spontaneous class identification was even less evident among working-class councillors than among working-class residents. The strong predominance of middle-class identification among Belfast councillors reversed the milder predominance of working-class identification among Glasgow councillors (51 per cent of whom placed themselves in the working class). The proportions among both middle- and working-class councillors who spontaneously placed themselves in a class were lower than in Glasgow – 0·35 compared to 0·47 for the middle-class, and 0·27 compared to 0·57 for the working-class.

Eighty per cent of Unionist councillors placed themselves in the middle- or upper-class, about the same proportion as Progressives in Glasgow. However only 3 per cent of Unionists compared with 18 per cent of Progressives regarded themselves as working-class. Roughly three quarters of Labour and Nationalist councillors identified themselves as working-class compared with only 5 per cent of Glasgow Labour, thus contributing to a more muted division in class terms between the council parties in Belfast. Even among Unionist middle-class councillors the proportion of 0·43 spontaneously identifying with their class was less than among Progressive middle-class councillors (0·50), and among non-Unionist working-class councillors it was 0·30 compared with 0·68 among Glasgow Labour working-class councillors.

At the level of both population and politicians therefore class consciousness was not only less extensive than in Glasgow, but also suffered a more rapid diminution among working-class identifiers compared with middle-class identifiers. Together with the presence (although not predominance) of a larger percentage of middle-class residents and councillors than in Glasgow, this evidence points to the prevalence of a middle-class ethos in Belfast which is stronger than that of any comparable industrial city. Such an ethos could well muffle the class differences which sustain local and national politics in the rest of Britain.

The middle-class identifications of councillors stemmed naturally from their high occupational status (Table 8.7). The division of Belfast residents between manual and non-manual occupations almost exactly parallels Glasgow, however.

TABLE 8.7

Belfast Residents and Councillors: Occupation and Self-perceived Class

(Percentage in each occupational class and proportion class-conscious in cell for middle- and working-class)

Residents Occupational class	No class named	Upper- class	Middle- class	Working/poor class
I Professional, administrative	—	—	86 0·50	14 0·00
II Semi-professional	6	3	55 0·56	36 0·33
III (1) Inspectors, supervisors and other non-manual	12	0	50 0·42	38 0·56
III (2) Skilled manual	8	3	30 0·23	57 0·33
IV Semi-skilled manual	5	0	14 0·40	75 0·30
V Unskilled manual	17	0	20 0·00	63 0·37
Councillors				
I Professional, administrative	50	0	50 1·00	0
II Semi-professional	6	10 0·33	61 0·37	23 0·29
III (1) Inspectors, supervisors and other non-manual	16	0	68 0·25	16 0·00
III (2) Skilled manual	25	0	25 0·00	50 0·50
IV Semi-skilled manual	0	0	0	100 0·00

Examining the relationship between occupational class and subjective class among residents more closely, the expected decrease in middle-class identification occurs with downward occupational status, the predominance of middle-class identification being reversed at the break between (non-manual) Class III (1) and (manual) Class III (2). While these tendencies were also apparent in Glasgow, an absolute majority of middle-class identifiers appeared there only in Class I, among professionals and employers. And only a fifth or less of any manual Class identified with the middle class compared in Belfast to a third among the skilled manual workers of Class III (2).

In the relationship between occupation and subjective class we again discover the strength of middle-class feeling in Belfast contrasting with the strength of working-class feeling in Glasgow. It should be noted however that this middle-class ethos cannot be unambiguously used as an explanation for the weakness of Labour and the strength of the conservative Unionists in Belfast. It is quite likely that the failure of Labour is itself the reason for muted working-class feeling: Unionist respondents are certainly less class-conscious, particularly among the working-class, than non-Unionists (Table 8.6).

If the weakness of working-class feeling is related to the relative insulation of Belfast from the mainstream of British politics, one might reasonably expect it to be stronger among the younger age groups brought up at a time when the city was increasingly affected by the economic and welfare policies initiated by the post-war Labour Government at Westminster. This is all the more plausible in that we have already traced the rise in Labour Party support among younger residents (Chapter 7). But working-class identification changes by only four percentage points (56 to 52) between the oldest and the youngest age groups, and middle-class identification by only 6 percentage points.

Discussion of class feeling can be clarified further by considering the characteristics associated by respondents with each class. In Table 8.8 we present responses from which a detailed comparison can be made of the ideas about each other held by various class groups. The main types of class description emerged from the original replies as linked to occupation, income or morals and attitudes. The 'morals and attitudes'

TABLE 8.8

Descriptions of People in the Middle- and Working-Class, by Various Subjective Class
Groups of Councillors and Residents in Glasgow and Belfast

(Percentages of total responses in each group)

	Middle-class characterised by:			Working-class characterised by:		
	Occupation	Income	Morals & Attitudes	Occupation	Income	Morals & Attitudes
Class-conscious middle-class						
Belfast residents	65	8	9	49	24	15
Glasgow residents	50	25	17	57	21	24
Belfast councillors	62	31	8	33	55	0
Glasgow councillors	78	9	6	90	10	0
Non-class-conscious middle-class						
Belfast residents	44	21	20	36	24	27
Glasgow residents	57	22	24	72	14	14
Belfast councillors	60	24	0	63	12	6
Glasgow councillors	59	6	9	63	21	15
Class-conscious working-class						
Belfast residents	52	29	5	58	18	12
Glasgow residents	50	35	10	57	20	17
Belfast councillors	73	0	12	84	0	0
Glasgow councillors	67	18	2	74	13	12
Non-class-conscious working-class						
Belfast residents	48	26	12	60	16	18
Glasgow residents	51	33	12	55	19	21
Belfast councillors	60	0	40	62	15	17
Glasgow councillors	56	25	7	64	20	6

Minor responses are omitted from the Table so percentages often total 80 or 90 rather than 100 per cent. The present groupings of responses differs from those used in Table 2.18 of *Class, Religion* in that descriptions of the working class as 'people who work' are coded as 'Occupation' rather than as 'Morals & Attitudes'.

category is of particular relevance to the question of whether class descriptions were covertly evaluative, since it groups perceptions of exploitation (only one per cent of the responses of only one Belfast group, however) with accusations of snobbery, laziness and commendations such as 'nice' or 'respectable' people. However, it will be seen that neither in Glasgow nor in Belfast were morals and attitudes mentioned in much more than a quarter of all responses: if such evaluations are taken as an indicator of class feeling it must be low in both cities, and somewhat lower in Belfast than in Glasgow.

Neutral non-evaluative descriptions of the classes included education as well as income and occupation. However, references to education never constituted more than 10 per cent of the replies of any group and so are not reported in Table 8.9 (with the omission of minor responses this accounts for percentages rarely totalling to 100 for any group). The main point which emerges about purely descriptive reactions to the classes is the extent to which occupational criteria were employed in all sets of responses – used, in fact, in double the cases in which any other criterion appears, except among councillors in Belfast who spontaneously identified with the middle class. For them income was the most useful class indicator. In other groups income tended to appear in a fifth to a quarter of the replies. The use of these criteria corresponds to the finding of Butler and Stokes in regard to their sample of British electors, 61 per cent of whom used occupation to describe the middle class and 74 per cent to describe the working class.[3]

No systematic differences in class criteria thus appeared between politicians and electors in either Glasgow or Belfast. Broadly the same view of class as primarily constituted by occupational status and secondarily by income differences was taken in both cities, by middle-class and working-class, by class-conscious and non-class-conscious. Some evaluative feeling crept in through comments on morals and attitudes but this was always limited and not concentrated in any one class group. The slight de-emphasis of morals and attitudes in Belfast compared with Glasgow fits with previous evidence on the lesser class-consciousness of Belfast residents and councillors.

Eighteen per cent of Belfast residents thought two classes

existed (compared with 22 per cent in Glasgow) and 59 per cent thought three classes existed (compared with 52 per cent in Glasgow). From 58 to 79 per cent of residents in the various class groups listed at the side of Table 8.9 mentioned three classes in all. Residents in the working-class groups were somewhat more inclined to mention two classes than residents in the middle-class groups (23 and 25 per cent compared with 10 and 15 per cent). These Belfast responses were almost exactly the same as those elicited in Glasgow.

More Belfast councillors in the middle-class mentioned three classes (80 and 71 per cent respectively) than councillors in the working-class groups (33 and 57 per cent). Working-class councillors, like residents, were more likely to see a two-class structure (43 and 33 per cent compared to 10 and 0 per cent). Again their perceptions did not differ markedly from those of Glasgow councillors.

Two thirds of working-class residents who mentioned only two classes saw these as being the working class and middle class, and about a fifth who saw a two-class structure split fairly evenly between viewing the other class as the middle or upper class. In Glasgow similar working-class residents saw the other class as upper or middle in fairly even proportions, while similar middle-class residents divided (again evenly) between working and upper class. Belfast councillors subscribing to a two-class structure mentioned middle and upper class in the ratio of 2:1 among the working class, and working to upper class in broadly the same ratio among the middle class.

Among all class groups of residents and councillors who viewed the class structure as three-tiered the actual classes were seen as working, middle and upper, which was exactly the situation obtaining in Glasgow.

Class perceptions thus showed no systematic differences between Glasgow and Belfast for any class group of residents or councillors. No class attracted substantial identification in Belfast which did not do so in Glasgow or in Britain as a whole – that is to say that middle- and working-class attachments predominated in Belfast, as elsewhere. The great difference lay in the lower class consciousness of Belfast residents compared with Glasgow residents, and in their more extensive middle-class identifications.

RELIGION AND CLASS

Religion undoubtedly helped soften the impact of class differences and so we now consider inter-relationships between religious differences and occupational and subjective class distinctions. First, the overall distribution of the population over different denominations should be examined.

Our sample figures, reported in Table 8.9, somewhat under-represent members of the Church of Ireland and over-represent Presbyterians in the population; actual proportions were in fact more comparable with each other and with Catholics. Each of these denominations accounted for about a quarter of the Belfast population. The 11 per cent of other Protestants were mainly Methodists, with adherents of minor Presbyterian sects. This last proportion was comparable with the Glasgow membership of minor Protestant sects. In Glasgow Catholics also constituted about a quarter of the population, but Presbyterians and non-believers appeared in much larger numbers – 44 per cent and 16 per cent. In the Province as a whole Catholics constituted 35 per cent, Presbyterians 30 per cent and Episcopalians of the Church of Ireland 25 per cent.

At 59 per cent of the population, church attendance of at least once a month was considerably more than 44 per cent among the Glasgow population, and larger than the 56 per cent of the English and Welsh population who attended church at least 'once in a while' in 1959.[4] The proportions reported in each cell of Table 8.9 related to those professing adherence to a denomination who had actually attended church in the last month. The Church of Ireland was obviously least patronised by its adherents while the Catholic Church attracted almost all. At roughly two thirds of adherents the attendance of Presbyterians and other non-episcopal Protestants was also high.

Half the Unionist residents were Presbyterian and about a fifth came from the Methodists and minor Presbyterian churches. The Church of Ireland and non-believers were represented by roughly similar proportions to those in the population, while Unionist Catholics hardly appeared. Within each denomination Unionist church-attendance increased in comparison with the general population. Labour adherents showed the reverse religious characteristics: disproportionately more Catholic –

TABLE 8.9

Religious Identification of Belfast Councillors and Residents

(Percentages of residents and councillors in each party: Proportions of church-attenders in each cell)

	Church of Ireland	Presbyterian	Other Protestant	Roman Catholic	Non-believer
All residents	21 / 0·31	33 / 0·60	11 / 0·68	25 / 0·91	7 / 0·00
Unionist residents	24 / 0·38	50 / 0·65	17 / 0·79	2 / 1·00	5 / 0·00
Labour residents	19 / 0·13	21 / 0·41	7 / 0·33	42 / 0·91	9 / 0·00
Liberal residents	11 / 1·00	0 / 0·00	0 / 0·00	78 / 0·91	0 / 0·00
Nationalist residents	0 / 0·00	0 / 0·00	0 / 0·00	100 / 1·00	0 / 0·00
All councillors	27 / 0·58	22 / 0·90	22 / 0·90	22 / 0·82	7 / 0·00
Unionist councillors	39 / 0·58	29 / 0·89	26 / 0·88	0 / 1·00	6 / 0·00
N.I. Labour councillors	0 / 0·00	25 / 1·00	50 / 1·00	0 / 0·00	25 / 0·00
Nationalist councillors	0 / 0·00	0 / 0·00	0 / 0·00	100 / 1·00	0 / 0·00
All Non-Unionist councillors	0 / 0·00	13 / 1·00	13 / 0·50	67 / 1·00	7 / 0·00

though perhaps as a result of residents' confusion between Northern Ireland and Nationalist Labour: less Presbyterian, although proportions for non-believers and Church of Ireland corresponded to those in the population. Church-attendance fell off among Labour adherents in every denomination except Catholic. Among Nationalists and Liberals Catholics were almost exclusively represented.

The religious loyalties of Belfast councillors corresponded fairly exactly to those of the population except that adherents of the minor Protestant sects were more numerous. The correspondence was greater than appeared in Glasgow where Presbyterians were over-represented at the expense of Catholics. As in Glasgow church-attendance was higher among councillors than among their coreligionists in the population. Whereas Presbyterians formed double the proportion of Church of Ireland adherents among Unionist supporters, the latter formed the largest single block among Unionist councillors – perhaps because it was traditionally the church of the Protestant elite and still carried an aura of greater social prestige. In 1966, though neither before nor since, N.I.L.P. councillors were exclusively Protestant in spite of their seemingly strong Catholic support; Nationalists were exclusively Catholic.

Marked occupational differences did not occur among adherents of the various denominations. Twenty-six per cent of Catholic residents fell into the non-manual Classes of the Registrar-General's Classification compared with 33 per cent of Presbyterians and 26 per cent in the Church of Ireland. Glasgow proportions were 21 per cent for Catholics and 38 per cent for Presbyterians. Nor were there marked discrepancies between the Belfast denominations at the level of any particular Class. Seventy per cent of Catholic councillors were professionals and supervisors in Class II, as were 70 per cent of Presbyterian councillors and 75 per cent in the Church of Ireland.

The absence of divergences in the occupational structure of any denomination is one indication of the absence of any marked relationship between occupation and denomination, which can be further checked by examining the religious composition of each occupational class. Presbyterian residents constituted half the members of the lower non-manual Class III (1) compared with the 13 per cent who were Catholic and

21 per cent Church of Ireland: in the exclusive Class I 43 per
cent were Presbyterian compared with 14 per cent Catholic and
Church of Ireland, respectively. But Catholics and Presbyterians both constituted a third of the more numerous and only
slightly less exclusive Class II from which the Church of Ireland
attracted a fifth. Presbyterians were also more numerous among
the skilled manual workers of Class III (2) (34 per cent compared with 20 per cent Catholic and 27 per cent Church of
Ireland) and drew a third, like the Catholic Church, from the
semi-skilled of Class IV. Only in the unskilled Class V were
Presbyterians outnumbered 27 per cent to 23 per cent by Catholics. From these two lowest Classes the Church of Ireland drew
13 to 14 per cent. Non-believers fluctuated from 3 to 7 per cent
of each Class. Actual attendance increased, though inconsistently, with higher occupational status within each denomination. This occurred also in Glasgow, where the proportions
drawn by Catholics from each Class corresponded closely to
those in Belfast, and non-believers were in a constant proportion within each Class (but much higher, about a third). The
different standing of the Protestant Churches in Belfast and
Glasgow unfortunately rules out close comparisons of their
comparative strength within each Class.

Presbyterians and Catholics each grouped a fifth of the two
thirds of all Belfast councillors in Class II: at 29 per cent the
Church of Ireland only slightly surpassed them. Other Protestant sects attracted 16 per cent, and non-believers 10 per cent.
Catholics and non-believers were more prominent in this
councillor Class than they were in Glasgow.

Over the combination of subjective class and membership
of a work-related association, which was the best class predictor
of Unionist support (Table 7.9), some denominational differences emerged. Catholics were overwhelmingly working-class
in their identifications but the majority were unorganised. The
non-Presbyterians among Protestants, and the non-believers
tended also to feel working-class (or at least not to feel middle-
class). Comparable proportions tended to membership of work-
related associations as did not, among the Protestants. Working-
class non-believers tended more to associations. Presbyterians
spread most evenly over all class groupings. The larger numbers
of Presbyterians enabled them to balance Catholics even among

the organised working class and they formed a dominant element in all the other class groupings.

Church-attendance was lowest among the organised working class and highest among association members who did not feel working-class. While denominational differences appear in regard to these class characteristics none show sharp divisions or any marked contrast with the situation existing in Glasgow. One difference which did appear among Glasgow councillors lay in the unanimous Catholic identification with the working class, while Protestant councillors split fairly evenly between working-class and middle-class identifications. In Belfast the difference was sharper: 78 per cent of Protestant councillors put themselves in the middle class and only 6 per cent in the working class, while 80 per cent of Catholics stated that they were working-class and 20 per cent placed themselves in the middle class.

As with class a central question in the estimation of the religious influences on Belfast politics is how far denominational loyalties showed a secular decline. Some insight can be gained by contrasting the identifications and church-attendance of the main age groups among residents. There was no decline in attendance – overall, or among Presbyterians and Catholics – between the oldest and youngest groupings. A marked diminution of zeal appeared among the minor Protestant sects, and to some extent in the Church of Ireland. Generally, no great changes in the religious equilibrium seemed in 1966 to be in the making. Again this is a case where the events of 1968–70 are unlikely to have diminished denominational solidarity among the young.

CONCLUSIONS

The guiding concern of this chapter has been to explain the stronger connection between religion and party support compared with the connection between class and party support in Belfast, which strikingly differentiates its politics from those of British cities. The leading possibilities explored have been first, that the class structure may take a different form in Belfast, or at least be perceived differently, or secondly that relationships between class and religion may be different.

The class structure did not appear to differ from that of Glasgow in particular (nor by extension from that of other British industrial cities) in terms of the underlying distribution of occupation, or in terms of the classes perceived to exist, their number, or the characteristics attributed to them. The difference lay first in the sheer extent of identification with the middle class in Belfast, and secondly in the low level of spontaneous class-consciousness – particularly of spontaneous working-class-consciousness – prevailing there.

Similarly religious loyalties showed the same relationships with occupational status and subjective class identifications in Belfast as in Glasgow. What is peculiar to Belfast is the low level of professed non-belief and the high level of church-attendance in all denominations.

Religion was then more salient in Belfast than in Glasgow or in Britain as a whole, and class less salient. In itself this finding is interesting and consonant with historical and commonsense observations. It is hardly enough to explain the divergant pattern of Belfast politics, however, without further exploration of the feelings and attitudes associated with different class and religious loyalties. These are investigated in the next chapter.

NOTES

1. For description of this cleavage in some Northern English communities see J. Bulpitt, *Party Politics in English Local Government* (London, 1966) *passim*; for Glasgow, *Scottish Political Behaviour*, especially Chapters 6 and 7.
2. *Political Change*, p. 67.
3. Ibid., p. 68.
4. *Scottish Political Behaviour*, p. 103.

9 Influences on Political Attitudes: Class, Religion, Party and Activism

CARRYING on the analysis of class and religious manifestations in Belfast, we are interested here in estimating the relative pull of class and religious feelings when these are compared directly. This analysis forms the first section, below. The comparative influence of class and religion can also be estimated indirectly, through their effect on a wide variety of preferences, perceptions and attitudes, at both activist and popular levels. The attitudinal investigation is also capable of showing whether the party divisions already examined are carried over into political outlooks and whether councillors as a group share preferences and perceptions which set them apart from the population. In the second section of the chapter, therefore, we shall compare the mutually independent effects of class, religion, party and activism (i.e. the councillor-resident distinction) over a wide range of attitudes.

CLASS COMPARED WITH RELIGIOUS FEELING IN BELFAST

Relationships between denominational and class identifications give some idea of the confluence of feeling on both dimensions. A direct comparison of the strength and direction of religious and class feelings will be undertaken in this section (Table 9.2 below). First, however, it is necessary to check whether the influence of religion does carry over strongly from voting behaviour to attitudes. The most strategic indication of the attitudinal effects of religion is formed by reactions to the question of whether Catholics and Protestants should be mixed

on Corporation housing estates. (In 1966 most estates were
either Catholic or Protestant.[1]) Reactions to this proposal can
be examined within each denomination, and among the
church-attenders of each denomination whose religious feeling
should be more intense.

The pattern of preferences which emerged was strongly
affected by religious loyalties but did not pit any one denomination directly against any other. Among residents Catholics and
non-believers were strongly for the proposal, in a ratio of
approximately 7:2. A majority in the Church of Ireland was
also for. But Presbyterians were evenly split, for and against,
and a majority of other Protestants were against. Churchgoing
Presbyterians produced a majority against integration, but a
slight majority of churchgoers in the Church of Ireland and
among other Protestants were for. Churchgoing Catholics
were of course practically indistinguishable from all Catholics.

Councillors of the Church of Ireland and other Protestant
churches were in a strong majority for the mixing of Catholics
and Protestants, and churchgoing did not substantially affect
their support. Presbyterian councillors as a whole, and also the
church-attenders among them, produced a less strongly marked
majority for integration. Non-believing councillors were
strongly for integration. Catholic councillors were unanimously
for. Thus there was substantially the same religious cleavage
of opinion among politicians as existed among the general
population.

Preferences on the housing question in Belfast can be contrasted with replies to an analogous question on mixing
Catholic and Protestant schoolchildren in Glasgow. There,
residents of all denominations agreed in an approximate ratio
of 6:3 that children should mix, and assent to this proposition
was practically unanimous among all religious groups of
councillors except Catholics, who split 50–50 on the proposal.
The suggestion of a religious confrontation on these central
social issues – which is present in Belfast in the sense that
different denominational loyalties threw up differently directed
majorities – was thus absent from the reactions of Glasgow
councillors and population. However, no clear-cut religious
division existed in Belfast, for no groupings except Catholic
councillors were fully united internally.

TABLE 9.1

Belfast Residents and Councillors: Religious Affiliation and Preferences on the Integration of Catholics and Protestants on Corporation Housing Estates

(Percentages of residents and councillors in each denomination)

	Agree very strongly	Fairly strongly	Not and DK how strongly	DK Neutral	Not and DK how strongly	Fairly strongly	Disagree Very strongly
All residents							
Presbyterian	17	21	11	1	7	11	28
Other Protestants	14	14	11	7	0	21	32
Church of Ireland	28	17	13	4	9	11	17
Non-believer	27	33	7	7	7	13	7
Roman Catholic	41	22	9	5	0	2	16
Churchgoing residents							
Presbyterian	7	18	13	2	7	11	34
Other Protestants	21	16	16	5	0	26	16
Church of Ireland	27	13	13	0	13	20	13
Roman Catholic	42	25	8	6	0	2	13
Councillors							
Presbyterian	30	0	20	0	10	0	30
Other Protestant	50	10	10	0	0	10	20
Church of Ireland	25	17	25	0	0	17	0
Non-believer	0	33	33	0	0	33	0
Roman Catholic	80	20	0	0	0	0	0
Churchgoing councillors							
Presbyterian	33	0	22	0	22	0	22
Other Protestants	56	11	0	0	0	11	22
Church of Ireland	29	0	43	0	0	14	0
Roman Catholic	80	20	0	0	0	0	0

Preferences were elicited through the question: Suppose somebody suggested that the Corporation should deliberately mix Catholic and Protestant tenants in the same housing estates. Would you agree or disagree with this proposal? How strongly would you feel – very strongly, fairly strongly, or not very strongly?

In order to examine the effects of class on the integration question in Belfast we employed the associational-subjective class combination previously used in connection with party support. However, hardly any difference appeared between members and non-members of work-related organisations, whether or not they felt themselves to be middle class or working class. The percentage agreeing to mix Catholics and Protestants varied only from 55 to 61 over all four groups. Sixty-five per cent of councillors who felt middle-class supported integration, while 91 per cent of working-class councillors gave their assent. However, councillors were so strongly middle-class in any case that this contrast had little substantive significance, especially as assent also came from 60 per cent of councillors who did not feel they belonged to a class.

Class and religious loyalties can be directly contrasted through a question also asked in Glasgow; it asked for first and second choices among four types of person – a Protestant of the same class, a Protestant of a different class, a Catholic of the same class, and a Catholic of a different class. An initial decision facing respondents was whether choices between individuals could be made on the basis of religious and class loyalties alone. The extent of willingness to use these oversimplified criteria gave some indication of intolerance and prejudice in Belfast compared with Glasgow, on the assumption that such feelings encourage judgement on the basis of crude social stereotypes. Persons adopting these stereotypes naturally preferred as their first choice individuals of the same class and religion as themselves. On their second choice such respondents had to choose between class characteristics similar to those they possessed themselves or similar religious characteristics. The percentages opting for persons of a similar class as against persons of a similar religion give a direct estimate of the comparative strength of the two types of identification in 1966.

Before comparing actual choices we can compare the proportion who refused to employ class or religious stereotypes. This proportion was greatest among non-believers (roughly 73 per cent) – possibly because their unconventional religious experiences had revealed the shallowness of social stereotypes. The next greatest proportion was found among Catholic

TABLE 9.2

Belfast Residents and Councillors: Religious Affiliation and Choices between Religious and Class Affiliations

(Percentages of residents and councillors in each religious denomination and percentages of churchgoing residents and councillors in each religious denomination)

	First choice prefer:				Second choice prefer:			
	Prot. same class	Prot. different class	Catholic same class	Catholic different class	Prot. same class	Prot. different class	Catholic same class	Catholic different class
All residents								
Presbyterian	73	0	1	0	3	24	40	0
Other Protestants	82	0	0	0	0	21	39	0
Church of Ireland	60	2	2	2	6	9	38	0
Non-believers	27	0	0	0	0	0	20	0
Roman Catholic	5	0	41	0	22	4	7	10
Churchgoing residents								
Presbyterian	80	0	0	0	0	23	26	0
Other Protestants	79	0	0	0	0	21	26	0
Church of Ireland	40	0	7	7	13	6	26	0
Roman Catholic	6	0	42	0	23	4	8	11
All councillors								
Presbyterian	60	0	10	0	10	60	10	0
Other Protestants	50	0	0	0	0	50	0	0
Church of Ireland	50	0	0	0	0	8	25	0
Roman Catholic	20	0	50	0	30	0	10	10
Churchgoing councillors								
Presbyterian	56	0	11	0	11	56	11	0
Other Protestants	44	0	0	0	0	44	0	0
Church of Ireland	43	0	0	0	0	11	29	0
Roman Catholic	20	0	50	0	30	0	10	10

Percentages making a first choice and percentages making a second choice are each reckoned out of 100 per cent.
Actual percentages do not sum to 100 per cent because of the proportions refusing to make choices on class and religious grounds.

residents (52 per cent): it was least among Protestants – 34 per cent in the Church of Ireland, 26 per cent among Presbyterians and 18 per cent among the minority denominations. The Protestant majority thus emerged as more addicted to stereotypes than the religious minorities. Churchgoing residents were also somewhat more likely to use stereotypes than non-churchgoing residents. Variation in denominational acceptance of the class and religious stereotypes was more marked among residents in Belfast, than it was in Glasgow where about 40 per cent in all denominations refused to use them. However, the overall proportion of refusals in Belfast was about the same as in Glasgow – 37 per cent compared with 40 per cent.

Those respondents who actually registered a first and second choice between coreligionists and members of the same class were probably all expressing prejudice in some form. The interesting question is whether their class or religious prejudice was the stronger.

As in Glasgow the vast majority of first preferences focused on persons of similar class and religious characteristics. A majority in all denominations of those residents who made a second choice, opted for persons of the same class characteristics but different religion. However, the majority varied interestingly between denominations. Most inclined to favour class over religion were non-believers, followed by members of the Church of Ireland and then Catholics. Presbyterians and other Protestants favoured class in the ratio of 2:1. While the original proportions did not change much for churchgoing Catholics or members of the Church of Ireland, Presbyterian and other Protestant churchgoers favoured a Protestant of a different class to almost the same extent as a Catholic of the same class. These tendencies were exactly the same as were observed in Glasgow.

Belfast Protestant councillors were less inclined to accept class-religious stereotypes than electors, but more inclined to accept them than Glasgow councillors. Catholic councillors plumped for class over religion, followed closely by councillors of the Church of Ireland. Presbyterian and other Protestant councillors on the other hand overwhelmingly chose a Protestant of different class. Churchgoing neither intensified nor reduced these tendencies. While in Glasgow Presbyterian councillors were certainly less inclined than Catholic councillors to opt for class affiliations, a slight majority did prefer the latter. Thus a greater difference opened up between Catholic and Presbyterian councillors in Belfast than in Glasgow. The difference between councillors' class or religious affiliations was also greater than appeared between Catholic and Presbyterian residents.

The whole tendency of our evidence is to reveal Belfast as no more and no less religiously tolerant than Glasgow, at least in 1966. The reason why religion entered into politics, even in that year, lay not in the general level of tolerance but in the fact that certain strategic groups had a greater potential for intolerance than others. These consisted of the majority religious groups of residents and particularly of councillors. The strong tendency of the latter to prefer coreligionists over members of the same class supports the interpretation that Protestant leaders rather than ordinary residents were at that time responsible for maintaining politico-religious divisions in Belfast. Their definition of the issues and mistrust of Catholics seem, however, on the basis of Table 9.2 to have found some response among majority groups at popular level.

Class effects on the choices reviewed in Table 9.2 can be estimated through their relationship with the combination of association membership and subjective class employed previously. The class and religious stereotypes used in the question were rejected by 45 per cent of unorganised middle-class residents compared with roughly a third of all other class groupings. On the crucial second choices of those who did employ the stereotypes an overwhelming 52 per cent of the organised working class chose a person of the same class compared with nine per cent choosing a person of different class. Forty-two per cent opted for the same class compared to 17 per cent opting for a different class among association members who did not identify with the working class. Thirty-three per cent chose the same class compared with 19 per cent choosing a different class among residents who were neither organised nor identified with the middle class. Of the unorganised middle-class identifiers 28 per cent chose a person of the same class compared with 18 per cent who chose a person from a different class. These results confirm the general preference for class over religious identifications among most groups of residents in Belfast.

Given the pattern of previous findings on the greater political influence of religion compared with class, it is anomalous that in a direct choice class loyalties were more commonly preferred over religious than religious over class by Belfast residents, although certainly by a slighter margin than by Glasgow residents. Why in this case did class not exert a political influence in other areas equal to that of religion?

The answer may lie in the stronger religious identifications of councillors, revealed in those same choices. Given two cleavages of more or less equal strength, party strategists have a certain latitude in choosing which to exploit. If their own preferences incline them to the judgement that religious cleavages are more salient, their choice of such cleavages may shape the pattern of support as much as the social divisions themselves. And quite apart from their own inclinations it is obviously more rational for Unionist politicians to muster all 70 per cent of Protestant residents rather than only 41 per cent of middle-class residents. The stress laid by the smaller parties on class rather than religious divisions underlines that point.

In seeking to explain Belfast politics it may be strategic to abandon the usual explanation of party support in terms of social factors which are implicitly assumed to be antecedent. For Unionist hegemony preceded modern social developments in Belfast (Chapter 2). It is more plausible to see the already existing Unionist hegemony as consistently depressing working-class consciousness and spreading middle-class identifications, than a depressed working-class consciousness producing Unionist hegemony. In the same way one can regard the salience of religion as maintained in part by the political consciousness surrounding it. In contrast, the strong working-class consciousness of Glasgow has surely been fostered by the Labour Party's predominance over a thirty-year period.

These interpretations can only be interim since all the available evidence has not yet been considered. In the second section we compare the influence exerted by class, religion, party and activism over a variety of political preferences and perceptions, in order to reach a broader understanding of the interpenetration of their effects than has been possible with the limited indicators used hitherto.

INFLUENCES ON POLITICAL ATTITUDES

An investigation of attitudinal effects can answer several questions relevant to any analytical assessment of Belfast politics. In the first place it produces further evidence on the effects of class compared with religion. Second, it shows whether the already wide cleavage between the parties is carried over into a consistent division of political preferences and outlook. Third, the analysis will enable us to discover whether councillors as a group display political characteristics, independent of their class, religious or party background, which set them apart from ordinary members of the population.

This last feature is particularly relevant because it bears upon widely accepted ideas about differences between persons highly active in politics (and thus termed for convenience political activists) and ordinary members of the population.[2] Because of their greater involvement, activists (in our case the Belfast councillors) can certainly be expected to be more knowledgeable and informed about politics. Such political expertise, reinforced by close contact in committee and council chamber, might prompt them on some occasions to agree more than the population on certain issues (such as the necessity of getting more money to maintain city services free of inflation). On the other hand, their stronger political involvement might render party and religious divisions even deeper and more consistent than those which appear among the population. There is a body of speculation about politicians' tendencies to agreement on procedural matters and on some policy matters, which we explore in greater detail below. Here we shall investigate the preliminary question of whether the fact of being a councillor exerts any effects independent of party, class or religious affiliations. This means that in subsequent analyses we shall treat the councillor-resident distinction as a background characteristic just like the difference between, for example, Unionists and non-Unionists.

The attitudes to which we relate class, religion, party and activism cover a wide range of political reactions. There are

first preferences on the politico-religious issues described at the
end of Chapter 5, and also on the annual proposal to increase
rates, the local property tax. Actual percentages for these
preferences are given in Table 11.3, below. Then there is the
degree to which councillors and electors were prepared to
support the Belfast majority on three of these issues (swings,
Mater, rates) against affected minorities. Issue perceptions are
also examined – on what constitutes the most important problem in Belfast, on popular agreement about that problem, on
the way in which the problem is viewed (in a general theoretical
context as against a highly specific limited context), and on
likely personal success on issues. The perceptions of voting
reported in Tables 7.12 and 7.13 were included, as well as
perceptions of local government performance – whether the
Corporation would be affected by the disappearance of political
parties, whether it is unduly influenced by pressure groups,
whether the Mayor represents everyone or only his party.
(This was of particular relevance in 1966, when Lord Mayor
Jenkins had publicly gone out of his way to advocate reconciliation with Catholics.) Finally, effects on the desire for change in
Belfast government were also brought into the analysis. All
these reactions to the Corporation are considered also in Chapter
13, where we explore support for established procedures in
Belfast in 1966.

We measure the mutually independent influence of class,
religion, party and activism on these attitudes by procedures
similar to those used to estimate the influence of class and
religion over Unionist and non-Unionist identifications in
Table 7.11. That is to say that proportional variation in the
dependent attitudes listed above was examined between social
class categories, under a control for religion, and vice versa (as
explained in the notes to Table 7.11). We can proceed in a
similar fashion to that used when Unionist support was the
dependent variable to examine the proportional variation
produced in, for example, preferences on the rates issue, as
between councillors and residents, under a control for party,
and vice versa. And we can measure the mutually independent
effects on attitudes of activism and religion, or of activism and
class, in exactly the same way.

We compare the effects of these background factors in this

pairwise manner, two at a time, because the numbers of respondents were too small to permit the imposition of simultaneous controls for all four at the same time. However, by averaging the effect of each variable under all relevant controls we were able to arrive at the comparative rankings reported in Table 9.3. Limitations of numbers also forced us to collapse the five-point religious classification used in Table 7.11, in order to conserve numbers in comparisons made under joint controls. A dichotomy between, on the one hand, Catholics, non-believers and non-church-attending members of the Church of Ireland, and, on the other hand, church-attenders in the Church of Ireland and all other Protestants, seems most fitted to maximise differences between respondents and forms the religious classification to which we refer in Table 9.3.[3]

TABLE 9.3

Comparison of the Effects of Class, Religion, Party and Activism over Political Attitudes in Belfast and Glasgow

(Sums of ranks assigned for relative influence over attitudes)

Belfast residents ranks summed:	Class	Party	Religion	Activism
Over all preferences and perceptions	34	32	33	—
Over preferences only	12	9	12	—
Over support for majority only	7	6	4	—
Over perceptions only	15	17	17	—
Belfast councillors ranks summed:				
Over all preferences and perceptions	44	29	33	—
Over preferences only	12	8	10	—
Over support for majority only	8	5	4	—
Over perceptions only	24	16	19	—
Belfast residents and councillors ranks summed:				
Over all preferences and perceptions	53	34	52	44
Over preferences only	15	7	14	15
Over support for majority only	9	5	5	11
Over perceptions only	29	22	33	18
Glasgow residents and activists ranks summed:				
Over all preferences and perceptions	39	—	44	37
Over preferences only	13	—	15	8
Over support for majority only	7	—	10	7
Over perceptions only	19	—	19	22

In order to make up the Table ranks were assigned to each factor in accordance with its influence, relative to the other factors, over the preferences and appraisals listed above. Thus on the last specific attitude considered – change in Belfast government – activism emerged as the strongest influence and was therefore given a rank of 1: relative to activism, class, religion and party exerted fairly equal effects and so tied on a rank of 2. When the ranks given to each of these factors, for all perceptions and preferences examined, are summed, they give the scores reported for 'Belfast residents and councillors' in Table 9.3. The sum gives a crude estimate of the overall influence, relative to other factors, of the factor under consideration. When considering effects on the attitudes of residents and councillors separately activism cannot, of course, be included in the comparison; therefore the sums of ranks giving the relative influence of class, religion and party over residents' and councillors' attitudes separately are rather different from those emerging in the overall comparison with activism, among the combined group of residents and councillors.

Since the numbers presented in Table 9.3 are essentially a rank-ordering, the smallest numbers mark the strongest effects (because they include more rankings of 1 and 2 than ranks of 3 and 4).

Among both residents and councillors, party emerged as the strongest influence over all attitudes, followed by religion and then by class. But party effects were only marginally stronger among residents than either class or religion. Among councillors religious effects approached those of party but class was much less influential than either.

It is probably more illuminating to consider the relative influence of background characteristics separately over preferences and perceptions, rather than mixing the two together. If we consider only issue preferences, the same general pattern of influence emerged for both residents and councillors: party exerted more effect than religion and class. Religion and class tied among residents while religion affected councillor preferences more sharply than class. Over all political perceptions considered the same order held among councillors while class emerged with slightly more effect than religion and party, among residents. In the case of support for the majority on issues – neither a clear-cut preference nor yet a perception – religion, party and class exercised relative effects in that order for both councillors and residents.

Generally, the effects of the background characteristics were almost indistinguishable among residents, probably reflecting the weak association between attitudes and other characteristics generally found at the popular level. Party, religion and class differed more sharply in their effects among councillors, and this may be a consequence of the greater consistency between the formal affiliation and political outlook of activists. One feature of this consistency which appears in most of the analyses with individual attitudes is the marked divisiveness of party and religion among councillors compared with residents.

When the influence of these background factors is compared for the whole group of councillors and residents combined, this resulted in a marked accentuation of party influences relative to other factors for attitudes overall, as well as for preferences and perceptions taken separately. The influence of religion, on the other hand, was reduced by the absence of strong differences among residents, so that in the combined group it exerted little greater effect than class. Interestingly, activism itself – the distinction between councillors and ordinary residents – produced effects which in aggregate strength fell midway between those of party and of religion and class. The political characteristics of party and activism thus emerge as affecting attitudes more directly than the social characteristics of religion and class.

Party emerges as the most influential variable because of the greater divisiveness of councillors compared with residents. There is a temptation to link this with the intransigence of politics in Belfast compared with other British cities. However, greater class and religious divisions also appeared in the attitudes of Glasgow councillors, relative to those of Glasgow electors. In Glasgow, on the other hand, activism exerted an influence which in many respects cross-cut those of class and religion and was comparable in strength. In order to see whether the influence of activism *vis-à-vis* class and religion was weaker in Belfast than in Glasgow we can compare the summed ranks of these background factors for residents and activists in the two cities. The comparison is facilitated by so many identical questions having been asked in the two surveys, but it must be remembered that party was not included in the comparison of attitudinal effect in Glasgow.[4]

Over the total number of direct comparisons between the effects of activism and those of other factors, activism emerged in Glasgow as slightly more influential than class, which was followed by religion. This compared with the more sharply defined lead of activism over class and religion in Belfast.

However, the aggregate comparison ignores the question of exactly what attitudes were affected most strongly by activism in each city. Examining rankings separately for preferences, appraisals and majority rule, activism appeared as far the strongest influence over issue-preferences in Glasgow. In Belfast, on the other hand, the influence of activism over preferences ranked almost on the same level with those of class and religion. In its effects on majority support activism in Belfast came last of all factors but in Glasgow activism tied for the most extensive influence with class. It is in its effect on perceptions that activism in Belfast led, while in Glasgow activism trailed class and religion.

The contrast between Glasgow and Belfast in terms of activism's influence over perceptions is anomalous because one would expect these relatively factual judgements to be invariantly affected by political knowledge and expertise regardless of other divergences. What does seem capable of explaining greater political intransigence in Belfast is the weaker influence of activism over preferences. In Glasgow activism exerted a stronger influence than either class or religion while in Belfast it was least effective of all the background factors. This implied a certain congruence of feeling and opinion among Glasgow councillors, which might counterbalance the class and religious divisions which still showed up as deeper than those at popular level. In Belfast, on the other hand, activism contributed mainly to political knowledge and expertise: intermingling in council and committees did not seem to have overcome class, religious and partisan cleavages. In the light of this analysis of attitudinal effects, activists in Belfast appeared more likely to emerge as opposed factional leaders than moderators joined by ties of common political sympathy.

NOTES

1. The Corporation had by 1966 made a few experiments with mixed housing. The subsequent riots caused minority families to leave these estates so that the effect of the present disturbances, as of nineteenth-century riots, is to reinforce the tendency to religiously homogeneous areas, which in turn helps perpetuate hostilities.
2. For a summary and discussion of such ideas see Ian Budge, *Agreement and the Stability of Democracy* (Chicago, 1970), Chapter 1.
3. This particular dichotomy was preferred because it is the one out of all possible dichotomies deriving from the original extended classification which maximises the effect of religion on party support.
4. This comparison is reported in Chapter 7 of *Class, Religion*.

10 Recruitment of Activists

In terms of its influence over attitudes, activism emerged as a factor in Belfast politics at least comparable with class, religion and party. Subsequent chapters will be concerned with exploring some of the implications of this finding. For if activists, by virtue of experiences in Council and administration which they share with each other but not with their followers, develop preferences and appraisals which differ from those of the general population, this will have immediate bearings on the question of representation – the extent to which councillors act on the preferences of their constituents (Chapter 11). It also indicates the presence of constraints on free communication between activists and population (Chapter 12). Different preferences may have evolved in procedural as well as other areas while patterns of conflict and agreement may also diverge (Chapter 13).

Before tracing these relationships between activists and population it will be useful to investigate the correlates of activism, just as we have already investigated the correlates of class, religion and party. By so doing we can enrich our explanations of why activism exerts the effects it does, and trace any differential opportunities for office holding conferred by membership of a particular class, denomination or party. An introduction to this question is provided by previous comparisons between councillors and population in terms of background characteristics (Chapter 8). Ultimately we shall undertake an extended analysis of the push towards office exerted by these characteristics. But a more immediate entry to the analysis of activist careers is provided by the recollections of councillors on why they first undertook political activity, why they first stood for Council and why they continued to stand. The answers of Glasgow councillors to identical questions provide a useful check on idiosyncracies of the Belfast responses.

SUBJECTIVE RECOLLECTIONS OF BELFAST
COUNCILLORS

(i) *Reasons for first entering politics*

The most striking finding from councillors' recollections of how
they first became active paradoxically relates to the half who
were inactive before standing for Council. This compares with
the mere fifth of Glasgow councillors who were similarly
inactive. All these Glasgow councillors were Progressives. In
Belfast, however, approximately half of both Unionists and
non-Unionists reported previous non-participation. The predominant Unionists were composed of slightly less than half of
formerly passive councillors, but in the case of Nationalists the
proportion rose to over three quarters. Only Northern Ireland
Labour comprised a strong majority of persons with pre-
Council experience.

In Belfast as in Glasgow a plurality of councillors who admitted prior activity named group prompting or affiliations as the
primary reason for initial involvement. However, the proportion of councillors giving group-related reasons did not greatly
outnumber the proportion attracted by abstract, ideological
reasons – 23 per cent to 13 per cent in Belfast compared with
47 to 20 per cent in Glasgow. And the 18 per cent of Belfast
councillors mentioning their general political interest compared
more closely with the proportion mentioning groups than the
15 per cent of councillors similarly drawn to initial involvement
in Glasgow. The pattern of influence which emerged among
Unionists was very similar to that among councillors as a whole.
Among non-Unionist councillors group influences tied with
ideological, and with general political interest (and were
outweighed by ideological influences among the reasons given
second).

(ii) *Reasons for First Standing for Council*

Group influences – and particularly party influences – outnumbered all others in the reasons for standing for Council
mentioned by Glasgow councillors, as a body and within each
party group. In Belfast this relationship was neatly reversed.
Concerns for causes which were largely ideological in nature
were cited by almost twice the proportion who mentioned

TABLE 10.1

Reasons Given by Belfast Councillors for First Becoming Active in Politics

(Percentages of all councillors and of party groups)

	Group influences				Promotion of causes			General interest in politics	Never active
	Primary group	Party related	Total group influences	Drawn in by political events	Policy-ideological	Helping people	Total Promotion of causes		
First mentioned reason									
All councillors	16%	7%	23%	2%	9%	2%	13%	18%	47%
Unionist councillors	19%	6%	25%	0	7%	3%	10%	19%	46%
N.I. Labour councillors	20%	20%	40%	0	20%	0	20%	20%	20%
Nationalist Labour councillors	0	0	0	11%	0	0	11%	11%	78%
All non-Unionist councillors	7%	7%	14%	7%	7%	0	14%	14%	58%
Second mentioned reason									
All councillors	7%	4%	11%	4%	9%	2%	15%	0	—
Unionist councillors	7%	3%	10%	3%	7%	3%	13%	0	—
N.I. Labour councillors	20%	20%	40%	0	20%	0	20%	0	—
Nationalist Labour councillors	0	0	0	11%	11%	0	22%	0	—
All non-Unionist councillors	7%	7%	14%	7%	14%	0	21%	0	—

Notes: Table 10.1. Questions on which the Table is based are:

When did you first become active in party work? Why did you first become active?
Respondents were allowed to reply freely and their answers were subsequently coded into approximately 50 detailed categories which are recombined into the broad headings in the Table. To avoid double-counting first-mentioned reasons are reported separately from second-mentioned reasons. In this and subsequent tables councillors who replied 'don't know' or for whom other data was missing are omitted, so percentages often do not total 100.

TABLE 10.2

Reasons Given by Belfast Councillors for First Standing for Council

(Percentages of all Councillors and of Party Groups)

	Group influences			Promotion of causes				General interest in politics
	Primary group	Party related	Total group influences	Drawn in by political events	Policy-ideological	Helping people and groups	Total promotion of causes	
First mentioned reason								
All councillors	16%	13%	29%	4%	33%	13%	50%	20%
Unionist councillors	19%	13%	32%	3%	39%	10%	52%	16%
N.I. Labour councillors	20%	20%	40%	0	40%	20%	60%	0
Nat. Labour councillors	0%	11%	11%	11%	11%	22%	44%	44%
All non-Unionist councillors	7%	14%	21%	7%	21%	21%	49%	29%
Second mentioned reason								
All councillors	4%	18%	22%	7%	13%	7%	27%	18%
Unionist councillors	6%	19%	25%	3%	16%	3%	22%	19%
N.I. Labour councillors	0	0	0	20%	0	20%	40%	20%
Nat. Labour councillors	0	22%	22%	11%	11%	11%	33%	11%
All Non-Unionist councillors	0	14%	14%	14%	7%	14%	35%	14%
Third mentioned reason								
All councillors	7%	0	7%	2%	4%	7%	13%	7%
Unionist councillors	6%	0	6%	0	6%	6%	12%	6%
N.I. Labour councillors	0	0	0	0	0	0	0	20%
Nat. Labour councillors	11%	0	11%	11%	0	11%	22%	0
All Non-Unionist councillors	7%	0	7%	7%	0	7%	14%	7%

groups. About a fifth of all councillors cited their fascination with politics as a reason for entering the Council, about the same fraction as related it to their initial entry into politics (Table 10.1). The distribution of replies again differed little between Unionist and non-Unionist councillors. Among the latter Nationalists laid proportionately more emphasis on general interest and ideology, and Northern Ireland Labour stressed general interest less and group influences more.

The heavily ideological motivations prompting entry to the Council, especially when compared with the influence of parties and other groups in Glasgow, can be seen as contributing to the more inflammatory style of politics in Belfast, compared with politics in Glasgow. It could be maintained that ideological and policy concerns would render politicians less inclined to compromise, more inclined to bitterness and internal division, than in the case where they were acting as brokers among the limited interests of concrete groups. The contention is plausible but it is also possible that the socialising effect of council activity might soften the clash of the original causes which prompted entry. Some evidence on the effects of Council life is contained in the replies of councillors to a third question, on why they continued to stand for re-election to Council.

(iii) *Reasons for Standing for Re-election to Council*

Certainly among councillors as a body, policy-ideological and related concerns showed a decrease among reasons for pro- longing Council activity compared with reasons given for first standing for Council. This reflected the decline in such reasons given by Unionists and Northern Ireland Labour. Nationalists cited the promotion of causes as much as their reason for continuing to stand as for first standing. Other reasons for continuing were almost totally lacking among non-Unionist councillors: groups attracted limited mention but no one mentioned interest in Council work except as an afterthought. More than half the Unionists who had been faced with a decision about standing again mentioned their interest in Council work, compared with a mere 16 per cent whose political interest prompted their initial entry. The contrast between Unionist councillors and members of the Opposition stemmed from the permanent minority status of the latter

TABLE 10.3

Reasons Given by Belfast Councillors for Continuing to Stand for Re-election to the Council

(Percentages of all councillors and party groups of councillors)

	Has not served more than one term	Group attachments			Promotion of causes				General interest and satisfaction from council work		
		Primary groups	Party-related	Total group attitudes	Continued influence of past political events	Policy-ideological	Helping people	Total Promotion of causes	Satisfaction from way of life as councillor	General interest in council work	Total general interest
First mentioned reason											
All councillors	27%	0	4%	4%	2%	24%	11%	37%	4%	24%	28%
Unionist councillors	16%	0	3%	3%	3%	23%	6%	32%	6%	36%	42%
N.I. Labour councillors	80%	0	0	0	0	20%	0	20%	0	0	0
Nat. Lab. councillors	44%	0	11%	11%	0	11%	33%	44%	0	0	0
All Non-Unionist councillors	57%	0	7%	7%	0	14%	21%	35%	0	0	0
Second mentioned reason											
All councillors	—	9%	0	9%	2%	13%	9%	24%	2%	4%	6%
Unionist councillors	—	10%	0	10%	3%	13%	13%	29%	3%	3%	6%
N.I. Lab. councillors	—	0	0	0	0	20%	0	20%	0	0	0
Nat. Lab. councillors	—	11%	0	11%	0	11%	0	11%	0	11%	11%
All Non-Unionist councillors	—	7%	0	7%	0	14%	0	14%	0	7%	7%
Third mentioned again											
All councillors	—	2%	0	2%	0	0	0	0	0	2%	2%
Unionist councillors	—	3%	0	3%	0	0	0	0	0	0	0
N.I. Lab. councillors	—	0	0	0	0	0	0	0	0	20%	20%
Nat. Lab. councillors	—	0	0	0	0	0	0	0	0	0	0
All Non-Unionist councillors	—	0	0	0	0	0	0	0	0	7%	7%

coupled with the reservation of Council offices for Unionists only. Non-Unionists were denied the opportunity to influence policy in any important way, and as a result derived little positive satisfaction from their Council activities. This contrast between the different parties' reasons for continuing did not hold in Glasgow, where about a third of the councillors in both parties mentioned their satisfaction in Council work. As a result only about a quarter of Glasgow councillors compared with a third of Belfast councillors found ideological or policy-related concerns sufficient to keep them going politically.

(iv) *Conclusions drawn from the Subjective Recollections of Belfast Councillors*

The general picture of Belfast councillors which emerges from these recollections about their political career is of inexperienced men suddenly pushed into activity at the time of their Council advent, largely for ideological reasons, which in the case of the opposition parties was not tempered by subsequent socialisation into Council activities. This picture fits well with the rigid ideological stands taken by many Belfast politicians, which in turn contributed to the continuing divisions underlying city politics. It is true it is the Nationalist rather than the Unionist councillor who is captured in this picture. Only half the Unionists compared with three quarters of Nationalists lacked pre-Council experience. While about half in each case ran for Council because of ideological reasons, a third of Unionists compared to only a tenth of Nationalists were attracted through groups. And Unionists' initial ideological zeal faded as interest in Council work increased. In all these respects Unionists resembled councillors of both the governing party and opposition in Glasgow, while Nationalists formed the deviant group. This was natural, for in Glasgow the opposition was associated with decision-making to an extent not evident in Belfast. Moreover, in the situation of vigorous two-party competition that existed in Glasgow the opposition had a realistic expectation of winning future power. Short of revolution the opposition had no hopes of power in Belfast. What emerges from these replies is a contrast between a competitive and flexible party system and rigid one-party dominance. In the first case the prospect of alternating in power gave most members of all parties a positive psychological investment in the system. In the second only members of the dominant party felt that the system belonged to them, and this feeling was reciprocated by the representatives of the permanent minority. We shall consider further manifestations of minority alienation in Chapter 13, in our discussion of support for the procedures underlying the system.

Apart from reflecting the influence of the party system, councillors' recollections also point to background factors influencing their recruitment into political activity. Party obviously requires close consideration. Our previous analysis suggests that the policy-related, ideological concerns which loomed relatively large for Belfast councillors were rooted in religious and to a lesser extent in class affiliations. Group-related motivations constituted only a minority of councillors' reasons for activity but were not negligible: these included not only religious and class affiliations but overt association memberships, linked often with occupation.

BACKGROUND FACTORS AFFECTING RECRUITMENT

(i) *Ways in which a Combination of Factors can Influence Recruitment*

Party, class and religious affiliations, work-related organisation memberships and occupation are all characteristics on which we previously compared councillors and electors. But simple comparisons on one characteristic are unlikely to provide more than indirect clues to the underlying processes whereby certain individuals decide to seek political office and others do not. For example, we have discovered that councillors are almost exclusively non-manual in terms of occupational status and thus that their work backgrounds sharply differentiate them from the population. But this finding does not allow us to discriminate satisfactorily between councillors and population, for the simple reason that so many non-activists also have non-manual occupations. The latter are a necessary but not sufficient cause for activism. The same can be said of the other characteristics mentioned above and of others on which councillors as a body markedly differ from the population, such as sex and education.

In attempting to make sense out of councillors' obviously a-typical characteristics, it is helpful to think of the factors promoting activism as falling under three headings: resources, motivations, opportunities.[1] In crossing the threshold to active participation an individual needs to be presented with opportunities as well as possessing certain resources: moreover, he is unlikely to take advantage of the openings which do appear unless he has sufficient motivation.

Many people have political resources. These include the speaking and writing skills associated with a longer education and certain non-manual occupations. Other characteristics such as the experience of organisational problems linked with association memberships, and childhood socialisation experiences, may also impart political skills. A father of non-manual occupational status is more likely to encourage the development of speaking and writing in his child: these skills are at any rate regarded as more appropriate in a son than in a daughter. Kinship with someone already politically active also places the individual in a situation where he can acquire skills very readily. Apart from socialisation experiences older persons have had more time to develop skills than younger persons. All these characteristics enhance the ability not simply to acquire skill but to make contacts, which are another important political resource. For example, persons who have lived their whole life in the city are more likely to have local contacts than incomers. Exposure to political events is also encouraged by these characteristics. The non-manual worker is more likely than the manual worker to have direct dealings with Corporation or Government; older persons are more likely to have had contact than younger: and so on. Kinship with an activist is likely to provide the greatest exposure of all. The more exposure the more likely are interest and concern about politics to be aroused, and these in themselves can constitute strong motivations for participation. Motivations can also be stimulated, as we noted above, by a desire to advance the interest of groups, of class and religious causes. Other policy-related reasons for participation can be generated by strong identifications with the community as a whole.

Motivations are more likely to be dampened and resources harder to employ in the case of non-Unionists compared with Unionists in a city dominated by one party. The same may be true for Catholics under Protestant domination, and for those who identify with the working rather than the middle class. Because of these affiliations political opportunities are more available for some individuals than others.

These theoretical considerations point out some character-istics from our survey data as likely to exert considerable effects on recruitment: these are the individual's own occupa-tion, father's occupation, work-related association membership, education, subjective class feeling, sex, age, religious denomina-tion, church-attendance, a longer residence in and satisfaction with Belfast (which together give some indication of the degree of identification with the whole community). Kinship with an activist is perhaps even more strategic than these (44 per cent of councillors claimed kinship) but we have no information on electors' kinships and so cannot use this factor in the comparison.

The fact that resources, motivations and opportunities are all essential to office-seeking also indicates that combinations of characteristics rather than any one single characteristic need to be operating before activity is undertaken. This points to the necessity of examining the effects of background factors con-currently and comparatively, rather than singly as we did in Chapter 8.

(ii) *Differentiation of Councillors from Ordinary Members of the Population in Terms of Background Characteristics*

To reach final conclusions about influences on their recruitment we should need to follow councillors through the whole of their careers, noting their changing life-styles, political relationships and motivations, at each stage of their public lives, Since the evidence derived from our survey was collected at one point in time we cannot therefore examine the direct influence over on-going recruitment of the factors we have named. What we can do is to see how far these factors in combination marked off the councillors in our survey from the sample of residents. Success in distinguishing these councillors from these residents cannot finally prove them causes of office-seeking but it does show that they could be causes. Lack of any association with office-holding even at one point in time does, on the other hand, provide evidence that they could not influence office-seeking over a more extended time period. In this sense the ability of the background factors in combination to distinguish between our councillors and our residents constitutes a minimal test of their influence on general recruitment processes in Belfast.

In combination the twelve factors listed above do distinguish our councillors fairly well from our residents. Sixty-two per cent of councillors possessed combinations of characteristics in terms of Unionist affiliations, non-manual occupation, high education, fairly exclusive background and so on – which were not shared with any residents. Seventy-eight per cent of residents possessed combinations of characteristics not shared with any councillors. Because such combinations were unique to either councillors or residents they enable a fairly successful prediction (or postdiction) to be made from an individual's background (in terms of the characteristics considered) to the fact of his being a councillor or resident. This success is reflected in a high value on appropriate statistics (0·82 on Goodman and Kruskall's Tau). So far as our evidence goes the background characteristics chosen for study do seem, as a whole, to influence recruitment in Belfast. The next questions concerns their relative influence. Is occupation, for example, more or less successful than party in distinguishing councillors from residents? And how do the other factors compare in their sensitivity to this difference?

(iii) *Relative Sensitivity of Background Characteristics to the difference between Councillors and Residents*

A method of estimating relative influence on a dependent, dichotomised attribute has already been used with the effects of class, religion, party and activism on attitudes and party support. In this case activism itself is the dependent attribute. Our procedure will again be to estimate average differences between the proportion of councillors out of all respondents characterised, for example, as male versus female, or Unionist versus non-Unionist, and so on. From such proportional differences we can infer the 'push' towards being a councillor which is exerted by each characteristic. By the method described in the preceding chapters we can estimate both the single 'effect' of each characteristic on activism (Table 10.4) and the 'effect' which it exerts independently of other characteristics (Tables 10.5 and 10.6).

TABLE 10.4

Single Effect Parameters for the Influence of Each Background Characteristic on the Distinction between Councillors and Residents in Belfast

	Own occupation	Father's occupation	Sex	Education	Subjective class	Party	Church-attendance	Assoc. Member	Satisfaction with life in Belfast	Spent life in Belfast	Denomination	Age
All councillors and all residents	0·35	0·26	0·25	0·24	0·16	0·13	0·13	0·09	0·09	0·06	0·05	0·05
Unionist councillors and Unionist residents	0·44	0·43	0·40	0·34	0·27	—	0·12	0·16	0·10	0·16	0·05	0·23
Non-Unionist councillors and non-Unionist residents	0·23	0·03	0·13	0·12	0·02		0·14	0·10	0·04	0·05	− 0·08	− 0·05

The first stage in the systematic analysis of effects is to rank characteristics on the relative size of the effect parameters produced for the single uncontrolled relationship with activism. The characteristic which produces most difference in the proportions of councillors clearly emerges from the single effect parameters of Table 10.4 as non-manual versus manual occupation. This pre-eminence is not surprising given the pervasive consequences of engaging in professional or white-collar occupations. Resources in the shape of time and skill, motivations stimulated by political exposure, opportunities produced by political contacts, are all more likely to be generated by non-manual compared with manual work. Even in terms of sheer physical effort expended on the job, and not on spare-time politics, workers by hand are more disadvantaged than workers by brain. At the same time, given that the full potential value of the parameter is 1·00, the 0·35 reported in Table 10.4 reflects the fact that most non-manual workers never become active.

Occupational effects seemingly extend from the past as well as the present, for father's occupation was the characteristic which produced the next most extensive change in proportions of councillors. The fact that education almost tied as the third most weighty background characteristic is obviously associated with the skills and self-confidence it imparts. The Council was so overwhelmingly a male preserve that the approximate equality of the influence exerted by sex and that exerted by education and father's occupation is not surprising. In less conservative societies than Belfast woman's role is defined as non-political and childhood socialisation implicitly diverts feminine attention from political topics.

Two points deserve note about the effects of other characteristics. Self-assigned class and satisfaction with Belfast, which are 'psychological' in the sense that they depend on the respondents' own assessment of his feelings, exerted only moderate effects compared to socio-economic characteristics such as occupation and education, which type the individual regardless of his own feelings. And religion exerted the least influence of all, indicating that the Council was not too unrepresentative of the population in terms of religious composition. In view of the religious cleavage in Belfast politics this is interesting, although it meant only that the permanent politico-religious minority in the population elected a permanent politico-religious minority on the Council: politically both were powerless.

The relative weight of background characteristics is roughly comparable as between Belfast and Glasgow. There, however, father's occupation was the leading factor, with a parameter of 0·33. Own occupation followed (0·28), and the higher proportion of women among Glasgow councillors produced a lower effect parameter (0·18). Education exerted almost the same effect in both cities, and in both religion was relatively unimportant in distinguishing activists from residents.

By separating Unionists from non-Unionists and calculating as before differences in the proportion of councillors produced by the change from one category to another, we are able to estimate the influence of background characteristics on the recruitment of councillors within each party. Comparisons of these effects show how far councillor selection differs between parties. Parameters for the effect of background characteristics among Unionists are reported on the second row of Table 10.4 and parameters for non-Unionists on the third row.

A sharp contrast can immediately be seen in the values for Unionists and non-Unionists. Most characteristics distinguished Unionist councillors from Unionist residents much more successfully, and therefore more sharply, than they did non-Unionist councillors from non-Unionist residents. Distinctions between the two latter groups were marginally stronger only on church-attendance and denomination. On other characteristics the effect-parameters for Unionists were double or more the size they assumed for non-Unionists.

The previous comparison of class and religious backgrounds of councillors and residents in the different party groupings (Chapter 8) has already indicated that Unionist councillors were more likely than other groups to originate from a relatively exclusive background. On the basis of the parameters in Table 10.4 we are able to expand and clarify the contrast. Non-Unionist councillors resembled their party following on all characteristics except their non-manual occupations (and, marginally, their sex, more assiduous church-attendance and longer education). The family background of these councillors resembled that of residents, judging by the fact that fathers' occupations were hardly linked to the councillor-resident distinction at all. In contrast, among Unionists, father's occupation was almost as important as present occupational status in distinguishing councillors from electors. The education of Unionist councillors had been much longer than that of Unionist residents, and (not surprisingly in view of this background) councillors were more strongly disposed to think of themselves as middle-class. The Unionist Council group also included a much higher proportion of males than did Unionist residents. We have already noted the greater tendency for women to support the Unionists at popular level (Table 7.7). Curiously Unionist councillors were less likely than Unionist residents to have lived in Belfast all their lives, probably because they were disproportionately drawn from the more mobile professional and managerial groups.

Father's occupation and present occupation, education and sex distinguished councillors from residents within both the Glasgow parties. The highest parameters attained values of only 0·36, however, and so did not distinguish so sharply as among the Belfast Unionists. Interestingly, subjective class was much less potent as a distinguishing feature among the class-based Glasgow parties (highest parameter 0·14 among Progressives) than among the Belfast Unionists at 0·27. Generally, the Glasgow parties showed much less contrast in the characteristics distinguishing councillors from residents than existed between Unionists and the rival parties in Belfast. While Unionist councillors emerged from a relatively exclusive and select background, the non-Unionists were much more men of the people. This sharp difference between the background of councillors may again be linked with the bitterness of Belfast politics. Councillors of different parties obviously had less in common in Belfast than they did in Glasgow. When background differences are considered in conjunction with the contrasts in motivation and socialisation to the Corporation revealed in councillors' recollections (Tables 10.1, 10.2 and 10.3) a considerable potential for cleavage is revealed. Except in the case of present occupation, moreover, the major social differences between councillors and residents as a whole obviously derived from the exclusive background of the Unionists. Thus the fairly high values of the effect parameters in the top row of

Table 10.4 are simply averages of the high values for Unionist distinctions and low values for non-Unionist distinctions, rather than mirroring a situation which applied to all councillors.

In estimating the relative success of background characteristics in distinguishing councillors from residents and extrapolating from this to the comparative weight of these characteristics in processes of political recruitment, we need to extend the analysis of single effects to take account of the association existing between many of the background characteristics themselves. Since, for example, fathers in non-manual occupations are able to afford a longer education for their sons, much of the effect exerted by father's occupation in isolation may be due to the link with education, or vice versa. In order to discover whether the influence exerted by the various characteristics in Table 10.4 is actually their own, we present in Table 10.5 estimates of the independent contribution made by each characteristic in combination with another characteristic towards distinguishing councillors from residents. We do not present all possible paired comparisons of contributions. Instead, to reduce complexity, we simply take those characteristics – own and father's occupation, sex and education – which exerted the greatest single effects in Table 10.4 and compare their independent effects with those of all other characteristics discussed. The values appearing in Table 10.5 are again effect parameters, calculated in the same way as for attitudinal effects in Chapter Nine. Values in the top right-hand corner of each cell in the Table give the independent effect exerted by the characteristic which heads the column in comparison with the row characteristic, the value for which appears in the bottom left.

Actually, the influence exerted under controls by the weightier characteristics (those heading the columns) differs remarkably little from the influence they exerted in isolation in Table 10.4. Present occupation emerged even more clearly as the prime characteristic distinguishing councillors from residents. For it retains its previous effect independently of father's occupation and education, while reducing their effects drastically. In direct comparison, these two characteristics exert independent effects which are almost equal in magnitude. The high proportion of male councillors ensures that this difference

TABLE 10.5

Mutually Independent Effects of Each Background Characteristic on the Distinction between Councillors and Residents

	Own occupation		Father's occupation		Education		Sex	
Father's occupation	0·32	0·08	—	—	—	—	—	—
Sex	0·27	0·25	0·18	0·25	0·26	0·25	—	—
Education	0·31	0·10	0·17	0·16	—	—	—	—
Subjective class	0·33	0·06	0·21	0·07	0·21	0·07	0·22	0·06
Party	0·32	0·09	0·20	0·16	0·21	0·12	0·25	0·14
Church-attendance	0·33	0·07	0·26	0·06	0·24	0·05	0·21	0·10
Association membership	0·36	0·12	0·28	0·13	0·22	0·09	0·27	0·07
Satisfaction with Belfast	0·34	0·09	0·25	0·10	0·21	0·08	0·23	0·09
Spent life in Belfast	0·34	0·03	0·26	0·05	0·22	0·01	0·23	-0·04
Denomination	0·34	0·01	0·21	0·07	0·20	0·05	0·23	0·02

TABLE 10.6
Mutually Independent Effects of Occupational and Other Factors on the Distinction between Councillors and Residents among Unionists and Non-Unionists

	UNIONISTS		NON-UNIONISTS	
		Occupation		Occupation
Father's occupation	0·17	0·36	−0·09	0·26
Sex	0·30	0·32	0·18	0·20
Education	0·15	0·35	0·00	0·26
Subjective class	0·22	0·26	−0·07	0·31
Church-attendance	0·05	0·41	0·13	0·19
Association membership	0·15	0·45	0·14	0·24
Satisfaction with Belfast	0·14	0·40	0·02	0·24
Spent life in Belfast	−0·01	0·44	0·10	0·24
Denomination	0·07	0·38	−0·15	0·23

from residents remains independent of occupation and comparable to its single effect. The values in Table 10.5 are almost identical with those obtained for the same pairings of characteristics in Glasgow.

Given the party contrasts which appeared for single effects of characteristics, it is likely that differences in the results of paired comparisons will also appear when Unionists are compared with non-Unionists. Since present occupation has emerged conclusively as the main influence on councillor-resident distinctions, we confine the analysis of party differences to paired comparisons of occupation with all other background characteristics. Again occupation appears as the major characteristic in regard to which councillors of both parties were differentiated from their supporters. Again characteristics such as father's occupation, education and subjective class distinguished Unionist councillors more sharply from Unionist supporters than they did non-Unionist councillors from non-Unionist supporters. The impression of Unionist councillors as a social élite and of non-Unionist councillors as – comparatively – men of the people, is not an artefact of occupational differences. In their main social characteristics, Unionist councillors were in 1966 a social élite. It remains to be seen whether their a-typical background cut them off from currents of popular opinion to a greater extent than their opponents.

CONCLUSIONS

Both in outlook and in social background the party groups of councillors differed sharply. Perhaps, indeed, the difference in background contributed to the difference in outlook. It would have been natural for the socially underprivileged to be less integrated into Council procedures and to be more concerned with ideological causes. Such symptoms of alienation derived also from Unionist hegemony in the city. They were absent in Glasgow partly because of the vigorous two-party competition existing there, but it is significant that no parallel contrast in social background existed there between councillors of different partisan loyalties. Conditions present in Belfast and absent in Glasgow have a prima facie connection with instability. We shall consequently pay particular attention in the following analysis of representation and communication to the question of whether the exclusive background of Unionist councillors affected their reactions to political opponents, and indeed even to their own supporters, in such a way as to exert any effect over the emergence of a crisis in 1968.

NOTE

1. J. D. Barber, *The Lawmakers* (New Haven, 1964), p. 15; and H. Jacob, 'Initial Recruitment of Elected Officials in the U.S. – a model', in *Journal of Politics* (1962), p. 708.

11 Representation

OUR comparison of councillors and residents in Belfast has revealed as many differences between councillors in the two parties as between councillors and residents *per se*. But this conclusion should not be overstated. While Unionist councillors were obviously drawn from more exclusive groupings than non-Unionist councillors, it remains true that the latter are not a mirror image of residents in terms either of present socio-economic characteristics or of origins. The party contrast resided in the fact that Unionists were sharply contrasted with the population on these factors, while non-Unionists were only mildly contrasted. On present occupation, however, which emerged as the most weighty factor differentiating councillors from residents under all controls, non-Unionists were quite sharply differentiated.

Given these differences between councillors and residents inside both parties and the peculiarly sharp differences between the majority Unionists and their following, the question of how far councillors' views reflected those of the population becomes particularly relevant. For if different social characteristics produce differences in political views, both sets of councillors are likely to diverge from their following, the Unionists more sharply than their opponents.

FORMS OF REPRESENTATION[1]

The notion just introduced – that policy views may be a reflection of social background – does in fact indicate one mode whereby popular views could be reflected at decision-making level. Representatives could be a microcosm of the population in terms of their social background and policy views, accurately reflecting diversity or homogeneity among residents as a whole. The evidence just reviewed makes it more likely, however, that Nationalists and Labour rather than Unionists would reflect opinions and background in that way. The latter, with their élitist background, are more likely to exercise their own judgement on the decisions confronting them, in the way originally recommended by Edmund Burke.

The potentiality for party differences in the style of representation and the pervasiveness of partisan feeling in Belfast call to mind the possibility that party may channel opinion. As in the classic case of British two-party competition, the party representatives may be sufficiently well disciplined to vote as a cohesive block and to carry through the party programme if elected. Under such conditions electors may very well vote for the party label rather than for the individual candidate – in effect seeking representation through the party programmes which best reflect their own views on salient issues.

The idea of representation by party conflicts to some extent with traditional forms of representation through the geographically defined constituency. Belfast is divided into fifteen wards, which form the focus of electoral competition. The views of ward electors presumably carry some weight with councillors, if only prudentially in the light of reprisals at future elections.

One could, of course, argue that communication constraints make it difficult or impossible for representatives to know what constituents are thinking in any case. Thus they are unlikely to make accurate judgements of constituency opinion or to reflect that opinion, however much they may wish to do so. Within the general context of their involuntary lack of response, representatives should, however, be more in touch with ward opinion where more constituents are active.

These five models of representation are not exhaustive of all possible practices, but they do cover the main forms whose presence has been detected in contemporary Western democracies. From our survey we know the preferences of Belfast councillors and residents on five current issues, and perceptions of the preferences held on each side. On the basis of this information we shall be able to discover which models, or combinations of models, best described the actual patterns of interaction between representatives and represented. This description can then form the basis of a comparison with relationships prevailing in other systems.

But just as with recruitment we prefaced our analysis of the characteristics actually differentiating residents and councillors with the latter's own perceptions of the recruitment process, so a highly relevant introduction to the question of representation is provided through perceptions of how councillors should act. The roles attributed to councillors should after all have some effect on their reactions. And since general expectations change less rapidly than preferences on relatively transient issues, they should also give some indication of the context within which issue-relationships evolve.

ROLES OF COUNCILLORS IN BELFAST

The question from which role orientations are inferred did not focus exclusively on modes of representation but inquired more generally what were thought to be the main responsibilities of councillors. As a result many responses stressed the overall running of the city, or specialised functions connected with this task, rather than representation as such. Thus, across all replies, 14 per cent of residents mentioned councillors' work for the city as a whole, as did 27 per cent of councillors themselves. Administrative control was stressed by approximately[2] 33 per cent of councillors, although by only 4 per cent of residents, and financial control by approximately 43 per cent of councillors compared with a mere 7 per cent among residents. On the other hand, only 18 per cent of councillors at most had orientations towards the provision of services, whereas 26 per cent of residents saw the general provision of services as a major responsibility. Over all replies mentioning general and specific services the proportion of residents increased to approximately 56 per cent. Party-related activity was stressed little on either side, nor were discrimination or the individual moral qualities of councillors.

Representative functions did, on the other hand, occur spontaneously to many respondents as an important responsibility of councillors. Such functions divided into two general types: representation of ward constituents and representation of the whole city population. This last function was mentioned by 22 per cent of councillors but by no residents. A greater equivalence existed between councillors and residents mentioning

TABLE 11.1

Responsibilities of Belfast Councillors as Perceived by Residents and Councillors

	First mention		Second mention		Third mention	
	Resd %	Cllrs %	Resd %	Cllrs %	Resd %	Cllrs %
Representation						
Represent his ward	23	29	4	7	1	4
Personal contact with constituents, surgeries	6	2	6	2	1	2
Represent populace	0	13	0	9	0	0
Get jobs for constituents	0	0	1	0	0	0
Get houses for constituents	0	0	1	0	0	0
Provide services						
Services in general	13	2	11	0	2	2
Provide housing	10	2	7	4	3	0
Provide schools	1	0	2	2	1	0
Look after old age pensioners	0	0	2	0	0	0
Help handicapped	1	0	2	2	2	2
Settle disputes	1	0	0	0	0	0
Provide other services	3	0	3	2	2	0
Administration						
Control officials	0	9	0	2	0	4
Contact higher authorities	0	0	2	2	0	0
Work on committees	1	4	0	7	0	4
Finance						
Keep down rents	0	0	0	0	0	0
Keep down rates	3	2	2	0	0	0
Represent ratepayers' interest	0	4	0	13	0	4
Attend to city finances	0	4	0	11	0	4
Govern City						
Keep business in city	2	0	1	0	1	2
Plan and develop city	0	0	0	0	0	0
Work for city as whole	11	18	2	2	1	7
Individual moral qualities						
Sincerity, honesty	0	0	0	2	0	0
Consider others	1	2	0	0	0	0
Be fair, non-discriminatory	0	2	3	2	1	0
Do very well	0	0	0	0	0	0
Party loyalty						
Represent party supporters in ward	3	0	0	2	0	0
Carry out Party policy	0	0	0	2	0	0
Carry out election promises	2	0	0	0	0	0
Be true to political ideology	0	2	0	0	0	0

Notes to Table 11.1. The question on which replies are based was – What would you say should be the main job of a councillor? Coding categories were devised on the basis of clusters in a sample of replies. Percentages in this and subsequent tables may not add exactly to 100 per cent because of rounding.

ward representation: 40 per cent among councillors and 27 per cent among residents.

The equivalence becomes closer – increasing to approximately 47 per cent of councillors and 43 per cent of residents – if ancillary ward functions such as contacting and serving constituents are taken into account. Thus, there is a strong emphasis placed by activists and ordinary residents on representation, particularly as conducted within the framework of the geographical constituency.

Compared with Glasgow, there was less of a tendency among councillors to focus heavily on certain responsibilities. On their initial replies 45 per cent of Glasgow councillors mentioned representation of the ward compared with 29 per cent in Belfast: 26 per cent said they should work for the city as a whole, compared with 18 per cent in Table 11.1. Proportionately more Belfast than Glasgow councillors mentioned the specialised functions of administrative and financial control, although relatively few in either city referred to party, individual qualities or the provision of services.

A real difference existed in the relative emphasis placed by residents on the provision of services. Approximately 27 per cent of Glasgow residents mentioned services at various stages of their reply, compared with 56 per cent in Belfast. The stress laid by Belfast compared with Glasgow residents on ward representation (approximately 43 per cent compared with 41 per cent) was much the same. Residents of both cities, like their activists, laid little stress on individual moral qualities or on the party attachments of councillors, in this no doubt reflecting a view of council membership as a public rather than as a partisan office. Unionist predominance did not affect replies here as it did so pervasively in other areas.

Neither Belfast nor Glasgow residents commented much on the discharge of specialised administrative functions. But 26 per cent from Glasgow mentioned general work for the city compared with only half that proportion in Belfast.

The lighter emphasis placed by Belfast residents on councillors' responsibility for governing the city, and their heavy stress on the provision of services, opened up a wider discrepancy than existed in Glasgow between their definition of councillors' roles and councillors' own definition. As we mentioned, councillors emphasised their governing functions and rather played down the provision of services. Only in the importance attached to ward representation did councillors' views overlap extensively with those of residents. In Glasgow, by contrast, the main clustering of both councillor and resident replies occurred on ward representation and governing the city.

Belfast residents differed little by party over the responsibilities they attributed to councillors. The latter themselves also showed an overall correspondence between party groups: somewhat less than half the Unionists and Nationalists mentioned ward representation at some point and proportions which approached 100 per cent in all parties mentioned functions connected with running the city. However, among such governing functions almost two thirds of Unionists placed financial control, compared with less than a quarter of Nationalists. A fifth of Unionist councillors mentioned the provision of services compared with only a tenth of Nationalists – no doubt because Unionists, as the dominant party, held themselves more responsible for services. Finally, while a third of Nationalists saw councillors as representing the whole population, only half that proportion of Unionists endorsed such a view. It may be that the political weakness of the Nationalists in 1966 forced them to stress the non-partisan or supra-party role of the Council. They certainly inclined to use Council channels to get their way on issues (Table 13.1).

In many ways the main contrast in Table 11.1 emerged between the approximately half of councillors and residents who mentioned councillors' representation of their ward and those councillors and residents who did not mention ward representation. For all other replies listed in the Table can be regarded as implying a city-wide role for councillors. There is an obvious city-wide focus implied in governance of the city, and financial and administrative control; less obviously, however, the provision of services is also a city-wide responsibility and so is representation of the whole population rather than constituents in any one ward. So basically replies can be regarded as ward-oriented or city-oriented. The type of orientation adopted is likely to have effects on each councillor's relationships with constituents on issues. Ward-oriented councillors are

Belfast: Approach to Crisis

likely to inform themselves of their constituents' opinions, and to bring their own views into line with those of constituents. City-oriented councillors would probably be less concerned with reflecting the preferences of constituents than with reaching agreement with council colleagues on the best course of action for the city. Of course, ward and city orientations could be held concurrently with different effects for different issues. Councillors with mixed roles may follow their ward orientation in regard to issues they conceive as particularly affecting the ward, but may not bother unduly about constituents' opinions on other issues seen to affect the whole city.

A first step towards testing these expectations is to take advantage of the natural trichotomy between city-oriented, ward-oriented and mixed replies. The very detailed categories of Table 11.1 can be regrouped broadly into the purely ward-oriented, purely city-oriented and mixed replies shown in Table 11.2.

TABLE 11.2

Perceived Responsibilities of Belfast Councillors as Divided between Ward Roles, City Roles and Two Types of Mixed Role

	Pure Ward Role	Mixed Ward Role	Mixed City Role	Pure City Role
All councillors	4	27	13	54
Unionist councillors	3	30	16	50
N.I. Labour councillors	0	20	0	80
Nat. Labour councillors	11	22	11	44
All non-Unionist councillors	7	21	7	57

Note to Table 11.2. Table 11.2 presents a computer recoding of the responses given in Table 11.1. 'Pure ward role' groups all respondents who at some point answered 'represent ward', 'personal contact with constituents', 'get jobs (houses) for constituents', in Table 11.1 and gave no other reply. All responses other than those termed 'ward responses' above are taken as 'city' responses. Respondents who gave 'city' responses without mentioning 'ward' responses are grouped under 'Pure city role'. Mixed roles (grouping respondents who mentioned both ward *and* city roles as now defined) are distinguished as 'mixed ward role' if the respondent mentioned a ward responsibility before mentioning a city responsibility and as 'mixed city role' if the respondent mentioned a city responsibility (as now defined) before mentioning a ward responsibility.

Actually two types of mixed replies are distinguished, on the assumption that placement of ward responsibilities before city responsibilities indicates that greater salience is being given to ward representation, and vice versa.

The interest in the adoption of ward-oriented as opposed to city-oriented roles naturally related to councillors, since it is their role conceptions which can be expected to shape relations with constituents. The predominance of pure city orientations in their replies is very noteworthy – over half the councillors did not mention ward-orientations at all: two thirds either did not mention ward representation or gave it less salience than city-wide responsibilities. The proportion mentioning the pure city role among Belfast councillors (54 per cent) was substantially higher than the proportion of councillors mentioning it in Glasgow (33 per cent), as was the proportion mentioning pure and mixed city roles in Belfast (67 per cent) compared with Glasgow (54 per cent). Few councillors in either city adopted a pure ward role (4 per cent compared with 8 per cent), but in Belfast only 27 per cent compared with 38 per cent in Glasgow gave greater salience to ward responsibilities in their adoption of a mixed role. Because of the predominance of the pure city role in Belfast replies only 40 per cent of councillors compared with 59 per cent in Glasgow adopted any kind of mixed role.

It might be felt that this emphasis on governing functions reflected the relatively exclusive origins of Unionist councillors, who because of dissimilarities in background would incline less to the desires of constituents. But as the party breakdown in Table 7.2 shows the emphasis on governing is equally prominent among non-unionist councillors. Northern Ireland Labour in fact stressed the pure city role to a much greater extent than Unionists. Councillors' conceptions of their own role were likely to have immediate effects on their desire to reflect constituency preferences. We spell out these effects immediately below.

SPECIFIC MODELS OF REPRESENTATION

Deriving from our introductory discussion and the analysis of roles we have six not wholly exclusive models of representation which could apply in Belfast. These models are briefly summarised below, together with the expectations they generate about the types of issue-relationship which should hold:

1. *The Role Model* of representation assumes that representatives act in accordance with the importance they attach to ward as against city responsibilities. Councillors attaching more importance to the ward would on these assumptions be more accurate in their appraisal of constituency opinion and would display a closer correspondence between such appraisals and their own preferences than councillors oriented more strongly towards governing functions.

2. *The Geographic Model*, in contrast, regards the constituency relationship as sufficiently pervasive to impose constraints on all councillors regardless of their orientation to ward or city. Concern for electoral prospects, if nothing else, would induce councillors to investigate the preferences of their constituents and to bring their own preferences into conformity, certainly on the more important issues.

3. *The Burkean Model* makes a further contrasting assumption that representatives would exercise their own judgement, regardless of ward or popular preferences. Councillors' issue preferences were therefore unlikely to coincide closely with those of the whole population or those of ward residents in 1966.

4. *The Microcosm Model* differs radically from the Burkean in expecting similar social backgrounds to cause councillors' opinions to mirror those of residents, and from the Role and Geographic Models in expecting social similarities to cause all residents' opinions to be reflected by the body of councillors, just as much as constituents' preferences by ward representatives.

5. *The Party Model* anticipates the main linkage of residents' and councillors' preferences to be through party. The correspondence between all residents' preferences and all councillors' preferences will be markedly increased when Unionist councillors are compared with Unionist residents, Nationalist councillors with Nationalist residents, etc.

6. *The Stratification Model* anticipates little correspondence between councillors' and residents' preferences, as a whole or inside each ward, owing to the blocks on communication between people at different levels of activity. The model assumes communication to be easier between persons at the same level of activity, so the convergence of preference among councillors of different parties and among electors of different parties should exceed any convergence between councillors and elec-

tors. Within the general non-convergence of preferences, however, residents and councillors should agree more within those wards where the level of political activity is higher, since there will be greater interaction between them.

To test these models we have reports from councillors and electors on their own preferences on the five issues already encountered. These are: (1) the proposal to open swings in public parks on Sundays, (2) the proposal to name the Lagan Bridge after Lord Carson, a Unionist hero, (3) the proposal to give State aid to the private, Catholic, Mater Hospital, (4) the increase in city rates, (5) the proposal to house Catholics and Protestants on the same estates. For the first four of these current issues we also have judgements of ward residents and councillors on what each others' preferences were.[3] Thus we can assess the accuracy of such judgements and also the correspondence between councillors' appraisals of ward preferences and councillors' own preferences. Since expectations derived from the models relate to these very points, the issue-responses provide an obvious way of determining which model, or which mixture of models, best describe councillor-resident relationships in Belfast in 1966. We adopt two basic ways of looking at the convergence of issue-preferences. First, we compare the preferences of all councillors, and of all councillors within a particular party, with the corresponding residents. Such a comparison tests expectations derived from the Burkean, Microcosm, Party and Stratification Models. Second, we compare the preferences of ward councillors, as a body and differentiated by party and role, with the preferences of their constituents. In connection with these comparisons we also examine councillors' appraisals of constituency opinion. This second group of comparisons tests further predictions of the four models just cited, and also expectations derived from the Role and Geographic Models.

OVERALL CONVERGENCE OF COUNCILLORS' AND
RESIDENTS' PREFERENCES

Table 11.3 presents the proportions of councillors and residents agreeing and disagreeing with the proposals stated above, on

TABLE 11.3

Preferences on Four Current Issues Expressed by Belfast Residents and Councillors

(Percentages of councillors and of residents)

	All	Unionist	N.I. Lab.	Nat. Lab.	All non-Unionist
SWINGS					
Residents					
% Agree	66	50	78	91	81
% Disagree	28	43	17	0	15
Councillors					
% Agree	74	66	80	100	93
% Disagree	24	32	20	0	7
LAGAN BRIDGE					
Residents					
% Agree	23	36	12	18	12
% Disagree	51	41	64	45	62
Councillors					
% Agree	22	32	0	0	0
% Disagree	67	55	80	90	86
MATER HOSPITAL					
Residents					
% Agree	78	69	86	100	87
% Disagree	16	24	9	0	8
Councillors					
% Agree	77	64	100	100	100
% Disagree	20	28	0	0	0
RATES					
Residents					
% Agree	10	9	14	0	11
% Disagree	75	77	72	64	71
Councillors					
% Agree	59	68	60	33	43
% Disagree	40	24	40	67	57
INTEGRATION					
Residents					
% Agree	56	48	65	64	65
% Disagree	36	45	27	27	27
Councillors					
% Agree	71	66	60	100	85
% Disagree	29	31	40	0	14
ALL ISSUES Product-moment correlation of cllrs' and electors' preferences	·61	− ·12	·80	·86	·68
ALL ISSUES BUT RATES Product-moment correlation of cllrs' and electors' preferences	·95	·70	·97	·89	·98

each of the five issues. The product-moment correlations at the foot of the table (already described in Chapter 6) summarise the general tendency for proportions agreeing or disagreeing among councillors to correspond to the proportions agreeing or disagreeing among residents.[4] The closer the correspondence between these proportions the nearer the correlation values approach 1·00. In actual fact, even a simple examination of percentages reveals a fair correspondence between councillor and resident proportions on all issues but rates. Residents were overwhelmingly against an increase which – among most groups – a small majority of councillors supported. Reflecting this dissonance on rates, the correlation between councillor and resident preferences shows a substantial rise when rates are omitted from consideration, among all respondents, Unionists and Labour. The absence of corresponding preferences on rates conforms best to the expectations of the Burkean or Stratification Models of representation. Either councillors did not know that residents opposed an increase or they chose to ignore that fact in formulating their own preference.

Leaving aside rates, the high correlation of 0·95 between the preferences of all councillors and all residents is best fitted by the Microcosm Model described previously. Whether or not councillors consciously took popular preferences into account while formulating their own position on these issues they certainly reflected general preferences. So high is this correlation that it can hardly be increased when purely party preferences are compared. A slight increase in correlations appears among non-Unionists and in particular among the Nationalist-Labour parties. That party does not automatically increase the convergence of preferences is nevertheless shown by the substantial diminution of the Unionist correlations compared with those for all respondents. A correlation of 0·70 for Unionists on all issues but rates is still reasonably high, however – too high to ascribe Burkean attitudes to most Unionist councillors. On most issues perhaps the situation here is best described by a stratification-microcosm model: certain constraints – probably linked to communication difficulties – hindered the tendency to full convergence which obviously existed on non-rates issues. Convergence might also be reduced by Burkean attitudes among a minority of Unionist councillors

In the case of non-Unionists, particularly the Nationalists, party did increase the overall correlations somewhat and hence a party-microcosm model described their relationships best.

The Stratification Model had mixed applicability over the correlations considered up to this point. The Burkean Model seems a rather better description of relationships on the rates issue. On other issues the high correlations between councillors' and residents' preferences go against stratification assumptions. Only in regard to the relative non-correspondence of Unionist councillors and residents' preference does the stratification model seem to have some relevance to the empirical relationships uncovered. We can more directly assess the Stratification Model by comparing correlations of preference between Unionist and non-Unionist councillors and between Unionist and non-Unionist residents, with the correlations between councillors and residents already shown in Table 11.3. For if communication is easier at the same level of activity, cross-party correlations at the same level of activity should be higher than any of the correlations between residents and councillors across their different levels of activity.

The correlation for the preferences of Unionist and non-Unionist councillors over all issues is 0.76 and for Unionist and non-Unionist residents 0.77. The greater magnitude of these cross-party correlations compared with most of the resident-councillor correlations for all issues reported in Table 11.3 lends considerable plausibility to an interpretation of issue-relationships in stratified terms. The exception remains the Nationalist parties, where councillor-resident correlations were higher than the cross-party correlations, and where, therefore, a microcosm model remains the best description.

Compared with a cross-party correlation between Glasgow councillors of 0.12 over all issues, the Belfast correlation of 0.76 is remarkably high. An inspection of percentage agreement and disagreement shows that it is due to the tendency of a majority of Unionist councillors to side with the non-Unionists on every issue-proposal except rates. Thus the internal divisions of Unionist councillors contributed to reasonably high cross-party agreement. In Glasgow councillors agreed highly (a correlation of 0.86) on non-partisan issues but on the two issues which were a focus of party controversy their internal solidarity on contrasting proposals reduced the cross-party correlation to -0.95. A strong contrast thus emerged between the effective parties of Glasgow and Belfast: the party solidarity of Glasgow activists contrasted with party disunity in Belfast. This difference between the cities has already been noted in Chapter 9 and will be discussed further in Chapter 13.

The cross-party correlation of 0.77 for Belfast residents was lower than the 0.88 correlation for Glasgow residents. This probably reflected deeper party divisions at popular level in Belfast compared with Glasgow.

CONSTITUENCY REPRESENTATION BY BELFAST
COUNCILLORS

As mentioned above, the geographical and role models of representation cannot be tested through comparisons of councillors' and residents' overall preferences. To discover how

TABLE 11.4

Correspondence of Councillors' and Ward Residents' Preferences on Five Current Issues

(Percentages of councillors whose preference is the same as or different from the preference held by the majority of residents in their ward on each issue)

	Swings	Bridge	Mater	Rates	Integration
% Same	66	51	64	35	58
% Different	30	33	22	51	38
% Indeterminate	4	16	14	14	4

Notes to Table 11.4. Ward constituent preferences are counted as 'for' or 'against' an issue if the modal opinion is 'for' or 'against' and is more than 10 per cent greater than endorsements of any other choice. Other cases are regarded as neutral. Illustrative examples of this procedure are tabulated below:

For	Against	Neutral	Ward Placement
%	%	%	
55	45	0	for
54	46	0	neutral
40	30	30	for
30	30	40	neutral
30	20	50	neutral
40	20	40	neutral

Councillors' and constituents' preferences are termed the same if the councillors' preference coincides with the decision on ward placement. These rules are followed also for Tables 11.5, 11.12, 11.14.

well they fit the situation we must examine the correspondence between councillors' and residents' preferences inside each ward.

On four out of five issues a majority of councillors shared the preferences of their constituents. The majority was not overwhelming, however. Only on one issue did the proportion endorsing different preferences from those of their constituents fall below 30 per cent. Generally, this pattern reveals a moderate fit with the expectations of the geographic model.

As always the rates question was exceptional. Here only a third of ward councillors agreed with their constituents and half disagreed. A similar but less marked divergence of opinion on rates appeared in Glasgow, where however the average level of councillor-resident agreement was almost the same as in Belfast (55 compared with 54 per cent over five issues).

Within the parties the ward model fits the relationships of non-Unionists more closely than it does the relationships of all councillors and residents. A majority of two thirds or more of the non-Unionist councillors agreed with non-Unionist residents in their wards on four issues and even on rates 14 per cent more councillors agreed with residents than disagreed.

In contrast a ward model can hardly apply to Unionist relationships at all. Only on two issues did a reasonable plurality of councillors agree with Unionists in their ward, but even on swings these were hardly more than half and on the Mater actually less than half. On the Bridge and Rates only a quarter of councillors agreed with ward Unionists. These findings reinforce the impression derived from the overall correlations in Table 11.3 that the Stratification and Burkean models fit the Unionists better than any description which emphasises an interplay between representatives' and constituents' preferences.

A further relevant breakdown of ward correspondences of opinion is by councillors' roles. The analysis of Tables 11.1 and 11.2 demonstrated that such roles polarised round ward representation on the one hand and governing functions on the other. In Table 11.5 Pure Ward Roles – an exclusive focus on ward duties shared by only two councillors – are combined with Mixed Ward Roles, which give priority to ward over city-wide functions. If role conceptions exert any influence those councillors whose focus is primarily on ward duties should

Representation 299

TABLE 11.5

Correspondence of Councillors' and Ward Residents' Preferences on Five Current Issues by Councillor Role

(Percentage of councillors with pure and mixed ward roles, mixed city roles and pure city roles whose preferences are the same as, or different from, the preferences held by the majority of residents in their ward on each issue)

	Swings	Bridge	Mater	Rates	Integration
Pure and mixed ward role					
% Same	64	57	71	21	59
% Different	30	21	14	59	42
% Indeterminate	6	21	14	21	0
Mixed city role					
% Same	50	50	33	33	66
% Different	50	50	33	50	34
% Indeterminate	0	0	33	17	0
Pure city role					
% Same	71	46	66	36	54
% Different	25	37	25	56	37
% Indeterminate	4	17	8	8	8

share preferences with ward residents to a greater extent than councillors putting less emphasis on ward roles (adapting a mixed city-role) or not mentioning ward responsibilities at all (those in a pure city role).

As it turns out, however, the naming of the Lagan Bridge was the sole issue where the correspondence declined steadily in the expected manner from those in ward roles through councillors in mixed city roles to those in a pure city role. On two other issues (swings and rates) the exclusively city-oriented councillors actually shared residents' preferences to a greater extent than those who placed their emphasis on the ward. While on the question of the Mater, Ward Roles did prompt greater correspondence than did city roles, councillors in mixed city roles shared residents' preferences to a noticeably lesser extent than councillors who failed to mention wards at all. Over these comparisons the Role Model cannot be said to fit actual relationships.

The general convergence of ward councillors' and residents' preferences, revealed earlier in Table 11.4, is shown by Table 11.6 to be associated with a convergence of personal preferences, and judgements of constituents' preferences, on the part of a

TABLE 11.6

Correspondence of Councillors' own Preferences and their Appraisals of their Ward Residents' Preferences on Four Current Issues

(Percentages of councillors)

	Own preference same as appraisal	Own preference differs from appraisal	Ward residents divided or have no opinion	DK NA
	All Councillors			
	%	%	%	%
Swings	49	11	31	9
Bridge	35	9	24	31
Mater	44	22	8	26
Rates	26	24	30	20
	Unionist Councillors			
Swings	32	16	39	13
Bridge	19	13	29	39
Mater	29	26	6	39
Rates	16	26	32	26
	Non-Unionist Councillors			
Swings	86	0	14	0
Bridge	71	0	14	14
Mater	78	14	7	0
Rates	50	21	28	0

plurality of councillors over three issues. Where personal preferences were not seen as positively coinciding with ward preferences, the latter appeared so divided or unascertainable as to leave the representative free to act. The correspondence between ward councillors' preferences and judgements of constituency opinion is of a similar magnitude to the correspondence observed in Glasgow. Unionist councillors in keeping with their rather Burkean attitude and exclusive background were less inclined to see a correspondence between their personal preferences and those of residents than non-Unionists.

Councillors as a whole were reasonably accurate in their impressions of ward feeling, as accurate as in Glasgow, where the proportion of correct appraisals averaged 43 per cent to 45 per cent in Belfast. However, inaccurate judgements accounted for half the replies on the Swings issue, for more than half on the Bridge and on the other issues for a third. Again the difficulties of communication revealed by this evidence and

TABLE 11.7

Accuracy of Councillors' Appraisals of Ward Residents'
Preferences on Four Current Issues

(Percentages of all councillors and of councillor in each
party group making accurate and inaccurate appraisals on
each issue)

	All councillors			
	Swings	Bridge	Mater	Rates
	%	%	%	%
Accurate	44	23	49	60
Inaccurate	51	55	33	33
DK, NA	4	20	18	7
	Unionist councillors only			
Accurate	32	13	35	55
Inaccurate	61	58	39	35
DK, NA	64	29	26	10
	Non-unionist councillors only			
Accurate	71	57	78	71
Inaccurate	29	43	21	28
DK, NA	0	0	0	0

An appraisal is considered accurate when it mentions the
category in which the ward has been placed by the procedures described in Notes to Table 11.4. This applies also
to Table 11.13.

theoretically associated with the Stratification Model were felt
more by Unionists than by non-Unionists, who were outstand-
ingly accurate in most of their judgements. The inaccuracy
of Unionist replies stemmed from a consistent tendency of
Unionist councillors to credit constituents with more opposition
to liberal policies on the various issues than actually existed.
This tendency is clearly revealed in Table 11.8.

Since on the Swings, Bridge and Mater issues the new policies were associated with conciliation the result of this misper-
ception was to make councillors supporting conciliation on each
issue much less confident that they enjoyed constituency support
than the diehards. Thus 60 per cent of those opposed to opening
Swings felt constituents also opposed their opening, compared
with the 21 per cent of those who supported opening who felt
that constituents shared their views. The contrast was sharpened
on the emotionally charged question of naming the Bridge:
62 per cent of the diehards felt they had constituency support

TABLE 11.8

Unionist Councillors: Appraisals of Constituents' Preferences over Current Issues, by own Preferences

Councillors think:

	Constituents agree %	Some agree Some disagree %	Constituents disagree %	Constituents preferences uncertain %
Opening Swings in Public Parks on Sundays				
Unionist councillors who agree	21	53	26	0
Unionist councillors who disagree	0	20	60	20
Naming Lagan Bridge after Lord Carson				
Unionist councillors who agree	62	0	0	38
Unionist councillors who disagree	23	46	5	23
Extending State aid to Mater Hospital				
Unionist councillors who agree	6	20	44	30
Unionist councillors who disagree	22	0	66	11
Increasing Rates				
Unionist councillors who agree	6	23	47	23
Unionist councillors who disagree	0	12	62	25

compared with 5 per cent of liberals: on the Mater the proportions were 66 per cent and 6 per cent. Lack of confidence in their grass-roots support no doubt influenced the moderates to press their policies less strongly than they might have done, with results for the development of the later political crisis which we explore at more length below.

Turning again to the performance of the Role Model of general ward relationships, we can discover first whether an emphasis on ward representation fostered greater congruence between councillors' personal preferences and their perceptions of ward preferences. There seems little indication that ward-oriented councillors brought their preferences into line with perceived constituency opinion any more than other groups of councillors. Also, councillors who endorsed pure and mixed ward roles were less accurate in appraisals of constituency opinion over three issues than councillors endorsing a pure city role, and no more accurate than those in a mixed city role. On the evidence reviewed here the Role Model is unable to account for many of the empirical relationships uncovered. Even a limited illusion of agreement with constituents is absent in Belfast although it appeared among ward-oriented councillors in Glasgow.

Over all the ward relationships which have been examined the Geographic Model is upheld by the moderate convergence between representatives' and constituents' preferences (Table 11.4). Communication constraints seem to have produced the inaccurate appraisals found among the strongly stratified Unionists among whom traditional Burkean attitudes may linger. The stronger convergence of preference among non-Unionists may be explained by the many background characteristics shared with residents by councillors, so that a microcosm description is still possible. The greater accuracy of non-Unionist perceptions of ward opinion and the stronger association of such perceptions with their own preferences also makes it likely that non-Unionist councillors experienced less difficulty in communicating with residents within the ward – perhaps again because of background similarities. We explore this point within the context of other evidence in the conclusion to this chapter.

KNOWLEDGE OF BELFAST RESIDENTS ABOUT
COUNCILLORS

So far we have analysed representative practices very much from the viewpoint of councillors, seeking to determine how far their opinions coincided with those of constituents and whether this was due to their conception of their role, their link with their ward, ability to communicate, and so on. Turning the question the other way we can ask what potential residents show for exercising control over councillors – for reviewing their actions and if necessary staging electoral reprisals for acts which violate their own preferences.

It is impossible to make a full investigation of residents' means of control without the use of information which we do not possess – on the interplay of constituency and representative preferences over time, for example, and of electoral reprisals which residents have actually enforced. Nevertheless it is obvious that electoral control requires a minimal amount of information without which it will be ineffective. Constituents could hardly exact reprisals if they did not know their representatives' identity or were ignorant of their position on issues. Knowledge of general party positions was also likely to be helpful in identifying councillors' issue stands. From our survey we can estimate the extent of residents' knowledge on all three points, and are also in a position to check its accuracy.

Only a third of residents could even hazard a guess at their councillors' names. Of these a further 14 per cent were unable to name even one out of their four ward representatives correctly. Thus only 20 per cent of all residents knew who one actual councillor was, a finding which hardly constituted a firm base for political action on their part.[5]

Given this widespread ignorance of councillors' identities the inability of an average 65 per cent of residents to identify ward councillors' issue-preferences is not surprising. Only between 10 and 17 per cent of residents in fact accurately judged their councillors' preferences. More Belfast than Glasgow residents were willing to hazard a guess at their councillors' issue-positions, but only about the same proportions were accurate in their appraisals.

Residents' inability to recall the most basic information about their councillors and their doings reflects on the validity of the ward model of representation discussed previously. If constituents lack the basic requirement for control over their ward representatives in the shape of accurate information it is unlikely that they will be able to take effective action in support of their preferences within the ward. There is, however, another institutional means of control available, through the parties. In describing the party model of representation we noted the possibility that electors might vote for a councillor because he was associated with a party whose overall programme exerted an appeal. In the same way as we have assessed the potentiality for control through the ward residents' possession of the minimal

TABLE 11.9

Belfast Residents' Perceptions of Northern Ireland Labour Party Position on Four Current Issues

(Percentages of all electors and of Unionist and non-Unionist electors)

	Perceived N.I.L.P. Position				
	For	No Position	Split	Against	DK
All Residents	%	%	%	%	%
Swings	55	3	15	5	22
Bridge	9	7	11	39	33
Mater	67	1	7	3	22
Rates	10	3	5	58	25
Unionists only					
Swings	49	4	15	4	29
Bridge	8	8	9	34	40
Mater	59	1	6	5	29
Rates	8	3	5	51	32
Non-Unionists only					
Swings	61	2	16	6	15
Bridge	10	6	13	44	27
Mater	74	1	7	2	15
Rates	12	2	4	63	18

TABLE 11.10

Belfast Residents' Perceptions of the Unionist Position on Four Current Issues

(Percentages of all residents and of Unionist and non-Unionist residents)

	Perceived Unionist position				
	For	No Position	Split	Against	DK
All Residents	%	%	%	%	%
Swings	9	1	24	52	14
Bridge	50	1	23	13	13
Mater	19	1	22	38	21
Rates	39	2	11	22	25
Unionist Residents					
Swings	9	0	29	50	12
Bridge	50	1	22	12	15
Mater	20	1	15	39	25
Rates	33	3	10	24	30
Non-Unionist residents					
Swings	9	1	20	54	15
Bridge	49	1	24	14	11
Mater	17	0	28	37	16
Rates	45	1	12	20	20

TABLE 11.11

Belfast Residents' Perceptions of the Nationalist Position
on Four Current Issues

(Percentages of all residents and of Unionist and non-Unionist residents)

	Perceived Nationalist position				
	For	*No Position*	*Split*	*Against*	*DK*
All Residents	%	%	%	%	%
Swings	67	3	2	3	25
Bridge	4	3	1	68	24
Mater	80	2	1	3	14
Rates	5	9	3	51	33
Unionist Residents					
Swings	64	2	3	6	25
Bridge	5	3	3	59	31
Mater	82	1	1	3	14
Rates	5	7	2	45	40
Non-Unionist Residents					
Swings	69	3	1	1	25
Bridge	4	2	0	75	17
Mater	79	2	1	3	14
Rates	4	10	3	55	26

information required for action, so we can assess the potentiality
for control through the party by analysing residents' knowledge
about party stands on current issues.

An immediately striking point about appraisals of party
stands is the third or less or all residents who expressed ignorance on any issue about Northern Ireland Labour and Nationalist Labour, and the quarter or less about the Unionists, Thus
the proportion claiming knowledge of party issue-stands is
greater than the proportion claiming knowledge of councillors'
names or preferences on issues.

We can measure the accuracy of these party-related appraisals by comparing responses in Tables 11.9, 11.10 and 11.11 with
the expressed preferences on issues of the majority of councillors
in each Party Group (Tables 9.1 and 11.3). On the basis of this
comparison all modal judgements of the Nationalist position
on all four issues, made by all residents and by Unionists and
non-Unionists, were correct. The same was true of all judgements of Northern Ireland Labour except for their position on

rates, where a plurality in all resident groups indicate that the party opposed the increase whereas a majority of their councillors supported it.

In contrast to these relatively accurate perceptions of opposition parties the modal judgement of Unionist position was wrong among all groups of residents for all issues except rates. Inaccuracy perhaps stemmed from the departure of a majority of Unionist councillors from the old rigid positions to an attempted rapproachment with Catholics and Liberals–towards opening swings and supporting the Mater and opposing the perpetuation of old grievances in the name of the bridge. But if accuracy of perception depends on conformity to stereotypes it is not likely to be useful in controlling councillors through their parties in any case. The inaccuracy of these modal appraisals contrasted strongly with Glasgow, where seven out of eight modal appraisals of the parties were accurate, compared with only eight out of twelve in Belfast. The contrast is further strengthened if we consider that only one out of four appraisals of the Belfast governing party were accurate, compared with all four appraisals of the Glasgow governing party.

All in all, party does appear to offer a stronger potential for control in Belfast than the ward. Compared with Glasgow, however, Belfast residents appeared to have a lower potential for control as such.

ALTERNATIVE CHANNELS OF PARTY INFLUENCES:
COMPETITION AND INTERNAL COMMUNICATION

In utilising parties to exercise influence, residents might convey their preferences to councillors in two ways. They might take advantage of situations where party competition was close and where councillors, seeking to buttress their opportunities for re-election might prove exceptionally responsive to constituents' wishes. This indeed is the generally held commonsense view of how influence is exerted through the parties. Alternatively one could argue that where one party enjoyed overwhelming support in the ward, and where therefore the mass of residents shared the same ideological attachments, communication would be facilitated and preferences more easily passed on. Of course, any greater convergence of views between councillors and residents in situations of one-party predominance might result, not from facilitated communication, but from the common ideology. But a broad ideology does not ensure greater agreement on detailed local issues. And communication flows can be examined directly to see if they were in fact greater under one-party predominance or in competitive situations.

Examining the convergence of preferences first it certainly appears to be greater in solidly one-party wards than in wards

TABLE 11.12

Correspondence of Councillors' and Ward Residents' Preferences on Five Current Issues, by Party and Competition within the Ward

(Percentages of councillors returned by solid Unionist wards, competitive Unionist wards, solid non-Unionist wards and competitive non-Unionist wards, whose preferences are the same as, or different from, the preferences held by the majority of residents in their ward on each issue)

Solid Unionist	Swings	Bridge	Mater	Rates	Integration
% Same	71	50	54	25	66
% Different	25	4	29	54	29
% Indeterminate	4	46	16	21	4
Competitive Unionist					
% Same	14	14	28	28	14
% Different	71	28	28	57	43
% Indeterminate	14	57	43	14	43
Solid non-Unionist					
% Same	100	100	100	71	100
% Different	0	0	0	28	0
% Indeterminate	0	0	0	0	0
Competitive non-Unionist					
% Same	86	43	100	43	43
% Different	15	0	0	57	57
% Indeterminate	0	57	0	0	0

which returned councillors of different parties in the three elections up to 1966. There is only one exception over all comparisons of the five issues undertaken for Unionists and non-Unionists: that relates to Unionists on rates and the reversal is by a mere three per cent.

The question now is whether the greater convergence in one-party wards stemmed from shared ideology or from facilitated

TABLE 11.13

Accuracy of Councillors' Appraisals of Ward Residents' Preferences on Four Current Issues, by Party and Competition within the Ward

(Percentage of councillors returned by solid Unionist wards, competitive Unionist wards, solid non-Unionist wards and competitive non-Unionist wards, whose preferences are the same as, or different from, the preferences held by the majority of residents in their ward on each issue)

	Solid Unionists			
	Swings	Bridge	Mater	Rates
	%	%	%	%
Accurate	29	12	30	62
Inaccurate	66	58	37	25
DK, NA	4	29	33	12
	Competitive Unionist			
Accurate	43	0	43	28
Inaccurate	43	72	57	71
DK, NA	14	28	0	0
	Solid non-Unionist			
Accurate	100	100	100	57
Inaccurate	0	0	0	43
DK, NA	0	0	0	0
	Competitive non-Unionist			
Accurate	57	28	57	71
Inaccurate	43	71	43	28
DK, NA	0	0	0	0

communication. Table 11.13 reveals a mixed situation. Among non-Unionists a fair case could be made for facilitated communication, since on three out of four issues councillors in non-competitive wards show a 100 per cent accuracy compared to the very mixed accuracy attained by councillors in competitive wards. The exceptional issue was rates, which is generally visible in any case.

Among Unionists, however, there was no greater accuracy in one set of wards than in the other and so we cannot but conclude that the more extensive sharing of Unionist ideology prompts the greater convergence of views in wards where the party dominates. This contrast between Unionists and non-Unionists is in line with previous conclusions about the blocks on communication between residents and councillors inside the Unionist Party.

THE STRATIFICATION MODEL: DIFFERENCES BETWEEN
HIGH AND LOW TURNOUT WARDS ON PREFERENTIAL
CORRESPONDENCE AND ACCURACY OF COUNCILLORS'
APPRAISALS

The importance of communication constraints inside ward and
party stresses the relevance of the model incorporating such
constraints. But although stratification assumptions anticipate
a block on messages between residents and councillors, they also
point to conditions under which the block can be more easily
circumvented. Where the level of general political activity is
higher there should be greater interaction between residents and
councillors, hence surer knowledge of each other's preferences
and alternatively more convergence of preferences.

The major type of activity on which we can differentiate
wards in order to test these assumptions is turnout at the triennial local elections. The estimation of turnout in Belfast has
considerable complications, however. The first relates to the
question of whether votes should be reckoned as a proportion
of local government electors in each ward, or of all residents.
Fortunately, the fact that local government electors formed a
relatively equal proportion of the population of all wards at the
start of the 1960s meant that the same results would have been
obtained whichever base was used in the calculation.

A further complication arose from the fact that some wards
were regularly contested by the parties, while others were
fought only irregularly. In a sense the absence of strong party
competition in a particular ward did objectively lower the
level of activity – residents did participate less. Equally, however, the lower level of activity hardly resulted from residents'
own volition.

The best way to meet this difficulty is to recognise the
possibility of differences arising both from contrasts in voluntary
levels of participation, and from contrasts in regular competition. Thus Table 11.14 divides wards into four groups:
regularly contested wards with relatively (1) high and (2) low
turnout and irregularly contested wards with (3) high and (4)
low turnout. In actual fact, levels of turnout vary to some
extent with regular competition. Thus wards in Group 2 with
a turnout extending from 41 to 34 per cent overlap with wards

TABLE 11.14

Correspondence of Councillors' and Ward Residents' Preferences on Five Current Issues in High and Low Turnout Wards

(Percentages of all councillors in regularly and irregularly contested high and low turnout wards whose preferences are the same as, or different from, the preferences held by the majority of ward residents)

	Swings	*Bridge*	*Mater*	*Rates*	*Integration*
Regularly contested high turnout					
% Same	50	12	75	37	25
% Different	37	50	0	62	62
% Indeterminate	12	37	25	0	12
Regularly contested low turnout					
% Same	80	80	70	10	70
% Different	20	10	20	70	30
% Indeterminate	0	10	10	20	0
Irregularly contested high turnout					
% Same	80	55	65	45	75
% Different	20	35	20	40	20
% Indeterminate	0	10	15	15	5
Irregularly contested low turnout					
% Same	43	43	57	43	43
% Different	43	43	28	43	57
% Indeterminate	15	15	15	15	0

in Group 3 with a range of 44–37 per cent. But all wards in Group 1 have a turnout higher than any ward in Group 3, and all wards in Group 4 have a lower turnout than any other wards.

When we examine the correspondence of preferences within each of these four groupings (Table 11.14) it appears that lower turnout in regularly contested wards was associated with a greater correspondence on three out of five issues. But the expected relationship emerged in the comparison of irregularly contested wards: higher turnout was associated with greater correspondence. As imposition of a control showed, the overall contrast between the four groups in Table 11.14 was very much affected by party. For example, all but two of the councillors in regularly contested low turnout wards were Unionists, and Unionists represented all wards which had irregular contests and low turnout.

In estimating the effects of differential activity on the

correspondence of preference among non-Unionists we are consequently able to make comparisons only between regularly contested high turnout wards and irregularly contested high turnout wards Although, as we noted above, high turnout in regularly contested wards is actually higher than high turnout for irregularly contested wards, the comparison turns out to be a repeat, in slightly disguised form, of Table 11.12. For regularly contested wards among non-Unionists were in fact those appearing as competitive non-Unionist in Table 11.12, and irregularly contested wards were of course solid non-Unionist wards. As before, we find that dominance by the non-Unionists increased correspondence of preference. Thus increases in activity cannot be said to have a general effect on correspondence, as asserted by the stratification model.

However amongst the Unionists higher turnout was associated with greater preferential correspondence on three out of five issues, among irregularly contested wards. No such relationship appeared for the comparisons (based on very small numbers) which can be made for regularly contested wards. Since the irregularly contested wards were those in which Unionists enjoyed a solid predominance, the trend which appears suggests that stratification assumptions may have a limited applicability to relationships between councillors and Unionist residents in Unionist one-party areas. But if it does apply, councillors' judgements of issue-preferences in these wards should be more accurate than in wards with lower turnout, and it appears that they are not. The absence of any consistent relationship between accuracy and type of ward among Unionist councillors makes it appropriate to apply the party-ideological interpretation already employed with Tables 11.12 and 11.13. That is, to regard the stronger convergence between councillors' and Unionist residents' views in the solidly Unionist, irregularly contested wards with high turnout as promoted by the stronger Unionist identifications of the more active residents, who exist in greater numbers in the strongly Unionist wards with high turnout. Stronger partisan commitments are liable to bring these active residents somewhat closer to councillors in their preferences on issues, thus producing the closer correspondence empirically noted. In none of the other groups of wards were active Unionists likely to have been present in such numbers – in low turnout wards because participation was less and in regularly contested wards because they were less solidly Unionist.

The wards appearing in the comparison of regularly and irregularly contested wards among non-Unionists are almost exactly those appearing as 'solid' and competitive wards in Table 11.13: thus no further comparison is necessary. In so far as non-Unionist councillors in irregularly contested or solid wards made more accurate appraisals than councillors in wards regularly contested, the relationship contravened stratification assumptions. Nor did the judgements of all councillors in wards with greater activity compared to those made in wards with lesser activity show as consistently more accurate. We can conclude only that political activity brings some Unionist councillors and residents closer, but through an enhanced partisan commitment rather than easing of communication constraints.

DIFFERENCES BETWEEN HIGH AND LOW TURNOUT WARDS ON KNOWLEDGE OF PARTY STANDS ON ISSUES

We saw from a previous discussion that Belfast residents had less information than Glasgow residents on the basis of which to control their representatives through parties. However, knowledge of party issue-positions did form the best basis they had for exerting control. Thus it is of some interest to see how far knowledge varied with the general level of ward activity, measured by turnout as in the immediately preceding analysis. Such an analysis also constitutes a test of stratification predictions as they apply directly to electors rather than to councillors. On stratification assumptions increases in activity should increase the proportion of ward residents making accurate appraisals of party issue-stands. As previously we can assess accuracy through the equivalence of a judgement of party position and the position actually taken by a majority of councillors in each party.

The general impression emerging from comparisons made with and without a party control is, however, that ward activity makes no difference to accurate perception. Some association between accuracy and activity does appear for certain subgroups, most notably for appraisals of the Nationalist position in irregularly contested wards. But overall there are more cases where accuracy is negatively rather than positively correlated with ward activity.

CONCLUSIONS

Having reviewed all available data, we can make a final assessment of the fit between theoretical models and actual constituency relationships. In this assessment we can interrelate the partial evaluations made on the basis of various analyses undertaken in this chapter, and also place them in the context of findings from previous chapters.

Discussion can be initially simplified by the role model's failure to meet any of the empirical patterns discerned here. Whatever the effect of role-conceptions in shaping political behaviour over time, in Belfast, they do not usefully describe constituency relationships at our time-point in 1966.

A second simplification is to note the markedly different relationships which prevailed among Unionists on the rates issue, as opposed to other issues. Here the majority of Unionist councillors appeared to be conscious of popular preferences (Table 11.7) yet consciously set against them (Tables 11.3, 11.6 and 11.8). This attitude was distinctly Burkean. Except for the few councillors of the Northern Ireland Labour Party a Burkean description did not apply to non-Unionists on rates nor to relationships on other issues for any party group or for councillors as a whole.

In order to simplify discussion further we next consider the ward model of representation. There is a moderate convergence of preference between ward councillors and residents on all issues but rates (Table 11.4) and a marked convergence between non-Unionist councillors and residents in each ward. More councillors' preferences coincide with their appriasals of ward opinion than flatly contradict their appraisals (Table 11.6) and appraisals were reasonably accurate (Table 11.7). Again these tendencies were more marked among non-Unionists than among Unionists. Thus a ward model does not reflect relationships among Unionists very well even when the rates issue is excluded. Even among non-Unionists, whose preferences corresponded closely to those of their constituents, correspondence with popular opinion appeared without reference to ward (Table 11.3). The general accuracy of non-Unionist councillors' appraisals of constituent opinion (Table 11.7) can also be explained on the assumption that they simply attributed their own issue preferences to residents in a ward where they had a party majority (Table 11.6). Thus the patterns revealed above can be interpreted without reference to ward relationships as we in fact interpret them below. Note, however, that further use of the ward model is inhibited not because it is directly refuted by our findings (for non-Unionists at least) but because (a) our findings are equally congruent with other models and (b) these other models have more generality applying to Unionists and non-Unionists alike, and are thus to be preferred in the interests of economical description.

Economical description is also facilitated by dropping the stratification model from consideration. Certain findings contradicted the stratification model more strongly than any findings contradicted the ward model. No association was discovered between ward activity and closer communication between councillors and residents nor between activity and knowledge of party positions. It is true that constraints on communication did exist. There was considerable ignorance on the part of Unionist councillors when they were asked about ward preferences (Table 11.7). And most residents were uninformed or misinformed about Unionists' issue-positions (Table 11.10). While such constraints existed the evidence already cited shows that they were not lightened by greater activity as the stratification model assumed. They were just as likely to be associated with differences in party or social background. Stratification emphases on communication constraints between councillors and residents, and on relatively easy communication among councillors, certainly receive support from the substantial correlation between preferences of councillors in different parties (Tables 11.3). For this is higher than the correlation between councillor and resident preferences inside the Unionist Party itself, although substantially lower than the comparable correlation for non-Unionists.

On the other hand, this particular finding is also inter-
pretable in terms of microcosm ideas, which have the advantage
of drawing on findings from Chapter 10. The microcosm model
states that representation is secured through a resemblance
between the social characteristics and general attitudes of
councillors and constituents, rather than through direct
communication or by party or ward agencies. In the case of
Belfast we have a group of Unionist councillors who were the
reverse of a microcosm, in that they came from a distinct and
exclusive background, and a group of non-Unionist councillors
who in most essential respects constituted a microcosm of their
constituents.

If preferences are influenced by social background it is logical
that preferences held by Unionist councillors should resemble
those of non-Unionist councillors rather more closely than they
did those of their own followers, since the councillor groups are
somewhat closer to each other in many background characteristics (though not in religious affiliation) than Unionist councillors were to their own followers. Since non-Unionist councillors resembled their own supporters more closely than they
did Unionist councillors it is also natural that the non-Unionist
intra-party correlation should be higher than the inter-party
correlation among councillors ($\cdot$98 compared to $\cdot$76).

The microcosm model thus shows a better fit to the overall
pattern of correlations revealed in Table 11.3 than does the
stratification model. But in itself it is not capable of describing
the total picture. For in spite of enormous disparities of social
background Unionist councillors did reflect the preferences of
Unionist residents on all issues but rates. The reflection is
imperfect but certainly evident and can be explained only in
terms of party ties. On four out of five issues the majority of
Unionist councillors shared the preferences of the majority of
their supporters. The validity of the party model also receives
support from the close convergence between the views of non-
Unionist councillors and residents, whose party ties acted as a
powerful reinforcement to similarities of social background.

The description which best fits Belfast at the time of our study
(leaving aside the rates issue) is therefore a party-microcosm
model of representation. Whereas for non-Unionists both party
and social influences worked together, in the case of Unionists

the strong social differences between councillors and residents limited any convergence of opinion. Earlier in the 1960s when Unionists were resting in the entrenched positions they had held for forty years, the convergence of opinion between councillors and residents was no doubt greater, and both had clear guidelines to the opinions held by the other. In the more fluid situation produced by O'Neill's opening to the Catholics the old positions changed. Communication constraints perhaps associated with differences in activity but more likely with differences in social background prevented a clear picture of the new Unionist policies from reaching the populace (Table 11.10). Doubts as to how far the new policies appealed to their following obscured Unionist councillors' perceptions of constituent feeling. In fact it seems from our evidence that a majority of Unionist followers in Belfast were favourable to a rapprochement, either spontaneously or following O'Neill's earlier lead.

The relatively low levels of intra-party communication and agreement among Unionists meant that the microcosm elements of the mixed party-microcosm model of relationships assumed greater prominence than in Glasgow, where a similar general description applied. There Progressive preferences correlated highly between all strata, as they did for Labour. Social differences between Glasgow councillors were also less marked and divided them almost equally from their following. In Glasgow, moreover, perceptual accuracy and convergence of preferences did vary with political activity, so that the stratification model had a congruence with findings which we have not discovered in Belfast. In both cities, however, role models were inapplicable: ward models fitted to some extent but not very exactly: and a Burkean model exactly fitted the reactions of the governing party on rates.

NOTES

1. The general shape of this analysis, and the specific models of representation employed, were suggested to us by the original work of Michael Margolis on the corresponding Glasgow data, cf. *Political Stratification*, Chapter 3. Professor Margolis' work forms the basis of the comparisons we undertake with Glasgow data in this and the following chapter.
2. Approximately, because there may be double counting involved once

we aggregate detailed replies into a more general category like 'Administration'. For example, someone who mentions 'control officials' in his first response may cite 'work on committees' on his second or third response.

3. We do not have these judgments on the question of housing integration because we had not originally envisaged that it would become an issue during the period of interviewing and hence asked only a question about personal preferences. As it happened the Corporation were actually making moves towards housing integration during interviewing, and so the topic can be regarded as a current issue.

4. We also ascertained the intensity of preferences and this is considered in Chapter 13, below.

5. Ignorance on this point is far from being confined to Belfast. In Glasgow 80 per cent of residents did not know the name of even one councillor.

12 Political Communication

ALTHOUGH they were associated with similarities and dissimilarities of social background rather than with levels of
political activity, information blocks emerged as central to
relationships between councillors, residents and constituents in
Belfast. Their importance stemmed not only from more or less
permanent effects on the practice of representation but also
from their influence on the major political development of the
1960s – the unsuccessful reconciliation of the Catholics attempted
by the O'Neill administration. Evidence reviewed in the
previous chapter revealed the tendency of Unionist councillors
to attribute more intransigent views to their followers than the
latter actually held (Tables 11.3, 11.7 and 11.8). The data
further showed the lack of popular impact made by moderate
Unionist initiatives (Tables 7.2, and 11.10). Moderate Unionists were probably inhibited from pressing their views strongly
against internal conservative opposition as the result of an
erroneous impression that O'Neill's initiative was not widely
supported at grass-roots level, while their failure to act decisively
led to the popular misapprehension that traditional Unionist
positions had not been basically affected. The feeling that no
real change had occurred seems to have led later, in 1968, to
direct Catholic action against what they felt to be an intolerable
Unionist *immobilisme*. Thus mutual misperceptions were integ-
rally linked with the explosive events of recent years. Their
genesis deserves close examination not only because of their
effects on usual politics but also because of their influences on
the development of the contemporary crisis.[1]

GATHERING POLITICAL INFORMATION

Our analysis of information-gathering links directly with the
previous discussion of representation since respondents were
encouraged to talk about activity in this area through questions

TABLE 12.1

How Belfast Residents and Councillors Heard about Four Current Issues

(Percentages of residents and councillors and of party groups)

	Daily papers	Sunday papers	Radio Television	Word of mouth	Pol. party	Ward agencies	Council and Council agencies	Official actions	Own efforts	DK NA
Swings										
All residents	65	1	24	7	1	0	1	0	0	1
Unionists	60	1	28	8	1	0	2	0	0	0
N.I. Lab.	67	0	24	6	0	0	1	0	0	2
All Non-Unionist	69	2	21	6	1	0	1	0	0	2
All councillors	7	2	0	4	9	2	65	0	9	2
Unionist councillors	10	0	0	0	3	3	78	0	3	3
N.I. Lab. councillors	0	0	0	0	40	0	20	0	40	0
Nat.-Lab. councillors	0	11	0	22	11	0	44	0	11	0
All non-Unionist councillors	0	7	0	14	29	0	28	0	21	0
Lagan Bridge										
All residents	63	0	31	4	0	0	1	0	0	0
Unionists	58	0	33	6	1	0	2	0	0	0
N.I. Lab.	69	0	29	1	0	0	0	0	0	1
All non-Unionist	68	0	28	3	0	0	0	0	0	1
All councillors	24	0	0	2	31	5	33	0	2	2
Unionist councillors	13	0	0	3	42	6	36	0	0	2
N.I. Lab. councillors	80	0	0	0	0	0	20	0	0	0
Nat.-Lab. councillors	33	0	0	0	11	0	44	0	0	11
All Non-Unionist councillors	50	0	0	0	17	0	35	0	0	7

TABLE 12.1—*continued*

Mater Hospital

	1	2	3	4	5	6	7	8	9	10
All residents	70	13	0	12	0	0	0	0	0	3
Unionists	68	17	0	14	0	0	0	0	0	1
N.I. Lab.	77	8	0	8	0	1	0	0	0	6
All Non-Unionist	71	9	0	11	1	0	2	2	1	6
All councillors	36	0	0	44	4	0	3	3	7	4
Unionist councillors	45	0	0	33	3	0	0	0	7	7
N.I. Lab. councillors	20	0	0	40	20	0	0	0	20	0
Nat.-Lab. councillors	11	0	0	89	0	0	0	0	0	0
All Non-Unionist councillors	14	0	0	72	7	0	0	0	7	0

Rates

	1	2	3	4	5	6	7	8	9	10
All residents	53	20	0	6	0	0	1	11	0	1
Unionists	49	20	0	8	0	0	3	19	0	1
N.I. Lab.	53	22	0	3	0	0	0	19	0	3
All Non-Unionists	57	19	0	6	2	0	0	16	0	2
All councillors	4	0	0	4	0	0	87	2	0	0
Unionist councillors	0	0	0	7	0	0	93	0	0	0
N.I. Lab. councillors	0	0	0	0	0	0	80	20	0	0
Nat.-Lab. councillors	22	0	0	0	11	0	67	0	0	0
All Non-Unionist councillors	14	0	0	0	7	0	72	7	0	0

on four of the current issues previously examined. These were the proposals to open swings, name the bridge, aid the Mater and increase rates. Examination of concrete information-seeking on live issues serves to check the validity of replies to the general questions on sources of information and media consumption, which we assess later.

(i) *Hearing of Specific Issues*

Table 12.1 reports the channels through which residents and councillors heard of the four issues. Two thirds of residents on all but rates heard from daily newspapers, and on rates more than half heard from dailies. Additionally a quarter to a third of all residents – on all issues but the Mater – heard from radio or television. Thus on all issues, over three quarters of residents were informed by the media in one form or another, and this applied overall and within each party group. Word of mouth played a noticeable part only on the Mater. Political agencies did little to inform residents, except through official action on the rates. This, however, was purely incidental – the despatch of notices of assessment.

Dependence on the media for knowledge about current issues was only slightly less marked among Glasgow compared to Belfast residents. A fifth to a tenth of the Glasgow sample had however heard by word of mouth. It is hardly surprising that councillors who in a sense were making local news should generally glean information from the media. A partial exception existed in regard to the Mater Hospital, where the Stormont Government was an important participant. Even on the Mater almost half the councillors got information directly by word of mouth, largely from associates. On Swings and Rates, institutional channels – the council and its agencies – were mentioned by overwhelming majorities of councillors. It is of interest that reliance on official channels varied strongly between party groupings of councillors. Unionist councillors relied on them most and councillors of the Opposition parties much less. Nationalist-Labour councillors in particular relied on a varied set of sources over the four issues – the parties, word of mouth and even – in regard to rates – the press.

The Bridge issue stands out as displaying less of a focus on one means of gaining information and also as the one case in which many Unionists relied on party sources. The explanation for both features lay in the sudden eruption of the issue on the political scene and the internal Unionist negotiations which preceded its settlement. Since the issue was raised and settled as an internal Unionist question, party sources assumed more prominence. Since it was not raised through regular channels, any source of information to hand was utilised.

Belfast councillors learned more through the Council and Council agencies compared to Glasgow councillors, for whom word of mouth and political parties were more consistently important. As in Belfast few Glasgow councillors heard of most issues through the media. Party differences in modes of information-gathering also occurred in Glasgow, where the governing Labour councillors relied heavily on their tightly organised party caucus, and the opposition Progressives on the Council and Council agencies. This pattern reversed the finding made in Belfast. Perhaps the Unionists, less organised and more faction-ridden than Glasgow Labour, were forced to rely more heavily on official Council machinery. For Unionists the Council may at any rate have appeared as an extension of the City Hall party, to which they naturally turned for the kind of information disseminated through the governing party in Glasgow. If correct this interpretation again, as in Chapter 10, stresses the extent to which opposition parties were forced outside the system in Belfast, unable to rely on the Council in the way Progressives could in Glasgow.

(ii) *Learning More about Specific Issues*

Awareness that a particular issue is being raised constitutes a useful but limited piece of information. For relevant action to be taken more knowledge is required. For this reason we were interested in asking how residents would set about getting more information on three of the current issues under review. Whereas the previous question on hearing about issues elicited reports of past behaviour, the question about getting more information is hypothetical. Lacking the anchorage of actual experience some of the methods suggested are unlikely to be ones which respondents had actually employed.

That this was indeed the case appears from the heavy concentration of replies for all issues on approaches to councillors

TABLE 12.2

How Belfast Residents Would Find Our More about Issues, as a Whole and by Party Groups

(Percentage of residents and party groups)

	Approach councillors	Corp. depts	Stormont Central Govt	Party assoc.	Other assoc.	Public meetings	Indiv. research	Personal contact	Do nothing	DK NA
Savings										
All residents	27	8	25	4	4	3	12	3	7	6
Unionists	24	10	24	5	6	3	10	4	7	7
N.I. Labour	29	3	28	4	4	3	12	1	9	6
All non-Unionists	30	7	25	3	3	4	14	1	8	6
Lagan Bridge										
All residents	20	7	32	4	0	3	12	3	13	5
Unionists	23	10	33	6	0	2	7	5	9	6
N.I. Labour	15	4	34	3	1	4	16	1	14	6
Non-Unionists	18	4	31	2	1	3	17	2	16	5
Rates										
All residents	26	24	20	2	3	3	7	4	5	5
Unionists	24	29	16	3	4	3	4	6	3	8
N.I. Labour	27	21	28	1	2	4	8	1	4	2
Non-Unionists	27	20	23	1	3	4	11	2	7	2

and the Corporation, and to the Provincial authorities at Stormont. The widespread ignorance of 80 per cent of residents about councillors' names revealed little actual contact. The fact that only a tenth of residents on average would have done individual research through the media from which half to three quarters in fact heard of issues also points to a lack of realism in replies. Nevertheless, these did reveal an awareness that representatives and officials could be contacted and used, and non-Unionists and Unionists would use them equally. Only a minority of residents – at maximum a fifth on the Bridge issue – had no idea what to do or would do nothing. And again there was no consistent tendency for non-Unionists to be more apathetic than Unionists.

Glasgow residents, in response to a similar hypothetical question about getting further information, showed an equal level of apathy, and a somewhat greater inclination than residents in Belfast to use public meetings and mass media. There being no devolutionary Parliament on their doorstep more said they would go to local councillors (an average of 37 per cent over three issues). Since Glasgow residents were just as ignorant of their councillors' names an even greater hiatus opened between their actual habits and professed modes of acquiring information. This can be interpreted in the same terms applied to Belfast: residents showed a potential for greater contact with councillors when they felt the need. But in neither Glasgow nor Belfast did that need appear to be felt in 1966.

Looking at the matter from another point of view, we can ask how councillors would have discovered more about their constituents' opinions. Although the question appears equally hypothetical we expect a greater correspondence in councillors' replies to actual modes of information-gathering, since most would have been confronted at some time with the problem of ascertaining constituency feeling.

A fair number of councillors, ranging from a tenth to a quarter on different issues, would have done nothing because they felt they knew their constituents' feelings in any case. This feeling was most widespread among Northern Ireland Labour, but was also general among Nationalist Labour except on the Bridge – with a fair degree of justification, in view of the accuracy of non-Unionist appraisals in this area (Table 11.7).

TABLE 12.3

How Belfast Councillors Would Find Out about Constituents' Opinions

(Percentage of all responses given by councillors and party groups)

	Through being pol. rep.	Party agency	Local leaders, people directly affected	Local organisations	See indivs directly	Mass media	Other personal contacts	Do nothing	Public meets
Swings									
All councillors	0	42	2	8	20	0	3	18	8
Unionist councillors	0	57	0	10	14	0	2	10	7
N.I. Lab. councillors	0	17	0	0	17	0	0	67	0
Nat.-Lab. councillors	0	7	7	7	35	0	7	7	14
All Non-Unionist councillors	0	10	5	5	30	0	5	25	10
Bridge									
All councillors	4	30	0	5	19	0	2	26	16
Unionist councillors	6	36	0	3	14	0	3	19	19
N.I. Lab. councillors	0	33	0	0	17	0	0	50	0
Nat.-Lab. councillors	8	15	0	15	39	0	0	23	0
All Non-Unionist councillors	5	29	0	11	32	0	0	32	0
Mater Hospital									
All councillors	2	39	2	2	20	2	2	17	25
Unionist councillors	2	51	0	2	15	2	0	13	15
N.I. Lab. councillors	0	29	0	0	29	0	0	43	0
Nat.-Lab. councillors	0	0	9	0	36	0	9	18	27
All Non-Unionist councillors	0	11	6	0	33	0	6	28	17
Rates									
All councillors	3	38	0	0	15	0	4	23	19
Unionist councillors	3	53	0	0	6	0	3	19	16
N.I. Lab. councillors	0	0	0	0	20	0	0	80	0
Nat.-Lab. councillors	0	9	0	0	36	0	9	18	27
All Non-Unionist councillors	0	6	0	0	31	0	6	38	19

Among councillors who would seek out constituency opinion, the modal strategy was to employ party agencies – talking to party workers, attending local committee meetings and so on. This course of action was endorsed by over half of all Unionist councillors on all issues except the Bridge. One of the attractions of this course for Unionist councillors no doubt lay in their more efficient party organisation. Regularised local committees and meetings meant that grass-roots opinion in the party could be relatively easily consulted. The disadvantage lay in the fact that party opinion by no means always coincided with popular feeling – a possibility strikingly supported by the inaccuracy of Unionists in regard to popular opinion (Tables 11.7 and 11.8). Here we may have an explanation for the ignorance of Unionist councillors about the extent of support for conciliatory policies. Unionist activists would naturally have been more diehard in their attitudes than the general population or even than Unionist identifiers in the population. Their own attitudes would naturally have affected these activists' own estimates of constituency opinion, and when passed on to councillors or M.P.s would have grossly inflated the extent of popular opposition.

Among non-Unionist councillors who would seek out opinion, a majority on all issues would see individuals directly or through public meetings. Again this probably reflected a mode of party organisation. Opposition parties were more personalised than the Unionists – Nationalist parties being often nothing more than personal machines. Since the running of these machines depended on a councillor's dispersed contacts it was natural for him to garner information on preferences at the same time as he disposed of other business.

Glasgow councillors were somewhat less inclined to do nothing than those in Belfast: on the other hand, about a quarter to a third, depending on the issue, would simply have relied on constituents coming to see them in the normal course of their functions as a political representative. This tendency was more marked among Glasgow Progressive councillors than among Glasgow Labour. Overall, therefore, Belfast councillors adopted somewhat more of an activist orientation in the search for constituents' opinions. The leading methods of active investigation among Glasgow councillors were through public meetings, seeing individuals directly and inquiring indirectly through local non-political organisations (each mentioned by a sixth to a fifth, depending on the issue). Party agencies were mentioned by about a tenth of Glasgow councillors on all issues – increasing to a sixth of the (better organised) Labour councillors. Even so, this proportion was far short of the half of Unionist councillors who would have worked through the party organisation. Labour councillors in Glasgow were, moreover, disproportionately inclined to see individuals directly or through public meetings, like the opposition parties in Belfast.

The major contrast between popular and élite modes of information-gathering which emerges from this review is the heavy reliance of residents on the media and of councillors on their personal contacts. Subsequent discussion bifurcates accordingly. First we consider communication between councillors, and then examine the type and quantity of the information that residents acquired from the media. These threads of discussion join when we finally consider how news got into the media in the first place, for reporters' prime contacts are, of course, local councillors.

COMMUNICATION WITHIN THE COUNCIL

We have seen that many if not most councillors heard about issues in the council (Table 12.1). Thus it appears that a great deal of communication went on between councillors. The question is, did all councillors communicate with each other, or did councillors communicate only inside their narrow party groups? If communication were widespread and untrammelled, we could assume that a certain amount of integration existed among councillors: to some extent, by virtue of being on the council, they were exposed to the same items of information and interpretations of events, however differently they then reacted. But if communication was partial and discrete, other differences between councillors were likely to be reinforced by divergent perceptions of political reality.

Too sharp a contrast between these situations should not be drawn. For Glasgow councillors, when asked whom they would go to see in policy areas related to current issues, showed considerable reluctance to cross party lines. The opposition

Progressives were forced to seek out the (exclusively Labour) convenors of committees, since they required specialised information which only convenors could give. But only one Labour councillor sought out a Progressive. Eighteen per cent of all designations named officials who, being in touch with both sides, perhaps helped to facilitate communication.

The fact that this inter-party hiatus was discovered among councillors prone to conciliation and compromise in their political dealings, must render interpretation of any similar hiatus in Belfast rather circumspect. However, the very size of the Glasgow Council may have helped to confine informal communication networks to the parties – each of which was about as large as Belfast Council itself.

A further note of caution relating to the interpretation of communication data follows from the somewhat different wording of the questions put to councillors in the two cities. In Glasgow they were asked: What other members of the council do you normally go to when you want to discuss something concerning (housing estates, Corporation schools, traffic problems, city rates)? In Belfast, for reasons connected with a possible extension of the survey in the event of not interviewing enough councillors the question ran: What other persons do you normally go to when you want to discuss something concerning (public parks, public works, health matters, city rates)? This wording was expected to elicit a wider range of designations than appeared in Glasgow. On the other hand, since we did not prejudge whether consultation occurred on or off the Council, we are still able to see how far the common institutional link actually shaped councillors' communications behaviour.

In actual fact, the contrasts with Glasgow were so striking that it is doubtful if they were affected by differences in question-wording. Council communication in Belfast focussed almost completely on the permanent officials. Councillors did not report asking questions of each other – even of the committee chairmen – they simply went straight to the relevant official. Thus on public parks 21 out of 32 designations named the Parks Director and three others named associated officials: on public works 58 out of 59 mentioned the City Surveyor, the City Architect, Town Clerk or other officials: on public health

40 out of 50 focussed on the Medical Officer of Health and a further eight on his subordinates: on rates 25 named the City Treasurer and 12 the Rates Superintendent, out of a total of 44.

These results point to such an atypical situation that it might well be asked whether Belfast councillors had properly understood the question – whether they misunderstood the reference as being to a strictly technical consultation. All one can say is that the very similar question asked in Glasgow was understood as referring predominantly to discussion with the political and partisan convenors of the important committees. In view of this, the difference between Glasgow and Belfast replies does seem genuine and unprompted by the question asked. It remains to interpret its significance.

For Unionist councillors, as we have already pointed out, the perpetual hegemony of their party on the Corporation probably induced a tendency to treat the Corporation as an extension of their party machine, and to consult with its officials as if they were party colleagues; they were after all selected by the City Hall party and had to be congenial to it. However, there was an important difference between Unionist councillors and Unionist-appointed officials. As we have seen, the Unionist party was divided by internal disagreements in the mid-1960s (Tables 9.1 and 11.3). As the major party in a one-party dominant system, factional clashes had been frequent in the past (Chapter 5) and in a sense constituted the normal process of decision-making (Chapter 13). Corporation officials could not afford to be too closely identified with any one Unionist faction, however much they were identified with Unionists as a whole. Thus the faction-ridden councillors could turn to the officials for the relatively unbiased information which they could not get from party colleagues.

Non-Unionists as well as Unionists consulted officials. On this interpretation they were simply making the best of a bad job. They needed information. They could not get it from their party colleagues who were in the same position as themselves. They had to seek it therefore from the officials who – though Unionist – were less objectionable than their flag-waving opponents on the Council.

The complete inability of the Belfast parties to communicate and their utter reliance on officials, obviously placed the latter in the key decision-making position which in Glasgow belonged to convenors of the ruling party. However well meaning the officials, this implied an exercise of power without electoral responsibility. Of themselves the officials could not push innovations, which would have meant allying themselves with one of the Unionist factions. None of these factions felt strong enough to take over the direction of policy. The opposition parties, far from attempting to negotiate with the Unionists, did not even speak to them. In the absence of free or general communication on the Council, we have another cause of the *immobilisme* which aroused Catholic discontent and which ruled out a flexible response to the initial symptoms of crisis.

BEST SOURCES OF POLITICAL INFORMATION
FOR RESIDENTS

From the information-gathering in which residents had actually engaged we inferred that their prime source of information was actually the media, rather than face-to-face contacts (Table 12.1). We can check this inference through residents' own reports about their best sources, as a preliminary to the analysis of popular reading, viewing and listening habits undertaken below.

TABLE 12.4

Belfast Residents: Best Sources of Political Information

(Percentage of all residents)

Sources	Politics in general	Local politics
Personal, non-media sources	*	6
Daily newspaper	41	61
Sunday newspaper	12	1
Newspaper (unspecified)	2	1
Television	30	20
Radio	9	5
Magazines	1	1
Other	1	0
Not interested, no best sources	2	1
Don't know, not ascertained	3	3

* On local politics a filter question was included, which asked the respondent if he used the media as his best source. No such filter was included for politics in general.

Table 12.4 confirms the heavy dependence of the population on the mass media, a dependence which was almost as marked in the case of local politics as for politics in general. Approximately 93 per cent of the population ranked the media as their primary source of information about general politics and approximately ninety per cent shared this dependence in regard to local politics. Respondents were explicitly allowed to name non-media sources of information for local politics, but only six and a half per cent took the opportunity to do so. Four fifths of these residents specified friends as their best source and the remainder mentioned workmates. These proportions hardly varied across party or educational lines.

Substantially more Glasgow residents (16 per cent) mentioned non-media sources in reply to a similar question. These sources were more various than in Belfast – party and government sources being mentioned by almost as many as cited workmates or friends.

In Belfast the two major purveyors of local political information emerged as daily newspapers and television, with five per cent of residents mentioning radio. Other media were named by negligible proportions. The media thus had the same relative importance for local politics as in Glasgow. In both cities daily newspapers assumed greater prominence compared to Sundays and to television and radio, as the focus passed from general to local politics.

The different party groups ranked media and non-media sources of information, and the various media themselves, in much the same order of importance. Non-Unionists turned to daily papers less for general political news, perhaps because the main Belfast paper (the *Belfast Telegraph*) was moderately Unionist. But for local political news they turned to dailies in the same proportions as Unionists.

Education as well as party loyalty may have affected information-seeking behaviour. But in fact little difference appeared between the groups with least schooling (who terminated education at less than fifteen) and those with medium schooling (who left school at fifteen). Those with most schooling were somewhat idiosyncratic in their habits as regards politics in general, but showed the same dependence as the others on daily newspapers in regard to local news. They were, however, less inclined to use non-media sources or television, and made heavier use of radio.

But overall, group variations were minimal. The population was uniformly dependent on the media for its local political information and particularly dependent on daily newspapers and television. Belfast residents in fact depended more heavily on these media than Glasgow residents, which renders the political role of mass communications even more crucial.

QUANTITY OF POLITICAL INFORMATION AVAILABLE FROM THE MEDIA

Indicators of the use made by residents of the media are therefore of high importance because they provide the best estimate of how much and what kind of general political information reached ninety per cent of the population. As Table 12.5 shows the number of daily newspapers read by the average person in Belfast in 1966 approached two, and of Sundays one and a half. Many residents did not read magazines and those who did stuck mainly to one type. On average two television news programmes were watched. Radio news attracted only a quarter of this attention. Unionists read less papers, particularly Sundays, than non-Unionists, and heard more radio news: otherwise the media consumption of the two groups hardly differed. The amount absorbed increased generally from the lower to the higher educational levels, as one would expect.

Glasgow residents' readership of dailies at an average of 2·20 compared closely with that of Belfast residents: the former, however, read more Sundays (2·20 compared with 1·63). Slightly more magazines were read in Belfast, and more news programmes were received on both television and radio. Contrasts between parties were equally limited in Glasgow: the spread in consumption between educational levels was, however, greater in Belfast.

The figures just reviewed give gross estimates of the total amount of material reaching residents. They do not reveal whether that material is political in nature or related to totally different areas of life. Reports made by residents on the part of the paper read first indicate whether the opportunity to read political news was taken or neglected (Table 12.6).

TABLE 12.5

Belfast Residents: *Quantity of Political Information Available from the Mass Media*

(Average numbers of newspapers and magazine types read and programmes heard or watched)

	All Residents	Unionists	N.I. Lab.	All Non-Unionists	Left School 15–	Left School 15	Left School 15+
Average no. daily newspapers read	1·94	1·85	2·00	2·07	1·84	1·90	2·03
Average no. Sunday newspapers read	1·63	1·32	1·80	2·00	1·53	1·62	1·73
Average no. of magazine types read	0·73	0·77	0·69	0·71	0·61	0·64	1·11
Average no. of television news programmes watched	1·97	1·94	2·04	2·06	1·53	1·81	2·20
Average no. radio news programmes heard	0·66	0·91	0·55	0·61	0·70	0·50	1·08

Types of magazines are: news or news analysis (including The *Economist*, *Statist*, *Time*, *Newsweek*, *New Statesman*, *New Society*, *Spectator*, *Tribune*, *Time & Tide*), union or party, Northern Irish or Irish, religious, general information (including *Punch*, *Life*, *Reader's Digest*, *Paris-Match*, *Time*) trade or professional, women's.

TABLE 12.6

Parts of Newspapers Read First by Belfast Residents

(Percentages of all residents and of party and educational groupings reading parts first)

	All Residents	Unionists	N.I. Lab.	Non-Unionists	Left School 15–	15	15+
No. of papers read	3	4	4	2	3	4	2
Local news	2	3	1	1	2	4	0
National news, Law reports	8	8	7	8	8	4	13
Editorials and letters	4	2	6	7	4	7	4
Religious, church news	1	1	0	0	1	0	0
Finance and industry, agriculture, fishing	1	1	0	0	1	0	0
Television, radio, books, theatre, arts	3	3	2	2	2	4	4
Accidents and crimes	7	9	4	5	8	7	4
Women's news, marriages, births	26	29	25	23	29	32	13
Sports, features, contests	20	14	27	26	22	11	20
Headlines, advertisements, other	19	19	16	18	14	18	32
Don't know, not ascertained	5	4	5	6	5	7	2
Read everything	2	4	2	1	2	3	5

It is obvious that news related to the politics of the locality assumed little prominence for residents, less even than national news. Perfunctory notice of local political events might have been taken by those residents who read everything, or by the twenty per cent who sought out headlines, advertisements and other prominent items. But for more than half the sample the areas of greatest salience – sports, births, marriages, accidents – were about as far removed from politics as they could be. Unionists were somewhat less disposed overall than non-Unionists to read about politics, although they focussed more directly on local news. Those with most education also read somewhat more about politics first, especially if the proportions reading headlines and advertisements are taken into consideration. Generally few large or interesting differences appear between subgroups. For all of them – and thus for residents as a whole – the extent to which political information was sought appeared to be severely limited. This situation is no different from that which appeared in Glasgow and is indeed what one would expect from general findings on the apathy and absence of political interest evident among the population of large cities.

QUALITY OF POLITICAL INFORMATION AVAILABLE FROM THE MEDIA

The amount of strictly political information taken by respondents from the media, as well as its quality, is also indicated by the type of newspaper read or programme received. Quality as opposed to popular newspapers, B.B.C. programmes as opposed to Independent Television, Home Service news bulletins as opposed to those on the Light (taking services as they existed in 1966), should all give more intensive and extensive coverage to political events. Other things being equal, a resident exposed to these types of media coverage should absorb more and better information than his fellows. Table 12.7 confirms previous impressions in demonstrating that, on the whole, the more informative media were patronised by a minority of residents. Newspapers are potentially the best qualified of all media to give continuous political coverage in depth, but those newspapers which do this – the 'quality' newspapers – were patronised by only three per cent of residents in the case of dailies and

TABLE 12.7

Belfast Residents: Quality of Political Information Available from the Mass Media

(Percentage of residents and of party and educational groupings)

	All Residents	Unionists	N.I. Lab.	Non-Unionists	Left School		
					15–	15	15+
Per cent quality out of all daily newspapers read	3	3	2	2	1	3	3
Per cent quality out of all Sunday newspapers read	7	6	5	8	3	4	2
Per cent News/Information out of all types magazines read	17	17	15	17	14	12	25
Per cent Union/Party out of all types magazines read	1	0	2	1	0	0	2
Per cent B.B.C. out of all television news/features programmes watched	64	65	62	64	61	65	74
Per cent Home Service/Third Programme out of all radio news/features programmes heard	79	82	75	76	74	68	95

Quality daily newspapers are the (Dublin) *Irish Times*, (Scottish) *Glasgow Herald*, *The Scotsman* and (London) *Daily Telegraph*, *The Times*, *Guardian*, *Financial Times*; Quality Sundays are the *Sunday Telegraph*, *Sunday Times*, *Observer*. In comparison with the popular press quality newspapers make a sharper separation between news reports and comments and give more detailed and extensive background coverage of events. The same can be said of B.B.C. Television in comparison with Ulster (Independent) Television programmes and the B.B.C. Home Service and Third Programme compared with the Light Programme.

by only seven per cent in the case of Sundays. Substantially more respondents, certainly, took informative magazines – but still less than a fifth of the total. These proportions correspond to those discovered in Glasgow, except that readership of quality dailies doubled there.

In terms of radio and television, the proportions displaying a preference for more informative channels increased markedly to two thirds and four fifths of all consumers. Preference for B.B.C. television was substantially higher in Belfast compared to Glasgow (64 per cent compared to 47 per cent), and preference for Home and Third programme news about the same. However, as indicators of exposure to political information these preferences are less revealing than preferences linked to newspapers and magazines. They show that the majority of the population are exposed to some serious news and comment, but associated reading habits do not provide an informational context within which disparate items of news can be retained and evaluated. Of course, Belfast is hardly atypical in this: certainly general patterns of media consumption are similar to those in Glasgow.

Unionists and non-Unionists in Belfast had similar viewing and listening habits. This contrasts to some extent with Glasgow, where more Progressives than Labour inclined to the better quality media. In part this can be seen as a reflection of educational differences in Glasgow, where the better educated strata inclined fairly consistently to more informative coverage. The same difference between educational groupings appeared in Belfast, but less markedly.

Two general findings emerge from this analysis of media usage. Political events percolate through newspapers, giving residents some inkling of local issues (Table 12.1). But purposive information-seeking through the media was limited, particularly in regard to local politics. Yet limited as such information-seeking appears, it was for over ninety per cent of residents the prime source of their knowledge about local affairs. Little wonder then that most were unable to specify either their councillors' names or their councillors' issue stands: or that the accuracy of residents' views about the parties depended more on traditional stereotypes than on their contemporary positions. Under such circumstances the Unionist moderates required to work very hard to get through to the masses. The evidence shows that their efforts were not sufficient.

MUNICIPAL CORRESPONDENTS: CHARACTERISTICS, OUTLOOK AND INFORMATION-SEEKING ACTIVITY

Our discussion has revealed the peculiarly marked dependence of Belfast residents on political information relayed through the mass media. The particular source of information varied to some extent with party and education but dependence on some media was always present and was as noticeable for local politics as for politics in general.

But if the media informed the population, who informed the media? In the sphere of local politics we can focus attention upon six men, the municipal correspondents of local newspapers, television and radio. It is from their reports that residents acquired what local information they got, and media controllers themselves obtained cues for their editorial stand. Obviously municipal correspondents cannot report all the news they hear: they must apply certain criteria of relevance and these criteria may be systematically related to their social and political characteristics. Obviously, also correspondents as much as other people experience constraints on their news-gathering activities. Because of the general dependence on the media such constraints are of central importance to the whole process of information-dissemination in Belfast.

As always in this investigation we are looking for factors peculiar to Belfast which may account for the unique politics of the city. In asking whether media reportage contributes to local tension we compare Belfast correspondents with Glasgow correspondents about whom we have similar information, on the assumption that Glasgow correspondents are more typical of reporters in British cities. The other groups with whom we shall be explicitly comparing correspondents are, of course, residents and councillors in Belfast itself. It is of interest to see which group correspondents resembled most closely, for political and social similarities – along with reported contacts between correspondents and councillors – may have affected the ability of councillors to emphasise some issues at the expense of others. Control or lack of control over publicity may have had profound consequences for the political stability of Belfast, which we detail below. Meanwhile we start by investigating the sociopolitical background of Belfast correspondents.

(i) *Social and Political Characteristics*

Four out of six Belfast correspondents had reported municipal affairs for less than four years (three for two or less). Another had reported for 10, another for 30 years. None of the Glasgow correspondents had worked less than five or more than fifteen years, with a fair spread between these extremes. Only one of the Belfast group and none of the Glaswegians had experienced an interruption in his municipal reporting. Three out of six correspondents in both Belfast and Glasgow had been political reporters before specialising in municipal affairs.

Classwise, all reporters occupied the same occupational status and possessed requisite educational qualifications. The massing of reporters in occupational class II, with other semi-professional groups, points to a close similarity in class terms with Belfast councillors. In terms of religion one Belfast correspondent regarded himself as a non-believer, two were Catholic, two Presbyterian and one Church of Ireland. All except the non-believer had attended church in the last month. The religious composition of Belfast Council as a whole showed a slight over-representation of members of the Church of Ireland, at the expense of Presbyterians and Catholics. The presence of two Catholics, two Presbyterians, and one non-believer, compared with only one adherent of the Church of Ireland among correspondents, thus distinguished them from councillors and almost as much from residents. In their assiduous church attendance correspondents resembled councillors.

In spite of diverse religious affiliations correspondents agreed strongly on the integration of Catholic and Protestant housing, which we used previously as an indicator of inter-denominational sympathy (Table 9.1). Glasgow correspondents agreed some-what less unanimously (four to one) on the comparable question of school integration. Belfast correspondents were definitely more in agreement with councillors than with residents on this point.

Among the correspondents all three Protestants were Unionists, the non-believer Northern Ireland Labour, and the

TABLE 12.8

Preferences of Belfast Municipal Correspondents over Five Current Issues

(Numbers of correspondents)

	AGREE			DK	DISAGREE		
	Very Strongly	Fairly Strongly	Not Strongly	Neutral	Not Strongly	Fairly Strongly	Very Strongly
Swings	5	1	0	0	0	0	0
Bridge	0	0	0	3	2	0	1
Mater	3	1	1	0	1	0	0
Rates	0	1	3	0	0	1	1
Integration	5	1	0	0	0	0	0

TABLE 12.9

Belfast Municipal Correspondents' Appraisals of Opinion over Four Current Issues

(Numbers of correspondents)

	Agree	Opposition of Prot. extremists to moderate Unionists and Catholics	Other groups opposed	Disagree	DK, No opinion
Population					
Swings	1	4	1	0	0
Bridge	0	3	0	0	3
Mater	0	4	0	1	1
Rates	0	0	0	4	2
Councillors					
Swings	0	5	1	0	0
Bridge	0	6	0	0	0
Mater	0	5	0	0	1
Rates	1	2	2	0	1

Catholics Republican Labour. Thus the politico-religious cleavages which divided councillors and residents were reflected among correspondents. In Glasgow three correspondents were Progressives, two less enthusiastically Labour, and one independent. It must be said that the Belfast correspondents saw much to criticise in their parties, all belonged to the moderate wings and condemned the extremists on both sides.

(ii) *Issue-preferences and Perceptions*

These remarks lead into a direct consideration of correspondents' political outlook. Table 12.8 gives their full preferences over the five central issues, which can be compared with those of residents and councillors (Tables 9.1 and 11.3). The remarkable point about correspondents' preferences is their unanimity. On three issues there was no opposition of preferences and on the Mater the single divergent voice was very muted. Only on rates was disagreement more obvious. Among Glasgow correspondents there was unanimity on only one issue, although opposition was muted on two others. The thrust of Belfast correspondents' preferences was always in support of the policies supported by the opposition parties and the O'Neill Unionists. In this respect they resembled councillors rather than residents. On the three issues on which questions were asked about decision by the Belfast majority or the affected minority, most correspondents supported majority decision: four – one on swings: three – two on the Mater: four – one on rates. Glasgow correspondents were similarly divided but in overall support of majority decision. Belfast councillors were also predominantly majoritarian though divided internally – more majoritarian, however, than residents.

Correspondents' perceptions of the state of opinion on current issues is important because it was the picture being communicated to their readers. Table 12.9 graphically reveals the extent to which correspondents saw a cumulative cleavage over politico-religious issues. This was perceived by fewer correspondents to exist among the population than among councillors, but was the perception adopted by a majority on each issue except the Bridge, on which half saw the population as unresolved. On rates the population was seen as widely disagreed but even here as many correspondents as endorsed any other view saw councillors falling into the familiar opposed groups.

In sharp contrast Glasgow correspondents saw issue-preferences in their city as generally consensual: on the pubs and fees issues four saw councillors as agreed and only two thought the population divided: on parking two thought that councillors and population clearly agreed with the proposals, and three thought councillors and population clearly disagreed. Five considered Glasgow residents to be opposed to the increase in rates: one thought councillors favoured the increase, two that they disapproved of the increase and two that they divided into opposing groups. There are obvious discrepancies between Glasgow correspondents' views of public and activist opinion, but the important point of the comparison with Belfast is the limited scope for inferring a consistent opposition between two clear-cut and cohesive bodies of opinion. This perception of a straight political confrontation over current issues linked with correspondents' general ideas about the running of Belfast. All thought preference in local government jobs was given to Protestants and supporters of the establishment. No Glasgow correspondents thought such preference was given in Glasgow. However five Glaswegians thought majority interests were sometimes ignored in favour of minority groups – three thought these were religious groups. The same number in Belfast endorsed the minority influence of religious groups and one correspondent attributed influence to the Right-wing Unionists: two, however, did not think the majority was ignored. A third of Belfast councillors but only a quarter of residents similarly felt that no minorities had undue influence.

Linked to this is the question of: Who ran Belfast? Five attributed power to more or less restrictive groups inside the City Unionist Party. In Glasgow only three correspondents credited the City Labour Party with running the city. Only sixteen per cent of Belfast residents named the Unionist Party – the question was not asked of councillors.

Parties as such were seen by five out of six correspondents as harmful in their effects on local government – as involving rule in the interests of Unionists and keeping sectarian squabbles alive. Four of the Glasgow correspondents saw parties as contributing to the orderly handling of Corporation affairs, as against only one Belfast correspondent. The view of parties as harmful was shared by a plurality of all Belfast groups – by 49 per cent of councillors and 41 per cent of residents. Not surprisingly five correspondents wanted change in Belfast government in the direction of taking power from party politicians and augmenting officials', by appointing a City Manager or at the extreme abolishing the elected Corporation in favour of Commissioners appointed by Stormont. As emerged in Chapter 5, such an action had solid modern precedents having been employed from 1942 to 1945. It was the method adopted to conciliate the minority in the more polarised city of Derry in 1968. Not surprisingly, only six per cent of Belfast councillors supported their own supersession. More surprisingly, only 14 per cent of residents wanted the Council abolished or weakened. In strong contrast Glasgow correspondents all suggested changes enabling councillors to function more effectively rather than involving a transfer to local officials.

With regard to the business rather than the process of government, the six correspondents unanimously rated housing as the most important problem facing the Corporation: 35 per cent of residents and 60 per cent of councillors concurred in this judgement. Three correspondents agreed further in naming traffic as second most important. Four correspondents also regarded housing problems as among the most newsworthy. Thus some connection appeared between their personal judgements in this area and the criteria which shaped their dissemination of news. Three Glasgow correspondents regarded housing as their most important problem and again there was a link with their criteria of newsworthiness.

In regard to the problems and issues mentioned above, correspondents divided on the exact nature of councillors' responsibilities. One thought that a councillor should simply represent his ward and two others that he should give priority to ward interests over general affairs. Two others reversed this ordering of responsibility while another stressed city responsibilities only. Correspondents thus stressed ward responsibilities more than councillors (Tables 11.1 and 11.2) but less than Glasgow correspondents, three of whom endorsed a pure ward role and three a mixed city role.

The salient conclusion derived from this analysis of Belfast correspondents' opinion is of their strong consensus on a particular view of the local government, in spite of the religious and political cleavages revealed in the preceding section. This shared view departed from that expressed by Glasgow correspondents in perceiving local political processes as shaped by a persistent cumulative division between entrenched Protestants and entrenched Opposition, with moderate Unionists between. Decision-makers were seen as favouring their own supporters: and thus greater changes were advocated than in Glasgow – changes which would have made local government less representative, because part of the trouble was seen as the propensity of the majority to support in power those extremists who victimised the minority.

On the whole, in their level of information and informed comment, and in their policy preferences, correspondents in Belfast resembled councillors rather than residents. Since councillors themselves were divided along the lines indicated by correspondents, similarities to councillors as a whole should not be overdrawn. The councillors whom correspondents resembled most were the moderate Unionists, the men in the middle. The overall resemblance between correspondents and councillors in Belfast was thus less strong than that which appeared between Glasgow correspondents and councillors.

The cleavage which correspondents perceived between moderate Unionists and diehards was on our evidence an accurate appraisal, which contrasted with the omnibus characterisation of all Unionists as diehards, made by a majority of residents. Nevertheless, it is revealing that correspondents regarded the moderates as weaker than their numbers on the council actually warranted (Tables 9.1 and 11.3). Correspondents saw the diehards as actually running Belfast and this perception, passed on through the media, must have contributed to the general impression that Unionist policies were basically unchanged. Once more it appears that the moderates' failure to convince others of their strength and determination was a fatal flaw in their programme of reform.

(iii) *Transmission of Information*

In descriptions of their own role Belfast correspondents were predominantly concerned with getting and relaying news: this was seen as a hard task, involving a breach in a 'conspiracy of silence' as one correspondent put it. Glasgow correspondents also (5 to 1) emphasised day-to-day news coverage. Since news was felt to be less difficult to obtain, four of the Glasgow correspondents viewed an important feature of their role as explaining the processes underlying each day's events. This was a feature subordinated in Belfast to the hard task of getting the real news.

Belfast correspondents were not crusaders. Asked what action they might take to get their way on current issues five out of six envisaged the possibility of using the media to influence events. Two of the five emphasised their paramount obligation to be fair, and two correspondents took a pessimistic view of press influence. Only one correspondent thought he was quite likely to succeed if he took action: the others felt they were unlikely to have any influence. In contrast four out of six Glasgow correspondents envisaged an aggressive newspaper campaign: three felt very or quite likely to succeed.

One problem which correspondents as well as councillors encounter is ascertaining what the population think. The most popular method in both cities was to get the views of organisations, such as the Churches, Tenants' and Ratepayers' Associations, Chambers of Commerce and so on. Systematic polling had more popularity in Belfast, and there was more reliance on the views of political activists (Table 12.10). Correspondents' use of organised non-political groups and their faith in polling markedly differentiated their methods from councillors' ways of contacting constituents through parties, and face-to-face meetings.

The general public was not the source of correspondents' information about current issues in either Glasgow or Belfast. Asked how they heard of four issues, five or six Belfast correspondents on all issues but the Mater mentioned the Council or councillors. On the Mater four had heard from M.P.s at Stormont.[2] No other sources were mentioned more than once. Similarly no more than one Glasgow correspondent mentioned sources other than the council on any issue. Reports of persons with whom correspondents discussed issues serve to confirm the impression of correspondents' reliance on councillors. On all issues but the Mater four or five Belfast correspondents had talked with a councillor and a similar concentration of discussion prevailed in Glasgow.

TABLE 12.IO

Methods used by Glasgow and Belfast Correspondents to Discover Popular Opinion, on Four Current Issues

(Number of responses)

	Opinion obvious	Organised groups	Councillors, political activists	Talking to people	Public meetings	Systematic poll	Other
			Glasgow				
Pubs	0	3	0	3	1	0	0
Fees	0	2	1	2	1	0	0
Parking	0	4	0	2	1	0	1
Rates	0	4	1	1	1	0	1
			Belfast				
Swings	0	2	2	1	0	4	0
Bridge	0	2	2	3	0	2	0
Mater	1	3	1	1	0	3	1
Rates	2	4	0	1	0	2	0

The impression that a predominant – almost sole – source of news for correspondents was the council is strengthened by their replies to a direct question about the main source of their local information. All six Belfast correspondents named councillors, two in conjunction with local officials and one in conjunction with Stormont M.P.s. All six Glasgow correspondents also named Council sources.

In disseminating the news thus gathered, three Glasgow correspondents felt they could get everything into their published reports and three remembered being cut. All Belfast correspondents felt they could get all they wanted into their newspapers: the two who reported for television as well as newspapers said they suffered cuts for reasons of time.

POLITICIANS' CONTROL OVER PUBLICITY

Overall, no great difference appeared between the news-gathering and disseminating activities of journalists in Glasgow and Belfast. The only significant contrast lay in the perceived difficulty of getting Corporation news.

Given this difficulty, in addition to correspondents' common dependence on councillors for their information about issues, the possibility arises that councillors might have been able to control the coverage given to a topic in the mass media: to emphasise some issues and to muffle others. Such a degree of control over media coverage would assume enormous importance where the population depended so heavily on the media for information, as in Belfast. In Glasgow most councillors in their own estimation enjoyed the ability to play up an issue, and about half thought they could also play issues down. Journalists agreed on the first point. On the second they stressed the inability of councillors to muffle issues without press co-operation, but in fact the majority turned out to have suppressed certain items of news at councillors' request.[3] Did the same situation emerge in Belfast?

We can first examine councillors' own estimates of their ability to publicise issues. Comparable proportions of Belfast councillors and Glasgow councillors (71 to 74 per cent) felt that they could bring issues to general attention. The ways in which these Belfast councillors thought they could gain atten-

TABLE 12.II

Belfast Councillors' Appraisals of Means and Obstacles to Bringing Issues to General Attention

(Percentages of all councillors and councillors in party groups saying issues can or cannot be brought to general attention, respectively)

	All Councillors		Unionist		N.I. Lab.		Nat.-Lab.		All Non-Unionist		
	1st	2nd	1st	2nd	1st	2nd	1st	2nd	1st	2nd	Mention
Issues can be brought to general attention through:											
Being a councillor	27	3	24	4	0	0	50	0	40	0	
Corporation, depts officials	0	0	0	0	0	0	25	0	20	0	
Central/Stormont Govt.	13	3	16	4	0	0	0	0	0	0	
Parties	16	6	20	8	0	0	0	0	0	0	
Non-Pol. local organisations	3	3	4	4	100	0	0	0	0	0	
Public meetings	23	19	24	24	0	100	25	75	20	0	
Mass media	10	29	8	20	0	0	0	0	20	80	
Direct Approach to public	3	0	4	0	0	0	0	0	0	0	
N.	30		25		1		4		5		
Issues cannot be brought to general attention because gained only through:											
Holding other position than Respondent holds	36	0	33	0	67	0	40	0	37	0	
Corporation, depts officials	9	0	0	0	0	0	0	0	13	0	
Central government	18	9	0	0	0	0	0	0	0	0	
Parties, which carry no weight	0	0	0	0	0	0	40	20	25	13	
Non-Pol. local organisations	0	0	0	0	0	0	0	0	0	0	
Public meetings which are ineffective	9	9	0	0	0	0	0	0	0	0	
Mass media not open to R.	27	0	0	0	33	33	0	0	13	13	
Public who are apathetic	0	0	67	0	0	0	20	0	13	0	
Gaining Electoral victory	0	0	0	0	0	0	0	0	0	0	
N.	11		3		3		5		8		

tion are detailed in Table 12.11. Belfast councillors as a whole were somewhat more confident of gaining attention by virtue of their public position than were Glasgow councillors but less confident of using the mass media. In contrast Belfast councillors felt they could get attention through the Stormont Government and through the parties. Reliance on public meetings was about the same in both cities.

The party groups on Belfast council diverged somewhat on the strategies open to them. Unionists felt Stormont and the parties were good channels for them, whereas non-Unionists placed heavier reliance on their status as councillors and the accessibility of the media. These contrasts between strategies were bound up with differences in the extent to which the party groupings were confident of gaining publicity: 87 per cent of Unionists compared to only 36 per cent of non-Unionists. The two thirds of non-Unionists who felt they could not get publicity felt more strongly than Unionists that their parties carried no weight. All who felt ineffective regarded other public positions as focusing more attention than their own from a population perceived as apathetic. Glasgow councillors who disclaimed influence over publicity placed more emphasis on public apathy.

Belfast correspondents confirmed – five to one – councillors' general opinion that they could bring issues to general attention. All five who agreed focussed exclusively on the press as the avenue to publicity, and emphasised the symbiotic relationship between councillors and journalists.

On the question of delaying or muffling issues councillors in Belfast were less confident than their counterparts in Glasgow. Only 33 per cent felt they could keep issues from attention compared to 44 per cent of Glasgow councillors. The proportion confident of muffling issues did not differ between the Belfast parties.

The main emphasis in both parties as in Glasgow was placed on the possibility of councillors of different parties agreeing to keep issues quiet: cooperation with the press was also mentioned. On the other hand, Belfast councillors sceptical about their ability to muffle issues emphasised the role of the Press in probing council affairs and finding councillors opposed to the prevailing view always ready to talk. These reactions were

TABLE 12.12

Belfast Councillors' Appraisals of Means and Obstacles to Keeping Issues from General Attention

(Percentage of all councillors and of party groups)

	All Councillors		Unionist		N.I. Lab.		Nat.-Lab.		All Non-Unionist	
	1st	2nd	1st	2nd	1st	2nd	1st	2nd	1st	2nd
Issues can be kept from general attention because:										
Councillors/officials agree/manoeuvre to keep issues quiet	60	0	50	0	50	0	67	0	60	0
Parties can agree/manoeuvre to keep issue quiet	13	0	10	0	0	0	33	0	20	0
Reporters can agree to keep an issue quiet/need not be informed	21	0	20	0	50	0	0	0	20	0
Public are ill-informed so their attention soon wanders	6	0	10	0	0	0	0	0	0	0
N.	15		10		2		3		5	
Issues cannot be kept from general attention because:										
Issues cannot be kept quiet	16	0	17	0	0	0	33	0	13	0
Issues should not be kept quiet	16	0	12	0	0	0	33	0	25	0
Councillors/officials will always talk	16	4	12	6	100	0	0	0	25	0
Party competition always brings issues into the open										
Reporters will always find out about an issue	32	0	35	0	0	0	33	0	25	0
Important issues cannot be kept quiet	4	4	0	6	0	0	0	0	13	0
N.	25		17		2		6		8	

again the same as those voiced in Glasgow. There was strong feeling, among non-Unionists particularly, that issues *should* not be left quiet.

Councillors' lack of confidence in their ability here was shared by Belfast correspondents. Four felt councillors could not keep issues quiet, because the press would always find out. The two who dissented observed however that councillors could agree not to say anything and could doctor the minutes of committees to make them quite unrevealing.

On the other hand, as in Glasgow, correspondents agreed almost unanimously (five to one) that if asked by a committee chairman to delay an item they would do so, if it was in their judgement appropriate. Only half the correspondents could think of problems best left unmentioned: vandalism and religion were each mentioned twice.

The general conclusions that emerge on councillors' ability to control political issues are thus much the same in Belfast as in Glasgow. There was general agreement on councillors' ability to gain attention for issues. There was considerable doubt whether they alone could keep issues quiet, but a distinct probability that they could do so with the cooperation of the press. Journalists were not unwilling to cooperate at least on certain occasions. The condition of mutual dependence between councillors and journalists was likely to stimulate mutual trade-offs that would enhance cooperation in the management of news.

It is tempting to discern differences in the potential for control over publicity of councillors in Belfast and Glasgow. Had a greater potential seemed available in Glasgow one could attribute greater stability there to a greater autonomy, freedom to maneouvre and ability to cooperate among councillors. Such conditions could have been seen as enabling politicians to avoid disruptive religious questions and to focus attention instead upon the more routine class cleavages underlying orderly two-party competition. In Belfast, on the other hand, the penetration of politico-religious divisions into the council chamber itself would have served as an explanation for the inability of leaders to choose the issues on which they could compete, with consequent effects on their ability to effect quiet compromise in any area.

In point of fact the evidence, though inconsistent, shows little difference between Glasgow and Belfast in councillors' control over publicity. True, Belfast councillors were somewhat less sure of keeping issues quiet. On the other hand, correspondents seemed just as ready to cooperate with councillors as in Glasgow. The absence of strong differences here reinforces the final conclusion of the Glasgow study that management of publicity is more a factor in the party struggle than an influence on politicians' autonomy.

CONCLUSIONS

In most respects communication processes in Belfast in 1966 were extremely similar to those of Glasgow. Councillors relied heavily on their personal contacts among other activists or officials: residents absorbed a thin diet of local information from the Press. The inaccurate ideas about each other's preferences uncovered in the last chapter were obviously fostered among residents and councillors by Unionist reliance on party agencies to uncover popular preferences. But this lack of direct contact was not unparallelled in Glasgow.

Where dissimilarities emerged in Belfast which seemed to have a significant connection with instability, were first the general images which municipal reporters had of politics in the city, that the diehards were in control, that every decision was a battle in which the intransigent majority elbowed aside the moderates and trampled the intransigent minority. Such images, consciously or unconsciously underlying the news appearing in the media, were not calculated to reconcile the minority to their present position nor to hearten the moderates. Nor did they wholly reflect a situation in which the majority of Unionist councillors did in fact support conciliatory policies. We have traced the resulting misperceptions (Tables 11.7 and 11.10) which ultimately crippled O'Neill's initiatives – a failure which ultimately did leave a more intransigent opposition confronting the diehards. In this respect correspondents' views of Belfast politics were self-fulfilling.

The other significant departure in Belfast from the situation prevailing in Glasgow was the complete absence of communication among councillors. While in Glasgow inter-party consultation was not absent, communication did flow strongly along party lines. But in Belfast the dearth of consultation even between party colleagues bespoke a situation of extreme fragmentation in which implicit understandings built up by frequent discussion were entirely lacking. In such a situation procedural understandings as well as policy agreements were likely to be impaired, with consequences for general stability which we shall explore in the next chapter.

NOTES

1. Again the analysis of this chapter draws heavily on the similar analysis carried through by Michael Margolis on Glasgow data, to which frequent reference is made in our text. See *Political Stratification*, Chapter 4.
2. As mentioned above, the question of support for the Mater Hospital was one which involved Stormont as well as the Corporation.
3. Of course, journalists did so only when, in their judgement, publication would have harmed affected individuals or the Corporation.

13 Support for Established Institutions, Cross-cutting and the Reaction of Political Moderates

SIGNS of the impending crisis in Northern Ireland are scattered through the evidence reviewed in previous chapters. When interpreted contextually, these give strong indications of how and why a crisis developed. The class division underlying politics in Britain was in Belfast overlaid by religious tension and Unionist hegemony (Chapter 8). That hegemony was seen as irreversible under existing procedures because it was based on the solid support of a popular majority – the Protestants (Chapter 7). Party divisions carried over (although not as clear-cut cleavages) into political attitudes and preferences on issues (Chapter 9). Unionist councillors formed a socioeconomic elite who ran the Corporation as their personal machine, where non-Unionist representatives seemed not to belong (Chapters 4, 5, 10). Certainly a majority of Unionist adherents and councillors – seconded by the press – wished in 1966 to make conciliatory moves towards the Catholics (Chapters 9 and 11), which if carried through might have defused the imminent crisis. But moderate councillors were discouraged and conservatives strengthened by an overestimate of intransigence among the population: while the resultant failure of the moderate leaders to act strongly reinforced popular impressions of Unionist intransigence and immobility (Chapter 11). In the last chapter we examined the communication processes which produced these mutually erroneous and damaging impressions, and noted their propogation by municipal correspondents and the dependence of the socially elitist Unionist councillors on party estimates of popular feeling (Chapter 12).

Certainly we must be careful to temper these impressions, taken from the analysis of survey responses, with observations of the actual behaviour of Unionist politicians during the late 1960s. The responses suggest that most Unionists favoured conciliation and it was only their failure to act – through the fatal lack of confidence existing between activists and residents – which fostered the crisis. But councillors' actions cast some doubt on their support for anything more than verbal conciliation. For four successive years a leading Unionist councillor nominated Alderman Daley, the most moderate Nationalist, as Vice-Chairman of the Parks and Cemeteries Committee, the least important on the Council. Daley was on each occasion defeated by the near unanimous opposition of the Unionists. While it is true that most large British cities have a winner-take-all distribution of Council offices, it is also true that acceptance of Daley would have been a more notable move towards conciliation than support of the moderate position on any of the issues examined. Our review of further survey evidence in this chapter suggests also that Unionists were muddled and inconsistent in their thinking about conciliation. Inaction was caused just as much by unwillingness to act as by indecisiveness and underestimates of popular support.

It was the absence of action to support Unionist promises which provided the immediate spur to events, together with the widespread feeling among Catholics that they were victimised (Chapter 7), and the lack of involvement which their representatives felt in existing institutions (Chapter 10). Some reaction by Catholics was inevitable after proposals for reconciliation had been aired but had seemingly bogged down. Expectations had been aroused but not satisfied, the classical conditions for revolution. A Catholic reaction was even more likely when a Labour Government at Westminster could be expected to sympathise with their situation.

In this chapter we examine two underlying conditions which could have encouraged violent reactions in the crisis from 1968 onwards. These are the extent of support for established institutions and the extent of cross-cutting between issue-preferences and background characteristics in Belfast, and among intransigents and moderates. We review the evidence on these points rather than present it in full because it has already been reported in detail elsewhere.[1]

One factor which we expected might encourage direct action on both sides was a lack of respect for constitutional conventions. Where such conventions are well established the political strategies even of those labouring under a strong sense of grievance are likely to emphasise action through existing institutions rather than direct self-help. In this section we review various manifestations of willingness to work through established institutions and the extent to which they were respected – again using the Glasgow situation as a touchstone by which to isolate features peculiarly associated with Belfast.

Strategies of Political Action

We first asked respondents what they would do to get their way on the issues of opening Swings, naming the Bridge, aiding the Mater or raising rates. Two thirds of both Unionist and non-Unionist councillors emphasised action through the council – a surprising similarity of response. One third of non-Unionist councillors said they would do nothing. Unionists were less inclined to passivity – only 13 per cent said they would do nothing, while groups of one sixth to one fifth mentioned action through the Party Group on Council, the party organisation, the media or informal groupings. Differences between the council groupings were in fact less than they appeared in Glasgow, where 50 per cent of the Opposition plumped for action through the Council but 56 per cent of Labour envisaged action through their party. There was little difference between alternatives favoured by residents of different parties.

Irrespective of party, residents were pessimistic of even moderate success from the actions they adopted – only 18 per cent thought they were very or quite likely to succeed. Fifty-three per cent of councillors thought they were at least moderately sure of success, but 64 per cent of Unionists felt this degree of confidence compared with only 28 per cent of non-Unionists. On the other hand, the contrast between council parties on this point was no greater than appeared in Glasgow, so the comparison isolates no peculiar features of Belfast politics which might serve as an explanation for the future course of events.

Changes in Belfast Government

A desire for governmental change might certainly indicate dissatisfaction with existing procedures, even if, in 1966, the Opposition groups reluctantly worked through them for lack of any better alternative. Astoundingly, many more Belfast residents than Glasgow residents (59 compared to 33 per cent) opposed any change at all. Two thirds of Unionist residents and half of the non-Unionists opposed change. Only 13 per cent of councillors – disproportionately Unionist – opposed change as such. But few councillors or residents supported any change which would subvert basic features of existing arrangements. The main support in all parties came for incremental reforms such as making councillors more efficient. These responses were highly analogous to those given in Glasgow, where indeed party differences on this question were slightly more marked than in Belfast.

A basic feature of local government in Belfast, as in Glasgow, is the influence of party. Party differences in Belfast were even more politically central than in Glasgow, for they ensured continuance of the Unionist hegemony. Reactions to the parties are therefore as good indicators of attitudes towards established institutions as the more direct desire for change in local government.

A more widespread distrust of the parties appears in Belfast compared with Glasgow. This was not evident from the analysis of party images carried through in Chapter 7 (Table 7.2), but from a direct question on whether the disappearance of parties would make any difference to the running of the Corporation. Answers were grouped according to whether (a) they implied that the disappearance of parties would produce bad effects, and thus that their presence was necessary and beneficial, (b) they implied their disappearance would be good, and thus that their existence was bad, (c) they implied that party activity as such was neutral. When proportions under (b) were subtracted from those under (a), no group in Belfast showed a balance of positive support for the parties. Unionist residents balanced support and hostility evenly (a – b═o). Non-Unionist residents were fairly critical (– 18), but non-Unionist councillors much more so (– 43) – especially Nationalist-Labour (– 67). Even Unionist councillors were critical (– 5).

As with municipal correspondents the comparison shows more hostility to parties among Belfast groupings than generally existed in Glasgow. There the Labour councillors, whose dominance stemmed from the existing party system, were overwhelmingly supportive of parties, showing an initial balance of support over hostility of 78 percentage points. Labour residents, with a score of – 1 on the same index, balanced considerable hostility to parties with considerable enthusiasm. Progressive residents were strongly critical, with an initial balance of – 33, but their councillors tempered criticism of parties with support, producing a net balance of – 11 points. Opposition Progressive councillors thus showed as much support for existing party arrangements as did the dominant Unionists in Belfast. Taken in conjunction with the strong divergence in a similar direction between municipal correspondents this finding represents the first major difference to emerge between Glasgow and Belfast on the question of support for procedures.

Impartiality of Belfast Government

The data reviewed previously suggests that the Corporation was viewed as an adjunct of the Unionist Party, even if non-Unionists were left no option but to work through it. This impression can be tested directly by examining answers to questions on the Mayor's impartiality, and on the influence of minorities on Belfast government.

Again, responses can be summarised by subtracting the proportion who feel the Mayor stands for his own party from the proportion who feel he stands for the whole city. Among both residents and councillors there was a strong balance of belief in the Mayor's impartiality (+61 and +46 respectively). This expression of trust was undoubtedly coloured by the activities of Lord Mayor Jenkins (1963–6), a moderate Unionist of the O'Neill variety, who had made many conciliatory gestures towards Catholics. That these had not gone unnoticed is shown by the belief in his impartiality expressed by non-Unionist

residents, which was almost as high as for Unionists (+56 and
+64). Naturally Unionist councillors also believed in the
Mayor's impartiality (+73) but endorsements dropped drastically among non-Unionist councillors (–14). No Nationalist
councillor believed in the Mayor's impartiality at all. Their
distrust is only slightly greater, however, than that expressed
by Glasgow Progressives about the Labour Provost.

Only slight differences from Glasgow similarly appeared in
residents' views on the point of who runs Belfast. Two thirds
of all groups in Belfast saw elected representatives as running
the city. Religious bodies attracted no more than seven per cent
of endorsements from any group. The ambiguities inherent on
this point were aptly paraphrased by one resident, who burst
out under questioning: 'Who runs Belfast? I don't know – no
one knows – God knows!'

Support for resolution of three current issues (swings,
Mater, rates) by the Belfast majority as opposed to affected
minorities was somewhat inconsistent, as in Glasgow, and
stronger among councillors than residents. Party ties affected
responses only to the same extent as in Glasgow. Support of the
majority was strongly affected by whether respondents agreed
with the policy that had majority support – again as in Glasgow.
If anything, Belfast respondents showed somewhat greater
enthusiasm for majority rule.

Answers to a question on whether minority groups had
undue influence threw up some striking differences. In terms
of the difference between the percentage seeing government as
representative and the percentage viewing it as unrepresentative, Belfast residents appeared more favourable to their
Corporation than Glaswegians to theirs (+16 compared to
–10). In Glasgow, however, both Progressive councillors and
Progressive residents were more disposed to think of the
Corporation as representative than members of the governing
Labour Party. But half of both the Unionist and non-Unionist
residents of Belfast were inclined to see local government as
representative, in the sense of responding only to groups which
should legitimately influence it. Unionist councillors were even
more confident – 61 per cent thought the Corporation was
properly representative. Only 14 per cent of non-Unionist
councillors shared this opinion.

The influence of religious groups was mentioned by almost half of the non-Unionist councillors, compared with no more than five per cent among any of the corresponding Glasgow groups.

Since job discrimination by local authorities in Northern Ireland is one of the most cited causes of the present crisis, some topical interest attaches to a question asked of both Belfast and Glasgow residents on discrimination in Corporation employment. Two thirds of Glasgow residents thought there was some discrimination to only 55 per cent of Belfast residents.

Cross-cutting between procedural attitudes

The comparisons between Glasgow and Belfast in terms of support for established institutions and procedures have proved largely negative. The greater distrust of parties in Belfast was probably an effect rather than a cause of Unionist hegemony and *immobilisme*. Fear of what change might bring no doubt helped to aggravate a political situation which would have benefited from constructive change more than most. However, it is hard to see it as a root cause rather than as a simple consequence of the confrontation between Unionists and Nationalists.

While the simple distribution of procedural support may not serve to differentiate Belfast, there remains the possibility that Belfast may be uniquely distinguished by the overall pattern of that support. This idea can be cast in terms which resemble the cross-cutting theory of political compromise discussed in the next section. A polity might be threatened not because its procedures failed to attract majority support (at either activist of popular level), but because the majority who consistently supported its procedures were confronted by a minority who consistently rejected them. Any sizeable and determined minority can make difficulties for a democratic system. The important factor in stability may consequently be the avoidance of a consistent cumulative split between two groups over procedures, rather than simply the attraction of majority support. Stable democracies, on the other hand, could be expected to generate cross-cutting attitudes to procedures among their population or political activists. We shall go further into the idea of cross-cutting below but the importance of cross-cutting for procedures lies simply in the idea that if everyone supports some aspects of democratic procedures, he is more inclined to favour continuation of the 'democracy' which embraces them all.

If cross-cutting is associated with greater stability we should expect to find cross-cutting higher on views about procedures in Glasgow than in Belfast, where a cumulative division should exist. The distributions of opinion already discussed provide a basis for estimating the degree of cross-cutting in both cities. All we need to know is 'the extent to which individuals who are in the same group (in regard to one aspect of democracy) are in different groups on (another aspect)'.[2] An estimate of this tendency is provided by Taylor and Rae's XC (for cross-cutting) statistic, which is simply the proportion of pairs, out of all pairs in a given collection of individuals, which fall into different opinion-groups on a comparison of two procedural attitudes.[3] In other words, it measures the extent to which individuals changed associates as their attitude towards different procedures varied.

To compare procedural cross-cutting between Glasgow and Belfast we took support for majority rule on current issues, attitudes to change in local government, positive and negative attitudes to parties and to the possibility that parties might disappear, appraisals of the impartiality of the Lord Mayor and of the extent to which the majority is ignored.

Answers on each were cross-tabulated with each of the others and XC calculated, giving 55 separate values for the different groups (Belfast residents and councillors, Glasgow residents and councillors). The most striking result was the overall similarity of results as between Glasgow and Belfast. Average cross-cutting between the procedural attitudes of residents of both cities was 0·49, and for councillors 0·47.[4] Thus there was no indication of a consistent procedural division between a well defined majority and minority in Belfast, contrasting with more diffuse procedural support in Glasgow. On the basis of the analysis reported so far in this chapter there are no grounds for attributing intransigence and political instability in Belfast to any very consistent minority opposition to the established institutions of city government.

CROSS-CUTTING OVER ISSUE-PREFERENCES

Cross-cutting arguments can also be applied to issue-preferences. Persons with different associates in different areas of policy are exposed to diverse arguments, which may induce moderation. Where preferences on different issues are superimposed or cumulative, only one viewpoint is heard, and this is more likely to promote intransigence. The social effect of cross-cutting is the creation of cross-pressures on the individuals involved. A person sharing preferences on class-related issues with a different group from the one he enters in regard to religious issues, for example, will either lapse into apathy or press for compromises in a class conflict which pits him against religious associates. Prudential considerations may also restrain members of the majority on one issue from bending the rules when they need their protection as a minority on the next issue. The explanation of instability in Belfast which emerges from this line of reasoning is then that a cumulative cleavage on current issues existed in Belfast, discouraging compromise and stimulating intransigence and violence.

Using the sets of issues in Belfast and Glasgow in 1966, we can directly assess the relevance of the cross-cutting explanation of political crisis. If the explanation is valid we should expect intransigence in Belfast to be associated with lower cross-cutting of issue-preferences, and moderation in Glasgow to be associated with higher cross-cutting. These expectations apply to the comparisons of both residents and activists, but particularly activists because policy compromises must be attained principally through their efforts. Care must also be taken to not simply compare issue-preferences as such, but also preferences of equal intensity and salience, and to discover how preferences cross-cut with party allegiances.

Using the XC statistics described above, comparisons on all these points were made between Glasgow and Belfast.[5] Most revealed similar levels of cross-cutting. The only point of difference lay in the higher cross-cutting of issue-preferences and party loyalties among Belfast councillors compared with Glasgow councillors, which stemmed in turn from the much higher level of internal disagreement among the Unionists compared with the two Glasgow parties (Table 11.3). Such disagreements obviously derived in part from the controversy on O'Neill's and Jenkins's overtures to Catholics, but probably also represented a normal tendency in the dominant party, since policy could only be made through factional clashes between Unionists.[6] In contrast, the Nationalist councillors showed considerable internal agreement – probably because, being excluded from policy-making, they were under little temptation to make compromises between practical constraints and their initial ideology.

Such a rigid consensus, however, rendered possible cooperation with any of the Unionist factions even more difficult, thus further lessening the possibility of political compromises other than those achieved inside the Unionist Party. But the minority parties' exclusion meant that there was little to tip the balance when Unionists were evenly divided, and the consequence was by 1966 an inability to take any decisive action. We have noted the influence of such *immobilisme* on the development of the present crisis. On the other hand, policy in the competitive two-party system of Glasgow was defined by clashes between the parties and finally decided by electors' choices between them. Considerable internal consensus was necessary for the party group to maintain its competitiveness but the necessity of making practicable and electorally appealing policies created some internal disagreement between diehards and opportunists. The result can well be seen as the moderate disagreement actually discovered among the Council groups.

CROSS-CUTTING BETWEEN BACKGROUND
CHARACTERISTICS

The analysis of cross-cutting between issue-preferences throws up interesting results, which confirm some of our previous inferences about the tendencies evident in Belfast politics. But cross-cutting as such does not play its anticipated part in distinguishing Glasgow from Belfast. Issue-preferences are not the only level at which we can examine cross-cutting, however. Social characteristics might be expected to shape individual behaviour more profoundly and to relate to a wider spectrum of attitudes than relatively transient issue-preferences. Again we only summarise the result of this analysis, based as before on use of the XC statistic, since it has been reported elsewhere.[7]

We searched for higher cross-cutting in Glasgow compared with Belfast at both popular and activist level, on a variety of indicators of social class (occupation, Register-General social class, home-ownership, trade union membership, level of education, subjective identifications), on a number of classifications of denomination, with and without church attendance, and party affiliation. Cross-cutting existed on all these characteristics at much the same levels in both cities, with two exceptions. Cross-cutting between subjective class and party was much lower among Glasgow councillors than Belfast councillors (0·24 compared to 0·32) but much the same among residents (0·45 and 0·47). A trichotomised religious classification (Protestant-Nonbeliever-Catholic) showed much lower cross-cutting with party among Belfast councillors (0·22 compared to 0·41 in Glasgow) and among Belfast residents (0·37 compared to 0·44 in Glasgow). The fact that a deeper cumulative cleavage existed between party and religion in Belfast than between party and any background characteristic in Glasgow offers powerful support to cross-cutting explanations of Belfast instability in terms of exposure to only one set of messages and an absence of contact with persons of different characteristics to oneself. The findings also support the contrasts already drawn between the class-based party division in Glasgow and the religious division in Belfast. At activist level the class-party correspondence in Glasgow (0·24) actually compared in value with the correspondence between religious and party loyalty in Belfast (0·22). However, unlike that religious conflict the class division in Glasgow is muffled by the absence of any marked carryover of class loyalties into party loyalties by Glasgow residents.

CROSS-CUTTING AMONG BELFAST MODERATES

The characteristics and attitudes of the moderate Unionists in Belfast have proved to be a key element in understanding the development of crisis. It appears to have been their misjudgements and indecisiveness which prevented positive action being taken to forestall Catholic grievances. We are interested in comparing cross-cutting among moderates and intransigents

TABLE 13.1

Belfast Unionist Councillors and Residents Adopting Conciliatory Preference on Politico-Religious Issues: Cross-cutting on Issue Preferences

Councillors	Opening Swings (agree) XC value	Naming Bridge after Carson (disagree) XC value	Aiding Mater Hospital (agree) XC value	Mixed Housing for Catholics and Protestants (agree) XC value	Moderates: mean for each issue pair XC value	Total Belfast mean for each issue pair XC value
Swings–Bridge	—	—	0·40	0·20	0·30	0·25
Swings–Mater	—	0·50	—	0·34	0·42	0·27
Swings–Rates	—	0·35	0·46	0·50	0·44	0·35
Swings–Integration	—	0·31	0·30	—	0·31	0·27
Bridge–Mater	0·50	—	—	0·37	0·44	0·24
Bridge–Rates	0·24	—	0·30	0·48	0·34	0·31
Bridge–Integration	0·35	—	0·39	—	0·37	0·30
Mater–Rates	0·46	0·37	—	0·50	0·44	0·28
Mater–Integration	0·31	0·39	—	—	0·35	0·38
Integration–Rates	0·49	0·48	0·50	—	0·49	0·33
Mean	0·39	0·40	0·39	0·40 (overall means 0·40)		0·29

Residents

Bridge–Mater	0·50	—	—	0·41	0·45	0·33
Bridge–Rates	0·49	—	0·50	0·46	0·48	0·37
Bridge–Integration	0·49	—	0·49	—	0·49	0·27
Mater–Rates	0·45	0·49	—	0·43	0·46	0·39
Mater–Integration	0·48	0·46	—	—	0·47	0·32
Integration–Rates	0·50	0·50	0·49	—	0·50	0·37
Mean XC	0·48	0·49	0·49	0·46 (overall means)	0·48	0·33 (overall means)

Notes to Table 13.1 Cross-cutting is calculated from a matrix formed by the joint distribution of individuals with opinions over the two classifications under consideration:

$$XC = \sum_{i=1}^{M} p_i^2 + \sum_{i=1}^{N} p_j^2 - 2\sum_{i,j} p_{ij}^2$$

where M is the number of categories in the first classification; N is the number of categories in the second classification; p_i are marginal proportions for the first distribution; p_j are marginal proportions for the second distribution and p_{ij} are the proportions in the cells of the matrix.

Since moderates were distinguished by their preference on issues, cross-cutting between other issues and the issue on which the moderate group was distinguished could not be estimated. This is the reason for the blank entries in Table 13.1 Cross-cutting between the other three issue-preferences could be calculated, however, for each moderate group.

in order to discover whether moderation was indeed fostered by cross-cutting, as previous arguments would imply, and whether the patterns revealed by cross-cutting analysis offer any further clue as to why moderates reacted as they did. If high cross-cutting promoted moderation there should be higher cross-cutting of background characteristics and issue-preferences among moderates than among the Belfast population and councillors as a whole.[8]

The identifying mark of moderates is their readiness to conciliate opposition on the four politico-religious issues previously examined. The only persons who could be identified as moderate in 1966 were those Unionists who adopted preferences supported by Nationalists and Catholics on the politico-religious issues. Nationalists almost unanimously supported preferences which favoured their side, so none could be identified for our purposes as conciliatory. We were unable to combine the four Unionist groups distinguished on politico-religious issues, since preferences showed no consistent ordering in terms of an underlying dimension.[9] Thus we could not score 'moderation' across all issues: hence we have to deal below with four separate though overlapping groups of Unionists distinguished by their pro-Catholic preferences on each of the politico-religious issues.

None of these groups displayed consistently higher cross-cutting on the background characteristics previously examined than Belfast councillors or residents as a whole. But as Table 13.1 reveals the moderate groups did on average show higher cross-cutting on issue-preferences than all councillors or residents.

On the face of it this result explains the moderation of these groups. Their extensive changes of associates between issues exposed them to diverse points of view which encouraged conciliation. But this interpretation is suspect because it does not fit in with other findings. Why, if changes of associates encouraged moderation, did these groups not show higher cross-cutting than intransigents[10] in terms of their background characteristics? Especially when the political contrasts between Glasgow and Belfast can be explained in part by the cumulative religious-party cleavage?

These apparent anomalies can be resolved if we remember the indecisiveness and inconsistency previously revealed by moderates and ask what is actually revealed by the high cross-cutting between their issue-preferences? It is obviously not a consistent tendency towards moderation, for if this were present there would be no cross-cutting at all – every moderate would endorse the conciliatory side on every issue, thereby retaining the same associates throughout. What is revealed by the high level of preferential cross-cutting actually discovered among moderates, is not generalised conciliation but greater confusion. They seem in 1966 to have been reacting inconsistently to each issue as it came up, rather than in terms of reasoned overall support for conciliation (hence the failure of preferences to scale). The moderates' lack of consistent conviction in 1966 helps to explain their later inability to offer steady support to moderate Unionist leadership in the Province, and hence the vacillating policies which led directly to the present crisis.

This reappraisal of Table 13.1 also explains the absence of higher cross-cutting on issue-preferences in Glasgow compared with Belfast. If such cross-cutting reveals vacillation rather than true moderation there is no reason why it should be higher in Glasgow. The contrast in the cumulative nature of religious-partisan divisions is enough to explain political differences between the cities – so far as they can be explained by cross-cutting.

CONCLUSIONS

The contrast in cross-cutting of background characteristics is indeed the main contribution of this chapter towards explanation of the current crisis. We have, however, also obtained illuminating confirmation of the extent to which internal splits among Unionists contributed to an inability to meet Catholic demands. The profound ambiguities among Unionist moderates as to how far they actually desired conciliation have been further revealed – ambiguities which impaired their ability to act decisively when they would not have seemed to be capitulating to Catholic intimidation. Our evidence shows that in 1966 Belfast Catholics were in a fair way to accepting established conventions and political arrangements. The tragedy is that vacillation on the part of the Unionist moderates inhibited them from timely concessions which would perhaps have finally confirmed that acceptance.

NOTES

1. For assessment of the procedural indicators see Ian Budge *et al.*, *Political Stratification*, Chapter 2. For some discussion of the contrasts in procedural support between Glasgow and Belfast see Ian Budge, 'Support for Nation and Government among English Children: An Alternative Interpretation', *British Journal of Political Science*, Vol. 1 (1971), pp. 288–392. On cross-cutting in Glasgow and Belfast see Ian Budge and Cornelius O'Leary, 'Cross-cutting Cleavages, Agreement and Compromise: An Assessment of Three Leading Hypotheses Against Scottish and Northern Irish Survey Responses', *Midwest Journal of Political Science*, Vol. XV (January 1971), pp. 1–30; Ian Budge and Cornelius O'Leary, 'Relationships Between Attitudinal and Background Cross-cutting: theoretical modifications suggested by further evidence from Glasgow and Belfast', *Midwest Journal of Political Science*, Vol. XVI (Summer 1972), forthcoming.
2. This characterisation of cross-cutting is employed by D. Rae and M. J. Taylor in *The Analysis of Political Cleavages* (New Haven, 1970), p. 92.
3. Ibid., pp. 90–7.
4. Average cross-cutting between procedural attitudes and party was 0·49 for Belfast residents, 0·47 for Glasgow residents, 0·48 for Belfast councillors and 0·47 for Glasgow councillors. Again there are practically no differences between the groups.
5. The detailed report is given in Budge and O'Leary, 'Cross-cutting Cleavages, Agreement and Compromise', cited in footnote 1.
6. This last interpretation receives support from the fact that Unionist disagreement extended to the non-religious issue of rates.
7. Budge and O'Leary, 'Relationships Between Attitudinal and Background Cross-cutting', cited in footnote 1, above.
8. This should be true even though the total extent of cross-cutting among moderates cannot be calculated. The cross-cutting statistic allows us to take into account only reciprocating pairs – i.e. no value can be obtained for moderate cross-cutting with intransigents which does not simultaneously reflect intransigents' cross-cutting with moderates. In practice we shall in the following analysis compare cross-cutting within each group of moderates with the values obtained for the total groups of councillors and residents in Belfast. The justification for so proceeding is that if moderates did change associates more over their characteristics and preferences, this general pattern should also appear among the moderates in isolation. Thus although XC values for moderates do not reflect their total change of associates, they do reflect their general tendency to change associates, which should be higher than among all councillors and residents.
9. The search-statistic for tendencies of preferences to form a Guttman scale was eta. For a cross-tabulation of dichotomised preferences

$$\text{eta} = \frac{\dfrac{P_{12}-P_{21}}{P_{12}+P_{21}} - E_I\left\{\dfrac{P_{12}-P_{21}}{P_{12}+P_{21}}\right\}}{1 - E_I\left\{\dfrac{P_{12}-P_{21}}{P_{12}+P_{21}}\right\}}$$

where P_{21} is the proportion of cases in the cell defined by moderate preference on the issue on which it is more difficult to be moderate, and by intransigent preference on the issue where it is easier to be moderate. If there were a consistent attitude towards Catholics P_{21} should be nearly zero. Expected values of this formula

$$E_I\left\{\frac{P_{12}-P_{21}}{P_{12}+P_{21}}\right\}$$

are included to safeguard against taking statistically independent issue-preferences as consistently related. The statistic varies from unity to zero, in accordance with tendencies of responses to form a Guttman scale. None of the eta values obtained were above 0·40 and most were close to zero.

10. Properly speaking, not intransigents but the total groups of councillors and residents: however cross-cutting for the total groups is presumably lowered by the presence of intransigents among them.

14 Conclusions

WE have attempted to give a general account of Belfast politics, historical and contemporary, which would serve in a sense as a terminal description of a system of some antiquity now about to disappear. This purpose has been fulfilled by the discussions of Belfast development and of political behaviour and attitudes in 1966, which form the staple of previous chapters. Inevitably, a major concern has been with religious tensions, violence and intransigence, since these constitute the salient feature of politics in the city. Our chapters have increasingly focused on possible causes of such phenomena, the centrality of which have become more apparent as our analysis, and events, unfolded. The purpose of these Conclusions is to interpret our findings on the correlates of political instability in Belfast, in order to provide an integrated explanation of contemporary events.

This concern dictates the form of our final discussion. First we shall review those major findings of the study which seem to link with political instability, suggesting an interpretation which draws equally on the historical and the survey evidence. Second, we shall derive from this interpretation an explanation of instability couched in fairly general terms, which may as a result have some theoretical interest in relating to instability elsewhere than in Belfast. If this aids the continuing diagnosis of Northern Irish problems, we shall consider our investigation justified.

INTERPRETATIVE REVIEW OF FINDINGS RELATING TO BELFAST INSTABILITY

Throughout our analysis comparisons with the stable city of Glasgow have been employed to isolate conditions peculiar to Belfast, and hence inferentially linked to instability there. Findings which are highlighted through these comparisons from the basis of discussion below:

    1. Violence and intransigence – in the sense of an inability

of politicians to work together or make lasting compromises advantageous to both sides – have been endemic in Belfast from the early nineteenth century right up to the time of writing. Violence and intransigence are manifestations of instability and thus constitute the explicandum of our discussion – the dependent variable of which the other conditions isolated below are prima facie causes.

2. In contemporary Belfast class feeling is low in comparison with British cities. Low levels of class consciousness are particularly evident among the working class. As a result middle-class identifications and feeling are more extensive than in Britain. Class had only a weak relationship with party attachments. Generally the low salience of class seems to have resulted from the salience of religion and the political success of the Unionists – predominantly middle-class in outlook and policy.

3. Denominational loyalties are, on the contrary, more widespread and intense in Belfast than in Britain.

4. The social salience of religion extends to politics. Rioting and parliamentary activity in the nineteenth and twentieth centuries have been linked with Protestant-Catholic differences. Party divisions have reflected religious divisions. In 1966 major images of the Belfast parties still related to politico-religious disputes, and four out of five current issues were of this nature.

5. Party divisions in 1966 obviously derived from the earlier divisions associated with nineteenth-century rioting, the Home Rule movements and the Irish Civil War. Historical analysis shows clearly that there was nothing in the basic nature of Irish religion to link it irreversibly with party conflict: had this been so, there would have been no alliance of Presbyterians and Catholics in 1798. The connection was fostered by politicians for their own advantage, first by the British Government's support for the Orange Order after 1798, and secondly by the Conservative Party under Bates from 1832. Obviously the influx of Catholic labourers gave rise to social tensions on which politicians could work. But in Glasgow the tensions arising from a similar influx were kept out of politics by the united action of the politicians.

6. Successful use of the religious appeal gave the Conservatives (and later Unionists) an inbuilt Protestant and electoral majority in Belfast, which was widely recognised in 1966.

7. As a result, the whole tradition of municipal decision-making in Belfast centred round Conservative and Unionist dominance. The modern Corporation was constituted in 1842 as a Conservative instrument and it remained a Unionist instrument in 1966. At no time was an opposition or minority party associated with the ruling of the city. From this developed a complete hiatus in communication between minority and majority politicians, a feeling of alienation on the part of minority politicians and a general distrust of parties and of party competition.

The permanent tenure of the Unionists blunted external perceptions of changing opinions and influences inside the City Hall Party, and is reflected in the municipal correspondants' expectation in 1966 that the Unionist diehards would always win.

8. One-party dominance secured efficient adaptation to changing circumstances in the period when popular political interest was limited and only one ideological tendency was represented inside the party – roughly the period from 1842 to the late 1860s. With the growth of Protestant populism in the shape of the Orange Order, and the admission of former Whigs in the late nineteenth century, the Unionist party tended to internal factionalism, a characteristic which was intensified in the 1960s (as witnessed by the absence of communication and policy-agreement among Unionist councillors). As a result of internal divergences the party became *immobiliste*: what all its members supported was the maintenance of the broad *status quo* against Nationalist threats, and so the party rested on support of the *status quo* in all its details. This stance was congenial to party leaders because of their privileged background, which made them insensitive to popular currents of opinion.

9. The Unionists were able to remain *immobiliste* because of the ideological rigidity of the Nationalist parties, which were also weakened by factionalism. Because of the social representitiveness of their leaders, however, the Nationalists in Belfast were more responsive to the changing wishes of their supporters and had by the 1960s shifted their main emphasis from irredentism to social welfare issues and discrimination. Such demands could no longer be dismissed by the Unionists leaders as illegiti-

mate, and indeed appealed to many Unionists as relatively cheap ways of winning the minority over to the existing system.

10. There was, however, no machinery for involving minority parties in decision-making. Any concession to the minority had to be pushed by one Unionist faction against the opposition of other Unionist factions. The moderate Unionists could not ally with Nationalists to secure concessions since this would have resulted in a hardening of Unionist opinion against them. The result was the strong solidarity of Nationalist opinion noted in Chapter 13, since being debarred from effective decision-making their councillors were under no need to make practical compromises.

11. Once involved in an internal struggle over the concessions to be offered to Catholics most Unionists found themselves caught in a web of conflicting loyalties and identifications, with their old verities gone. The resulting cross-pressures impelled most Unionists towards moderation but also vacillation, since they were too confused to have clearly attainable objectives. On the part of activists such internal vacillation was compounded by pessimism about the popular support they enjoyed, while for the population and indeed for reporters the diehard Unionists were more visible than the moderates.

12. Verbal assurances and gestures were thus easier for moderate Unionists than action, but roused hopes among Catholics which remained unfulfilled. The impediments to moderate initiatives were popularly ascribed to the unshakable dominance of diehards, buttressed by the electoral invincibility of the Unionists. Despairing of successful action through established channels Catholics dramatised their grievances in demonstrations. Although such demonstrations did eventually produce desired concessions they also – by provoking Protestant fear and hostility – inadvertently stimulated the present violence and led to renewed intransigence on both sides.

EXPLANATIONS OF BELFAST INSTABILITY

Our review of findings begins with Belfast violence and ends with Belfast violence. This is not tautological, for a major lesson of our historical analysis is the extent to which violence is self-perpetuating. Not only does it form a precedent for the action to be taken by aggrieved individuals, but it arouses prejudices in each of the opposed groups, which are passed on with other group traditions, and strengthened by the residential segregation fostered by inter-group tensions. It is possible that religious-ethnic animosities, once aroused, are more likely to produce violence than pure class feeling, which can be assuaged by a timely redistribution of material and symbolic rewards. This is debatable, but what is certain from our evidence is that, historically, political hostilities preceded and precipitated religious hostilities. This is true both on the macro-historical level of general Conservative Party policy in Belfast, and on the micro-historical level of the events preceding each major riot (Table 3.1).

Historically, therefore, politics preceded violence, and violence produced more violence. There seems a certain inevitability to events from the first riot of 1813 and the hardening of Presbyterian feeling towards Catholics – a high probability of conflict whether or not the eventual outcome was the predominance of Catholics or Protestants in Belfast. Compromise only appeared really feasible at the outset of this sequence of events in the period about 1800 and in the 1960s. Such a multiplicity of eventual causes of violence emerge prior to 1800 that any reasonably compact explanation has to take its start from that period of relatively free choice on the part of Protestant leaders. We have earlier discussed the reasons which made them withdraw their support for Catholic aspirations and substitute a political confrontation. From that decision the rioting, the civil war, and its poisoned aftermath followed.

Of our own time, and therefore more interesting and accessible to analysis, is the second moment of decision, the brief period in the mid-1960s when politicians were relatively free to break the weakened hold of the past. Such an opportunity for choice arose from the very success of the Protestants in consolidating and administering their Northern Irish State, a success which finally convinced the Catholics that they must work within its framework. This realisation gave the Unionist politicians the opportunity, frustrated for 150 years by religious-ethnic animosities, of winning over the minority by the same timely redistribution of benefits which in Britain had conciliated the working class. In Belfast, whatever was the position in the rest of the North, politicians had the advantage that the majority of their supporters also favoured a conciliatory policy. In contrast to the earlier period, violence followed not from the aggression of Protestant leaders but from the vacillating moderation which has been described in relation to cross-cutting effects.

Slightly broadening the Belfast and Northern Irish experience, we can suggest general lessons from the failure of conciliation. These apply only under circumstances similar to those of Belfast, where an entrenched dominant party was trying to extend the basis of its support by conciliating a previously alienated minority. In this case it appears from our investigation that moderate leaders should verbally as well as behaviourally continue hardline policies towards the minority right up to the moment when they have sufficient popular and activist support to initiate effective conciliatory measures. A delay in conciliatory gestures should not prove fatal, for if conciliation is feasible at all the situation must have stabilised sufficiently for the minority to comply with the *status quo* even if they do not support it. Developments in Belfast indicate that empty verbal gestures stimulate feelings of relative deprivation to a level where they are bound to be disappointed by delays in action, and to result eventually in renewed minority action against the regime. This may be the future course of development in countries like Italy as it is by now a historical development in Belfast.

A further precaution to be taken by moderate leaders is to ensure that communication has been effectively opened up with minority representatives. This strategy is not inconsistent with the one recommended above, for communication might as easily cover the reasons for interim hardline decisions, as for conciliatory ones. Yet in a situation where lines of communication are non-existent (as in Belfast in 1966) moderates in the dominant party have no means of ascertaining what the responses of the minority are likely to be. If the conciliatory gestures which are politically practicable are not likely to conciliate the minority then they may be positively harmful.

Associated advice is to ensure that communication with party supporters in the population is effective and that realistic estimates can be made of their sentiments. The importance too of ensuring that at the right moment the press will not only be friendly but optimistic need not, after our detailed examination, be too strongly stressed.

The most theoretically interesting of the findings from our analysis is undoubtedly the correlation of high cross-cutting particularly among moderates, with instability in Belfast. It is significant that such high cross-cutting was associated with party and issue-preferences: the cross-cutting of religion and party was less in Belfast than in Glasgow.

The general conclusion from our findings was that cross-cutting theories generally ignored the tendencies to withdrawal associated with cross-pressures. Certainly these on our evidence induced moderation, but moderate inaction rather than action. The question raised by our investigation is, therefore, when does cross-cutting provide openings for genuine conciliation, rather than empty gestures without real policy substance? From our analysis two conditions suggest themselves:

First, genuine opportunities for new alignments open up when all relevant groups experience cross-pressures. In Belfast the concentration of cross-pressures among Unionists implied that the only group able to make effective decisions was paralysed. If all groups experienced cross-cutting all might be equally vacillating, but that very fact should give like-minded individuals the opportunity to form new alliances across group barriers. The importance of considering all relevant groups is stressed by the finding that major class conflicts in Glasgow – which might have been provoked by the cumulation of class and party divisions among activists – were dampened by high cross-cutting on these two characteristics among the population. One can imagine situations where cumulative divisions among the population were blurred by cross-cutting among the leaders. Something like this might account for the moderation of Conservative and Labour leaders in Britain between the wars.

Second, cross-cutting is also unlikely to produce similar effects in relation to social characteristics and preferences on current issues. The logical status of the two situations is actually quite different. Cross-cutting on issues implies that no firm lines of policy can be pursued, that no leader can maintain a cohesive coalition because nobody has consistent preferences. Such a situation does not indicate moderation but chaos. To talk of political principle at the tail-end of an empirical investigation may sound incongruous, but it seems likely that politicians who lack any unifying guidelines will dissipate their efforts because of the shifting nature of the alliances they try to form.

Cross-cutting on social characteristics may well, on the other hand, foster moderation in the anticipated ways by bringing people into contact with different types of associates and stimulating intercommunication and exposing each individual to diverse points of view. But the moderation so produced would surely be consistent when expressed in terms of issue-preferences. In other words, if high cross-cutting of religious and other characteristics fosters a conciliatory attitude to other religious groups, this should be expressed by consistent adoption of moderate preferences on politico-religious issues. Seen in this light, high cross-cutting on such issues implies an absence of consistent pressures towards moderation. This reinterpretation of cross-cutting hypothesis certainly accords with the Belfast and Glasgow evidence.

In this refinement of cross-cutting hypotheses the Belfast investigation has, hopefully, contributed to the general theoretical interests of political science. We have also attempted to relate our findings in a useful way to the developing situation. Admittedly, at the time of going to press (August 1972) the pace of events is so rapid and their impact so grave that it is not impossible that before the publication of this book Belfast, Northern Ireland and indeed the whole of Ireland may be engulfed by civil war. In the last few months the policy options of moderates have been progressively destroyed by extremist groups, which scarcely existed at the time of our investigation. The danger is all too apparent that the bomb and the bullet may replace the ballot. As Ireland's greatest poet wrote during the last civil war:

'The good lack all conviction, while the bad are full of passionate intensity.'

But if, as we hopefully aver, democracy is not destroyed and Belfast and Ireland reduced to the level of Cyprus, Jordan or Bolivia, then our study may be useful to those involved in any future Irish rapprochement. At least they may be helped to avoid the errors and omissions of the past.

Appendix A

SURVEY METHOD

As mentioned in our Introduction, the Belfast survey was designed from the start to replicate as closely as conditions would allow the Glasgow survey designed by Brand, Budge, Margolis and Smith and carried out from February to October 1966. Limitations of time and resources obliged us, however, to omit interviews with party workers from the Belfast study and to reduce the original sample of the population from 749 to 334. In the event we obtained interviews with 229 Belfast residents, 45 municipal councillors and six municipal correspondents.

Because of the common design of the surveys the description of questionnaires and procedures contained in Appendix A (Study Design) of *Political Stratification and Democracy* also covers the main features of the Belfast research design. Against that general background we are concerned here with highlighting modifications in the Belfast design, giving a brief chronological account of its development, and assessing the validity and reliability of the results obtained.

CHRONOLOGY AND SURVEY PROCEDURES

The notion of parallelling the Glasgow survey in Belfast was conceived as part of the original research framework. The comparison sprang naturally from the many similarities between the historical and cultural backgrounds of the two cities, and the sharp contrasts in their politics. Like Glasgow, contemporary Belfast is primarily a creation of nineteenth-century industrialism, the legacy of which has partly contributed to depressed twentieth-century conditions. The culture of both cities derives from a similar amalgam of Irish and Scottish influences. Religious differences are an important feature of the life of both: in both the ratio of Catholics to Protestants is similar, and Presbyterianism one of the dominant Protestant sects. Yet in spite of social similarities the politics of Glasgow seemed to emphasise class differences as the basis of party cleavage, while in Belfast religion appeared as the predominating political division.

Because of this comparative interest, plans for the Belfast survey were first discussed in December 1965, before the main interviewing in Glasgow had begun. The design of the questionnaires was settled in February 1966 while interviewing in Glasgow was under way. Since this was to be the first political survey either at population or activist level ever to be undertaken in Northern Ireland, various contingency plans in case of non-response were also laid at this point. These entailed minor modifications in the wording of certain questions. Uncertainties about responses to the survey also prompted the major decision to draw a relatively small sample of residents to allow for more concentrated interviewing and detailed investigation of non-contacts.

With regard to residents' non-response, arrangements were made to check all non-contacts to ensure that failures did not derive from defects in the Register of Electors (see below). The possibility that many councillors might refuse interview meant that we had to consider broadening our selection of activists to Belfast political notables, generally, and to Stormont M.P.s. Most questions which in the corresponding Glasgow schedule had referred only to 'councillors' were therefore worded to include 'political leaders in Belfast' as well. This extension of their scope extended to questions about persons consulted on current issues. Since we might possibly find ourselves comparing the replies of Stormont M.P.s with those of other groups, we also asked an entirely new question about the role of Stormont M.P.s.

Other modifications to the questionnaire resulted from the objective political differences between Glasgow and Belfast. The Irish Nationalist groupings formed an important political influence which had to be taken into account. Questions on likes and dislikes about the parties were therefore extended to Nationalists as well as Unionists and Northern Ireland Labour. Questions about Nationalist stands on issues were also inserted.

Obviously, the set of issues current in Belfast at the time of interviewing were likely to differ somewhat from those in

Glasgow, although increases in rates form a hardy perennial in most cities. The other issues were altered to those discussed in the text.

The above constitute the only modifications made to the basic Glasgow questionnaires, so that the content of interviews remained very much the same. Although satisfactory informal pre-tests of the modified questionnaires were made in Belfast before the main interviewing took place, no extensive pilot was felt to be necessary, since the basic design and wording had stood up to extensive use in Glasgow.

Interviewing of ordinary residents began in the first week of June 1966, and was completed by the first week of July. During the first two weeks of June a series of disturbances involving Protestant extremists took place in Belfast, culminating in a riot in Cromac Square, and the murder of a young Catholic barman in a related affray. The disturbances did not seem to exert a substantial affect on the willingness of residents to respond to the schedule, nor even to influence the content of their replies.

Final year students in politics and social administration conducted all residents' interviews on a payment-by-time basis. For most, two initial trial interviews with residents not in sample provided their first experience in the field. Students with some prior interviewing experience followed up the more difficult cases.

The residents initially drawn for interview constituted a systematic selection of 334 from the Register of Electors (1964) of the City of Belfast. Of these 229 were successfully interviewed. The remaining 105 from the sample consisted of 69 electors and 36 non-electors. Twenty-two out of the 105 had died since the Register was made up, 11 were too ill for interview and 27 had moved out of the population. Nine had moved and could not be traced, while three were away for reasons connected with their occupation. Thirteen refused an interview and sixteen could not be contacted. Suspected false entries in the Register, contradicting folklore, accounted for only four of the missing electors.

Assessment of these results rests on the fact that – in contrast to the annual local elections in Britain – Belfast municipal elections were held at three-year intervals when all councillors were elected in each ward. The Belfast local government Register (as distinct from the Register for Westminster and Stormont elections) was thus revised only at the end of three years, and effectively the Register from which we drew our sample was already two and three quarter years from the date of its compilation by mid-1966. During this time quite extensive changes could have taken place, and in particular many persons listed on the Register in 1964 could have moved out of the population. We were careful therefore to establish as precisely as possible why contacts could not be made, especially whether persons had moved outside Belfast, and thus effectively out of the population with which we were concerned. The check was also made necessary by widespread rumours of false entries in the Register, made to increase the voting strength of various political parties. Actually only the four cases of suspected false entries were found (about one per cent of the original sample). These, of course, could be immediately eliminated from the population we were concerned to examine. Deceased residents had removed in a peculiarly final way: added to those who had left Belfast, the numbers of those no longer in the population with which we were concerned came to 53 out of 105, or almost half the non-contacts. Allowance for this group raises the response rate from 68·5 per cent to 80 per cent, a figure which compares with the 76 per cent attained in the Glasgow electoral survey, and in most British political surveys. As with Glasgow, this percentage is the strictest possible response rate one could apply. Several of the non-contacts were with persons whose physical or mental disabilities or occupations (e.g. seamen) removed them from effective political activity in the city. Some of the untraceable removals were probably out of the city. (We have explicitly taken into account only those moves about whom we had definite information.) Given these additional considerations, the response appears reasonably satisfactory.

One peculiarity of the Belfast sample compared with that from Glasgow should be noted here. The restrictive property qualifications on the Belfast franchise have the consequence of excluding an estimated 24 per cent of the adult population from the municipal franchise. The Register of Electors lists all residents and not only local electors, however, since it also covers the less restrictive Stormont franchise and the universal Westminster franchise. (The different categories of elector are distinguished in the Register by letters placed after their name.) Our sample of residents thus includes both local electors and local non-electors. The proportions of each contained in our final sample form another statistic through which the degree of survey bias is ascertained below.

Councillors began to be interviewed immediately after completion of the population survey. Most had been seen by the end of October 1966, but because of the difficulty of arranging suitable times a few were staggered until as late as January 1967. Interviewing of councillors was carried through entirely by academic and research staff of Queen's University, under the direction of Cornelius O'Leary. The final total of interviews was 45 out of 60 councillors on the Corporation (both ordinary councillors and aldermen). As in Glasgow, few of the non-contacts represented direct refusals: most were simply too elusive to fix a definite appointment.

Experience gained in the Glasgow study indicated that municipal correspondents of the local press were an important link in the communication channels linking activists and electors. Accordingly, the Glasgow schedule devised for correspondents was adapted to conditions in Belfast and administered during early 1968 by Dr R. Baxter of the Queen's Politics staff.

Since essentially the same schedules and questions had been used in Belfast as in Glasgow, the codes which had been tested and developed for Glasgow and which had stood up to production coding could be employed on all schedules, with some modifications to Belfast conditions. Modifications were evolved on the basis of trial runs with randomly selected sub-sets of population and activist schedules. Since the overall number of interviews (274) was small compared with that obtained for Glasgow, the reliability of coding was increased by employing one person to process all schedules except 25 from the population sample. Coding bias is not therefore eliminated but it is kept the same throughout, and to the extent that analysis rests on comparisons between population activists and their sub-groups, results should be unaffected by the uniform bias. The validity of coding was ascertained by having 10 per cent of the schedules coded independently and checking the correspondence of results. Most single column codes had nearly 100 per cent correspondence, as in Glasgow, and double and triple column codes had a satisfactory correspondence in almost all cases. The degree of correspondence between the independent coding attempts fell below 80 per cent only for Solutions to Problems facing Belfast (77 per cent), Role of a Stormont M.P. (76 per cent) and Reasons for standing for Council the first time (70 per cent).

Once punched, verified and made up to magnetic tape the data were subjected to computer and hand checks for consistency and wild coding. Few mistakes emerged at this stage – one indication that previous operations had been carried out satisfactorily. The cleaned data, together with codebooks, are now deposited with the British Social Science Data Bank at the University of Essex, which can also provide a full table of coding correspondences, on request.

ESTIMATES OF SURVEY ERROR

Bias creeps into survey statistics at every stage of preparation and processing. However perfectly drawn, a random sample does not in any case give wholly correct estimates of population figures, being always subject to variation deriving from the fact that it is a sample. For a sample of 229 the range of variation reaches a maximum of 6·5 per cent at the 0·05 level of probability, i.e. the population percentages can be expected to be within a range of ±6·5 per cent of the sample statistic for 19 out of 20 of possible random samples that could be drawn, of size 229.

However – as clearly emerges above – our 229 residents are not a random sample of people living in Belfast in 1966. For one thing, names were taken from a Register made up some time previously. Many people drawn in our original sample had moved out of the population, but many people not listed in the Register had moved in – quite apart from those missed in the enumeration for the Register itself.

Second, there is the problem of non-contacts. Twenty per cent of our effective sample either could not be contacted or refused interview. These non-contacts are very likely to be persons with common social or personality characteristics which render them more elusive than the residents we did interview, and which also systematically affect their political reactions.

Even if problems of obtaining interviews did not exist there would undoubtedly be some errors through incorrect reporting by interviewers or by respondents' desire to give answers pleasing to interviewers, which revealed themselves in a good light. Finally, at each stage of coding and punching the data, inaccuracies may creep in. These may be kept down to an acceptable level by the checks mentioned above, but may still seriously compound original interviewing mistakes.

A partial test of how far sampling and survey errors affect our results is provided by a comparison of sample statistics with census and election data for Belfast. With regard to purely social characteristics it emerges that the sample percentages are within the permissible range of variation around population percentages (i.e., ±6·5) except for the youngest age group, and the lower occupational classes.

The under-representation of young adults (paralleled in the Glasgow study) is most easily explained in terms of difficulty in making contact with a relatively mobile and less politically aware section of the population. It should also be noted that the census figure includes those who were 20-year-olds in 1966 while the sample starts from those who were 21 in 1964 – a discrepancy which goes a fair way towards accounting for the non-coincidence of survey and census percentages.

One can also partially explain the over-representation of Class III (2) and under-representation of Class IV in our sample in terms of greater ease in contacting those in higher occupational groups, who are more settled, better educated and more interested in politics. However, this would only be the case if members of the higher classes were also substantially over-represented, which they are not. It is better to say frankly that no obvious reason for this sample bias occurs to us. But it should not seriously affect the analysis of class effects on political behaviour, since the great divide lies between the professional and clerical workers of the top three Occupational Classes, and the manual workers of the lower three, rather than between the skilled manual workers of Class III (2) and the semi-skilled in Class IV.

TABLE A.1

Comparison of Sample and Population Percentages, Various Characteristics

Characteristic		Sample	Census 1961	Census 1966
Occupational class	I	3·06	2·32	
	II	14·41	12·05	
	III(1)	10·48	15·61	
	III(2)	37·55	28·50	
	IV	15·72	27·23	
	V	13·10	14·33	
Education	15 −	67·69	72·47	
	15	12·23	7·84	
	16	6·11	6·24	
	17	6·11		
	18	2·62 ⎱	9·46	
	18+	4·80 ⎰		
Sex	M	48·03	45·35	45·12
	F	51·97	54·64	54·87
Marital Status	Married	70·74	64·09	64·66
	Single	20·96	24·85	24·02
	Widowed	8·30	10·75	10·89
	Divorced	0·00	0·29	0·32
Type Housing	Rents Privately	50·66	53·54	
	Rents Council	12·23	13·91	
	Owns	34·5	31·60	
			Other 1·0	
Religion	Non-believer	6·55	4·35	
	C. of I.	20·52	20·75	
	Presbyterian	32·75	29·91	
	Other Prot.	11·35	17·00	
	'Prot.'	0·87		
	R.C.	25·33	22·95	
Age	20–29	10·04	20·16	20·77
	30–39	16·60	18·41	16·28
	40–49	21·83	18·98	17·96
	50–59	23·57	18·85	18·82
	60–69	13·98	14·12	15·39
	70+	12·23	9·44	10·75
Local elector	Local Elector	80·20		76·48
	Local non-Elector	19·80		23·52
1964 Municipal Election votes cast	Unionist	31·88		12·90
	N.I. Labour	17·47		7·67
	Rep. Lab.	3·06		1·90
	Other	1·75		3·18
	Non-voter and non-franchised	43·67		73·9

The first basic political statistic to consider in regard to the sample of residents is the proportion of local non-electors. In our original systematic sample of 334 this proportion was 21 per cent: the proportion in the interviewed sample is 19 per cent, so that non-responses have not especially biased the sample in regard to this characteristic. The actual proportion of local non-electors in the population in 1966 was 23·52: both of the two sample statistics closely approach this.

The comparison of reported local votes in 1964 with actual voting figures carried inherent difficulties, since the sample percentages are based on reports of the way individual respondents acted, while the figures are based on votes cast. Since each individual had at least three and sometimes more votes (where he had additional business qualifications) the derivation of the individual preferences reported in the table rests on the perhaps tenuous assumption that most individuals cast their plural votes for the same party, so that division of the original figures by three will give the correct distribution of voting preferences, as well as a figure for those not voting. These processed figures yield percentages (in the final column of the table) which reveal an obvious overestimate of turnout by our sample and a consequent inflation in the percentages voting Unionist and Northern Ireland Labour. Since voting is a valued act in Western culture a reluctance on the part of electors to confess to non-voting is widespread, however permissive the tone of the relevant question. The same over-report of voting was encountered in Glasgow and has been met in most political surveys, but in Belfast it is compounded by the greater period of time which had elapsed since the last municipal election and by the intervention of two British General Elections and one Northern Irish General Election in the intervening period. The figures are not as bad an overestimate as they might seem, for some of the persons removed from our original sample by death, illness or emigration would also have been unable to vote in the municipal election, although they are not included to swell the estimate of non-voting in our sample.

With councillors as opposed to residents our intention was not to interview a sample but as far as possible to see all 60. We succeeded in interviewing all Republican Labour and National Democratic Party representatives on the Council (three in each case), all Northern Ireland Labour Party and Independent Labour councillors (four in each case), one of the four Independents, one of the two Protestant Unionists, and 29 out of 40 Unionists. The Unionist percentage of our interviewees is 64 per cent and the Unionist percentage of the whole Council 66 per cent. Forty-seven per cent of interviewees are current office-holders compared to 45 per cent of the whole Council. Twenty-two per cent are aldermen compared with 25 per cent on the full Council. With regard to party, office and Council status therefore it appears that the 45 councillors interviewed constitute a reasonably unbiased selection from the whole.

Index